EUROPEAN CONTRACT LAW AND THE CREATION OF NORMS

For Jack Balkin,
with sincere gratitude,

Mateusz

Hamburg, 2021

EUCOLATH
European Contract Law and Theory Series

European Contract Law and Theory Series, Volume 5

EUROPEAN CONTRACT LAW AND THE CREATION OF NORMS

Edited by
Stefan Grundmann
Mateusz Grochowski

INTERSENTIA
Cambridge – Antwerp – Chicago

Intersentia Ltd
8 Wellington Mews
Wellington Street | Cambridge
CB1 1HW | United Kingdom
Tel: +44 1223 736 170
Email: mail@intersentia.co.uk
www.intersentia.com | www.intersentia.co.uk

Distribution for the UK and
Rest of the World (incl. Eastern Europe)
NBN International
1 Deltic Avenue, Rooksley
Milton Keynes MK13 8LD
United Kingdom
Tel: +44 1752 202 301 | Fax: +44 1752 202 331
Email: orders@nbninternational.com

Distribution for Europe
Lefebvre Sarrut Belgium NV
Hoogstraat 139/6
1000 Brussels
Belgium
Tel: +32 (0)800 39 067
Email: mail@intersentia.be

Distribution for the USA and Canada
Independent Publishers Group
Order Department
814 North Franklin Street
Chicago, IL 60610
USA
Tel: +1 800 888 4741 (toll free) | Fax: +1 312 337 5985
Email: orders@ipgbook.com

European Contract Law and the Creation of Norms

Artwork on cover: Keith Corrigan / Alamy Stock Photo

ISBN 978-1-78068-965-4
D/2021/7849/20
NUR 822

British Library Cataloguing in Publication Data. A catalogue record for this book is available from the British Library.

CONTENTS

LIST OF CASES

SUPRANATIONAL

COURT OF JUSTICE OF THE EUROPEAN UNION

NATIONAL

BRAZIL

FRANCE

GERMANY

UNITED KINGDOM

POLAND

USA

LIST OF AUTHORS

Hugh Collins
Cassel Professor of Commercial Law, London School of Economics, United Kindgom

Hanoch Dagan
Stewart and Judy Colton Professor of Legal Theory and Innovation and Director of The Edmond J. Safra Center for Ethics, Tel-Aviv University, Israel

Mateusz Grochowski
Senior Researcher at the Max Planck Institute for Comparative and International Private Law in Hamburg, Germany; Assistant Professor at the Institute of Law Studies of the Polish Academy of Sciences in Warsaw, Poland; Fellow of the Information Society Project at Yale Law School, United States

Stefan Grundmann
Professor of Transnational Law & Theory at the European University Institute in Florence, Italy; Professor of Private and Business Law at Humboldt-University in Berlin, Germany

Lorenz Kaehler
Professor for Private Law, Civil Procedure and Legal Philosophy at the University Bremen, Germany

Daniel Markovits
Guido Calabresi Professor of Law and Founding Director of the Center for the Study of Private Law at Yale Law School, United States

Hans-W. Micklitz
Finland Distinguished Professor at the University of Helsinki; Professor for Economic Law at the Robert Schuman Centre for Advanced Studies, European University Institute, Florence, Italy

Florian Möslein
Director of the Institute for Law and Regulation of Digitalisation (www.irdi.institute) and Professor of Law at the Philipps-University Marburg, Germany

Horatia Muir Watt
Professor, Sciences Po, Paris; Fellow, Institut Universitaire de France

Jerzy Pisuliński
Professor of Civil Law at the Faculty of Law and Administration of the Jagiellonian University, Poland; Member of the Civil Law Codification Commission (CLCC), a body attached to the Ministry of Justice of the Republic of Poland, since October 2006, and Vice-Chairman of the CLCC in 2011–2015

Camelia Toader
Professor, Private Law Department, Faculty of Law of the University of Bucharest, Romania; Judge at the Court of Justice of the European Union since January 2007

Aneta Wiewiórowska-Domagalska
Senior Researcher at the European Legal Studies Institute, Osnabrück University, Germany, and Co-Chair of Consumer Forum established by the Polish Human Rights Commissioner

PART I

ARCHITECTURE

THE CREATION OF NORMS

An Evolutionary View on European Contract Law

Stefan GRUNDMANN and Mateusz GROCHOWSKI

When creation of norms is the theme, European contract law shares a development that is global, that can be summarised as the advent of a variety of competing rule-setters and that has characterised the last five or six decades. It has moved from *one government* contract law until the second half of the 20th century to *complex governance*, which also embraced contract governance structure.[1] At the same time, European contract law is special within this broad global flow – strongly propelled mainly on the two sides of the Atlantic – in that it has added considerable complexity to this already rich picture. It has done so, for instance, with respect to multi-level contract law, optional codification and with a strange body of adjudication of contract law at the federal level, with a strong command from above, namely a relatively activist European Court of Justice (ECJ). This first overall account of the vast picture takes up both the global flow *and* the added European 'jewels'. It does so in an order inspired rather by substance than by origin. In other words, global and European developments are not segregated, but rather a substantive logic is followed.

1. LAW, STATE AND CONTRACT: BETWEEN THE OLD AND THE NEW PICTURE

1.1. REGULATORY 'MONOPOLY' vs. PRIVATE LAW 'BEYOND STATE'

The beauty of the theme lies in the change from an old to a new picture. What is perhaps the *summa* of the 'old picture' was described most beautifully in the *Ancien Régime*, in 1748. The book referred to – dealing with the very concept of law(s) (*l'esprit des lois*) – contains as its most famous (set of)

---

1 Path-breaking, O. Williamson, 'Transaction-Cost Economics: The Governance of Contractual Relations' (1979) 22 *Journal of Law & Economics* 233; on this contribution, its significance, context and the discussion it triggered, see S. Grundmann in S. Grundmann, H.-W. Micklitz and M. Renner, *New Private Law Theory: A Pluralist Approach*, Cambridge University Press, Cambridge 2020, chapters 3 and 17. See also, today from a broadly contextual and interdisciplinary perspective, S. Grundmann, F. Möslein and K. Riesenhuber (eds.), *Contract Governance: Dimensions in Law and Interdisciplinary Research*, Oxford University Press, Oxford 2015.

phrase(s): '*Mais les juges de la nation ne sont ... que la bouche qui prononce les paroles de la loi; des êtres inanimés, qui n'en peuvent modérer ni la force ni la rigueur. C'est donc la partie du corps législatif ... [l']autorité suprême à modérer la loi, en faveur de la loi-même*'.[2] All is centred on the sovereign legislature. This may be the 'old picture', but it stems from a genius that has also clarified the concept of separation of powers – albeit with a very weak judicial power, still rather an instrument of the other two powers than one on its own merits. Some 20 years later came the declaration of independence, by one side of the Atlantic to the other; some 30 years later, the first two declarations of human rights, on both sides of the Atlantic; and some 50 years later, the start of the grand codifications, kicked off in Europe in 1797 (in Austrian, formerly Polish, Galicia)[3] and, on a much grander scale, in 1804 in France. The picture, however, remained the old one: the prime responsibility for rule-setting rests with the sovereign (democratic or not); moreover, the judge remains mainly the mouthpiece that simply pronounces the words formulated by the sovereign. There might, of course, have been a little germ of future developments that continued to flourish, the so-called law merchant (*lex mercatoria*), mainly on the seas, for instance the Atlantic and the Mediterranean Sea,[4] where the sovereign power and monopoly over rule-setting and 'ordering' seemed to be questioned to some extent.

The germ for a 'new picture', however, remained weak, without strong offspring, at least in conceptual terms, for the whole of the 19th and half of the 20th centuries. The power of trade and of globalisation remained the drivers, drivers that flourished over these 150 years (suffering, of course, during the political catastrophes). These drivers, however, found a powerful new conceptualisation only in the second half of the 20th century (admittedly with some timid predecessors). This new conceptualisation – and with it the 'new picture' – rests on two pillars: private party autonomy coupled with practice on the one hand, and cross-border transnational perspectives on the other.

The first pillar of the new picture can be seen in the re-conceptualisation of the *lex mercatoria* in the 1960s. At that time, *lex mercatoria* was re-conceptualised by Frenchman Berthold Goldman and Anglo-German Clive Schmitthoff as a

---

2 Montesquieu (Charles-Louis de Secondat, Baron de La Brède et de Montesquieu), *De L'Esprit des Loix [Lois]*, Barrillot, Geneva 1748 (typically quoted: Paris, Garnier, 1777), Book XI, chapter VI.

3 The West Galician Code (*Westgalizisches Gesetzbuch* or *Bürgerliches Gesetzbuch von Westgalizien*) enacted by Austria in a part of Galicia incorporated after the partition of Poland in 1795, which subsequently became the main basis for development of the *Allgemeines Bürgerliches Gesetzbuch* of 1811 – see F. Korkisch, 'Die Entstehung des österreichischen Allgemeinen Bürgerlichen Gesetzbuches' (1953) 18 *Zeitschrift für ausländisches und internationales Privatrecht* 266, 282 et seqq.

4 See S.P. Donlan, 'The Mediterranean Hybridity Project: Crossing the Boundaries of Law and Culture' (2011) 4 *Journal of Civil Law Studies* 355, 383–95.

body of law created by merchants, based on their practice and their free will (autonomy), without sovereign empowerment.[5] The core problem was (and remained) how free will as such, and thus party autonomy and practice based on it, without being grounded in a legal order established by sovereign power, could be seen as a legally binding and legitimate source of law. This free-floating legitimation – without a *Grundnorm* (basic norm) – despite being advocated for in the so-called free law movement (*Freiechtsschule*), had remained a rather a weak minority, even marginal, view, at least after World War II. However, also on the grounds of a basic (foundational) norm, *lex mercatoria* as law – i.e. private party ordering – did not seem unthinkable any longer. There were indeed endeavours to base certain parts of *lex mercatoria* – namely the sets of terms and conditions codified by neutral international bodies, such as Incoterms – on the acknowledged set of legal sources and basic norms of public international law or European Union law.[6] A second perspective where the acknowledged account of sources of law was taken into consideration relates to certain sub-sets, which will also be discussed in this volume. These are cases where a delegation took place – as in the case of standardisation (below section 5. and Grochowski's chapter) – or where regulation driven by private parties (self-regulation) was enacted with a view to abiding by it voluntarily, often also to avoid public (sovereign) regulation, i.e. under a threat of imminent state regulation (below section 5.2 and Micklitz's chapter). All these approaches

---

5 B. GOLDMAN, 'Frontières du droit et lex mercatoria' *Archives de philosophie du droit* 1964, 177; C. SCHMITTHOFF, 'International Business Law. A New Law Merchant' (1961) 2 *Current Law and Social Problems* 129; review of the rich literature in K.P. BERGER, 'Einheitliche Rechtsstrukturen durch außergesetzliche Rechtsvereinheitlichung', *Juristen-Zeitung (JZ)* 1999, 369; more conceptual H.-J. MERTENS, 'Lex Mercatoria: A Self-applying System Beyond National Law?' in G. TEUBNER (ed.), *Global Law Without a State*, Dartmouth, Aldershot 1997, pp. 31–44; id., 'Nichtlegislatorische Rechtsvereinheitlichung durch transnationales Wirtschaftsrecht und Rechtsbegriffe', *Rabels Zeitschrift für ausländisches und internationales Privatrecht (RabelsZ)* 56 (1992), 215. Roots already in L. GOLDSCHMIDT, *Universalgeschichte des Handelsrechts*, 3rd ed., Ferdinand Enke, Stuttgart 1891) – based, of course, on the historical school so prominent in Germany and that so strongly deviated from the all-pervasive codification movement on the continent; on Goldschmidt and this way of its own (*Sonderweg*), see K. SCHERNER, 'Lex mercatoria – Realität, Geschichtsbild oder Vision?', *Zeitschrift der Savigny-Stiftung für Rechtsgeschichte, Germanistische Abteilung* 118 (2001), 148; id., 'Goldschmidts Universum' in *Festschrift für Knut Wolfgang Nörr*, Böhlau Verlag, Köln 2003, pp. 859–92; L. WEYHE, *Levin Goldschmidt, Ein Gelehrtenleben in Deutschland; Grundfragen des Handelsrechts und der Zivilrechtswissenschaft in der zweiten Hälfte des 19. Jahrhunderts*, Duncker & Humblot, Berlin 1996.

6 In public international law, this was namely section 38 of the Statute of the International Court of Justice (ICJ), in European Union law namely the fundamental freedoms. On these endeavours, see S. GRUNDMANN, 'Lex mercatoria und Rechtsquellenlehre – insbesondere die Einheitlichen Richtlinien und Gebräuche für Dokumentenakkreditive', *Jahrbuch Junger Zivilrechtswissenschaftler (JJZ)* 1991, 43; id., 'General Principles of Private Law and Ius Commune Modernum as Applicable Law?' in *Essays in Honour of Richard Buxbaum*,: Kluwer, The Hague/London/Boston 2000, pp. 213–34.

and concrete examples, however, did not advocate – as Goldman and Schmitthoff did – for a legally binding force of standardisation and self-regulatory schemes based on practice and private party autonomy alone. They rather still searched for a chain of legitimacy grounded in sovereign power or legal sources. They have, however, already led, in practice and in substance, to a huge extension of rule-setting by private parties.

Still more radical are social sciences approaches questioning the need for a basic norm legitimation – initially more rooted in sociology in the 1960s, then also in economics in the following decades. Such approaches either claim that ordering in certain or even many social contexts does not require legal instruments or that certain communities have their own system of ordering, equally equipped with (state-like) sanctioning power. This will be taken up below in the section devoted to genuine private ordering (below section 5.1).

The second pillar of the new picture consists of a new conceptualisation and a changed vision of the arena of rule-setting reaching beyond the national sphere. In 1956, Philip Jessup coined the term and the concept of a 'transnational law'.[7] Besides the power and emancipation of the private parties, the crossing of borders and the conceptualisation of this potential constitute the second core responsible for a more diversified, less nation- and sovereign-state-oriented concept of creation of norms, for the 'new picture'. This has a global side (below section 1.2) and a genuinely European side (below sections 2 and 4).

In parallel to these two pillars, which account for the stronger empowerment of private party rule-setting, one more development instead accounts for a shift between two of the three powers, from the legislature to the judiciary. This is the conceptualisation of more activist courts – even though, in fact, courts before the second half of the 20th century may also already have been activist to a comparable extent. This arguably considerable shift from a judge who simply pronounces the will of the legislature to a partner in rule-setting constitutes a shift between two forms of sovereign power from a state theory perspective. It may, however, also be viewed as yet another form of increased variety in a surging number of rule-setters. Moreover, in some respects, such as knowledge of facts on the spot, judges as rule-setters may be seen to be closer to private parties as rule-setters than to the legislature.[8] For instance, internet platforms,

---

7 P. Jessup, *Transnational Law*, Yale University Press, New Haven 1956; on this book, the concept and the discussion it triggered, see lately M. Renner in S. Grundmann, H.-W. Micklitz and M. Renner, above n. 1, chapter 25.

8 For this aspect – not further developed in the following – see, for instance, R. Podszun, 'Regelsetzung durch Gerichte als evolutionärer Prozess – Von Darwin zur Dashcam' in F. Möslein (ed.), *Regelsetzung im Privatrecht*, Mohr Siebeck, Tübingen 2019, pp. 255–300. On the huge literature on the role of judges as creators of norms and on the factors influencing their decision-making, see (mainly from common law contexts): A. Hill, 'The Law-Making Power of the Federal Courts: Constitutional Preemption' (1967) 67 *Columbia Law Review*

when proposing the rules of the platform, may also be starting from a concrete set of facts, much more like judges – and the legislature's approach may diverge from both the judicial and platform-based schemes.

1.2. CIVIL LAW CODIFICATION AND ITS CHANGING ROLE IN A MULTI-CENTRIC LEGAL ORDER

When Philip Jessup coined the term 'transnational law', the phenomenon of a globalised world – albeit with a strong split into blocs – was by no means new as such. Nor did his book completely depart from the traditional image that the nation state and public international law mainly based on bilateral and multilateral, even global, treaties and charters constituted the two core sources of 'law'. Instead, the revolutionary germ rested, on the one hand, in the fact that other actors, such as powerful multinational enterprises, were taken into consideration – even though it took some time until they were seen as genuine legislatures themselves (see below section 5.1), and, on the other hand, in the new term, 'transnational law'. Transnational law as a concept left some room alongside genuine public international law based on sovereign power as the basic norm and legitimation. The last six decades have seen a constant struggle to conceptualise this realm that exists alongside genuine public international law, and that started as a remainder, but may well in fact occupy a large, perhaps even the largest, space today. Concepts such as the multinational enterprise, constitutionalisation of the global sphere, competition of legislatures and corporate social responsibility are testaments to the extension of this arena (see more below sections 3.2, 4.2 and 4.3).

The single most important instrument based on sovereign power that accounts for much of this newly discovered 'transnational law freedom' can be seen in the fundamental freedom of choice of law in contract law. Seen from a European perspective, transnational law as a multi-centric legal order is characterised by a freedom of choice of law in contract law. Article 3 of the Rome Convention on choice of law in contract law, supplemented by Article 3 of the Rome I Regulation[9] establish this very far-reaching principle. Outside

1024; L.L. Jaffe, *English and American Judges as Lawmakers*, Clarendon Press, Oxford 1967; M.A. Loth, 'Who Has the Last Word? On Judicial Lawmaking in European Private Law' (2017) 25 *European Review of Private Law (ERPL)* 45. Still seminal for interpretation in codified systems: J. Esser, *Vorverständnis und Methodenwahl in der Rechtsfindung. Rationalitätsgrundlagen richterlicher Entscheidungspraxis*, Athenäum, Frankfurt am Main 1972, esp. pp. 7–9, 116–41; for a contextualisation and the discussions ensuing, see S. Grundmann in S. Grundmann, H.-W. Micklitz and M. Renner, above n. 1, chapter 1.

9 See Regulation (EC) No. 593/2008 of the European Parliament and of the Council of 17 June 2008 on the law applicable to contractual obligations (Rome I) [2008] OJ L177/6;

specific fields of contract law and regulation, any meaningful cross-border element in the transaction suffices to allow parties to freely choose any national law of the world, even without any connection to the case and with no need for justification.[10] If an arbitration clause is included, any set of rules at all can be chosen – so long as the arbitral court is empowered to judge *ex aequo et bono.*[11] In any event, the extension of the freedom of choice of law is such that many questions ensue. Why, for instance, should an internationally discussed and drafted set of rules created by a body that (in many cases) well represents the main constituencies involved be less legitimate as the chosen law than the law of a state without rule of law and that, for instance, openly discriminates against the interests of certain member of society?[12]

The complete freedom of choice under Article 3 is subject to two modifications. Firstly, it is limited in its extent through various exceptions, the most important for contract law being the two contained in Articles 6 and 9 Rome I Regulation. In consumer contracts, the law in force at the consumer's place of habitual residence sets the baseline below which no rule chosen may fall. Moreover, those rules that protect a common interest, namely those that protect market functioning or proper disclosure, apply (without freedom to deviate by choice of law) whenever the contract impacts on the territory where they have been enacted (so-called impact principle).[13] Secondly, besides freedom of choice

---

Convention 80/934/EEC on the law applicable to contractual obligations, opened for signature in Rome on 19 June 1980 (Rome Convention) [1980] OJ L266/1; and ample literature in G.-P. Calliess (ed.), *The Rome Regulations,* 2nd ed., Kluwer, Alphen aan den Rijn 2015.

10 See G.-P. Calliess, above n. 9, Art. 3 para. 12, 34 and 52; H.E. Yntema, '"Autonomy" in Choice of Law' (1952) 1 *American Journal of Comparative Law* 341; F. Maultzsch, 'Party autonomy in European private international law: uniform principle or context-dependent instrument?' (2016) 12 *Journal of Private International Law* 469; K. Kroll-Ludwigs, *Die Rolle der Parteiautonomie im europäischen Kollisionsrecht,* Mohr Siebeck, Tübingen 2013; H. Muir Watt, '"Party Autonomy" in international contracts: from the makings of a myth to the requirements of global governance' (2010) 6 *European Review of Contract Law (ERCL)* 250, esp. 260–264.

11 See K. Berger, *Formalisierte oder „schleichende" Kodifizierung des transnationalen Wirtschaftsrechts – zu den methodologischen und praktischen Grundlagen der lex mercatoria,* De Gruyter, Berlin/New York 1996, pp. 50–58; P. Lagarde, 'Approche critique de la lex mercatoria' in *Études offertes à Berthold Goldman* 1983, pp. 125–50, at pp. 140 and 146; on the large number of (the most important) international conventions on arbitration that allow for such choice, see J. Bonell, 'The relevance of courses of dealing, usages and customs in the interpretation of international commercial contracts' in Unidroit (ed.), *New directions in international trade law,* Reports 1977, pp. 109–137, at p. 118.

12 For a summary of the debate and further readings see G.-P. Calliess, above n. 9, Art. 3 para. 33.

13 The so-called effects doctrine ('impact' principle) – as opposed to the principle of territoriality (seat of the actors or place of actions taken) – was most prominently introduced in antitrust law: see Joined Cases 89, 104, 114, 116, 117 and 125–129/85, *Woodpulp* [1988] ECR 5193. It is paramount, however, also in other areas, such as capital market law or unfair competition law.

in its basic sense (free choice at will), there is not just its extreme opposite, i.e. internationally binding law. Rather, there are many shades in between. For example, the applicable law can often be chosen only by adopting a certain arrangement. For instance, by choosing a certain seat for the internet platform – or by choosing the location of the headquarters under the real seat theory in (certain) company law(s) – the applicable law of that place is also chosen even though free choice at will is not accepted there.[14]

Along with the growing heteronomy of sources of private law – and the gradual withdrawal of the state from direct regulatory activity – the significance of the freedom to choose the applicable law has also seen a parallel evolution. Muir Watt, in her contribution to this volume, explores this phenomenon further against the background of the present-day transnational markets. The classic conceptual agenda of private international law, confined to the idea of the state's monopoly in the creation of contractual norms, is no longer able, in Muir Watt's view, to embrace the normative landscape of contract law in its entirety. Against this background, the freedom of choice is not merely a freedom to set oneself free from state-made law (as it would be considered in the classic terms), but rather a freedom to choose between several competing modes of governing contracts. In the EU legal sphere, freedom in choosing the applicable law is intertwined with single market freedoms, as a component of a wider autonomy-based edifice. At the same time, the whole heterogeneous structure of the modern transnational law remains in constant flux, animated by a tension between various state and non-state actors, each competing for a stronger grasp of the governance of market relations.

The openness to choice – direct and free choice of law where not limited, or choice of law via the choice of a certain way of arranging the relationship – accounts for much of what constitutes the variety of rule-setters in the transnational sphere to be discussed in the remainder of this overall summary and throughout much of the book. And this arena is in constant flux – namely if it includes the many national law choices that are thus opened. In Europe, both the old codifications (like those of France, Germany and now Italy) must adapt to new trends,[15] and the codifications of the ex-communist Central European countries often are re-enacted (like in Hungary)[16] or are in the course

---

[14] See on the EU law position/framework on real seat theory (on the basis of freedom of establishment), with comparative law indications where the theory is still applied, see S. Grundmann, *European Company Law – Organization, Finance and Capital Markets*, 2nd ed., Intersentia, Cambridge/Antwerp/Portland 2012, §7 paras. 6–10, 20, 25, and §25 paras. 32–37, 43, 46.

[15] See S. Grundmann and M. Schäfer, 'The French and the German Reform Compared' (2017) 13 *ERCL* 459, 470–72.

[16] The Civil Code of Hungary of 2013, which replaced the Civil Code of 1959 (founded on the combined influence of classical civil codes, especially the ABGB, and the socialist ideology

of being re-enacted (like in Poland).[17] Pisulinski's contribution shows how the reform of the Civil Code in Poland is motivated by two perceived shortcomings: the not fully adequate regulation of service contracts – which are increasingly so rich and important – and the equally not fully adequate regulation of formation of contract (with e-formation techniques abounding, but also with new marketing techniques). The European Union texture of rule-setters adds another dimension to this picture (below section 2).

1.3. CONTRACT LAW IN ITS RELATION TO VALUES, POLICIES AND NEW FUNCTIONS

In the first two sections, one major – arguably *the* major – overall change in the process of the creation of norms was identified as a twofold extension of power. Firstly, the influence that contract partners have on the regime that is to be applied was seen to have increased, because the number of rule-setters has also increased, extending to private law subjects as well (i.e. there is *larger participation in rule creation*). Secondly, these subjects were also seen to be much more in control of the legal arrangement because of a largely extended freedom of choice of law in the transnational legal arena (i.e. there is *larger choice*). In what follows, a countervailing trend that now needs to be addressed will be taken up. Contract law will recurrently be described as the vehicle via which new values, policies and also new functions or preferences enter the market and the transactions on it, namely its legal constitution. Via the advent of such new value bases and functions, new modes of creating the content of contract are also addressed.

The most basic traditional kind of private and contract law norm that is open for such new developments, and indeed is designed to adapt to them, can certainly be found in general clauses, and most prominently in the duty of good faith. This – old – private and contract law rule and standard already has a highly influential history over the last century, discussed in the following (see below section 3.1 and the chapter by Markovits). A second powerful route via which value- and function-based considerations have been 'infused' into contract law is recourse to constitutional values, namely concrete fundamental rights, be it directly, as seen at the national level first in Germany, then in other countries and at the EU level (see below sections 3.2 and 4.1), or be it indirectly,

---

and legal doctrine); see also A. Menyhárd and E. Veress (eds.), *New Civil Codes in Hungary and Romania*, Springer, Cham 2017; see also L. Vékás, 'Hungary' (2006) 2 *ERCL* 112.

17 On the rebirth of the codification idea in Europe, along with recently enacted national civil codes, see also R. Schulze and F. Zoll (eds.), *The Law of Obligations in Europe: A New Wave of Codifications*, Sellier, Munich 2013; E. Hondius, 'Recodification of Private Law: Central and Eastern Europe Set the Tone' (2013) 21 *ERPL* 897.

as was the case in the approach to the constitutionalisation of transnational law, which has been guided by an idea of a transnational constitution inspired by concrete constitutional regimes (see also below section 3.2).

These guiding principles, that infuse an additional value basis into contract law, are themselves subject to dynamic evolution, as are general standards like good faith, as well as more concrete concepts like the (agreed-upon) quality of the good in sales law or reasonable care for the interests of the contract partner. Two examples are illustrative of this. Consumers may, in considerable, large or even majority numbers, start to oppose the fact that certain products on offer are manufactured in conditions that do not respect basic human rights standards and/or do not show care for their ecological footprint. If this can be ascertained with sufficient certainty, these values would eventually filter into contract law if below-average performance in this respect came to be seen as a defect of the good or service delivered.[18] Similarly, insolvency might arguably be seen as a considerable inroad into human dignity and this might impact on interpretation of contract law if high enough a number of borrowers rather obviously did succumb to unrealistic forecasts of their future capacity to pay back loans. In such a situation, the value of better protection of human dignity might arguably be infused into contract law if the good faith principle (or a duty of loyalty) at the contract formation was interpreted as to contain a duty of responsible lending.[19] Using such concepts would imply that contract law serves as a vehicle to fostering new values cherished by contract partners.

2. EUROPEAN UNION: CREATOR OF CONTRACT LAW AND EMPOWERING CONTRACTUAL SHAPING

This is not an essay on EU treaty law, but it includes the question of what role the EU law framework may (also) play in the creation of contract law norms.

18 Proposals in this sense in H. Collins, 'Conformity of Goods, the Network Society, and the Ethical Consumer' (2014) 22 *ERPL* 619, esp. 634–40.

19 Proposals in this sense very clearly: C. Hofmann, 'Die Pflicht zur Bewertung der Kreditwürdigkeit', *Neue Juristische Wochenschrift (NJW)* 2010, 1782, esp. 1785 et seq.; similar, at least in their result: Y. Atamer, 'Duty of Responsible Lending – Should the European Union Take Action?' in S. Grundmann and Y. Atamer (eds.), *Financial Services, Financial Crisis and General European Contract Law – Failure and Challenges of Contracting*, Kluwer Law International, Alphen aan den Rijn 2011, pp. 179–202, at pp. 191 et seq. and 199–202 et passim; J. Pottow, 'Private Liability for Reckless Consumer Lending' (2007) *University of Illinois Law Review* 405, 431 et seq.; C. Sunstein, 'Boundedly Rational Borrowing' (2006) 73 *University of Chicago Law Review (U. Chi. L. Rev.)* 249, 267. For the EU, the dispute is obsolete at least with respect to the economically most relevant consumer loans, since this rule has also been inserted into the Mortgage Credit Directive 2014/17/EU, which clearly protects private parties.

Therefore, a short summary of the rule-setting framework and architecture should suffice – complemented by some considerations on the CJEU's role as a creator of contract law that is more on the substantive contract law side (below section 6).

2.1. CONTRACT LAW AND EU COMPETENCES: THE ROLE OF AUTONOMY AND OF REGULATION

The well-known starting point is that there is no specific legal basis for contract law, but only the general internal market legal basis contained in Article 114 TFEU. The large majority of contract law measures enacted within the EU legislative process are based on this norm. The second most important legal basis is de facto sector-specific and concerns those contract law issues that have to do with financial services (Art. 53(1) TFEU).[20] Both legal bases require that the measures taken reduce the burden of cross-border transfers and thus facilitate such transfers – even though, whenever this condition is satisfied, it is universal and unquestioned practice that the measures taken may also harmonise national law for all domestic transactions. Conversely, mere harmonisation of cross-border transactions forms the rare exception, and where it had occurred, as for instance in Directive 97/5/EC on (cross-border) credit transfers, it was later typically changed to also encompass harmonisation of domestic transactions, for instance when Directive 97/5/EC was replaced by the Payment Services Directive 2007/64/EC. Moreover, whenever the EC/EU legislature confirmed that such facilitation of cross-border transfer was the aim, the CJEU also confirmed this view, giving large legislative discretion in assessing the facilitation aspect. In all the proceedings where the legal basis was challenged, the Court struck down a 'harmonisation' measure only in one case and this was a case where an outright ban of publicity for tobacco products had been pronounced, i.e. a measure clearly aimed at the exact opposite of facilitation.[21]

Despite this generous practice on the interpretation of the legal basis by the Court – apparently giving much leeway – the design of the legal basis (aimed at cross-border empowerment) has nevertheless strongly influenced the kind

---

20 In addition, Art. 53(1) TFEU allows (only) for measures 'for the coordination of the provisions laid down by law … in Member States concerning the taking-up and pursuit of activities as self-employed persons', for instance providers of financial services, 'in order to make [such activities] easier'. Among the three most important EU law measures for banking contract law, two are also based on Art. 114 TFEU, namely Directives 2014/17/EU on Consumer Mortgage Credits and 2015/2366/EU on Payment Services (II), while MiFID II (Directive 2014/65/EU) on investment services (including advice) and on markets for financial instruments is based on Art. 53(1) TFEU.

21 See Case C-376/98, *Tobacco I* [2000] ECR I-8498.

of measures taken. They have all been designed in such a way that facilitation of cross-border trade was at least plausible. The background of the design consists of Articles 3–6 and 9 Rome I Regulation (and its forerunner, the Rome Convention) and of an old ECJ judgment that held that all those national rules that could be opted out from in cross-border transactions did not constitute obstacles to cross-border trade.[22] The design opted for in the legislative contract law agenda was harmonisation only in areas of consumer protection and areas where some kind of public good, namely the regulated market, was at stake. These are areas where free choice of law under Article 3 Rome I Regulation is restricted – namely under Articles 6 and 9 Rome I Regulation – and where the protection of consumers or a public good is at stake. The common denominator is that risks stemming from professional activity are regulated, at the national level mostly in a mandatory way – mandatory also for cross-border transactions, which hence creates a potential obstacle, for which the EU legislature has increasingly and rather systematically provided harmonisation.[23] Hence, European private law and European contract law are different from classical private and mainly contract law where default rules are dominant, facilitating a choice of solutions ultimately based on party autonomy. The European agenda concentrates in essence on the regulatory part of any contract, hence the concept of European regulatory private law[24] – a part of contract law that, however, has to be seen and has already been seen for a few decades as an integral part of contract law.

With this divide comes one important consequence. The regulatory part of contract is typically harmonised, and hence regulated at the EU level, which takes precedence over national contract law. However, while this constitutes an important consequence for the character of contract law – including commercial contracts – it does not change the hierarchy of norms that much. EU contract law is regulatory in character, i.e. it is about shaping necessary safeguards in markets and contracts.[25] This part of contract law would, however, takes

22 See Case C-339/89, *Alsthom Atlantique* [1991] ECR I-107.

23 For this interpretation, see already S. Grundmann, 'The Structure of European Contract Law' (2001) 9 *ERPL* 505; and (positive for this design) id., 'Europäisches Handelsrecht – vom Handelsrecht des laissez faire im Kodex des 19. Jahrhunderts zum Handelsrecht der sozialen Verantwortung', *Zeitschrift für das gesamte Handelsrecht (ZHR)* 163 (1999) 635; main lines also in id., 'European Contract Law(s) – of What Colour?' (2005) 1 *ERCL* 184; and the same thrust, for instance, in K. Riesenhuber, *EU-Vertragsrecht*, Mohr Siebeck, Tübingen 2013, pp. 86–93.

24 See H.-W. Micklitz, 'The Visible Hand of European Regulatory Private Law – The Transformation of European Private Law from Autonomy to Functionalism in Competition and Regulation' (2009) 28 *Yearbook of European Law* 3; H. Dagan, 'Between Regulatory and Autonomy-Based Private Law' (2016) 22 *European Law Journal (ELJ)* 644; also S. Grundmann, above n. 23.

25 For this interpretation, see already S. Grundmann, above n. 23.

precedence in any event, even within one unitary – for instance – national system. Thus, the divide is more one of responsibilities – internal market making and safeguarding the proper market mechanism at the EU level, facilitating the use of party autonomy rather at the national level – and not one that creates a *new* hierarchy.

2.2. THE DYNAMICS OF LAW-MAKING BETWEEN THE EU AND THE MEMBER STATES

This divide also shapes the dynamics of law-making between the EU and the Member States. While EU law formally takes precedence – national law having to transpose and adapt it, namely via the concept of direct or indirect effect (interpretation in conformity with the EU law measure, namely EU Directives) – the dynamics are more substantially shaped by the substantive split of labour.

A general trend that can be found in each new generation of legislation, however, is that the coverage of EU law tends to extend. The development from the EC Directive 97/5/EC on (cross-border) credit transfers to the third-generation EU Payment Services Directive II 2016/64/EU is an excellent example of this trend. The 1997 regime was restricted to one payment instrument, only to cross-border transactions and only to the few major obstacles and problems that had been identified in cross-border transfer of credit. Conversely, the 2016 regime covers all major payment instruments (encompassing well over 99 per cent of transactions in both number and volume), including on the domestic market (and notably even when third states are affected) and does so for each and every important issue in the arrangement of payments – a true mini-codification. A similar development can be found in 2019 in the realm of sales and digital contracts with EU Directives 2019/770/EU and 2019/771/EU, as well as with a good number of other measures.

This twofold trend towards much increased density and substantially broader coverage (both in substance and in extent of application) is sometimes coupled with a transition from harmonisation via Directives to harmonisation via EU Regulations. The difference between the two modes of harmonisation, however, while doctrinally meaningful, is not in practice so important (given that Directives also have direct and indirect effect). In contract law, EU Regulations are still rare, although they can increasingly be found in market regulation proper. Such regulations have already been traditionally in use with respect to antitrust measures, and lately also for the regulation of financial markets where Regulations now abound (covering prospectuses, insider dealing, market manipulation, financial benchmarks, short sales and OTC markets, etc.).

3. CONSTITUTION AND CONSTITUTIONAL VALUES AS A SOURCE OF CONTRACT LAW

3.1. GOOD FAITH AND FAIRNESS AS PRIVATE LAW CONSTITUTION

When it comes to contract law that is inspired by values outside the two basic principles of (a) binding force of consent (with legal certainty) and (b) correcting flaws in the formation of consent and in the performance of the contract, the natural starting point would seem to be the good faith principle (and other similar general clauses). This is often forgotten amid all the discussion of the impact of constitutional values and principles on contract law or of the constitutionalisation of contract law more generally, which certainly are also important driving forces (below sections 3.2. and 3.3).

It has been shown for financial contracts, which have played such an important role in the German Constitutional Court's case law on developing direct or indirect effect of fundamental rights in contract law, that very much the same results can be reached – in jurisdictions other than Germany – by private law principles such as good faith and standards of fairness in contract law.[26] The good faith principle constitutes a powerful source of new values that go beyond mere (formal) consent – namely testing substantive consent, rewriting contracts in extreme situations, or seeing contract as a legally binding instrument that is embedded in a social relationship and to a certain extent dependent on it. The good faith principle has its own long history, one that is particularly strong in Germany, where it was seen for all of the 20th century as an overarching principle that inspires all phases and all aspects of contract making and contract law: namely the formation of contract and including the pre-contractual phase, as well as trust created in it,[27] but also interpretation and performance of contract (including its rewriting in extreme cases of change), and eventually also the post-contractual phase.[28] This overarching concept of a good faith principle

---

26 This was the case, for instance, in the United Kingdom and in the Netherlands. See O.O. Cherednychenko, *Fundamental Rights, Contract Law and the Protection of the Weaker Party: A Comparative Analysis of the Constitutionalisation of Contract Law, with Emphasis on Risky Financial Transactions*, Sellier, Munich 2007; id., 'EU Fundamental Rights, EC Fundamental Freedoms and Private Law' (2006) 14 *ERPL* 23.

27 See also on the density of case law (due to the provision's role as a 'starting point' for judicial engineering and institution building): C. Schubert in F.J. Säcker, R. Rixecker, H. Oetker and B. Limperg (eds.), *Münchener Kommentar zum Bürgerlichen Gesetzbuch – Band 2,* 7th ed., C.H. Beck, Munich 2016, §242, paras. 24–29. Linking 10 per cent of all German Supreme Court cases to Art. 242 of the new German Civil Code: D. Looschelders and D. Olzen in J. von Staudinger, D. Looschelders and G. Schiemann (eds.), *Staudinger BGB – §§241–243,* 15th ed., Sellier/De Gruyter, Berlin 2014, §242, para. 79.

28 See last footnote.

has in recent times been implanted with a similarly broad scope into the much older French Civil Code, in the first truly fundamental reform in contract law for this grand old Code.[29]

While the common law, namely in England, is traditionally seen as being opposed to attributing to good faith the character of an overarching principle,[30] Markovits, in his contribution, argues precisely for this for the common law of contracts in the US. He sees good faith as 'contract's core value' – one could say, the value that constitutes the essence of contractual binding force and promise. His argument would suggest that this is so more generally in contract law in countries that see the well-intended and understandable interest of each party as the guideline for contract interpretation. His argument is, however, limited to performance, where the core idea would seem to be that not sticking to the letter of an agreement and not punishing the party that might not have specified all the potential details of the agreement also implies that good faith can serve as a fall-back solution. Good faith would comprise what each party would have understood as the natural content of the agreement, had each party taken the understandable and visible legitimate interest of the other party into account. What may seem far-reaching for common law legal scholars is, however, arguably much less demanding than the continental concept of good faith as an overarching principle and indeed the core value basis for the whole relation, starting before the formation proper and ending well after the execution proper.

3.2. THE ROLE OF CONSTITUTION IN CONTRACT LAW

Nowadays in Europe, including the United Kingdom, it would seem as if good faith as the 'constitution' of contract law (Markovits) has been pushed a bit into

29 Arts. 1104 and 1112 of the new French Civil Code (as of 2016); see, for instance N. Dissaux and C. Jamin, *Réforme du droit des contrats, du régime général et de la preuve des obligations, Art. 1112 Code Civil,* Dalloz, Paris 2016; S. Grundmann and M. Schäfer (2017) 13 *ERCL* 459, 470–72. For the prominent role the good faith principle plays in Italian private law as an overarching and general concept, see, for instance, M. Barcellona, *Clausole generali e giustizia contrattuale. Equità e buona fede tra codice civile e diritto europeo,* Giappichelli, Turin 2006. For a (rather detailed) overview of good faith in a European and international context: C. Schubert, above n. 27, §242, paras. 151–68. Investigating the role of good faith in European contract law while considering PECL, UNIDROIT and CISG: O. Lando, 'Is Good Faith an Over-Arching General Clause in the Principles of European Contract Law?' (2007) 15 *ERPL* 841.

30 Proposals in this sense in G. Teubner, 'Legal Irritants: Good Faith in British Law or How Unifying Law Ends Up in New Divergences' (2003) 61 *Modern Law Review* 11; M. Piers, 'Good Faith in English Law – Could a Rule Become a Principle?' (2011) 26 *Tulane European & Civil Law Forum* 123, esp. 130–38; H. Collins, 'Good Faith in European Contract Law' (1994) 14 *Oxford Journal of Legal Studies* 249, esp. 238–54.

the background – at least in the general perception – by a (more prominent) instrument referring directly to constitution and its values for contract law. This line of thinking was first developed by the German Constitutional Court which characterised constitutional law, with its fundamental rights, not only as a limit on state power, but as the prime and general basis of legal values in all areas of the law, including contract law (taking precedence over all other sources). It did so early on in the *Lüth* case of 1958 on freedom of opinion in political questions with respect to tort and unfair competition law. It reinvigorated this idea for contract law in the 1990s, namely in the *Surety* case on situations of so-called structural imbalances in contractual relations, the legal evaluation of which case law it assessed against the fundamental rights of human dignity and freedom of the person.[31] The conceptualisation of this idea in the literature – with particular reference to contract law and an economic constitution – started in Italy in the 1960s, and in the 1990s the so-called *Schutzpflicht* theory was famously developed.[32] The approach was also followed outside the EU (for instance in Brazil, where the direct impact of the constitution on private law is the dominant approach). Even in the common law country of the United Kingdom, private law is tested against fundamental rights, albeit on the basis of the European Convention on Human Rights (ECHR), which takes precedence over the common law.[33]

---

31 See Bundesverfassungsgericht (BVerfG, German Constitutional Court), BVerfGE (official reports) 7, 198. Then BVerfG, BVerfGE 89, 214 (*Bürgschaftsfall* – surety case); BVerfG, BVerfGE 81, 242 (*Handelsvertreterfall* – commercial agent case); in 2018: BVerfG, BVerfGE 148, 267 (*Stadionverbotsfall* – ban on entry to stadium case). For Brazil see, for instance, Constitutional Court (Suprêmo Tribunal Federal), *RE (Recurso Extraordinário)* 201.819-8 (2nd senate) (reporter G. Mendes) of 11.10.2005 ('due process'). There is a broad survey in C. Mak, *Fundamental Rights in European Contract Law. A Comparison of the Impact of Fundamental Rights on Contractual Relationships in Germany, the Netherlands, Italy and England,* Kluwer, Alphen aan den Rijn 2008, pp. 75–81 et passim.

32 See first L. Mengoni, 'Forma giuridica e materia economica' in id., *Diritto e Valori*, Mulino, Bologna 1985 (first published in two articles of 1963 and 1966). The *Schutzpflicht* theory opines that all the state bodies (of Germany), including courts, have the duty not only to refrain from violating the fundamental rights of the Constitution, but also to safeguard them, for instance in court proceedings, and to do so universally, in all relationships on which they are adjudicating. See C.-W. Canaris, 'Verfassungs- und europarechtliche Aspekte der Vertragsfreiheit in der Privatrechtsgesellschaft' in *Festschrift für Peter Lerche,* C.H. Beck, Munich 1993, pp. 873–91. For Italy (with its particularly rich literature), see G. Comandé (ed.), *Diritto Privato Europeo e Diritti Fondamentali – Saggi a ricerche,* Giappichelli, Turin 2004; P. Laghi, *L'Incidenza dei Diritti Fondamentali Sull'Autonomia Negoziale,* Cedam, Padua 2012; F. Macario, 'L'autonomia privata nella cornice costituzionale: per una giurisprudenza evolutiva e coraggiosa', *Questione Giustizia* 2016, 52–76; more broadly see also G. Brüggemeier, A. Colombi Ciacchi and G. Comandé (eds.), *Fundamental Rights and Private Law in the European Union,* Cambridge University Press, Cambridge 2012; S. Grundmann (ed.), *Constitutional Values and European Contract Law*, Kluwer International, Alphen aan den Rijn 2008.

33 See e.g. *Lee v. Ashers Baking Company Ltd and others* [2018] UKSC 49, where the UK Supreme Court juxtaposed the principle of non-discrimination (in the context of refusal to make an

Collins, in his contribution, prominently defends this line of thinking (both for the UK and the EU). In the examples he discusses and his system-building, he identifies several groups, among which two would seem to stand out. In the first group, constitutional values play a role where traditional private law already requires the balancing of interests, introducing a new powerful argument as evidenced in the *Alemo-Herron* case. In this case, it was asked whether a new employer, when being constrained to take on posted workers in an enterprise it has acquired, should moreover be forced to accept later salary increases bargained for by trade unions whose bargains were binding in the old enterprise, but with whom the new employer does not want to enter into an agreement. In the second group, however, constitutional values play a more radical role when they infuse a new idea into a rather concrete norm from a different context, like the right to a home (Art. 7 EU Charter) when assessing the termination of a credit agreement (*Aziz* and *Kušionová* cases).[34] Collins points to the fact that such value bases at times are not spelt out explicitly, but would still seem to have an impact (along with *Aziz*, Collins also mentions *Putz/Weber*). Collins' contribution, however, deals mainly with CJEU case law and the EU level, which are taken up separately, as a source for the creation of law on its own merits and of rather high complexity (see below section 6).

The idea of constitutional values impacting on private law is, however, not restricted to well-defined catalogues of fundamental rights in national or international instruments or other principles also found there. Entirely to the contrary, and specifically in the transnational arena, a broader and less concretely grounded reference to the 'constitutionalisation' of this arena is made.[35] If contexts matter, it may be clarified that the approaches are often rooted in concepts developed in sociology, system theory and political science. The overarching idea is as follows. Where a system of law develops with party autonomy at its centre and with the claim to function as a system of law – namely in transnational markets and enterprises – it is to be taken at its word and as a full legal system.[36] Only the completeness of the system as a legal

agreement) with the freedoms of expression and of religion, derived from the ECHR; see also a broader survey, within the Society of European Contract Law (SECOLA), in: H. Collins (ed.), *European Contract Law and the Charter of Fundamental Rights*, Intersentia, Cambridge/Antwerp/Portland 2017.

34 See C. Mak, 'One and the Many: Translating Insights from Constitutional Pluralism to European Contract Law Theory' (2013) 21 *ERPL* 1189.

35 See C. Mak, above n. 31, pp. 191 et seqq.; H.-W. Micklitz, 'Introduction' in H.-W. Micklitz (ed.), *The Constitutionalization of European Private Law*, Oxford University Press, Oxford 2014; O.O. Cherednychenko, 'The Constitutionalization of European Private Law: Gateways, Constraints, and Challenges' (2015) 23 *ERPL* 797; A. Colombi Ciacchi, 'The Constitutionalization of European Contract Law: Judicial Convergence and Social Justice' (2006) 2 *ERCL* 167.

36 See E. Gaillard, 'Transnational Law: A Legal System or a Method of Decision Making?' (2001) 17 *Arbitration International* 59, esp. 66–68; G.-P. Calliess, 'Reflexive Transnational

system allows for its fairness, but also for its moral claim. Its embeddedness in a legal culture – here, of a fair market economy in (typically) democratic systems under the rule of law – is of core importance, as the main actors shaping the transnational system live in such a legal culture. This allows for the construction of a realm in which basic constitutional principles apply, including a balance of powers, care for a common good (for instance in environmental issues), fairness and social aspirations. Where there are universal rules – such as the universal declaration of human rights – the basis for such an approach becomes more concrete, and the line of legitimacy would seem to resemble more that of the *Lüth* and the *Surety* cases. In yet another way, contract law becomes potentially more value loaded, and this implies a meaningful shift in regulatory techniques and in division of labour between rule-making actors. It develops more compound and heterogeneous ways of integrating values and policy goals into its domain, especially through the involvement of non-state actors in framing and reframing its policy agenda. In this way, contract law may not only shape purely economic matters, but also create broader social effects (e.g. by becoming more inclusive towards fundamental rights, economic equality and environmental issues addressed by CSR and, still more targeted, via sustainability clauses).[37] This is also the case for non-discrimination measures developed in a bottom-up way by sharing economy platforms, such as Uber and Airbnb.[38] Consequently, the classic political legitimisation of a policy agenda in contract law is partly replaced by 'legitimisation' based on market dynamics or decentralised decision-making.

3.3. IN PARTICULAR: NEW TYPES OF CONSTITUTIONAL RIGHTS IN AN EVOLVING CONTRACT LAW

How dynamic a development in contract law such a value basis stemming from the realm of constitutions might trigger, how evolution in the constitutional setting might have strong overspill effects in contract law, can be illustrated well with just one example. This is the right to informational self-determination developed by constitutional courts around the world, specifically in the context

Law. The Privatisation of Civil Law and the Civilisation of Private Law', *Zeitschrift für Rechtssoziologie* 23 (2002), 185, esp. 194 et seq.

37 See K. Peterková Mitkidis, *Sustainability Clauses in International Business Contracts*, Eleven International Publishing, The Hague 2014.

38 For more on the non-state creation of protective mechanisms in this regard, see e.g. N. Schoenbaum, 'Law and Norms in the Market Response to Discrimination in the Sharing Economy' (2019) 13 *Law & Ethics of Human Rights* 1; K. Sargeant, 'Alternative Dispute Resolution in Short Term Rental Accommodations: Is Binding Arbitration Appropriate in the Sharing Economy for Racial Discrimination Cases' (2019) 34 *Ohio State Journal on Dispute Resolution* 575, esp. 580–82.

of data protection.[39] Originally, it was seen as being fully in the hands of the person to whom the personal data referred – hence the full legitimising effect of consent, at least informed consent. One conceptual problem from the outset was, however, that private parties could not, in the case of many fundamental rights, validly renounce those rights of their own motion (autonomy) – even more so when they could not really have full knowledge of the degree to which they were renouncing such rights. The development of a form of consent that needs to be thicker and that can be challenged at all[40] was particularly understandable – and even necessary – against this background, even though such reasoning is not completely alien to recent contract law either. The example shows, however, how change in constitutional values may also trigger change, or at least fall onto fertile ground, for contract and thus facilitate the evolution of contract law.

4. THE SELECTION OF NORMS: FROM DEFAULT RULE TO OPTIONAL CODES AND REGULATION

4.1. OPTIONALITY AS AN INTRINSIC FEATURE OF DEFAULT REGIMES AND CONTRACT LAW

The ongoing evolution of rule-setting schemes brought strongly back to the fore one more foundational layer of contract law: the division between mandatory and non-mandatory rules. On the classic view, the law of contracts is by nature 'facilitative', i.e. designed merely to provide instruments for the efficient expression of the parties' intent. This entails a general aversion towards any form of compulsion within the classic conceptual framework, understood as the lack (or scarcity) of mandatory rules.[41] In other words, contract law should focus on facilitating rather than on limiting the parties' freedom of choice. This aim is pursued in two interconnected ways.

---

39 G. González Fuster, *The Emergence of Personal Data Protection as a Fundamental Right of the EU*, Springer, Cham 2014, pp. 55–105; J. Eichenhofer and C. Gusy, 'Courts, privacy and data protection in Germany: Informational self-determination in the digital environment' in M. Brkan and E. Psychogiopoulou (eds.), *Courts, Privacy and Data Protection in the Digital Environment*, Edward Elgar, Cheltenham/Northampton, MA 2017, pp. 101–19.

40 See e.g. D. Clifford, I. Graef and P. Valcke, 'Pre-formulated Declarations of Data Subject Consent – Citizen-Consumer Empowerment and the Alignment of Data, Consumer and Competition Law Protections' (2019) 20 *German Law Journal* 679, esp. 690–707.

41 See also M. Fornasier, *Freier Markt und zwingendes Vertragsrecht. Zugleich ein Beitrag zum Recht der Allgemeinen Geschäftsbedingungen*, Duncker & Humboldt, Berlin 2013; M. Renner, *Zwingendes transnationles Recht. Zur Struktur der Wirtschaftsferfassung jenseits des Staates*, Nomos, Baden-Baden 2011, pp. 35–42; O. Remien, *Zwingendes Vertragsrecht und Grundfreiheiten des EG-Vertrages*, Mohr Siebeck, Tübingen 2003.

Firstly, in the vast majority of legal orders, the core part of contract law consists of a menu of contract types, which provide parties with ready-made sets of rules to be used in drawing up the actual structure of their contract. The theoretical foundations of this concept are thoroughly discussed by Dagan, who in his contribution advocates for the view of contract law as an institution of liberal society, which assists in making choices by providing an array of options that can be used in designing actual agreements.[42] Perceived in this way, contract law is an instrument of individual autonomy, which is the ultimate value of all contract law in its entirety. From this perspective, the principal task of contract law is to provide parties with well-designed options to choose between, and thereby enhance the exercise of their autonomy – and arguably, as Dagan and Heller put it, Anglo-American law would be enhanced by more of this, especially in non-economic areas.

Secondly, the choice schemes are also established through various forms of optional rules. Contract law is populated with various normative elements, which bind the parties only conditionally and yield to their decision.[43] The textbook example of this approach is non-mandatory (default) rules based on opt-out scheme, which are binding on the parties as long as they do not decide to exclude these rules or replace them with an idiosyncratic contract clause. The actual toolbox of non-mandatory contract law is, however, much more diverse and encompasses a broad range of rules that are optional to varying degrees, such as regulatory menus[44] and semi-mandatory (*halbzwingende*) rules.[45] This design allows contract law not only to be inclusive of the idiosyncratic interests of the parties, but also to allow for easier incorporation of evolving policy and values.[46]

---

42 See, more extensively, as well H. Dagan and M. Heller, *The Choice Theory of Contracts*, Cambridge University Press, Cambridge 2016.

43 Cf. e.g. G. Bachmann, 'Optionsmodelle im Privatrecht', *JZ* 2008, 11; L. Kähler, *Begriff und Rechtfertigung abdingbaren Rechts*, Mohr Siebeck, Tübingen 2012, pp. 81–93; from a partly different vantage point I. Ayres and R. Gertner, 'Strategic Contractual Inefficiency and the Optimal Choice of Legal Rules' (1991) 101 *Yale Law Journal (Yale LJ)* 729, esp. 765 et seq.

44 I. Ayres, 'Menus Matter' (2006) 73 *U. Chi. L. Rev.* 3.

45 Today, this instrument is particularly characteristic of EU consumer law, which perceives default rules as overall detrimental for a weaker party (due to his/her inferior bargaining power) and attempts to restrain the parameters of choice. See for instance M.E. Storme, 'Freedom of Contract: Mandatory and Non-Mandatory Rules in European Contract Law' (2007) 15 *ERPL* 233, esp. 237 et seq.; U. Mattei, 'Efficiency and Equal Protection in the New European Contract Law: Mandatory, Default and Enforcement Rules' (1999) 39 *Vanderbilt Journal of International Law* 537, esp. 546–51; G. Wagner, 'Mandatory Contract Law: Functions and Principles in Light of the Proposal for a Directive on Consumer Rights' (2010) 3 *Erasmus Law Review* 47, esp. 48–51 and 57–66; further on semi-mandatory rules see e.g. H. Krejci, 'Konsumentenschutz und Gewährleistung' in B. Blaschek et al. (eds.), *Konsumentenpolitik im Spannungsfeld von Liberalisierung und Sozialer Verantwortung. Festschrift für Gottfried Meyer*, Neuer Wissenschaftlicher Verlag, Vienna/Graz 2004, pp. 127–36; L. Kähler, above n. 43, pp. 81 et seq.

46 See M. Grochowski, *Default rules and the transformative potential ofprivate law* [unpublished manuscript].

Increasingly, however, with respect to default rules, the question of rule-setting is also raised. In the classic conceptual framework, the creation of default rules remains exclusively within the law-making capacity of the state, which decides to include private actors in the co-creation of the regulatory design of contracts. Such downstream allocation of regulatory capacities does not, however, exhaust the spectrum of possibilities for inclusion of private actors into the creation of contract law. The erosion of the state's law-making monopoly can also be sensed here. The globalisation of markets and contracts has entailed the creation of default rules at the transnational level, through various entities and in a variety of forms.[47] Apart from the more traditional modes of rule-setting (such as CISG, incorporated into international public law treaties),[48] the practice of transnational law has developed a variety of de facto default rules, of different scope and created by various actors (see the examples below in section 4.2). These default rules, created without state authority, can be recognised ex post as a binding part of contract law and incorporated through legislation[49] or case law.[50]

Although all these state- and privately created rules are designed in a one-size-fits-all form (i.e. for all contracts of a particular type and all possible contractors), the picture of default rules would be incomplete without mentioning rules with a narrower ambit. These are in particular typical of more close-knit communities, where contractual rules can be created either through a community's consent[51] or by imposition by one of parties. This phenomenon may be vividly illustrated by the example of online platforms (such as Uber, Airbnb and Amazon). At the same time, as Grochowski observes in his

---

47 See F. MÖSLEIN, 'Dispositive Regeln im transnationalen Privatrechtsverkehr – Same same, but different?' in G.-P. CALLIESS (ed.), *Transnationales Recht*, Mohr Siebeck, Tübingen 2014, pp. 155–71.

48 See e.g. F. FERRARI, *The CISG and its Impact on National Legal Systems*, Sellier, Munich 2008, pp. 11 et seq.; A.M. GARRO, 'Gap-Filling Role of the Unidroit Principles in International Sales Law: Some Comments on the Interplay Between the Principles and the CISG' (1994–95) 69 *Tulane Law Review* 1149.

49 See e.g. F. MÖSLEIN, 'Legal innovation in European contract law: within and beyond the (draft) Common Frame of Reference' in H.-W. MICKLITZ and F. Cafaggi (eds.), *European Private Law After the Common Frame of Reference*, Edward Elgar, Cheltenham/Northampton, MA 2010, pp. 173–200.

50 See M. SANTOS SILVA, *The Draft Common Frame of Reference as a 'Toolbox' for Domestic Courts. A Solution to the Pure Economic Loss Problem from a Comparative Perspective*, Springer, Cham 2017, pp. 57–98; M. GROCHOWSKI, 'The practical potential of the DCFR Judgment of the Swedish Supreme Court (Högsta domstolen) of 3 November 2009, Case T 3–08' (2013) 9 *ERCL* 96; more generally also M. HESSELINK, 'A Toolbox for European Judges' (2011) 17 *ELJ* 441.

51 In this way, for instance, the digital market communities create reputation-based schemes – see e.g. D. COOLICAN and L. COFFMAN, 'Trust, the Sharing Economy and Behavioral Economics', available at https://www.behavioraleconomics.com/trust-the-sharing-economy-and-behavioral-economics, with a reference to a previous study.

contribution, although contracts of this kind are composed predominantly of inalterable ('mandatory') rules, some of the rules are also optional in nature, allowing one or both contractors to make choices regarding their application to an agreement.

4.2. OPTIONALITY VS. AUTONOMY IN CONTRACT LAW

Closely related to these considerations is the question of on what grounds the content of default rules ought to rest – or, to put it differently, what values and policy considerations a default rule should adhere to and how these can be identified. The classic answer to this question is that default rules should by nature be free of any substantive policy considerations and should reflect the typical preferences of average contractors.[52] The European legal tradition phrases this assumption such that default rules should reflect the optimal and the most balanced allocation of rights, duties and risks between parties. Approached in this way, default rules may be seen as a paradigmatic pattern (*Leitbild*),[53] which, for this reason, also constitutes the natural benchmark for judicial control of standard contract terms that diverge from a default rule.[54] This also encompasses the unfairness control under Directive 93/13/EEC, as expressed explicitly, for instance, in §307 (2) BGB (German Civil Code).

---

52 See e.g. I. Ayres and R. Gertner, 'Filling Gaps in Incomplete Contracts. An Economic Theory of Default Rules' (1989–90) 99 *Yale LJ* 87, esp. 89–93; I. Ayres and R. Gertner, 'Majoritarian vs. Minoritarian Defaults' (1989–90) 51 *Stanford Law Review* 1591, esp. 1592, 1611 et passim; I. Ayres, 'Preliminary Thoughts on Optimal Tailoring of Contractual Rules' (1993–94) 3 *Southern California Interdisciplinary Law Journal* 1, esp. 5 et seq.; A. Schwartz and R.E. Scott, 'The Common Law of Contract and the Default Rule Project' (2016) *Vanderbilt Law Review* 1523, esp. 1527. This attitude refers back to the most classic perception of default rules as gap-fillers, created in order to supplement lacunae in incomplete agreements (see e.g. I. Ayres and R. Gertner, 'Filling Gaps', above in this note, p. 87 et passim; D. Medicus and J. Petersen, *Allgemeiner Teil des BGB*, 11th ed., C.F. Müller, Heidelberg et al. 2016, p. 194.

53 On the potential of default rules to serve as a paradigm (*Leitbildfunktion*), see J. Schapp, 'Die Leitbildfunktion des dispositiven Rechts für die Inhaltskontrolle von Allgemeinen Geschäftsbedingungen nach §9 Abs. 2 AGB-Gesetz', *Der Betrieb* 1978, 621; F. Möslein, *Dispositives Recht: Zwecke, Strukturen und Methoden*, Mohr Siebeck, Tübingen 2011, pp. 40 et seqq., 118 et seqq.; id., 'Optional Regulation of Standard Contract Terms' in K. Purnhagen and P. Rott (eds.), *Varieties of European Economic Law and Regulation. Liber Amicorum for Hans Micklitz*, Springer, Cham 2014, pp. 86–92; M. Hesselink, 'Non-Mandatory Rules in European Contract Law' (2005) 1 *ERCL* 44, esp. 58, 63, 83; J. Schürnbrand, 'Muster im Recht: Gesetzliche Muster und Modellgesetze' in F. Möslein (ed.), *Regelsetzung im Privatrecht*, Mohr Siebeck, Tübingen 2019, pp. 205–26; on the pattern-setting through DCFR rules, see also M. Hesselink, above n. 50, p. 460.

54 See e.g. J. Cziupka, *Dispositives Vertragsrecht: Funktionsweise und Qualitätsmerkmale gesetzlicher Regelungsmuster*, Mohr Siebeck, Tübingen 2010, pp. 212 et seqq.

Apart from the obvious questions of democratic legitimacy and the balance of powers (regarding opposition between statutory defaults and rules created ad hoc by courts to supplement lacunae in contracts), this approach also poses a foundational epistemic issue. Under what premises can the law-maker be assumed to have better access to knowledge about the market and extra-market social realities, hence being able to create more just and well-balanced default rules?[55] This concern may be partly mitigated when self-regulatory communities of contractors step in, for instance in online commerce (see above section 4.1). This allows micro-majorities, peculiar to a particular group of contractors, to be established, and default rules to be created in a much more situation-specific way. This thrust can still be strengthened, for instance, via the development of IT-based techniques of gathering and analysing data about the needs and preferences of individual market actors and their groups. This, in turn, allows speculation about the feasibility of more 'granular' sets of rules (related to the specific characteristics of particular communities) and even fully personalised rules (tailor-made for particular contractors).[56]

The 'majoritarian' concept encompasses, however, only the more classical part of the conceptual agenda of default rules. In the current contract law discussion, default rules are frequently perceived as also constituting an instrument of achieving particular regulatory goals. Contract law scholarship recognised some time ago that the decision to opt out from a default rule may be influenced by the procedural requirements that should be met to change a default rule (often referred to as 'altering rules').[57] In his contribution, Kähler delves more deeply into this issue and analyses various instruments that shift contract rules from full defaults to certain degrees of mandatory character. Apart from the classic forms of altering rules, he also focuses on less obvious ways of proceduralising opt-outs, such as making an option offer to a counterparty or employing

---

55 On the skepticism regarding the epistemic dimension of the majoritarian theory see e.g. A. Schwartz and R.E. Scott, 'Contract Theory and the Limits of Contract Law' (2003) 113 *Yale LJ* 541, esp. 594.

56 See A. Porat and L.J. Strahilevitz, 'Personalizing Default Rules and Disclosure with Big Data' (2014) 112 *Michigan Law Review* 1417; C.R. Sunstein, 'Impersonal Default Rules vs. Active Choice vs. Personalized Default Rules: A Triptych', available at https://papers.ssrn.com/sol3/papers.cfm?abstract_id=2171343; M. Seligman, 'Personalized Choice of Private Law', Cardozo Legal Studies Research Paper No. 596; A.J. Casey and A. Niblett, 'The Death of Rules and Standards' (2016–17) 92 *Indiana Law Journal* 1401, 1406 et passim.

57 I. Ayres, 'Regulating Opt-out: An Economic Theory of Altering Rules' (2011–12) 121 *Yale LJ* 2032; see also B. McDonnell, 'Sticky Defaults and Altering Rules in Corporate Law' (2007) 60 *SMU Law Review* 383; J.A.E. Pottow and O. Ben-Shahar, 'On the Stickiness of Default Rules' (2006) 33 *Florida State University Law Review* 651, esp. 660–70; G. Klass, 'Interpretation and Construction in Altering Rules', Georgetown Public Law and Legal Theory Research Paper No. 12-153/Georgetown Business, Economics and Regulatory Law Research Paper No. 12-038; more generally also C.R. Sunstein, 'Switching the Default Rule' (2002) 77 *New York University Law Review* 106, esp. 111–15.

'response rules', which set particular consequences for opting out from a default rule insofar as the parties have decided to exercise this choice in a particular contract.

Recently, the idea of stiffer defaults, located in between the classical mandatory and non-mandatory rules, has been further reconceptualised under the influence of behavioural insights into decision-making patterns. From this perspective, default rules take into account the biases and other cognitive constraints of the parties[58] and try to steer the parties' choice (in particular, by making them stick to the default content of a rule). In this way, default rules may be turned into an instrument of market and social steering, framing the choice in a way that will channel individuals' decisions towards particular ends,[59] maintaining at the same time the formal freedom of choice. The growing awareness of the behavioural premises of default rules has been translated into the idea of a 'libertarian paternalistic'[60] ordering, which replaces classic mandates with optional schemes, based on the conceptual pattern of a default rule. The idea of regulation through non-mandatory rules, endorsed especially strongly in public law, is proliferating to a growing extent in the horizontal market relations between individuals.[61] In this way, non-mandatory rules take an intermediary position along the mandatory/non-mandatory spectrum and situate themselves between simple 'facilitation' on the one hand and the fulfilment of policy goals in contract law on the other hand.

---

58 See e.g. K. Mathis and P.A. Burri, 'Nudging in Swiss Contract Law? An Analysis of Non-mandatory Default Rules from a Legal, Economic and Behavioural Perspective' in K. Mathis and A. Tor (eds.), *Nudging – Possibilities, Limitations and Applications in European Law and Economics*, Springer, Cham 2016, pp. 121–51, esp. 134–42; A.-L. Sibony and A. Alemanno, 'The Emergence of Behavioural Policy-Making: A European Perspective' in A.-L. Sibony and A. Alemanno (eds.), *Nudge and the Law. A European Perspective*, Hart Publishing, Oxford 2015, pp. 1–25, esp. 14–16; R. Korobkin, 'Status Quo Bias and Contract Default Rules' (1997–98) 83 *Cornell Law Review* 608, esp. 609–32.

59 See C.R. Sunstein, *Why Nudge? The Politics of Libertarian Paternalism*, Yale University Press, New Haven 2012, pp. 151–54; R. Korobkin, 'Behavioral Economics, Contract Formation and Contract Law' in C.R. Sunstein (ed.), *Behavioral Law and Economics*, Cambridge University Press, Cambridge 2000, pp. 137–43; L. Kähler, 'Regelformulierung und Regulierung durch abdingbares Recht' in F. Möslein (ed.), *Regelsetzung im Privatrecht*, Mohr Siebeck, Tübingen 2019, pp. 185–204, esp. 195–99; B. Lurger, 'Empiricism and Private Law: Behavioral Research as Part of a Legal-Empirical Governance Analysis and a Form of New Legal Realism' (2014) 1 *Austrian Law Journal* 20, esp. 29 et seq.

60 See e.g. C.R. Sunstein and R.H. Thaler, 'Libertarian Paternalism Is Not an Oxymoron' (2003) 70 *U. Chi. L. Rev.* 1159; H. Eidenmüller, 'Liberaler Paternalismus', *JZ* 66 (2011), 814; C.R. Sunstein, 'Nudges.gov: Behaviorally Informed Regulation' in E. Zamir and D. Teichmann (eds.), *The Oxford Handbook of Behavioral Economics and the Law*, Oxford University Press, Oxford 2014.

61 See e.g. K. Mathis and P.A. Burri, above n. 58; C.R. Sunstein, 'Nudging and Choice Architecture: Ethical Considerations', Harvard John M. Olin Discussion Paper Series, Discussion Paper No. 809, January 2015, pp. 11 et seq.; H. Eidenmüller, above n. 60, pp. 819 et seq.

4.3. OPTIONAL CODE: THE BETTER OF SEVERAL WORLDS OR MERE EPISODE?

Over the last two decades, the theme of norm creation in contract law has been dominated by the idea of an optional code in Europe – with most sympathy probably for a regime that would cover contracts overall, but not more. This was the design of the Principles of European Contract Law (PECL), which triggered the discussion, but also of the Unidroit Principles.[62] It was also the scope of the (academic) Draft Common Frame of Reference (DCFR) (with some rather marginal and not really meaningful extensions), which led to the EU Commission Proposal of a Common European Sales Law (CESL), i.e. with a considerable reduction in the scope of application.[63] From a more theoretical perspective on the creation of norms, the interesting part lies in the discussion on optionality, rather than in the contents of the proposals, which did not really take up such modern developments as chains and networks of contracts, long-term contracts, the digital world of contract, or even the full range of service contracts.[64]

With respect to optionality, the European approach sharply differs from the one taken in the US Uniform Commercial Code (UCC) – certainly its most important counterpart, were it not for the fundamentally different design of the option. While the UCC allowed US states to opt in (and all have now so), the European model was one of giving private parties – i.e. users – this power. The European approach thus raised questions relating to competition between legislatures – in this case competition with national contract laws, i.e. vertical competition, coupled with horizontal competition.[65] Irrespective

62 Unidroit, *Principles of International Commercial Contracts*, 1994 (revised editions in 2004, 2010, 2016); O. Lando and H. Beale (eds.), *Principles of European Contract Law*, Part I and II, revised ed. 2000 and Part III (with R. Zimmermann), 2003, Kluwer, The Hague/London/Boston; student edition 2019 of all three parts (now with Wolters-Kluwer) edited by O. Lando, H. Beale, A. Prüm, E. Clive and R. Zimmermann.

63 C. von Bar, E. Clive, H. Schulte-Nölke et al. for the Study Group on a European Civil Code and Research Group on EC Private Law (Acquis Group) (eds.), *Principles, Definitions and Model Rules of European Private Law – Draft Common Frame of Reference (DCFR)*, Sellier, Munich 2008, then revised version with commentaries; Proposal for a Common European Sales Law (CESL), 11.11.2011, COM (2011) 635 final; see Y. Adar and P. Sirena, 'Principles and Rules in the Emerging European Contract Law: From the PECL to the CESL, and Beyond' (2013) 9 *ERCL* 1; D. Staudenmayer, 'Der Kommissionsvorschlag für eine Verordnung zum Gemeinsamen Europäischen Kaufrecht', *NJW* 2011, 3491; M.W. Hesselink, 'The Common Frame of Reference as a Source of European Private Law' (2009) 83 *Tulane Law Review* 919.

64 While the former are completely missing (see S. Grundmann, 'Costs and Benefits of an Optional European Sales Law (CESL)' (2013) 50 *Common Market Law Review (CMLR)* 225, 234–37), for the area last mentioned at least a partial collection can be found (however not very influential in the DCFR): M. Hesselink et al., *Principles of European Law: Commercial Agency, Franchise and Distribution*, Sellier, Munich 2006.

65 See more generally: S. Grundmann, above n. 64; F. Gomez and J. Ganuza, 'An Economic Analysis of Harmonization Regimes – Full Harmonization, Minimum Harmonization or

of whether such competition could really function or which obstacles were to be faced, theoretically this refined 'European' approach was a big step in the question of creation of norms because three core features were combined for the first time. The combination comprised: (a) freedom of choice for users, (b) low information costs plus the legal certainty ensuing from one uniform (even though optional) regime, and (c) an integrated regime of facilitating rules and of regulation of the typical problems of market structure and weaker parties.[66] The reasons why the endeavour failed – as one of the few cases where an EU Commission proposal was definitively dropped – need not be discussed here.[67]

Optional Instrument?' (2011) 7 *ERCL* 275; and already D. Cunning and J. MacIntosch, 'The role of interjurisdictional competition in shaping Canadian corporate law' (2000) 20 *International Review of Law and Economics* 141; W. Kerber and S. Grundmann, 'An Optional European Contract Law Code – Advantages and Disadvantages' (2005) 21 *European Journal of Law and Economics* 215. For company law, see G. Bachmann, 'Vertikaler Regulierungswettbewerb im Europäischen Gesellschaftsrecht' in *Festschrift für Hommelhoff*, Verlag Dr. Otto Schmidt, Köln 2012, pp. 21–44; L. Klöhn, 'Supranationale Rechtsformen und vertikaler Wettbewerb der Gesetzgeber im europäischen Gesellschaftsrecht', *RabelsZ* 76 (2012), 276, 301 et seq.; H. Fleischer, 'Supranational Corporate Forms in the European Union: Prolegomena to a Theory on Supranational Forms of Association' (2010) 47 *CMLR* 1671, 1700–03.

66 For a map of the advantages of centralised and of decentralised rule-setting that were rather ingenuously combined in such design, see for instance: O. Bar-Gill, M. Barzuza and L. Bebchuk, 'The Market for Corporate Law' (2006) 162 *Journal of Institutional and Theoretical Economics* 134; R. Cooter, *The Strategic Constitution*, Princeton University Press, Princeton 2000, pp. 130–39; D. Esty and D. Geradin, 'Regulatory Co-opetition' (2000) *Journal of Economic Law* 235, 240 et seq.; F. Gomez, 'The Harmonization of Contract Law through European Rules – a Law and Economics Perspective' (2008) 4 *ERCL* 89, 95–103; K. Heine and W. Kerber, 'European corporate laws, regulatory competition and path dependence' (2002) 13 *European Journal of Law and Economics* 47; W. Kerber, 'Rechtseinheitlichkeit und Rechtsvielfalt aus ökonomischer Sicht' in S. Grundmann (ed.), *Systembildung und Systemlücken in Kerngebieten des Europäischen Privatrechts*, Mohr Siebeck, Tübingen 2000, pp. 67–97, at pp. 84–87; H.R. Romano, 'Law as a product – some pieces of the incorporation puzzle' (1985) 1 *Journal of Law, Economics, and Organization* 225; H. Siebert and M. Koop, 'Institutional competition – a concept for Europe?', *Aussenwirtschaft* 45 (1990), 439; J.-M. Sun and J. Pelkmans, 'Regulatory competition in the Single Market' (1995) 33 *Journal of Common Market Studies* 67; on innovation and experimentation in particular, see S. Cleveland, 'Process Innovation in the Production of Corporate Law' (2008) 41 *U.C. Davies Law Review* 1829, esp. 1868.

67 For such explanations, see D. Anagnostopoulou, 'The Withdrawal of the Common European Sales Law Proposal and the European Commission Proposal on Certain Aspects Concerning Contracts for the Online and Other Distance Sales of Goods' in M. Heidemann and J. Lee (eds.), *The Future of the Commercial Contract in Scholarship and Law Reform. European and Comparative Perspectives*, Springer, Cham 2017, pp. 127–59, esp. pp. 152–59; A. Colombi Ciacchi, 'Contents and Effects of Contracts: Lessons to Learn from the CESL' in A. Colombi Ciacchi (ed.), *Contents and Effects of Contracts – Lessons to Learn from the Common European Sales Law*, Springer, Cham 2016, pp. 3–10, esp. pp. 8–10; K. Norris, 'Common European Sales Law: A Missed Opportunity or Better Things to Come' (2016) 37 *Business Law Review* 29. Ample background discussion would suggest that the strategic exclusion of much of the elite of contract law in the Member States by the organisers of the drafting groups strongly fired back.

One core finding in the process would seem to be in any case that an optional code would have left many of the advantages of decentralised rule-setting intact, while also reaping most of the advantages of centralised rule-setting.[68] When, however, the CESL proposal itself was discussed, fears were expressed that the adopted version, despite its optionality and because of some features favouring its application, might impose itself as the quasi-exclusive model on the European market via so-called network effects.[69] In that case, no second try would probably have been possible (in which case the non-inclusive method of drafting would have been more problematic).

5. THE EVER-STRONGER PRIVATE CREATOR OF NORMS

5.1. THE MODEL OF PRIVATE LEGISLATURE

The model of private legislature grounds its legitimacy in the finding that, in certain contexts, ordering by a sovereign body has less convincing results than rule-setting by bodies not endowed with sovereign legitimacy. The reason may be the superior information possessed private parties – and this is arguably a very powerful aspect, given that the superiority of a market economy over a planned economy can probably best be explained by the advantages of a more dispersed distribution of information (and decision-making power).[70] A further reason may also be that the parties affected have more legitimacy to regulate than those not affected (subsidiarity)[71] – an argument that potentially has to be

---

68 For the combination as such (as a win-win situation), see the contributions above n. 65 et seq., namely by F. Gomez and J. Ganuza, by S. Grundmann, and by W. Kerber and S. Grundmann, as well as K. Röpke and K. Heine, 'Vertikaler Regulierungswettbewerb und europäischer Binnenmarkt – die Europäische Aktiengesellschaft als supranationales Rechtsformangebot', *ORDO (Jahrbuch für die Ordnung von Wirtschaft und Gesellschaft)* 56 (2005), 157, 173–74 (in the case of an optional EU Code, the market mechanism also decides the question of how much rule-setting is needed at the central level and how much at the decentralised level).

69 See A. Engert, 'Networks and Lemons in the Market for Contract Law' in H. Eidenmüller (ed.), *Regulatory Competition in Contract Law and Dispute Resolution*, Bloomsbury Publishing, London 2013, pp. 317–25; S. Grundmann, above n. 64, pp. 232–34; questioning the idea of a 'free trial run' also J. Cartwright, '"Choice is good." Really?' (2011) 7 *ERCL* 335.

70 Path-breaking and still in principle the accepted base line: F. von Hayek, 'The Use of Knowledge in Society' (1945) 35 *The American Economic Review* 519; contextualisation and further discussion in S. Grundmann in S. Grundmann, H.-W. Micklitz and M. Renner, above n. 1, chapter 12.

71 See I. Bartle and P. Vass, 'Self-Regulation Within the Regulatory State: Towards a New Regulatory Paradigm?' (2007) 85 *Public Administration* 885, esp. 902; B. Gabor, *Regulatory Competition in the Internal Market. Comparing Models for Corporate Law, Securities Law*

weighed against the concern that certain parties among those affected are in need of protection. Finally, for a combination of reasons, the public administration of justice may be too costly as compared to private ordering. Private ordering in this sense, however, must be distinguished from absence of ordering – as often advocated by economic theory and free market proponents. Private ordering is regulation, with a weighing of interests by the rule-setter – just by another type of rule-setter that arguably has advantages and disadvantages.

While in the 1960s it would seem that the view still completely prevailed that ordering, even if aimed at setting free private initiative, had to be sovereign ordering (setting the rules of the game neutrally or allocating property rights efficiently),[72] this appraisal changed considerably from the 1970s onwards. One of the first authors claiming the superiority of regimes established by private parties in certain situations – between contract parties, but also in larger communities – was Williamson. He thereby also triggered research into how the quality of rules may be related to the authorship of rules – and this was a link typical of the governance research agenda kicked off at that moment too.[73] The scenario he claimed such superiority for was long-term relationships, as nobody can truly know the future and as, for this reason, parties should rather establish governance regimes for the solution of problems later on. Williamson had forerunners, interestingly not in (institutional) economics, but in legal sociology, which already had described how – empirically – certain contexts are handled more satisfactorily with little or without any recourse to law.[74] Without recourse to law is not, of course, the same as private ordering. Therefore, this path becomes more interesting once economist Bernstein and social scientist Ellickson analyse how it is a strong system of sanctioning power

and Competition Law, Edward Elgar, Cheltenham/Northampton, MA 2013, pp. 276 et seq.; L. Gibson, 'Subsidiarity: The Implications for Consumer Policy' (1993) 16 *Journal of Consumer Policy* 323, esp. 328.

72 Probably the two outstanding figures on both sides of the Atlantic with respect to legal institutions ordering markets are F. Böhm and R. Coase, namely with F. Böhm, 'Privatrechtsgesellschaft und Marktwirtschaft' (1966) 17 *ORDO* 75 and R. Coase, 'The Problem of Social Cost' (1960) 3 *Journal of Law and Economics* 1. Both clearly attribute this task exclusively to sovereign power (legislature, judges), against private party 'usurpation'. For this see S. Grundmann in S. Grundmann, H.-W. Micklitz and M. Renner, above n. 1, chapters 3 and 6.

73 See O. Williamson, 'Transaction-Cost Economics: The Governance of Contractual Relations' (1979) 22 *Journal of Law & Economics* 233; id., *The Economic Institutions of Capitalism – Firms, Markets, Relational Contracting*, Free Press, New York 1985, chapter 1; see S. Grundmann in S. Grundmann, H.-W. Micklitz and M. Renner, above n. 1, chapters 3 and 17.

74 Path-breaking, S. Macaulay, 'Non-Contractual Relations in Business – a Preliminary Study' (1963) 28 *American Sociological Review* 55; for the reactions and later development, see references in the last footnote.

outside the law that makes 'order without (sovereign) law' more feasible[75] – and this is typically the case in more homogeneous and well-confined communities. In parallel, in new economic sociology and in sociology more generally, one of the important findings would seem to be that the comparative advantages of different kinds of ordering speak strongly for a mixture of strategies. Moreover, these mixtures can be found empirically in highly successful compounds, a mixture of social norms, private ordering (both paramount for the creation of trust) and public ordering.[76] Even though this constitutes only an extremely brief summary of a few key elements and structures, the finding reported would seem to explain quite a bit of the success or non-success of private ordering in key examples that can be found over the last decades.

5.2. PRIVATE ORDERING, SELF-REGULATION AND STANDARDISATION AS A FIRST GENERATION

While, of course, voluntary access to pieces of private ordering raises completely different issues, private ordering with some coercive power can be found early on in two phenomena that are explored in more detail in this book. The finding in economic sociology that a convincing mixture might give superior results can be tested in these cases. Private regulation may unfold along two lines of state – market and state – society interaction. The first model builds on regulating 'under the shadow of law', where the non-state regulation applies in a soft or non-coercive way.[77] The paradigmatic illustration of this approach is default

---

75 See L. Bernstein, 'Opting Out of the Legal System: Extralegal Contractual Relations in the Diamond Industry' (1992) 21 *Journal of Legal Studies* 115; R. Ellickson, *Order Without Law: How Neighbors Settle Dispute,s* Harvard University Press, Cambridge, MA 1991; see also L. Bernstein, 'Private Commercial Law in the Cotton Industry: Creating Cooperation Through Rules, Norms, and Institutions' (2001) 99 *Michigan Law Review* 1724, esp. 1728–34, 1739–45; a strong application namely on transnational enterprises in L.C. Backer, 'Economic Globalization and the Rise of Efficient Systems of Global Private Law Making: Wal-Mart as Global Legislator' (2007) 39 *Connecticut Law Review* 1739. On transnational value chains and their social sciences conceptualisation and legal construction, see recently K. Eller, *Rechtsverfassung globaler Produktion*, Mohr Siebeck, Tübingen 2020.

76 See e.g. G.-P. Calliess, 'Transnational Consumer Law: Co-Regulation of B2C-E-Commerce', CLPE Research Paper 3/2007, pp. 4 et seqq.; N. Dorn, 'Capital cohabitation: EU Capital Markets Union as public and private co-regulation' (2016) 11 *Capital Markets Law Journal* 84, esp. 94–97; B. Canno and H. Chung, 'A Framework for Designing Co-Regulation Models Well-Adapted to Technology-Facilitated Sharing Economies' (2014–15) 31 *Santa Clara Computer & High Technology Law Journal* 23; see also more generally S. Augsberg, 'Regelsetzung als staatlich-privater Prozess – Vom 'Steuerungsdurcheinander' zur Regulierungsstrategie?' in F. Möslein (ed.), *Regelsetzung im Privatrecht*, Mohr Siebeck, Tübingen 2019, pp. 95–119, esp. pp. 97–107.

77 See especially the seminal paper by R. Mnookin and L. Kornhauser, 'Bargaining in the Shadow of Law – the Case of Divorce' (1979) 88 *Yale LJ* 950, as well as R. Cooter,

rules, which allow straightforwardly for an interchange between state- and party-made rules (see also above sections 4.1 and 4.2). The general optionality of private law however also allows for other types of non-state ordering, where parties may take advantage of the lacunae left deliberately or accidentally in the private law architecture, in the domain described famously by Jean Carbonnier as '*non-droit*'.[78] The filling-in of this area by private actors is 'embedded' in the cultural context of contracting.[79] It requires that rules set in this way have to comply with underlying moral values and customs,[80] which frame and limit the regulatory activity of private actors.

Private regulation emerges at the crossroads of these dynamics, being both 'embedded' in the fabric of social normative patterns, as well as 'overshadowed' by the state-enacted rules and their judicial enforcement. Möslein, in his contribution, builds on this observation, investigating how private and state-made ordering cohabit and supplement each other (referring specifically to third-party certification). As he observes, the actual architecture and functioning of both types of rule-setting are much closer to each other than might appear from a merely theoretical perspective. The conundrum of public- and private-set elements in social and economic ordering is tested further by Micklitz, who delves more deeply in his contribution into the tensions between private, public and mixed (co-regulatory) schemes. None of them, he argues, emerge in isolation from one another, but rather exist in a constant, dynamic interdependence. The pivotal elements of this system are state law and judicial enforcement, which provide a discursive framework for various forms of non-state rule-making and adjudication. In this way, classic contract law is not only 'under siege', but also creates an incentive for constant evolution and refinement of the entire heterogeneous order.

S. Marks and R. Mnookin, 'Bargaining in the Shadow of the Law: A Testable Model of Strategic Behavior' (1982) 11 *Journal of Legal Studies* 225; contextualisation and history of the idea in S. Grundmann in S. Grundmann, H.-W. Micklitz and M. Renner, above n. 1, chapter 27 – see also the same chapter for discussion of the authors J. Carbonnier and M. Granovetter quoted below. Amongst the more recent continuations and discussions of the concept of bargaining 'under the shadow of law', see for instance G. Bosch and S. Lehndorff, 'Autonomous bargaining in the shadow of the law: from an enabling towards a disabling state?' in D. Grimshaw at al. (eds.), *Making work more equal. A new labor market segmentation approach*, Manchester University Press, Manchester 2017, pp. 35–51; A. Porat and L.J. Strahilevitz, 'Personalizing Default Rules and Disclosure with Big Data' (2014) 112 *Michigan Law Review* 1417, 1459.

78 J. Carbonnier, 'L'hypothèse du non-droit' in id., *Flexible droit – Pour une sociologie du droit sans rigueur*, LGDJ, Paris 2001, pp. 25–47.

79 See M. Granovetter, 'Economic Action and Social Structure: The Problem of Embeddedness' (1985) 91 *American Journal of Sociology* 481, esp. 495–98; with a reference to the concept of 'embeddedness' coined by Karl Polanyi in *The Great Transformation*, Farrar & Rinehart, New York 1944.

80 So for instance J. Carbonnier, above n. 78.

5.3. PRINCIPLES AND OPTIONAL CODES AS A (LOST) SECOND GENERATION

The idea of an optional code (of European contract law) (above section 4.3) was not created within a discussion that was open to new schemes of optionality of sovereign rule-setting. Rather it was triggered by an endeavour that aimed at a traditional (but European) code that would replace all national law and that was proposed and designed by academics, namely in the so-called von Bar group – some observers spoke of an (envisaged) European *Code Napoléon* (and European Portalis). This endeavour, as a first step and to trigger the first moves towards 'adoption', contained, however, an element of optionality. Specifically, in the Unidroit Principles the idea was expressed that this set of rules, designed without sovereign legitimacy, and hence rule-setting by private parties (more specifically: scholars) could be chosen by parties (see the Preamble to the Principles). In this way, the optionality proposed here is one that refers to texts that are clearly to be seen as private ordering.

The successful examples of private ordering named above (section 5.1) are designed such that they are not of general application and do not compete with sovereign rule-setting, but rather target groups with alternative sanction regimes, including arbitration – typically, well-defined homogeneous groups (the latter with the one exception of international arbitration). This factual statement would seem to explain the divergence in success of the European Principles and of the Unidroit Principles. The endeavour of European Principles would seem to be obsolete – it was in strong competition with an active sovereign legislature, and the Principles were not targeted at hot-spot lacunae where there was insufficient sovereign rule-setting. When the attempt to capture the sovereign legislature failed, the endeavour also failed. Conversely, the much more cautious approach of the Unidroit Principles, strongly referring to *lex mercatoria*, did not directly aim at competition with and replacement of a sovereign legislature, and instead aimed at a constituency that often chooses international arbitration. The Unidroit Principles are still livelier and are also revised periodically. Machnikowski, in his presentation at the Secola conference and upon which this publication is based, saw optionality as typically doomed to failure (with only one exception: the UN Convention on the International Sale of Goods of 1980), primarily because legal certainty was so difficult to build up. Again, within the realm of international arbitration, mechanisms differ in precisely this respect. The arbitration board's prudence and a sensible solution are typically more trusted in this context than foreseeability and legal certainty.[81]

---

81 See e.g. C.R. Drahozal and S.J. Ware, 'Why Do Businesses Use (or Not Use) Arbitration Clauses' (2010) 25 *Ohio State Journal on Dispute Resolution* 433, esp. 450–53; G.-P. Calliess and P. Zumbansen, *Rough Consensus and Running Code. A Theory of Transnational Private Law*, Hart Publishing, Oxford 2012, pp. 112 et seq.

5.4. THE DIGITAL ARENA AS A THIRD GENERATION

The digital arena has powerfully developed into a third generation of ample private ordering. Some of its features might even indicate that we are currently entering into the golden age of private ordering. Contract law – for instance European contract law – in the digital age or arena is even a topic on its own merits, including its aspects of private ordering.[82] Therefore, only three particularly salient features should be highlighted here.

The nature of private ordering is indeed particularly radical when – as Lawrence Lessig famously declared – the technical code is code itself,[83] shaping the contract inexorably, without escape. No chance for opposition is left at the negotiation period: computer screens used for the conclusion of contracts ban any deviation even more comprehensively than the practice of standard contract terms already did. There is also no chance for opposition in the performance phase. Anyone who does not stick meticulously to the prerequisites for registration literally foregoes his seat (for instance, in the airplane) and any benefit from the contract. Standardisation may already be similar to this in the analogue world, but the technical code not only shapes the contract and the definition of the required quality (as standardisation does), but even executes it. Finally, breach and litigation on breach phase is also limited to computer input screens, at least de facto. Complaints are constrained to forms accepted by the provider; the client can no longer formulate them herself. Otherwise, in court proceedings, it will be claimed that the possibility offered of dispute resolution had not been taken up – however burdensome it may be. Of course, all these hurdles to evade the technical 'code' are owing also to other factors – namely consumer apathy because of low damages – but the characteristics of the 'code' add to this set of reasons powerfully and in a quintessential way.

A second salient feature is how the legal rules of a contract are often written into the DNA of an IT instrument, for instance an algorithm or blockchain. Often the execution of a contract (for instance, payment or release of a service or good) is completely structured and triggered within and by the electronic set

---

[82] See indeed, within the Society of European Contract Law (SECOLA), S. Grundmann (ed.), *European Contract Law in the Digital Age*, Intersentia, Cambridge/Antwerp/Portland 2017; but as well A. de Franceschi (ed.), *European Contract Law and the Digital Single Market*, Intersentia, Cambridge/Antwerp/Portland 2017; A. de Franceschi and R. Schulze (eds.), *Digital Revolution – New Challenges for Law*, C.H. Beck et al., Munich et al. 2019; a broader conceptualisation of contract law sources also in S. Grundmann and P. Hacker, 'The Digital Technology as a Challenge to European Contract Law – From the Existing to the Future Architecture' (2017) 13 *ERCL* 255.

[83] See indeed L. Lessig, 'The Law of the Horse: What CyberLaw Might Teach' (1999) 113 *Harvard Law Review* 501; for a discussion of the concept, see H.-W. Micklitz in S. Grundmann, H.-W. Micklitz and M. Renner, above n. 1, chapter 16.

of rules,[84] creating a strict and inseverable parallel between factual execution and legal arrangement. Another examples are blockchains, which for instance underlie the transfer of cryptocurrencies, into which the consent mechanism required for the ('legal') validity of such transfer is embedded. Smart contracts may even trigger changes in the contract, for instance a declaration of termination in the event of cross-default.

A third type of particularly powerful provider of regulatory services has arisen with the advent of digital platforms. Airbnb, Amazon and others for contracts, and Google, Facebook and others for discussion and social fora, provide for a full set of rules, a true regulatory set for the relationships of their users – whether contractual or going beyond contract. Courts struggle with conceptualising whether, how and with what kinds of safeguards they indeed form the law between the parties.[85] Are they incorporated via the parties' will – i.e. do the parties, by using the platform, implicitly shape their contractual relations according to the terms issued by the platform? Are such platforms subject to legal standards – at least the most fundamental ones, i.e. basic fundamental rights – and, more importantly, do they have to make them the basis of platform activities? Grochowski, in his contribution, observes that platforms do not merely act as intermediaries in establishing contracts and other social links, but also massively impose regulatory frameworks for the agreements concluded between their users. The platforms thus establish specific types of contracts (e.g. sales 'under Amazon rules'), which are binding only by virtue of the consent of community of contractors who accept this regulatory design by joining a platform and accepting its user agreement.[86]

---

84 For this mechanism, see for instance K. Werbach and N. Cornell, 'Contracts Ex Machina' (2017–18) 67 *Duke Law Journal* 313, esp. 363–74; R. de Caria, 'The Legal Meaning of Smart Contracts' (2018) 26 *ERPL* 731, esp. 746–49. More generally on smart contracts as a new genre of (self-)regulatory structure and its ramifications for assets allocation, see K. Pistor, *The Code of Capital. How the Law Creates Wealth and Inequality*, Princeton University Press, Princeton/Oxford 2019, pp. 183–204.

85 For the alternative concepts of how to integrate these terms into the customer relationship, see for instance M. Cohen and A. Sundararajan, 'Self-Regulation and Innovation in the Peer-to-Peer Sharing Economy' (2015–16) 82 *University of Chicago Law Review Dialogue* 116; A. Sundararajan, *The Sharing Economy. The End of Employment and the Rise of Crowd-Based Capitalism*, The MIT Press, Cambridge/London 2017, pp. 131–58; M. Grochowski, 'Spontaneous Order in the Sharing Economy? A Research Agenda' (2018) 13 *Studies in Private Law* 75, esp. 77–80; C. Busch, 'Self-regulation and regulatory intermediation in the platform economy' in M. Cantero Gamito and H.-W. Micklitz (eds.), *The Role of the EU in Transnational Legal Ordering. Standards, Contracts and Codes*, Edward Elgar, Cheltenham/Northampton, MA 2020, pp. 115–34; M. Cantero Gamito, 'Regulation.com. Self-regulation and Contract Governance in the Platform Economy: A research agenda' (2017) 9 *European Journal of Legal Studies* 53.

86 On the regulatory competition between state-enacted contract law and standard contract terms, see also M. Radin, *Boilerplate: The Fine Print, Vanishing Rights, and the Rule of Law*, Princeton University Press, Princeton 2014, pp. 33–51.

The emergence of such community-specific types of contracts widens the overall menu of options available to parties on the market, although the cognitive constraints and market competition dynamics may further limit the ability to make meaningful choice between the various modes of regulatory architecture available for an agreement.

It can already be foreseen that this third generation will not only be much more successful than the second generation, but will also go beyond all generations, i.e. including the first generation, in that full integration into the system of sources of law will be deeply discussed. It is already clear that digital sources with legal content – unlike what happened with standardisation and also with self-regulation – will themselves be questioned. It will be asked how far fundamental parameters of legality are respected within the codes of these third-generation of private ordering. They are tested against anti-discrimination laws when, for instance, the AI is trained via old practices and case law (when discrimination was still omnipresent). They are tested against unfair competition law when their algorithms increase prices after identifying from big data that users are domiciled in a particular country ('geo-blocking').[87] Even the prerequisites of consent are questioned in a particular way in the arena of personal data and disclosure of such data. All this implies that the power of private ordering – whether legal or de facto – in the digital arena has triggered a discussion on how to defend the objective legal architecture to an extent that private ordering had never done before in other areas.

6. CJEU CASE LAW AS A SPECIFIC SOURCE OF EU LAW: A BIRD'S EYE PERSPECTIVE

6.1. THE CJEU AS CREATOR OF CONTRACT LAW IN EUROPE

A theme on its own merits, CJEU case law as a specific source of EU contract law has to be prominently kept in mind in the context of creation of norms,

87 For the EU, see first steps in Regulation (EU) No. 2018/302 of the European Parliament and of the Council of 28 February 2018 on addressing unjustified geo-blocking and other forms of discrimination based on customers' nationality, place of residence or place of establishment within the internal market and amending Regulations (EC) No. 2006/2004 and (EU) 2017/2394 and Directive 2009/22/EC [2018] OJ L601/1. On a more general ban on geo-pricing (discriminating against Brazilian residents), see the so-called *Decolar* case (Decolar.com): Inquérito Civil no. 247/2016 5ª PJDC of 25 January 2018 and Inquérito Civil no. 359/2017 5ª PJDC of 6 December 2018; 7th Chamber of Poder Judiciario do Estado do Rio de Janeiro of 19 August 2019, Recourse no. 0002693-88.2019.8.19.0000; see also Br Na Rede, 'Brazil's Decolar.com Is in Hot Water for Geopricing Allegations', 22 June 2018, available at http://brnarede.com.br/en/brazils-decolar-com-is-in-hot-water-for-geopricing-allegations/.

but an in-depth analysis would go beyond the limits of this volume.[88] It can be considered by way of paradigm, rather than systematically. But as two contributions in this volume are dedicated to it, at least some developments of significant importance should be highlighted in this survey chapter. As an overall assessment, what needs to be stated in our view is that the CJEU also plays a particularly activist role in the realm of contract law. Four roles might be illustrative of this view – even though they clearly do not exhaust the CJEU's case law developments.

The earliest role the CJEU took on in the realm of contract law was that of a strong facilitator of party autonomy across borders. Having attributed to EU treaty law direct applicability and direct effect, and moreover also primacy over national laws, the Court soon also applied this to fundamental freedoms as well. This implied that party autonomy was extended across borders within the EU,[89] putting all national norms that hindered the validity and execution of a contract to a twofold test. This was a test of substantive justification (all such national norms had to be based on mandatory reasons of public good) and a test of proportionality of all such justifications (both limitations being controlled by the CJEU).[90] This move was often criticised, for instance because it was seen as primarily deregulating and thus promoting an ultra-liberal agenda, or because it was seen as being only instrumental for the market and not related to contractual justice.[91] It did, however, clearly constitute a powerful new paradigm of contract law and did indeed create markets.

Two other roles that the CJEU took on later instead point into the opposite direction, namely towards re-regulation. In both roles, the CJEU strongly accompanied the path towards re-regulation taken by the EU legislature from 1986 – with Directives on (among others) consumer credit, unfair terms, package travel, investment services, consumer sales, and e-commerce (in the first 15 years). In the first role, the Court followed a model already established by the German Constitutional Court (as described above

---

[88] For this theme, see, within the Society of European Contract Law (SECOLA), in parallel S. Grundmann (ed.), *The European Court of Justice as Creator of Contract Law*, Intersentia, Cambridge/Antwerp/Portland 2020 – for the following, see also more in detail the introduction to this volume.

[89] P. Müller-Graff, 'Europäisches Gemeinschaftsrecht und Privatrecht – das Privatrecht in der europäischen Integration', *NJW* 1993, 13, 14.

[90] Seminal in this respect (and since then consistent and broadly accepted practice), and extended namely with respect to proportionality (information rules are typically sufficient): Case C-212/97, *Centros* [1999] ECR I-1459; see, for instance, S. Grundmann, 'Information, Party Autonomy and Economic Agents in European Contract Law' (2002) 39 *CMLR* 269, 281–85.

[91] See C. Joerges, 'The Impact of European Integration on Private Law: Reductionist Perceptions, True Conflicts and a New Constitutional Perspective' (1997) 3 *ELJ* 395; A. Furrer, *Die Sperrwirkung des Gemeinschaftsrechts auf die nationalen Rechtsordnungen*, Nomos, Baden-Baden 1994, pp. 161 et seqq.

in section 3.2); in the second, however, it acted in a highly innovative way itself. The first tool for re-regulation via adjudication – the use of fundamental rights as an overarching set of principles and indeed the core value bases also for private and contract law – must be seen as an adaptation by the CJEU of a conceptualisation that had earlier taken place in the literature of several Member States. The CJEU took up the main arguments, but now on the basis of EU fundamental rights, namely on the basis of the newly enacted EU Charter of Fundamental Rights. In doing so, however, it not only changed the legal argument to some extent, but moreover also (massively) extended the line of reasoning to the whole of Europe.[92] The second instrument for re-regulation via adjudication breaks new ground more freely and is based (mostly) on the EC Unfair Terms Directive of 1993, the Directive that is of overwhelming importance for the CJEU's case law on contract law.[93] The Court would seem to have taken the stance that this Directive – within the setting of standard term contracts, i.e. more generally within the setting of virtually all consumer contracts – serves as an underlying legal value basis. This comes close to the role attributed to the one played by fundamental rights in the German and European case law just mentioned. The leading case of *Mohamed Aziz* illustrates this beautifully.[94] As the contract underlying the transaction was based on standard contract terms (and therefore the above-mentioned EC Directive applied), the CJEU held that Spanish law (indeed enacted by the national legislature) could not introduce a particular regime of interim legal protection (of creditors). The Spanish rule struck down by the CJEU had allowed for the eviction of a purchaser of a flat and a borrower of a mortgage on the basis of summary proceedings (within a forced execution procedure), before, often years later, the validity of the credit agreement was ascertained by a final substantive decision by the court competent in substance. The CJEU opined that this regime did not allow for efficient testing of contract terms used in the underlying credit agreement.

---

92 See Case C-144/04, *Mangold* [2005] ECR I-9981; Case C-555/07, *Kücükdevici* [2010] ECR I-365; Case C-617/10, *Åkerberg Fransson*, ECLI:EU:C:2013:105; Case C-414/16, *Egenberger*, ECLI:EU:C:2018:257; good analyses, for instance, in B. Heiderhoff, S. Lohsse and R. Schulze (eds.), *EU Grundrechte und Privatrecht*, Nomos, Baden-Baden 2016; D. Jarass, 'Die Bedeutung der Unionsgrundrechte unter Privaten', *Zeitschrift für Europäisches Privatrecht (ZeuP)* 2017, 310; J. Knox, 'Horizontal Human Rights Law' (2008) 102 *American Journal of International Law* 1; B. Moutel, *L'effet horizontal de la Convention européenne des droits de l'homme en droit privé français: essai sur la diffusion de la CEDH dans les rapports entre personnes privies*, dissertation, University of Limoges, 2006, available at http://www.theses.fr/2006LIMO0516; M. Starke, *EU-Grundrechte und Privatrecht*, Mohr Siebeck, Tübingen 2017.

93 Council Directive 93/13/EEC of 5 April 1993 on unfair terms in consumer contracts [1993] OJ L95/29. For the enormous amount of cases adjudicated on the basis of this Directive (more than 50 per cent according to the authors), see H.-W. Micklitz and B. Kas, 'Overview on cases before the CJEU on European Consumer Contract Law (2008–2013) Part I and II' (2014) 10 *ERCL* 1 and 189.

94 See Case C-415/11, *Mohamed Aziz*, ECLI:EU:C:2013:164.

Finally, in a fourth dimension, the CJEU also plays the role of an (often considerably innovative) interpreter of contract law. The following case law example may illustrate this. In *Weber/Putz*, the Court had to decide a case where a producer of tiles was at fault regarding defects in the tiles (which changed colour when exposed to sunlight), but where the seller himself could not (yet) have known about these defects when selling the tiles. The case was paradigmatic because the tiles had already been installed, and the main costs accrued were not for the materials (the tiles), but for the installation and replacement of the tiles. The question was whether damages in the form of the cost of removing the defective tiles and installing new tiles without these defects could be awarded even if fault was normally the prerequisite of contract law and even if privity of contract would impose a solution where the purchaser could only sue the seller (who was not at fault), and not the producer (who in this case was responsible for the defects). At least in terms of its outcome, the Court answered this question in a positive way, pointing also to the fact that sellers can have recourse against producers.[95] In other words – and though the Court was unfortunately not very explicit on this – the position was taken that fault requirements have to be reconsidered in situations where there is split of labour and that split has been chosen – as is normal – on the seller's side.

Toader, in her contribution giving a CJEU's judge's view, sees the Court mainly as the body that not only applies the harmonisation measures, but also performs the task of systemisation of the individual measures enacted in a certain piecemeal approach. The contribution considers this in relation to three issues, namely the scope of application, duties during the performance phase proper, and how far the courts should actively seize questions (ex officio). One core feature that is taken up systematically is that protection of the weaker party and a certain thinking in terms of subsidiarity should be weighed against each other. This is exemplified, for instance, by the *Berliner Kindl* case and the question whether a surety – who takes on a similar risk of repayment as the borrower, but does so as a third party – should enjoy the protection of the Consumer Credit Directive and in what circumstances. Aneta Wiewiorowska-Domagalska's contribution serves as the national counterpart and asks the core question of how well CJEU case law – and the underlying EU law measures – can be integrated into national legal orders. She strongly advocates that only via such integration can EU law indeed take full effect – or, in the words of the CJEU, have its '*effet utile*'. The rich picture drawn sees the interpretation of general clauses or the filling of gaps – i.e. questions of scope of

---

95 See Joined Cases 65/09, *Weber* and 87/09 *Putz* [2011] ECR I-5257; for an extensive explanation and critique of this decision, see S. Grundmann, 'Consumer Sales: The *Weber-Putz* Case-Law – From Traditional to Modern Contract Law' in E. Terryn, G. Straetmans and V. Colaert (eds.), *Landmark Cases of EU Consumer Law – In Honour of Jules Stuyck*, Intersentia, Cambridge/Antwerp/Portland 2013, pp. 725–42.

application – as the areas where the integration is most difficult. More generally, the picture drawn is one of rather difficult integration into national regimes. The contribution, however, is quite reserved in terms of making statements about where the CJEU has actively created European contract law.

6.2. THE CJEU'S ROLE COMPARED

In significant parts of what has been reported – and potentially also beyond them – the CJEU would seem to act more broadly as a (rather) autonomous creator of the most varied forms and aspects of contract law than its counterparts in the common law world, namely the US Supreme Court and the UK House of Lords, now the Supreme Court. This view is striking, as the latter two certainly also consider themselves to be rather more activist than traditional courts, and to be proponents of global development as well. Just a few words of brief explanation of this view. The role of facilitator and creator of new markets – namely the internal market as an integrated compound of (formerly and still to some extent) national markets – does not seem to have a fully compatible counterpart. This is obvious for the case of the UK Supreme Court (overseeing a centralised jurisdiction), but would seem to apply even to the US Supreme Court (despite the importance of a federal system and namely of the commerce clause).[96] Obviously, the UK and mainly the US Supreme Court also have important case law on cross-border issues, namely far-reaching recognition of forum and standing (in the US), considerable extension of their own jurisdiction's application in choice of law issues, and long-arm statues that impose regulatory policies on factual situations considerably outside their own jurisdiction.[97] These issues, however, would seem to be of a kind that

---

96 See for instance P.C. McGinley, 'Trashing the Constitution: Judicial Activism, the Dormant Commerce Clause, and the Federalism Mantra' (1992) 71 *Orlando Law Review* 409; M.S. Knoll and R. Mason, 'The Economic Foundations of the Dormant Commerce Clause' (2017) 103 *Virginia Law Review* 309, esp. 353 et seq.; R.E. Barnett, 'The Original Meaning of the Commerce Clause' (2001) 68 *U. Chi. L. Rev.* 101.

97 The typical feature of the long-arm application of US law is that the fact patterns – typically a tort – as such did not have any genuine link with the US, but that the tortfeasor – often a multinational enterprise – has some economic interests in the US (sec. 302 CPLR New York requires only 'transacting any business in New York') and that the US wants to police the case. Thus, for instance, for the alleged crime of financing a terrorist attack between Lebanon and Israel, a Lebanese bank was seen to fall under US jurisdiction and US liability standards were seen to apply – in this case the anti-terrorism Alien Tort Statute – on the basis of an account which this Lebanese bank owned in the US and via which it transacted with US banks. Application of US law does not require that the fact pattern itself which is tried has an impact in the US – here the terrorist attack – see *Licci v. Lebanese Canadian Bank*, SAL, No. 183 N.Y. of 20 November 2012; the contact was also rather fortuitous in *Deutsche Bank Securities, Inc. v. Montana Board of Investments*, 7 N.Y.3d 65, 850 N.E.2d 1140 (mere use of a New York-based messaging wire sufficient to apply New York law/jurisdiction). Developing a set of five

is more generally dealt with by courts of last instance (including the CJEU), specifically when they have competence in relation to a large economic power such as the US or the EU.[98]

Moreover, with respect to the transfer of human rights aspects and more generally constitutional values into private law, both the UK and the US Supreme Court seem much less activist and certainly less innovative than the CJEU (and German courts). This is true despite the fact that the UK Supreme Court indeed took up the pan-European trend – now using not so much EU primary law but rather the European Convention on Human Rights (ECHR), a source of public international law that takes precedence over national UK law, as the benchmark against which to assess UK private law.[99]

7. CONCLUSIONS AND CAVEATS

The creation of norms constitutes just as much an overarching, highly fascinating and timely theme as it forms an ocean that can only be mapped out from an extreme bird's eye view. Two topics, however, stand out in how broad a brush had to be used when giving this survey. These are the role of the CJEU and of the digital arena. Both are oceans themselves (and topics of books on their own merits).[100] Therefore, the general caveat that the accounts in this overall survey are very much a summary apply to these two topics even more than to the others. Even in this highly summarised form, they have nevertheless been included both in this overall survey (see above sections 7 and 5.4, respectively) and in three contributions to the book (two chapters and one, respectively). These two topics are so powerful because the CJEU is a relatively activist court in the realm of contract law and the digital arena has quite simply revolutionised rule-setting in contract law. The CJEU plays a relatively activist role in the realm of contract law because of its having taken on at least four roles: it acts (a) as a strong facilitator of party autonomy across borders, (b) as a strong protector of constitutional values (namely of weaker parties), (c) as a proponent of a holistic view of the entirety of a legislative regime (from

(rather general) criteria: *Asahi Metal Industry Co. Ltd. v. Superior Court*, 480 U.S. 102 = 107 S.Ct. 1026 (1987). Leading cases by the US Supreme Court on the conflict-of-laws side are *International Shoe v. Washington*, 326 U.S. 310 (1945) and *World-Wide Volkswagen Corp. v. Woodson*, 444 U.S. 286 (1980). Still worth reading, R. Casad, 'Long Arm and Convenient Forum' (1971) 20 *Kansas Law Rev* 1; and the monograph by J.-P. Schmidt-Brandt, *Zu den long-arm statutes im „Jurisdiktions-Recht' der Vereinigten Staaten von Amerika und zu ihrer Bedeutung für wirtschaftsrechtliche Streitigkeiten*, Peter Lang, Frankfurt am Main 1991.

98 See references above n. 13.

99 See above n. 33.

100 See indeed, within the Society of European Contract Law (SECOLA), S. Grundmann (ed.), above n. 88; and id. (ed.), above n. 82 (the latter, however, with more emphasis on substantive law than on the particular role of the digital arena in revolutionising rule-setting).

contract to forced execution), and (d) often as quite an innovative interpreter of contract law as well. Conversely, the digital arena constitutes so powerful a topic for our theme as it has transformed the creation of rules in contract law. To name just three salient features of the digital arena that show this powerful effect, firstly, (a) the code (of IT programs) – privately created – sets such high hurdles for changes to the formation, execution and even termination and administration of claims that it de facto replaces sovereign law to a considerable extent. Moreover, (b) the shaping of the contract via algorithms, blockchains, etc. can be such that the legal arrangement of the contract is largely encrypted in these instruments and is thus executed automatically. Finally, (c) digital platforms (including social media) often completely regulate exchanges and actions undertaken on them – leaving little of the outside world of law, and thus, for instance, both de facto and via anonymity features, hate speech largely has immunity online, where it would otherwise be punished in the analogue world.

Besides these two caveats, the theme of the creation of norms in European contract law is so rich and fascinating because it encompasses two flows of ideas coming together: on the one hand, a global flow (propelled by US and by European ideas and developments), and on the other, specifically EU law-related developments of considerable (regional, but also paradigmatic) importance. The global flow is one from a sovereign monopoly over law-making to a variety of rule-setters. This trend has been triggered on the one hand by a stronger understanding of the advantages of rule-setting by the private law circles most affected (see sections 1.1 and 5.1). On the other hand, it has also been triggered by the discovery of the fact that in the transnational sphere, it is not only public international law and national law applied across borders that shape legally transnational arrangements and transactions (see section 1.2). These developments have, since the 1960s, shaped the intellectual architecture of rule-setting beyond the state. In substance, contract law rule-setting is characterised by another 'beyond', and this is beyond 'contract law'. This development – also starting in the late 1950s and continuing since then – is linked to a re-writing of contract law under the influence of new democratic constitutions and also of international instruments, and to an overspill that lead to the idea of a constitutionalisation even of the transnational sphere (see sections 1.2 and 3). These three elements – the better understanding of the advantages of private influence in rule-setting (see section 5.1), globalisation and a clearer focus on the multiplicity of instruments in the transnational sphere, and the constitutionalisation of contract law – can finally be spelt out in two ways. On the one hand, there is the much wider choice given to private parties, as a result of which they become more the masters of their own contractual arrangement than the sovereign legislature, which may now be seen to provide (only) the legal raw materials (see section 4). On the other hand, we have seen the advent of private parties and communities as rule-setters proper – already shaping the raw materials that (other) private parties then use (see section 5). For both dimensions, individual contributions in the core parts of the book (Parts III and IV) take up the most salient examples that have been summarised in the introduction.

The European flow, besides also propelling the global flow, adds a few 'jewels' – certainly the CJEU, which, in important respects, can be seen as a relatively activist 'creator' of contract law on the international market, to which one part of this book is devoted (see above section 6 and Part V). Besides this, the idea of an optional code – though not successful in the form of the CESL – has its more general appeal as a particular mode of regulation between public and private ordering. Finally, the more day-to-day interaction between national and supranational rule-setting and adjudication that is typical of European contract law would also seem to be rather unique and worth special consideration in the world of the 'creation of norms'.

PART II

BASIS OF NORMS

Values and Jurisdictions

GOOD FAITH AS CONTRACT'S CORE VALUE

Daniel Markovits*

The common law of contract has long recognised a duty of good faith in performance.[1] This chapter argues that this duty is contract's core value – that good faith *constitutes* the distinct form of legal obligation that contracts establish. An initial section introduces the duty of good faith in performance through a series of doctrinal examples. Subsequent sections examine the metes and bounds of good faith and elaborate a theory of this duty. The theory explains that the duty of good faith in performance neither adds to the obligations that contracts impose nor recasts the substantive terms of actual contracts to fit any ideal. Instead, good faith is an attitude that contracting parties might take to the agreements that they have in actual fact made. When contracting parties approach their agreements in good faith, they at once respect freedom of contract and establish their contractual relations as sites of intrinsically valuable reciprocal recognition. Good faith thus constitutes contracts as what I have elsewhere called *collaborations*.[2]

---

* This chapter derives from Chapter 19 of my *Contract Law and Legal Methods* (Foundation Press, New York 2012) and abridges Daniel Markovits, *Good Faith as Contract's Core Value* in Gregory Klass, George Letsas, and Prince Saprai, eds., The Philosophical Foundations of Contract Law (OUP 2014).

1 A seminal authority is Lord Mansfield's opinion in *Boone v. Eyre* (1777) 126 Eng. Rep. 160 (KB); 1 H. Bl. 273. An early case imposing this duty in an American jurisdiction is *Kirke La Shelle Co. v. Paul Armstrong Co.*, 188 N.E. 163, 167 (N.Y. 1933).

2 D. Markovits, 'Contract and Collaboration' (2004) 113 *Yale Law Journal (Yale LJ)* 1417.

1. GOOD FAITH IN CONTRACT DOCTRINE

In the United States, the Uniform Commercial Code (UCC) imposes a mandatory duty of good faith in performance on 'every contract' within its scope.[3] The Restatement (Second) of Contracts similarly says that '[e]very contract imposes upon each party a duty of good faith and fair dealing in its performance and its enforcement.'[4] Moreover, the two authorities elaborate good faith in similar terms. The UCC thus adds that 'good faith' means 'honesty in fact and the observance of reasonable commercial standards of fair dealing'.[5] The comments to the Restatement explain that good faith 'excludes a variety of types of conduct characterized as involving "bad faith" because they violate community standards of decency, fairness or reasonableness.'[6]

While the Restatement sensibly takes the position that a 'complete catalogue of types of bad faith is impossible', it nevertheless provides representative examples. These include: 'evasion of the spirit of the bargain, lack of diligence and slacking off, willful rendering of imperfect performance, abuse of a power to specify terms, and interference with or failure to cooperate in the other party's performance.'[7] The comments add that good faith

> is violated by dishonest conduct [in enforcing contract rights] such as conjuring up a pretended dispute, asserting an interpretation contrary to one's own understanding, or falsification of facts. [Good faith is also violated by] dealing which is candid but unfair, such as taking advantage of the necessitous circumstances of the other party to extort a modification of a contract for the sale of goods without a legitimate commercial reason. [Good faith is also violated by] harassing demands for assurances of performance, rejection of performance for unstated reasons, willful failure to mitigate damages, and abuse of a power to determine compliance or to terminate the contract.[8]

Good faith forbids parties from hiding behind indefinite contract terms, either by construing them in an excessively self-serving light or by claiming that the indefiniteness renders the contracts containing them void, *tout court*. Instead, where a contract leaves the particulars of performance to be specified by one of the parties, that party is constrained to make the specification in good faith,[9] which, as the comments to the UCC say, entails that 'the range of permissible variation is limited by what is commercially reasonable'.[10] In the context of sales

---

3 Uniform Commercial Code §1-304 (2003).
4 Restatement (Second) of Contracts §205 cmt. [a] (1981) (hereinafter Restatement).
5 UCC §§1-201, 2-103.
6 Restatement §205 cmt. [a].
7 Restatement §205 cmt. [d].
8 Restatement §205 cmt. [e].
9 UCC §2-311(1).
10 UCC §2-311 cmt. 1.

contracts that measure quantity by the output of the seller or the requirements of the buyer, good faith requires that the quantity a party orders or delivers not be unreasonably disproportionate to the legitimate expectations of the counterparty.[11] Contracts for exclusive dealings in some class of goods similarly require parties to use their best or at least reasonable efforts to supply or promote the goods in question.[12]

A comparable regime governs contracts in which terms essential to operating the contracts as circumstances have developed are not just left indefinite but are not included at all.[13] Where the parties have failed to make adequate arrangements for some contingency ex ante, they must employ good faith in making arrangements ex post. For example, termination is governed by good faith,[14] at least where the contract does not establish any specific regime. A party seeking to terminate may not do so before the non-terminating party has had 'reasonable notification',[15] which is to say a 'reasonable time to seek a substitute arrangement'.[16]

The warranties concerning title that a seller provides her buyer are also governed by good faith. In particular, where a contract does not specify otherwise, a seller warrants that her title is good and its transfer is rightful, and that the buyer will not be unreasonably exposed to litigation based on third parties' colourable claims or interests in the goods.[17] Similarly, good faith requires a seller to disclose known material but hidden defects in goods sold.[18] The disclosure may be waived by a disclaimer that asserts that there may be hidden defects, but this of course puts the buyer on notice that goods may not be as they appear. And although contracting parties generally can, 'if they consciously desire, make their own bargain as they wish',[19] good faith precludes a party from using one clause to undo a promise made in another, at least in circumstances in which honouring the undoing cannot be understood except as implementing the manipulative term of a bait and switch. This principle applies with especial force to preclude sellers' efforts to disclaim warranties that their selling methods are designed to convey the impression

---

11 UCC §2-306(1).

12 See UCC §2-306(2); *Wood v. Lucy, Lady Duff-Gordon*, 118 N.E. 214 (N.Y. 1917).

13 A similar principle may be found in English law, although not necessarily under the header 'good faith'. An example is the rule that '[w]here in a written contract it appears that both parties have agreed that something shall be done, which cannot effectually be done unless both concur in doing it, the construction of the contract is that each agrees to do all that is necessary to be done on his part for the carrying out of that thing, though there may be no express words to that effect.' *Mackay v. Dick* (1881) 6 App. Cas. 251 (HL) (Blackburn J).

14 See UCC §2-309 cmt. 8.

15 UCC §2-309 cmt. 5.

16 UCC §2-309 cmt. 8.

17 UCC §2-312(1) and cmt. 1.

18 UCC §2-314 cmt. 4.

19 UCC §2-313 cmt. 6.

of having given. The comments to one of the UCC sections on warranties thus observe that 'a contract is normally a contract for a sale of something describable and described. A clause generally disclaiming "all warranties, express or implied" cannot reduce the seller's obligation for the description and therefore cannot be given literal effect.'[20] Rather, 'in determining what [the parties] have agreed upon good faith is a factor and consideration should be given to the fact that the probability is small that a real price is intended to be exchanged for a pseudo-obligation.'[21]

In all these ways, the duty of good faith in performance regulates advantage-taking within the contract relation. Unsurprisingly, therefore, good faith becomes particularly important where structural circumstances make it impracticable or even impossible for the parties to regulate such advantage-taking directly and expressly, because prior agreements cannot effectively reach them.

Thus, although contracting parties generally remain free to renegotiate or rescind their contracts, good faith precludes one party from employing this freedom strategically, to exploit vulnerabilities of the other that are themselves created by (indeed creatures of) the contracts to be renegotiated.

For example, it is bad faith for an employer to discharge a sales employee who is paid on commission after the employee has obtained an extraordinarily large order but before completion of all the formalities required to make the commission come due.[22] Similarly, it would be bad faith for an employer to fire an employee just before the employee meets a performance quota that triggers a substantial bonus. In each case, the employee has expended effort that the employment contract contemplated and indeed was designed to induce and, by rendering this effort a sunk cost, eliminated her power to bargain for a share of the return to the effort. In refusing to pay the commission or the bonus, the employer has deprived the employee of the share of the return to her effort that the contract had allocated to her ex ante and exploited the employee's weakened bargaining position ex post. This is bad faith.[23]

Insurance contracts present similar patterns. Typically, an insurer assumes duties both to pay damage awards or settlements secured against the insured

---

20 UCC §2-313 cmt. 6.

21 UCC §2-313 cmt. 6.

22 See *Fortune v. National Cash Register*, 364 N.E.2d 1251 (Mass. 1971).

23 Other cases display a similar, and similarly clear, pattern, in different fact settings. Thus, it is bad faith for a buyer who has contracted to purchase a specific asset from a middleman subsequently to buy this asset directly from the middleman's supplier in order to save having to pay his profit. To do so would be to exploit the vulnerability to which the contract has exposed the middleman – the revelation of the asset to the buyer – in order to deprive the middleman of the very gain that the contract was designed to secure him. See e.g. *Patterson v. Meyerhofer*, 97 N.E. 472 (N.Y. 1912). Similarly, it is bad faith for a financing-dependent buyer to fail to make adequate efforts to seek financing. See e.g. *Fry v. George Elkins Co.*, 327 P.2d 905 (Cal. App. 2d 1958); *Goldberg v. Charlie's Chevrolet, Inc.*, 672 S.W.2d 177 (Mont. Ct. App. 1984).

by injured third persons in connection with covered events, up to some limit, and to defend the insured against claims for such damages. This makes it bad faith for the insured to exploit the insurer's position by insisting on accepting unreasonably large settlement offers, and refusing to cooperate in any further defence, on the ground that this costs her nothing and saves her the burden of the lawsuit. And, much more practically important, it is bad faith for the insurer to reject reasonable settlement offers near the policy limit, on the ground that it bears none of the litigation risk associated with rejecting the offers.[24] In each case, one party exploits a strategic vulnerability of the other that arises inside the insurance contract (and indeed is caused by the contract) to secure its private advantage. Once again, this is bad faith.

Finally, good faith applies to create effectively mandatory duties in circumstances in which the parties' contractual relations have broken down in ways such that no prior agreement could reliably govern conduct. The most common such circumstances involve a party's response to his counterparty's breach, and thus in particular concern the party's efforts to recover damages. The parties cannot contract ex ante for the case in which a promisor denies her contractual obligations entirely, because this denial would cover any agreement that they had made for such a case. The promisor's denial of the contract does not, however, disentangle the parties from each other's affairs. The disappointed promisee will continue to insist on her contractual rights and to take steps to vindicate these rights. Insofar as the steps that she takes might impose costs on her promisor, the law must regulate her conduct (as the parties' agreement cannot). A mandatory duty of good faith figures prominently in this regulation.

For example, although a seller whose buyer has breached may, in appropriate circumstances, avoid the burden and expense of proving up market damages and instead resell the goods and recover damages based on the contract-resale price difference,[25] the resale must be made in good faith.[26] Relatedly, although sellers whose buyers breach may recover consequential damages, their recovery is limited according to their duty to make a good faith effort to minimise (including by resale) the consequential damages suffered as a result of the breach.[27] Analogous duties of good faith apply to buyers with respect to cover when their sellers breach[28] and to buyer's duties to mitigate (including by purchasing cover) their consequential damages from breach.[29]

These examples may be multiplied. And they all reaffirm the general lesson drawn earlier. The duty of good faith polices advantage-taking within the

24 See e.g. *Comunale v. Traders & General Ins. Co.*, 328 P.2d 198 (Cal. 1958) (en banc).
25 UCC §2-706.
26 UCC §2-706(1).
27 See UCC §2-708 and cmt. 6 thereto.
28 See UCC §2-712(1) and cmt. 4.
29 See UCC §2-715 and cmt. 2.

contract relation. It seeks to prevent the frame of the contract relation – the fact that the parties to this relation rely on each other's expressed intentions – from becoming itself an opportunity for manipulation or exploitation. Good faith steps in to *require* contracting parties to respect each other's contractual intentions even where they, preferring manipulation, are disinclined to do so.

2. THE METES AND BOUNDS OF GOOD FAITH

The examples all share the general sentiment that it is bad faith for one party to use the fact of the contract to exploit the other going forward. Thus it is said that good faith precludes a party from using its inevitable room to manoeuvre within the contract 'to recapture opportunities forgone upon contracting'.[30] Bad faith in performance, that is, 'consists of an exercise of discretion in performance to recapture opportunities forgone at formation'.[31] Most importantly, a party cannot use the very fact that after negotiations had concluded in an agreement, his counterparty took steps (pursuant to that agreement) that rendered her more vulnerable than she was in the negotiations, now to renegotiate aspects of the agreement on more favourable terms. In the words of a prominent early American opinion, '[i]n every contract there is an implied covenant that neither party shall do anything which will have the effect of destroying or injuring the right of the other party to receive the fruits of the contract, which means that in every contract there exists an implied covenant of good faith and fair dealing.'[32]

This formulation provides an important warning against an attractive error. It is tempting to think that the duty of good faith in performance *adds* to the content of contractual obligation – to this obligation's metes and bounds – concretely and in the context of particular contracts. Courts and commentators both occasionally succumb to temptation on this point. They treat good faith as what Allan Farnsworth and then-Judge Scalia, reciprocally quoting each other, have called 'implying terms in the agreement'.[33] Some even go so far as

---

30 S.J. Burton, 'Breach of Contract and the Common Law Duty to Perform in Good Faith' (1980) 94 *Harvard Law Review (Harv. L. Rev.)* 369, 373.

31 Ibid., p. 387.

32 *Kirke La Shelle Co.*, above n. 1, p. 167. The case involved a silent-film era agreement to share 'motion picture' rights to a play and the question whether rights to make a 'talkie' based on the play were within the scope of the agreement. The court held that they were not. It has seemed to many that this is a mistake on the facts. See *L.C. Page & Co. v. Fox Film Corp.*, 83 F.2d 196, 199 (2d Cir. 1936) (words 'motion picture' in pre-'talkie' contract held to include 'talkies'); *see also Bartsch v. Metro-Goldwyn-Mayer, Inc.*, 391 F.2d 150 (2d Cir. 1968), cert. denied, 393 U.S. 826 (1968).

33 *Tymshare Inv. v. Covell*, 727 F.2d 1145, 1152 (D.C. Cir. 1984); E.A. Farnsworth, 'Good Faith in Contract Performance' in J. Beatson and D. Friedmann (eds.), *Good Faith and Fault in Contract Law*, Clarendon Press, Oxford 1995, p. 161.

understanding the duty of good faith in performance to import one or another conception of what Todd Rakoff has called 'exchange justice' into contract law.[34] On this view, now expressed in Daniel Friedmann's words, good faith imposes 'restraints on self-interest in deference to a much heavier interest of another party'.[35] Jack Beatson has offered a similar account of certain limits on advantage-taking within contracts that have made their way into English law.[36] Even legislatures have gotten into this business, as in the English Unfair Contract Terms Act, which (in Hugh Beale's words) has the 'substantive content' that some clauses 'cause such an imbalance that they should always be treated as being contrary to good faith and therefore unfair'.[37] This approach adopts a substantive regime very similar to that which jurisdictions in the United States have imposed through substantive unconscionability; but it imposes this regime under the heading 'good faith'.

Such approaches possess a natural appeal. To understand good faith as inserting an additional, mandatory obligation into every contract would be to be able to use the duty to decide (close) cases. Being practical, lawyers and judges naturally seek guidance and assistance in resolving concrete disputes. Good faith understood as a distinctive additional contract term promises to provide both.

This promise is unlikely to be fulfilled, however.

To be sure, it is possible to fix the inner and outer bounds of good faith. On the one hand, it is commonly and rightly observed that 'conduct that might not rise to the level of fraud may nonetheless violate the duty of good faith in dealing with one's contractual partners'.[38] Good faith must require more of the parties than just that they abjure fraud, because good faith refers to rights established by a completed bargain rather than only to rights against being misused in bargaining.

On the other hand, it is equally familiar that good faith requires less than fiduciary loyalty and devotion.[39] A fiduciary, as it is sometimes said, is 'required to treat his principal as if the principal were he'.[40] In fact, a fiduciary must treat

34 T. Rakoff, 'The Implied Terms of Contracts: Of "Default Rules" and "Situation-Sense"' in J. Beatson and D. Friedmann (eds.), above n. 33, p. 195.

35 D. Friedmann, 'Good Faith and Remedies for Breach of Contract' in J. Beatson and D. Friedmann (eds.), above n. 33, p. 400.

36 J. Beatson, 'Public Law Influences in Contract Law' in J. Beatson and D. Friedmann (eds.), above n. 33, p. 288.

37 H. Beale, 'Legislative Control of Fairness: The Directive on Unfair Terms in Consumer Contracts' in J. Beatson and D. Friedmann (eds.), above n. 33, p. 245. Beale points out that the statute 'does not require that the significant imbalance be caused by the absence of good faith' (n. 91).

38 *Mkt. St. Assocs. Ltd. P'ship v. Frey*, 941 F.2d 588, 594–95 (7th Cir. 1991).

39 But see *Parev Prods. Co. v. I. Rokeach & Sons, Inc.*, 124 F.2d 147 (2d Cir. 1941), which comes close to taking a fiduciary duty view, seeking 'the really equitable solution' as opposed to 'a limited rule of good faith' (at 150).

40 *Mkt. St. Assocs.*, above n. 38, p. 593.

his principal more carefully still: there is any number of risks that a person might (even reasonably) take on his own account that he may not, acting as fiduciary, take on his principal's. Good faith, by contrast, does not require contracting parties to display substantive other-regard or altruism, preferring their partners' interests over their own, or even weighting the two interests equally, within their contracts. Good faith, in the words of one prominent opinion, 'does not mean that a party vested with a clear right is obligated to exercise that right to its own detriment for the purpose of benefiting another party to the contract.'[41] Another prominent American court draws the contrast between good faith and fiduciary loyalty more directly still. '[G]ood faith', the court observes, 'does not envision loyalty to the contractual counterparty, but rather faithfulness to the scope, purpose, and terms of the parties' contract.'[42] English law takes a similar approach. As Jack Beatson has pointed out, '[o]ne of the hallmarks of English common law is that it does not have a doctrine of abuse of rights: if one has a right to do an act then, one can, in general, do it for whatever reason one wishes.'[43] This has the consequence that '[e]xcept where the contracting parties are also in a fiduciary relationship, self-interest is permissible, and indeed is the norm in the exercise of contractual rights.'[44] Mere self-interest therefore cannot be bad faith.

Judge Richard Posner puts this point more colourfully, observing in *Market Street Associates Limited Partnership v. Frey* that '[t]he contractual duty of good faith is thus not some newfangled bit of welfare-state paternalism or the sediment of an altruistic strain in contract law.'[45] Similarly, 'even after you have signed a contract, you are not obliged to become an altruist toward the other party.'[46] Nor does good faith require contracting parties to adopt even an attitude of substantive impartiality between their contractual interests and the interests of their contracting partners. The duty of good faith in performance applies, after all, to every contract, including to contracts among sophisticated parties who can take good care of their own interests. The law does not seek, 'in the name of good faith, to make every contract signatory his brother's keeper'.[47] Good faith is not a principle of substantive fairness even just in the face of new contingencies that arise within the contract relation. Good faith thus leaves the parties free to be self-interested within their contracts – as self-interested as they were without them, subject only to honouring the terms of their agreements.

---

41 *Rio Algom Corp. v. Jimco Ltd.*, 618 P.2d 497, 505 (Utah 1980).

42 *ASB Allegiance Real Estate Fund v. Scion Breckenridge Managing Member, LLC*, 50 A.3d 434, 440–41 (Del. Ch. 2012) aff'd in part, rev'd in part on other grounds, 68 A.3d 665 (Del. 2013). I owe this reference to Andrew Gold.

43 J. Beatson, above n. 36, pp. 266–67.

44 Ibid., p. 267.

45 *Mkt. St. Assocs.*, above n. 38, p. 595.

46 Ibid., p. 594.

47 Ibid., p. 593.

The inner and outer bounds of good faith are thus easy to discern. But it is not possible to say in general precisely where good faith falls in between these inner and outer bounds, at least not in a way that mechanically decides cases. In any concrete case, party conduct will slide seamlessly from clear bad faith, which undermines the contract, to clear good faith, which embraces the contract's purposes. The thought that good faith protects the reasonable contractual expectations of the parties cannot insert a seam.[48] The root reason

---

[48] A classic example of the problem appears in *E. Airlines, Inc. v. Gulf Oil Co.*, 415 F. Supp. 429 (S.D. Fla. 1975).
Eastern Airlines had contracted with Gulf Oil Corporation for Gulf to supply Eastern's requirements of jet fuel over a several-year period. The contract fixed the purchase price by reference to a price indicator called 'West Texas Sour' reported in a trade publication called Platts Oilgram Service-Crude Oil Supplement. In the middle of the contract period, the 1973 OPEC oil embargo surprised world oil and fuel markets, causing prices to rise unexpectedly. However, and layering a second surprise on top of this first, the West Texas Sour price indicator did not reflect the hike in prices. (This was due to intricacies involving price controls implemented following the crisis.) The contract price therefore came to depart dramatically from the market price, and litigation ensued.
This raised the question how much fuel Eastern might demand consistent with good faith. In particular, Eastern's aeroplanes had taken on more fuel at certain airports than required to reach their next destinations, in order to refuel less frequently and to avoid refuelling at certain other airports entirely. This practice, known as fuel-freighting, had allowed Eastern to avoid the inefficiencies associated with frequent refuelling and with refuelling at awkward locations. On the other hand, by increasing the flying weight of its aeroplanes, fuel-freighting had also increased Eastern's total fuel consumption. By lowering Eastern's fuel prices (through the anomalous West Texas Sour indicator), the contract with Gulf had shifted the balance of these costs in a fashion that increased the amount of fuel-freighting that was optimal for Eastern. Gulf claimed that Eastern's fuel-freighting violated its obligation to set its requirements reasonably and in good faith.
As in general, the inner and outer bounds of good faith might be confidently identified in this case also. Thus it would have been clear bad faith, for example, for Eastern to use the contract to support fuel arbitrage, buying at below market prices from Gulf and selling to its competitors at market prices. The contract, after all, unambiguously concerned Eastern's jet-fuel requirements as an *airline*, that is, for use in its aeroplanes, and not as a jet-fuel *dealer*. At the other extreme, it would have been clear good faith for Eastern to fuel and fly in precisely the patterns that it would have adopted, pursuant to the contract, had the contract and market prices not diverged. Eastern had no affirmative duty, under the contract, to adjust its fuel requirements downward to serve Gulf Oil's interests.
But these extremes mark out an immense middle ground, and assessing the extremes leaves it unclear where in this middle ground the line between good and bad faith lies.
Would it have been bad faith for Eastern to increase its requirements in connection with acquiring a competitor, where the acquisition was motivated exclusively by Eastern's access to cheaper fuel? Presumably so, since such an acquisition (with its exclusive motivation) looks like fuel arbitrage by other means. But if this is so, then surely the same argument applies to render it bad faith for Eastern to add aeroplanes or even just flights to its operations, at least where the growth is driven by cheap fuel. (The aeroplanes and routes, after all, will be won – and sometimes even literally bought – from Eastern's competitors; and it cannot matter to Eastern's good faith whether its expansion occurs by buying the competitor's stock or by acquiring its business assets.) And now it is only a small, and seemingly inexorable, step to calling it bad faith for Eastern to increase its fuel requirements in any way (or indeed to fail to decrease them in any way) on account of its advantageous price. This conclusion, however,

why the idea that good faith in performance 'protects the reasonable contractual expectations of the parties against ex post advantage-taking' cannot fix the boundaries of good faith in a fashion that can decide close cases is that good faith is required precisely because the contractual intentions of the parties, and hence also their reasonable expectations, are not complete or clear. An account that understands good faith as a *rule of decision* thus commits a circle: it supposes what it purports to determine, that is, how much the terms of the contract allow each side to exploit subsequent developments to its unilateral advantage.

Good faith thus provides little help in drawing a line between permissible and impermissible conduct in between the outer and inner bounds (fraud on the one hand, and fiduciary loyalty on the other) just set out. Nor could it be expected to. Indeed, the additional duty conception of good faith does not simply initiate a fruitless quest but furthermore rests on a fundamental mistake. Good faith simply does not determine the *content* of contract obligation, and certainly not at the margins of performance (by adding an incremental duty or right to what the contract would have required in its absence). The Official Comment to UCC §1-304 makes this plain:

> This section does not support an independent cause of action for failure to perform or enforce in good faith. Rather, this section means that a failure to perform or enforce, in good faith, a specific duty or obligation under the contract, constitutes a breach of that contract or makes unavailable, under the particular circumstances, a remedial right or power. This distinction makes it clear that the doctrine of good faith merely directs a court towards interpreting contracts within the commercial context in which they are created, performed, and enforced, and does not create a separate duty of fairness and reasonableness which can be independently breached.[49]

The UCC's formulation invites theoretical reflection. The task of legal theory is not simply to help decide (close) cases. Legal theory also seeks to illuminate the character of legal relations. It seeks, speaking a little loosely, to reveal the meaning of the law. An account of good faith might therefore have great theoretical value even if it provides only limited assistance in deciding cases. An understanding of good faith thus does not so much help to decide cases as to understand what has been decided.

Good faith thus characterises contract obligation's *form* and identifies an *attitude* towards contractual obligations: good faith supports the parties'

---

cannot be right, as one of the points of a requirements contract – one of the benefits that the contract is intended to confer on a buyer and hence something that it must be good faith for her to insist on – is surely to allow a buyer to improve its business position (and hence among other things to grow) on account of having a reliable supply of inputs. The examples slide seamlessly from clear bad faith, at odds with the contract's purposes, to clear good faith, which embraces these purposes.

49 UCC §1-304 cmt. [1].

contractual settlement, working to 'effectuate the intentions of the parties, or to protect their reasonable expectations'.[50] It is thus, fundamentally, an attitude of respect for the contract relation, and the measure of good faith is the contract itself. Good faith thereby establishes the character of the contract relation. It involves a distinctively contractual form of recognition and respect and fixes the character of contractual collaboration. A non-conclusory account of good faith explains, directly and without reference to other theory-laden terms, how contracting parties must balance self- and other-regard as they interpret, fill out, and implement their contractual arrangements.

3. GOOD FAITH, FREEDOM OF CONTRACT, AND CONTRACTUAL SOLIDARITY

Good faith requires contracting parties to vindicate reasonable contractual expectations but cannot be called on to fix the content of the expectations in whose terms it is defined. The measure of each party's good faith is the agreed purpose memorialised in the contract, which is to say the legitimate contractual expectation of the other. Good faith so understood is not a principle of substantive fairness in the face of new contingencies. The parties thus remain free to be self-interested within the contract – as self-interested as they were without it, subject only to the demand that they honour the terms of their agreement. A party may not use unanticipated contingencies to deprive his counterparty of a benefit that the contract allocated to her. But the parties equally need not sacrifice anything in the face of new contingencies that the contract does not require, nor need they assist the other parties in gaining from contingencies.

This feature of good faith – that it does not establish affirmative duties of other-regard so much as articulate respect among parties who remain at arm's length – will turn out to be essential to good faith's character, and indeed to the character of the contract relation generally.

The arm's length nature of good faith is itself rendered concrete in doctrine, for example in the expectation remedy and the associated practice of 'efficient breach'.[51] The expectation remedy establishes a default that promisors insure their

---

50 S.J. Burton, above n. 30, p. 371. For cases, see e.g. *Sessions, Inc. v. Morton*, 491 F.2d 854, 857 (9th Cir. 1974); *Ryder Truck Rental, Inc. v. Cent. Packing Co.*, 341 F.2d 321, 323–24 (10th Cir. 1965); *Perkins v. Standard Oil Co.*, 383 P.2d 107, 111–12 (Or. 1963) (en banc).

51 The account of the expectation remedy that follows receives a more elaborate development in D. Markovits and A. Schwartz, 'The Myth of Efficient Breach: New Defenses of the Expectation Interest' (2011) 97 *Virginia Law Review (Va. L. Rev.)* 1939; D. Markovits and A. Schwartz, 'The Expectation Remedy and the Promissory Basis of Contract' (2012) 45 *Suffolk University Law Review* 799 (symposium in honour of the 30th anniversary of the publication of *Contract as Promise*); and D. Markovits and A. Schwartz, 'The Expectation Remedy Revisited' (2012) 98 *Va. L. Rev.* 1093.

promisees against breach by guaranteeing the promisees' value of performance – through it, the law vindicates promisees' contractual expectations. At the same time, the remedy allows a promisor who confronts an opportunity to increase overall surplus by diverting the promised performance to a higher-valuing third party self-interestedly to appropriate the gains from dealing with the third party for herself.

As long as she transfers to the promisee an amount equal to the expectation remedy, a promisor who commits such an 'efficient breach' surely displays no bad faith. The transfer vindicates the promisee's reasonable contractual expectations. After all, the parties, bargaining in the shadow of the remedy, will have reduced the contract price (and increased the promisee's contractual expectations) in light of the promisor's right to retain the gains from the 'efficient breach'.[52] The parties' contractual intentions will have contemplated that the promisor retains such gains ex post, and she will have paid for them ex ante. Her payment will have been memorialised in a lower price term, which is to say that the promisor's entitlement to the gains from efficient breach is made express in the contract, or at least implied in fact rather than in law. (This approach to the expectation remedy thus sounds in the parties' actual rather than ideal agreement, a point that will become important in a moment.) Indeed, given this arrangement, it would be bad faith for a promisee to insist on specific performance, as this would give the promisee a benefit that he did not pay for and deprive the promisor of one of the benefits that the contract expressly gave her.[53] The expectation remedy thus does not eliminate contractual sharing (including of the surplus generated by 'efficient breach') but instead cabins contractual surplus-sharing according to the parties' agreement, ex ante.[54]

---

52 The parties will generally prefer this, as the overall gains from trade (which the parties may divide however they can agree) will be greater under the expectation regime than under a property right regime.

53 Moralists who criticise the expectation remedy and 'efficient breach' for, in effect, encouraging promisor bad faith miss this point. Examples include: R.R.W. Brooks, 'The Efficient Performance Hypothesis' (2006) 116 *Yale LJ* 568; M. Eisenberg, 'Actual and Virtual Specific Performance, the Theory of Efficient Breach, and the Indifference Principle in Contract Law' (2005) 93 *California Law Review* 975; M. Eisenberg, 'The Disgorgement Interest in Contract Law' (2006) 105 *Michigan Law Review (Mich. L. Rev.)* 559; D. Friedmann, 'The Efficient Breach Fallacy' (1989) 18 *Journal of Legal Studies* 1; S. Shiffrin, 'Could Breach of Contract Be Immoral?' (2009) 107 *Mich. L. Rev.* 1551; S. Shiffrin, 'The Divergence of Contract and Promise' (2007) 120 *Harv. L. Rev.* 708.

54 Specific performance is not different in this respect. Rather, it simply shifts the control over the contractual trade from the promisor to the promisee, whom it empowers to be self-interested within the contract in just the manner in which the expectation remedy empowers the self-interest of the promisor.

At least in the general run of cases, such a reallocation would reduce overall contractual surplus, for reasons having to do with transactions costs. The traditional specific performance remedy draws the promisee into the promisor's perform-or-breach decision, by giving the promisee a right to demand performance. But it does not exclude the promisor from that

In this way, the expectation remedy vividly embodies the attitude towards contractual obligation associated with good faith and brings the structure of the contract relation into line with this attitude. Good faith thus establishes a contrast to what the contract relation would be like were it governed by a regime of reciprocal fiduciary obligation between promisor and promisee. The fiduciary regime would require each party to display affirmative other-regard within the contract and to adjust its conduct not only to vindicate whatever expectations were fixed by the parties ex ante but also fairly to balance its and its counterparties' interests as these develop ex post. Such fiduciary arrangements are possible, and indeed are recognised in law. But they remain starkly and expressly different from the contract relation.[55]

Contractual good faith is thus thin (being limited to respect for an antecedently and independently agreed surplus allocation) and flexible (being open to any surplus allocation on which the parties have so agreed). But it is neither inconsequential nor slight. Indeed, contractual recognition, although it arises at arm's length, possesses a value in which more intimate forms of recognition cannot share. Among other things, thinness reconciles the mandatory duty of good faith with freedom of contract. In addition, the structure of good

---

decision, as she retains her right simply to perform. This is an odd way of speaking, but it matters. Where a promisee entitled to specific performance demands too great a share of the gains from an efficient breach, a promisor will threaten to deprive the promisee of the gains entirely, simply by performing. The strategic setting associated with traditional specific performance thus requires a transaction's costly, and hence inefficient, ex post renegotiation.

This reveals that in order to be as efficient as the expectation remedy, a specific performance rule would have to give promisees a right to *require* promisors to deal with third parties (committing an 'efficient breach') and disgorge the gains from such dealing. See R.R.W. Brooks, above n. 53; D. Markovits and A. Schwartz, above n. 51. This requirement renders vivid that the entitlement to self-interest within the contract – and the associated insistence on sharing ex ante rather than ex post – survives the reallocation of gains associated with replacing the efficient expectation remedy with an efficient regime of specific performance.

55 For more on the nature of fiduciary loyalty, including as it appears in contrast to good faith, see D. Markovits, 'Sharing Ex Ante and Sharing Ex Post: The Non-Contractual Basis of Fiduciary Relations' in A. Gold and P. Miller (eds.), *The Philosophical Foundations of Fiduciary Law* (2014).

Commentators do not always appreciate the structural difference between good faith and fiduciary loyalty and sometimes understand the two as what D. Gordon Smith calls 'variations on a theme.' D.G. Smith, 'The Critical Resource Theory of Fiduciary Law' (2002) 55 *Vanderbilt Law Review* 1399, 1487. More specifically, Smith proposes that '[b]oth [fiduciary duty and good faith] are judicially imposed loyalty obligations designed to attack the potential for opportunism in relationships' (at 1487–88). Smith further asserts that good faith 'requires each contracting party to consider the interests of the other contracting party when contemplating self-interested actions. To that extent, the duty of good faith is similar to fiduciary duty' (at 1488).

This is error, both about doctrine and about doctrine's deeper normative structure. Good faith, once again, looks backwards, to the contract and its allocation of benefits and burdens; fiduciary loyalty looks forwards, to balance the parties' interests as conditions develop.

faith corresponds to the formal equality that contract law embeds elsewhere in doctrine. Most importantly, good faith (rightly understood) establishes contract as a collaborative relation and places this relation at the centre of the distinctive form of social solidarity established through market exchange.

The contrast between contractual good faith and fiduciary obligation – the principle that good faith does not establish intimacy or affection so much as articulate respect among parties who remain at arm's length – is worth exploring in the light of these claims. To begin with, this contrast illuminates the relationship between good faith in performance and freedom of contract – the fashion in which the duty of good faith serves as the core doctrinal expression of freedom of contract. Furthermore, the contrast reveals the character of contractual recognition and market solidarity.[56]

It is commonly said that the degree of other-regard required by contract is *less* than that required of fiduciaries. In one sense, the account just elaborated supports the commonplace view: if a beneficiary asks his fiduciary to walk a mile with him, she must, altruistically, walk with him twain; a contractual promisor, by contrast, may self-interestedly walk only the mile that she promised, and not an inch further. But contractual good faith is not simply a lesser version of fiduciary other-regard – altruism light, as it were. Rather, contractual good faith involves a distinctive form of recognition of the other to whom it is owned – a form of recognition that fiduciary altruism forecloses, or at least impedes.[57]

A fiduciary's obligation to take the initiative on her beneficiary's behalf is coupled with an entitlement to pursue the beneficiary's interests as the fiduciary sees them, including even where the beneficiary takes a different view. These are two sides of fiduciary intimacy's single coin, as altruism becomes quite literally a nonsense in the absence of a right, in the altruist, to promote the other's true interests rather than false ones. This thought is reflected in fiduciary law, through doctrines that limit the terms on which a beneficiary might engage a fiduciary. Broadly speaking, fiduciary arrangements must hold fiduciaries to standards of reasonable care on their beneficiaries' behalves and must give fiduciaries a right to pursue their independent judgments in their exercise of this care. Doctors must sometimes override the choices of their patients, for example, and lawyers must override the choices of their clients; at least, they must both sometimes refuse to go along with self-destructive or even just imprudent

56 See generally D. Markovits, 'Market Solidarity', Inaugural Lecture as Calabresi Professor of Law, Yale University, 09.04.2012, available at <http://vimeo.com/40731104>.

57 Doctrine sometimes recognises and implements this point. One can thus find cases that expressly associate certain rights to good faith in performance with arm's length contracts, by observing that these rights do not arise within joint ventures. See e.g. *Ray-Tek Services, Inc. v. Parker*, 831 N.E.2d 948, 953 (Mass. App. Ct. 2005). The fiduciary character of the joint venture entails rights and duties of its own, of course. But these squeeze out, rather than simply add to, certain of the rights and duties associated with contractual good faith.

client initiatives. Beneficiaries cannot impose their unreasonable preferences or beliefs on their fiduciaries.

By contrast, a contractual promisor's entitlement to good faith self-interest comes with an obligation to take her counterparty's intentions at face value. Both are, equally, expressions of the contractual arrangement – to go only the distance, and only along the path, that the contract to which she and her collaborator agreed specifies. The contractual promisor's freedom from any altruistic obligation thus also deprives her of any entitlement to promote her perspective over her promisee's. Just as fiduciary altruism carries with it paternalism and associated limits on the freedom of the beneficiary, so good faith self-interest (the fact that a promisor may, within the constraints of the contractual agreement, remain as self-interested within the contract as she was without it) carries with it anti-paternalism. Anti-paternalism is, in fact, just another facet of freedom of contract, as a promisee subjected to the mercies of her promisor's paternalism within the promise would be deprived of promise as a reliable mechanism for pursuing her own purposes (a deprivation that the promisor's altruism reduces not one whit).

Finally, returning to the connection between good faith and freedom of contract casts the inter-subjective recognition involved in every contractual exchange in a revealing light. Fiduciaries, because of their altruism and the paternalism that this carries with it, recognise their beneficiaries in terms of their peculiar, idiosyncratic needs and interests – one might say, as the particular persons they are. Contractual promisors, by contrast, proceeding anti-paternalistically and in good faith, recognise their promisees for their general intentional capacities to pursue whatever interests and needs they have – one might say, for their generic moral personalities.[58]

In a nutshell, once again, good faith allows contracting parties to remain as self-interested, and as much at arm's length, within the contract as they were without it, *except* that they must accept, as a side-constraint, that the best interpretation of what they agreed to in contracting binds them to limit their self-interest. And the distinctive balance of self-interest and other-regarding constraint articulated by good faith elaborates a particular form of interpersonal recognition and respect.

This chain of characterisations – from good faith to self-interest to anti-paternalism to freedom of contract to recognition of generic personality – generates a striking conclusion, moreover. Contractual recognition (the basis of contractual solidarity) is not lesser but rather different from more intimate forms of recognition. Indeed, the contract relation – precisely because good faith is thinner, more generic, and more abstract than particular, concrete

58 I elaborate this thought in greater detail and argue that the structure of promissory recognition renders promising incompatible with intimacy in D. Markovits, 'Promise as an Arm's Length Relation' in H. Scheinman (ed.), *Promises and Agreements*, 2011, p. 295.

altruism – opens up possibilities for solidarity at arm's length that intimates cannot achieve. Good faith thus underwrites a distinctive form of recognition in which contracting parties recognise one another's expressed intentions, at face value. When they do so, the parties to contracts recognise one another as sovereign wills, whose freedom and hence also choices must be respected. Fiduciary relations lack this variety of respect, not in spite but rather because of the substantive other-regard that they involve.

The connection between good faith and freedom of contract – including through its emphasis that the boundaries of good faith in particular cases are determined by rather than determining the actual intentions and expectations of the parties – goes to the core of good faith and to its structural role in the contract relation. The duty of good faith in performance, once again, is not a separate undertaking of the parties to a contract but an attitude towards whatever undertakings the parties have adopted. To display good faith in contract performance is simply to recognise the authority of the contract, and hence the authority of one's counterparty to insist on performance according to the contract's terms.

The duty of good faith in contract performance thus expresses a commitment to a particular normative (and indeed legal) relation. Honouring the duty involves internalising the authority structures of that relation and implementing them in one's own practical life. This, incidentally, is why good faith, even as its content may be varied almost arbitrarily by the parties (to take on any substance consistent with there being a contract between them), remains a mandatory rule that cannot be waived. Good faith in performance just is the attitude of taking contractual obligation appropriately seriously. To reject good faith is, in effect, to deny the contractual obligation to which good faith attaches. To make such a denial at the moment of contract formation, as would be involved in a waiver of good faith, is to forswear the intent to obligate. And that necessarily causes contractual obligation to fail from the get-go.

4. GOOD FAITH AS A PEDESTRIAN IDEAL

Good faith, so understood, is a private analogue – as between the contracting parties – of the public duty to obey the law that arises among citizens generally (and the rejection of good faith is a private analogue of the revolutionary's denial of the political obligation to which the duty to obey the law attaches). The analogy between faithfully performing a contract and dutifully obeying the law reveals something important about good faith. The duty to obey the law is not simply a duty to act in accordance with justice or natural law, but rather attaches (defeasibly, of course) to *positive law*. Similarly, the duty of good faith in performance is not simply a duty to coordinate optimally but rather attaches to the *positive contract* – to the contract that was actually agreed rather than to some ideal alternative. Good faith in performance is thus a *pedestrian* ideal, which takes as its lodestar the actual contract that the parties' intentions established rather than the *utopian* contract that it would have been optimal for them to establish. Indeed, good faith underwrites a distinctive, intrinsically valuable relation among the parties, at all, *only* in respect of its pedestrian connection to their actual, concrete intentions.

This is not a trivial or obvious point, and it is not always understood. It is tempting to idealise good faith by connecting it not to what the parties intended – to their actual joint plan – but to what they ought, rationally or ideally, to have agreed, or even just to what they would have agreed ex ante had they known then what they have discovered ex post. But overlooking the actual in favour of the ideal – rejecting pedestrian good faith (based on the parties' actual agreement) in favour of a utopian alternative (that invokes the agreement that the parties ideally would have struck) – introduces confusions into discussions of good faith.

Natural justice has long tempted political thinkers towards scepticism concerning the authority of merely positive law. Similarly, the rational idealisation of good faith has, at various times, attracted all manner of thinkers to resist the positive terms of actual contracts. In private law, the utopian approach to the contract relation is at the moment especially tempting to writers in the economic tradition.

Consider again, and in this light, Judge Posner's opinion in *Frey*. According to Judge Posner, the duty of good faith 'is a stab at approximating the terms the parties would have negotiated had they foreseen the circumstances that have given rise to their dispute.'[59] Good faith, on this approach, is thus just another 'way[] of formulating the overriding purpose of contract law, which is to give the parties what they would have stipulated for expressly if at the time of making the contract they had had complete knowledge of the future and the costs of negotiating and adding provisions to the contract had been zero.'[60] This is as clear a statement of the utopian approach as can be made: good faith, for Judge Posner, is the doctrinal pathway for making the ideal actual.

That vision of good faith cannot be the right one, however. At least, it cannot be right without in effect eliminating contract as a distinctive legal category, which expresses a peculiar face of human freedom and constructs a distinctive human relation.

As a shallow matter, the utopian conception of good faith simply does not fit the doctrine. According to the utopian view, the duty of good faith in performance *adds* to the substantive content of every contractual obligation. A utopian duty of good faith would entail that contractual promisors owe their promisees

59 *Mkt. St. Assocs.*, above n. 38, p. 595.
60 Ibid., p. 596.

performance that they would not owe otherwise. The additions reflect the gaps between the perfectly efficient contracts that the parties would have made had they reasoned ideally without transactions costs and the inefficient contracts that the parties, given their positive transactions costs, actually did make. But doctrine, once again, expressly denies this: recall the UCC's insistence that good faith 'does not create a separate duty of fairness and reasonableness which can be independently breached.'[61] The doctrinal duty of good faith in performance is not a separate or additional undertaking of the parties to a contract but an attitude towards whatever undertakings the parties have adopted.

This feature of the doctrine is no accident, moreover. Rather, utopian conceptions of good faith would betray the deep structure of contract law.

To see why good faith cannot be understood in this utopian fashion, begin by observing that a gap inevitably exists between the ideal contract and the contract that the parties have actually made. In some cases, parties expressly adopt optimal terms. (Quantity terms set by sophisticated parties are likely optimal, for example.) In others, there exist good reasons to suspect that silent parties have in fact struck the optimal agreement. (One such case, familiar from earlier discussion, concerns the expectation remedy, which may profitably be understood in terms of a legal presumption that otherwise silent parties have, through a contract's price term, adopted an efficient liquidated damages clause.) But in many cases, it will be clear (or even just on balance the best view) that the parties are interacting on terms that are not optimal. In some cases, parties who have established no contractual relation at all would be better off had they established one. In others, parties have made a contract but on terms whose departure from the optimum has been undeniably memorialised in the express terms of their agreement. In still other cases, the parties' intentions receive only implicit expression, in the interstices of their express agreement, but the best reconstruction of the parties' real contractual intentions again departs from the ideal, optimal contract.

This is not just contingently but necessarily so. Parties to contracts, needless to say, do not reason perfectly or costlessly in their contractual practices; and the costs that they face are reflected in the divergence between agreements that the parties actually make and the ideal agreements. This divergence is inevitable and indeed a transcendental condition of the parties' contracting at all. If persons really could reason perfectly and costlessly in the manner that utopian good faith imagines, they would have no need of, and hence would not (and could not rationally) resort to contract. Rather than ordering their affairs by private agreements, perfectly and costlessly rational parties would engage in ideal public social planning to arrange all their affairs maximally well (efficiently, let us say) for all time. For perfectly, costlessly rational parties, private law, including

61 UCC §1-304 cmt. [1].

contract law, is otiose: the only contract that they require is the social contract. Perhaps (and foreshadowing an argument to come) even the social contract would be otiose for such creatures, as they might all instantly agree to live by a unanimously affirmed principle of natural justice.

So actual contracts *necessarily* and indeed *constitutively* depart from the ideal. And in all cases in which the actual departs from the ideal – involving suboptimal failures to contract *tout court*, suboptimal express contract terms, and suboptimal implied-in-fact contract terms – good faith depends, at least partially, not on what would have been optimal for the parties to agree but rather on what they did agree. Whenever the actual depart from the ideal contractual intentions, the obligations that these intentions create turn not on what would have been optimal for the parties to agree but rather on what they did agree. Treating imperfectly rational parties as if they were perfectly rational, by giving good faith in their contractual relations a utopian bent, therefore undermines their actual contract practices in the service of an ideal whose content is fixed not according to the contracting parties' intentions, but rather according to the court or other lawgiver that determines what is ideal. A utopian standard of good faith, which looks to an ideal rather than to the parties' actual contract, thus violates the parties' contract under the guise of perfecting it. In this way also utopian good faith turns its back on contract.

This recounting of good faith's insistently pedestrian character is not just a pedantic emphasising of the contingent and concrete against the universal and abstract, moreover. The distinction between pedestrian and utopian is essential to the character of good faith – really, to the character of the contract relation elaborated in terms of good faith. A utopian standard of good faith, which looked to an ideal rather than to the parties' actual contract, would undermine rather than promote contractual values. Indeed, just as pedestrian good faith promotes freedom of contract and constitutes the contract relation as a site of recognition, so utopian good faith undermines both contractual freedom and recognition.

The connection between the pedestrian account of good faith and freedom of contract is easy to see (and reaffirms that good faith, in spite of being a mandatory rule, *promotes* freedom of contract). Pedestrian good faith protects the parties' actual contractual intentions against ex post exploitation, thereby allowing the parties to project their intentions into the future. Good faith is of a piece with contract law's negative libertarian elements. Pedestrian good faith serves rather than limiting freedom of contract by insistently refusing to require the parties' agreement to adopt any particular terms, or even to make any particular division of contractual surplus, but only to respect whatever division they have agreed. By contrast, utopian good faith imposes on the parties a bargain that they did not make. That the parties would be better off under the ideal bargain than under their actual one does by itself eliminate the imposition. Nor does the possibility that the parties would have chosen the ideal bargain had they perfected their deliberations. The fact that pedestrian and utopian good faith come apart entails that the parties did not perfect their intentions.[62]

Utopian good faith thus necessarily encroaches on actual freedom, in the sense associated with negative liberty, in the name of ideal freedom, or positive liberty. This is just the private law analogue of the more familiar public law thought that the utopian social contract – the idea that the state is constructed perfectly to instantiate ideal justice and that merely positive law can have no free-standing authority of its own – undermines collective political freedom, replacing democratic sovereignty with a tyranny of rights. The economic focus of utopian good faith in private law – the effort to attribute to the parties whatever intentions would have maximised the value of their bargain – is just a reference to positive liberty dressed up in negative libertarian clothes. That is the commonest apology of the paternalist.

The connection between pedestrian good faith and contractual recognition travels only slightly farther afield. Utopian good faith, recall, reconstructs contracts according to ideal efficiency, that is, without reference to the actual intentions of the contracting parties. A party who applies utopian good faith to her own contractual performance can thus proceed without engaging her counterparty at all – she can reason in isolation rather than together with him. This is rendered vivid by imagining a world in which persons deliberate in the fashion that utopian good faith envisions. If persons could deliberate and coordinate ex ante in the perfect and costless style that utopian good faith attributes to them ex post, then all contracts would be unambiguously complete, so that it would be possible to perform and assess them purely mechanically, with no faith at all, either good or bad. Contracts would, literally, cease to involve a leap of faith. They would also cease to involve respect or recognition among the parties to them, or indeed to involve communication at all. The parties, being ideal and costless deliberators, would each know the other's intentions without needing to be told, just as ideal reasoners would all commonly know the entire truth without needing to communicate. This is why, as I observed earlier, persons who deliberated in the perfect and costless fashion imagined by utopian good faith would not pursue individual engagements with one another at all.

62 None of this is to deny that contracting parties might, *in some instances*, form the actual intention that gaps in their contractual understandings shall be filled in using ideal terms. Once again, the discussion of the expectation remedy that appears in the following paragraphs illustrates just such a case. But there will also arise cases in which the parties' actual intentions either expressly or by clear implication depart from the ideal. (The case discussed just following this note is such a one.) And a contract cannot arise simply out of a *general* intention in favour of optimal exchange, as this necessarily remains too abstract to resolve concrete questions. The analogy to the law is again helpful here. As a public order cannot be established simply by justice but requires positive law, so a contract cannot be established simply by ideal intentions but requires actual ones. Like utopian politics, so utopian contract is quite literally impossible – both practices are by their nature pedestrian.

Creatures capable of planning perfectly do not need private, obligation-based coordination mechanisms to supplement public coordination. They can simply make their public arrangements perfect, and then optimally achieve all their purposes by living perfectly within them.

Good faith is, in this respect, a practical analogue to the principle of charity in interpretation of theoretical communications, a point that sometimes comes out in the cases.[63] Thus, Judge Posner observes that 'whether we say that a contract shall be deemed to contain such implied conditions as are necessary to make sense of the contract, or that a contract obligates the parties to cooperate in its performance in "good faith" to the extent necessary to carry out the purposes of the contract, comes to much the same thing.'[64] Note, further, that the analogy to the principle of charity again rejects utopianism in favour of a pedestrian reconstruction of good faith. The principle of charity requires placing a favourable gloss on what has been said rather than assuming that the truth is always and already known. The utopian assumption would undermine the principle's connection to interpretation, by depriving it of a text to interpret. Once again, if the truth is always known even without being said, then communication becomes otiose.

These observations merely emphasise in an extreme case a basic objection to utopian good faith quite generally. By drawing its content out of the thin air of reason and quite apart from any concrete intentions or contractual engagements, utopian good faith replaces contractual recognition and solidarity *among the parties* with each party's substantively identical but wholly separate relation to right reason. Parties who operate their contracts according to utopian good faith might, to borrow a form of words from Hume, be *in agreement*; but there is not *an agreement* among them. And without a contractual agreement to serve as a substrate to sustain it, there can be no contractual recognition, either.

The analogy between private contracts and the social contract once again usefully develops this point, by illuminating the private contract relation in the brighter light of its more familiar public counterpart. Just as utopianism has tempted theorists of good faith in private contract, so it has been tempting for political philosophers to idealise the social contract. Indeed, the dominant strains of the social contract tradition have succumbed to and even embraced this temptation. The perfect social contract is not political but rather replaces

63 An exchange with Charles Fried helped me to recognise the importance of this analogy.

64 *Mkt. St. Assocs.*, above n. 38, p. 596. The connection between good faith and contextual interpretation also figures in the history of the doctrine. Harold Dubroff thus observes that many of the earliest American cases on good faith employ the doctrine 'to avoid the sometimes harsh results that would otherwise have occurred under the conservative interpretation and gap-filling rules prevalent in the Nineteenth and early Twentieth Centuries.' H. Dubroff, 'The Implied Covenant of Good Faith in Contract Interpretation and Gap-Filling: Reviling a Revered Relic' (2006) 80 *St. John's Law Review* 559, 562. I would like to thank Paul MacMahon for pointing this argument out to me.

politics, supplanting the actual (republican or democratic) exercise of collective sovereignty with an idealised or just social order (whose terms, enforced by technocrats or philosopher-judges) are designed precisely to constrain actual, concrete politics. The perfect completeness of the social contract thus eliminates the need for political action and agreement in the everyday sense. And the social contract enjoys its authority on the basis of its rationality or justice and not in virtue of having been adopted by any politically constituted sovereign. For the utopian, as Rawls admits, we 'submit our conduct to democratic authority only to the extent necessary to share equitably in the inevitable imperfections of a constitutional system.'[65]

Perfectly rational and reasonable creatures would not require politics or any political agreement – they would coordinate perfectly justly, but also perfectly separately, being once again in agreement without reaching an agreement on a constitution for their political life. Imperfectly rational and reasonable creatures subject to rule by an idealised social contract fail even to be in agreement and hence experience the constraints on their sovereignty that the social contract imposes as politically alienating. That is why preventing political alienation in our imperfect world requires actual politics.

Politics, moreover, must proceed on formally rather than substantively egalitarian terms. More specifically, the formal equality of democratic citizenship is the only conception of public equality compatible with collective sovereignty in an open political community populated by imperfect moral deliberators and hence condemned to pluralist collective life subject to non-ideal positive law. The utopian social contract – the idea that the state is constructed perfectly to instantiate ideal justice and that positive law can have no authority of its own – thus threatens to deny citizens the capacity to constitute themselves, communally, as a sovereign. And private contracts, once again, resemble the social contract. Good faith measures reciprocal recognition among formally equal private contractors just as the duty to obey democratic law measures reciprocal recognition among formally equal public citizens.

It is a mistake, for all these reasons, to treat our actual private law, which is very much required, as simply an effort (not very successful) to approximate the state of affairs in which it did not exist at all. Rather, private law establishes real relations among parties in their actual, imperfectly rational state. These relations have value – intrinsically – and not just as tools. They in fact have value precisely because they are relations of recognition among imperfectly rational creatures, who yet respect one another's rationality. (At the root of this thought

---

[65] J. Rawls, *A Theory of Justice*, 1971, p. 355. Rawls gives this thought practical effect in his theory of justice, by removing virtually all important collective decisions from politics in its ordinary sense. Justice, for Rawls, determines the substantive content of policy concerning not just basic liberties but the distributions of all primary goods, including income and wealth, powers and opportunities, and even the social bases of self-respect. See ibid., p. 62.

is the insistence that the thing to be made sense of is *the contract* and not some idealisation thereof – that the entities to be respected are the persons and not some idealisations thereof.) Utopian good faith thus disintegrates contractual recognition just as surely as pedestrian good faith instantiates it.

The contractual duty of good faith in performance is thus necessarily a pedestrian ideal rather than a utopian one, whose content is fixed according to the actual intentions of the imperfect parties rather than the counterfactual intentions that the parties would have formed had they deliberated perfectly.[66] This explains why, as doctrine makes plain, good faith cannot add much to deciding close cases: although the duty of good faith in performance requires the parties to respect each other's reasonable contractual expectations, good faith cannot be called on to identify the reasonable expectations in terms of which it is defined. Whereas utopian good faith might usefully decide cases, by specifying the content of reasonable contractual expectations according to its own free-standing substantive principle, pedestrian good faith simply directs a court to contractual intentions whose content must be gleaned from elsewhere, using other means.

---

66 Even those who propose utopian reconstructions of good faith in theory accept the ideal's pedestrian limitations in practice. Judge Posner, indeed in the very opinion in *Frey* that cast good faith in terms of 'complete knowledge' and 'zero' contracting costs, is a case in point.
The case concerned what good faith required in connection with a contract for the sale and leaseback of a shopping centre. The contract expressly contemplated a further negotiation concerning financing to support additional improvements to the centre and stipulated that, should this negotiation fail, the lessee might repurchase the property at roughly the original contract price. That turned out, given movements in the local real estate market, to be a very low price. The lessee initiated the financing negotiations without notifying the lessor of the repurchase option; the lessor refused financing; the lessee sought to exercise the repurchase option; and the lessor refused to convey the land on the ground that the lessee's failure to inform the lessor of the option when it initiated the refinancing negotiations constituted bad faith.
Judge Posner held that the lessee's duty of good faith, on these facts, required only that its silence concerning the repurchase option did not arise out of a subjective intention to trick the lessor into unwittingly triggering the option, which rendered the lessee's good or bad faith a question for the fact-finder. He reached this conclusion even though subjecting the lessee to an affirmative duty to disclose would likely have been efficient, as it would have saved the costs of duplicative efforts by both sides to keep track of the terms of their agreement. Certainly the subjective (no trickery) standard of good faith that Judge Posner settled on is inefficient, as it makes assessing good faith require extensive and expensive fact-finding, and hence dramatically increases litigation expenses ex post. These points follow T. Rakoff, 'Good Faith in Contract Performance: Market Street Associates Ltd. Partnership v. Frey' (2007) 120 *Harv. L. Rev.* 1187.
One suspects that Judge Posner, in deciding the case, had at the back of his mind the actual commercial practices of sophisticated developers, which do not require affirmative other-regard but reject outright trickery. As the opinion says, good faith does not 'make every contract signatory his brother's keeper'. *Mkt. St. Assocs.*, above n. 38, p. 593. This is language steeped in the reconstruction of actual cultural practice rather than in critique aimed at rationalising practice according to idealised reason.

5. GOOD FAITH AS CONTRACT'S CORE

The thinness of good faith in performance – the fact that good faith does not require altruism or even modest affirmative other-regard but rather is consistent with remaining as self-interested within the contract as without it – connects good faith to formal rather than substantive conceptions of equality. And the fact that good faith nevertheless requires promisors to recognise the authority of their contracts, and hence also of their counterparties to insist on contract rights, connects good faith to equality of status – namely to the shared status of possessing full and equal contractual capacity.

Certainly contractual good faith remains possible even under conditions of substantive inequality. Nothing in the patterns of recognition and respect immanent in the contract relation depends on the substantive fairness of the division of contractual surplus. Even where one side to a contract has leveraged undeserved bargaining advantages in contract formation, so that the substantive terms of an exchange unfairly favour her over the other, she may perform her contract in good faith. Doing so requires only that she respect the contractual settlement, and hence her counterparty's authority to insist on that settlement, and so declines to exploit additional strategic advantages that arise within the contract (and are perhaps even obtained through it) to revise that settlement still further to favour her. In spite of the substantive unfairness that lies behind contracts in such cases, each party (including the exploiter) continues to assume duties to adjust, in good faith, to new contingencies, in order not to deprive the other party of the benefits that the contract was intended to secure. (That these benefits are unevenly, and indeed unfairly, divided, does not mean that the division has no normative force within the contract, or that either party may undo it to her unilateral advantage.) Contract obligation, one might say, does not depend on setting the world right before contracts are made, or improving the world through contracting, but can instead arise equally in non-ideal as in ideal contracting. In this way, contract possesses the power to launder injustice, creating legitimate entitlements between parties where previously there were none and, moreover, inducing the parties to recognise these entitlements.

Such a formal equality of status is likely the only conception of private equality compatible with freedom of contract in a dynamic open economy populated by non-ideal costly economic deliberators. (Similarly, the formal equality of democratic citizenship is likely the only conception of public equality compatible with collective sovereignty in an open political community populated by imperfect moral deliberators and hence condemned to pluralist collective life subject to non-ideal positive law.) Good faith is thus the measure of equal arm's length relations among free contractors in private law (just as the duty to obey democratic legislation is the measure of equal arm's length relations among free citizens in public law). Good faith in contractual performance thus connects the solidarity of the contract relation (solidarity within the contract, one might say) to the broader formal equality that lies at the bottom of the democratic, market-oriented societies in which contract typically flourishes. The doctrinal order and the economic structure thus converge.

The pedestrian account also returns the idea of good faith to its doctrinal beginnings. The discussion of good faith began by observing that it is a distinctively contractual notion, as opposed to an ideal from either tort on the one hand or fiduciary law on the other. This is what it means for good faith to be bounded below by fraud (which even tort law forbids) and from above by fidelity (which fiduciary law requires). Good faith applies not among strangers and is not owed to everyone (like tort duties) nor does it apply only among intimates (like fiduciary fidelity). Rather, it applies among persons who have forged a relationship with each other, structured around a shared understanding of a voluntary obligation, that they do not have with the general mass of humanity. Good faith applies only in respect of this obligation relation, and not in respect of other unrelated dealings and interests even among these persons. This, finally, is why good faith makes no independent contribution to the content of the contract obligation. The measure of good faith is the shared project of the contract; apart from this shared project, the persons' relation continues to be characterised by arm's length dealing.

Good faith thus takes the shared perspective of the contract – the joint activity of the contract's performance – as its lodestar. It is an attitude that the parties display towards each other in virtue of, one might even say (by) respecting, their agreement.[67] Good faith requires the parties to take a certain attitude with respect to whatever terms, whatever division of surplus, they have adopted (to honour these terms, roughly). A promisor cannot, that is, abandon her contractual intentions, including the intention to adjust to unanticipated contingencies in a fashion that secures the success of the contractual collaboration's shared plan. To return to the language of Judge Posner's opinion in *Frey*, and this time to agree with it, contracts

> set in motion a cooperative enterprise, which may to some extent place one party at the other's mercy. The parties to a contract are embarked on a cooperative venture, and a minimum of cooperativeness in the event unforeseen problems arise at the performance stage is required even if not an explicit duty of the contract. The office

67 Note that the account here rejects the long-dominant (but perhaps now more generally retreating) view that good faith 'has no general meaning or meanings of its own,'" but instead merely 'serves to exclude many heterogeneous forms of bad faith.' R. Summers, '"Good Faith" in General Contract Law and the Sales Provisions of the Uniform Commercial Code' (1968) 54 *Va. L. Rev.* 195, 196. Good faith does have a general content, which is set out in the main text.

> of the doctrine of good faith is to forbid the kinds of opportunistic behavior that a mutually dependent, cooperative relationship might enable in the absence of the rule.[68]

This thought underlies the common view that good faith is essential for preventing the contract relation from becoming a locus of exploitation. In fact, good faith plays a more fundamental role still in contract obligation, although this role remains unacknowledged. Good faith does not just prevent exploitation; it is essential for contract to exist at all. For imperfect planners, who cannot plan clearly for every contingency but whose plans inevitably involve haziness and have gaps, good faith is required to make joint planning possible. Good faith in performance is the attitude that imperfect planners must adopt towards their plans in order for the plans to be joint plans at all. It is, quite literally, the matrix in which a shared perspective is possible.[69]

One is tempted to say, in light of all of this, that good faith is the very essence of contractual solidarity, and hence of contract's contribution to social solidarity overall. To make a contract with another *just is* to adopt attitudes of solidarity in favour of the joint project fixed by the contractual intentions. To make a contract *just is* to accept the duty of good faith in its performance.

---

68 *Mkt. St. Assocs.*, above n. 38, p. 595 (internal quotation marks and citation omitted).

69 It is no coincidence, then, that good faith was often used to overcome the requirement of mutuality of obligation. See e.g. *Imperial Ref. Co. v. Kanotex Ref. Co.*, 29 F.2d 193 (8th Cir. 1928). That requirement reflects the fact that contracts must be joint endeavours. Good faith is the measure of the *ongoing* jointness.

THE RULE OF LAW AND THE CHARTER OF FUNDAMENTAL RIGHTS AS A SOURCE OF EUROPEAN PRIVATE LAW

Hugh COLLINS

Can the Charter of Fundamental Rights of the European Union (CFREU)[1] provide a source of contract law and other rules of private law in the legal order of the European Union (EU)? Assuming that the Charter can perform that role of being a source of private law norms, we must ask whether it should it be used by the courts for such a purpose. In particular, under the competences or powers conferred by the Treaty of European Union (TEU),[2] we need to question whether it is lawful for the courts to draw upon the CFREU as a source of private law rules or would it be contrary to the laws laid down by the Treaty? These are the three main questions considered in this chapter. My answer to those questions will be, respectively, yes, we can use the Charter as a source of contract law rules, though, secondly, we should only use this source with due caution; and yes, the CFREU is a legitimate source of private law in the EU, though its legitimacy depends on a fresh understanding of the meaning of the core value of the Rule of Law in the EU.[3] Before explaining the reasoning behind those answers to my

1 Charter of Fundamental Rights of the European Union [2012] OJ C326/391.
2 Treaty on European Union (Consolidated) adopted by the Treaty of Lisbon, signed on 13 December 2007 (consolidated version) [2012] OJ C326/13 (TEU).
3 Article 2 TEU.

questions, however, it is helpful to explain the special context in which they arise in connection with the EU legal order and its private law.

1. GAP-FILLING IN EU PRIVATE LAW

Scholars of national systems of private law have frequently considered the extent to which constitutional bills of rights or binding international treaties such as the European Convention on Human Rights (ECHR) can be used to modify or develop private law. In national legal systems, there is considerable uncertainty about the justification and proper scope for this movement towards the 'constitutionalisation of private law.'[4] While some would prefer to reject entirely the insertion of references to fundamental rights in private law disputes,[5] the general view in European nation states appears to be that although private law claimants cannot rely upon such fundamental rights to create new claims or causes of action against other private parties (as opposed to the state), it is possible that fundamental rights may influence the interpretation of existing private law at least to the extent that interpretations of private law rules and principles should not contradict fundamental rights. There are different degrees

---

4 T. Barkhuysen and S. Lindenbergh (eds.), *Constitutionalisation of Private Law*, Martinus Nijhoff, Leiden/Boston 2006; H.-W. Micklitz, 'Introduction' in H.-W. Micklitz (ed.), *Constitutionalization of European Private Law*, Oxford University Press, Oxford 2014, p. 1. Many other books describe this phenomenon in jurisdictions around the world, though not always using the same terminology of the constitutionalisation of private law: D. Oliver and J. Fedtke (eds.), *Human Rights and the Private Sphere: A Comparative Study*, Routledge-Cavendish, London/New York 2007; M. Hesselink, 'The Horizontal Effect of Social Rights in European Contract Law' in M. Hesselink, *The New European Private Law*, Kluwer Law International, The Hague/London/New York 2002, p. 177; D. Friedmann and D. Barak-Erez (eds.), *Human Rights in Private Law*, Hart Publishing, Oxford 2001; C. Mak, *Fundamental Rights in European Contract Law: A Comparison of the Impact of Fundamental Rights on Contractual Relationships in Germany, the Netherlands, Italy and England*, Wolters Kluwer, The Netherlands 2008; S. Grundmann (ed.), *Constitutional Values and European Contract Law*, Kluwer Law International, The Netherlands 2008; G. Bruggermeier, A. Ciacchi and G. Comande (eds.), *Fundamental Rights and Private Law in the European Union*, vol. I, *A Comparative Overview*, Cambridge University Press, Cambridge 2010; D. Hoffman (ed.), *The Impact of the UK Human Rights Act on Private Law*, Cambridge University Press, Cambridge 2011; H. Collins (ed.), *European Contract Law and the Charter of Fundamental Rights*, Intersentia, Cambridge 2017; L. Siliquini-Cinelli and A. Hutchison (eds.), *The Constitutional Dimension of Contract Law: A Comparative Perspective*, Springer 2017.

5 D. Nolan, 'Negligence and Human Rights Law: The Case for Separate Development' (2013) 76(2) *Modern Law Review* 286, esp. 302; J. Smits, 'Private Law and Fundamental Rights: A Sceptical View' in T. Barkhuysen and S. Lindenbergh (eds.), above n. 4, p. 9; J. Morgan, 'Privacy, Confidence and Horizontal Effect: "Hello" Trouble' (2003) *Cambridge Law Journal* 444; R. Bagshaw, 'Tort design and human rights thinking' in D. Hoffman (ed.), above n. 4, p. 110. For discussion of these views: H. Collins, 'Private Law, Fundamental Rights, and the Rule of Law' (2019) 121 *West Virginia Law Review* 1.

to which fundamental rights might have this kind of 'indirect effect' or impact on the interpretation of existing private law.[6]

In practice, however, the issue of whether such declarations, charters, or bills of fundamental rights should be employed to modify national private law arises fairly rarely. One reason for that absence of claims is that national private law systems usually provide a comprehensive set of answers to the sorts of issues that arise in disputes between private individuals. For the most part, private lawyers prefer to stick to the established rules of private law, usually consolidated in a code or statute, together with a case law that provides further interpretive guidance. It is often a sign of desperation when a litigant relies upon a constitutional bill of rights or an international charter of fundamental rights. In such cases, the reason for reliance on charters of fundamental rights may well be that all other legal avenues in private law seem blocked, because the relevant private law seems clear or at least cannot be interpreted in the way favoured by the claimant. Accordingly, the litigant appeals to the highest national constitutional court, or to the European Court of Human Rights (ECtHR), or to another court that is empowered to assess the conformity of private law with fundamental rights, in the hope that the claim can be reconsidered in terms of a contradiction or inconsistency between the rules of private law and the court's duty to respect and protect the observance of fundamental rights. A similar appeal to fundamental rights may arise in the context of a dispute between private parties that is regulated at least in part by EU legislation. Article 51 CFREU has been interpreted to require courts to pay due regard to Charter rights when interpreting and implementing EU law.[7]

Inside the European Union, however, the context for questions about the constitutionalisation of private law differs considerably. This question arises within a legal framework that does not confer on the EU the full competence to develop its own civil code to cover matters such as general contract law, torts, and property law. Instead, Directives that have an impact on the private law of Member States are justified as falling within the competence of the EU to create a free internal market in goods and services. The most common justification for Directives in relation to consumer transactions is that the EU legislature hopes that by providing equal consumer protection measures throughout the EU, consumers will be emboldened to shop across borders, thereby opening up the market for consumer goods and services. Whether or not EU measures have helped this process of expanding consumer markets is unclear,[8] but what

---

6 For an exploration of the different strengths of indirect effect: A.L. Young, 'Mapping Horizontal Effect' in D. Hoffman (ed.) above n. 4, p. 16.

7 Case C-617/10, *Åklagaren v. Hans Åkerberg Fransson*, ECLI:EU:C:2013:105; Case C-198/13, *Víctor Manuel Julian Hernández and Others v. Reino de España (Subdelegación del Gobierno de España en Alicante) and Others*, ECLI:EU:C:2014:2055.

8 H. Collins, *The European Civil Code: The Way Forward*, Cambridge University Press, Cambridge 2008, pp. 64–65.

is certain is that various EU Directives have provided a substantial framework for consumer protection in contract law, thereby to some extent necessarily displacing national private law systems.

Although there are many significant Directives that steer the contract law of Member States, these Directives are not, strictly speaking, really deserving of the name 'contract law'.[9] If contract law is understood as the legal rules that regulate contracts or determine rights and obligations between the parties to a contract, such directly applicable rules are not the normal mechanism by which the EU pursues its internal market policy. As it is composed of Directives, in general, EU contract law regulates the law of contract found in Member States, not the contracts between private parties themselves. The EU Directives usually set minimum standards or goals that the national contract laws of the Member States are supposed to implement properly and for which suitable remedies should be made available in order to ensure their effectiveness. EU contract law is therefore mostly a meta-law: it does not usually regulate contracts directly, but rather regulates national contract laws that regulate contracts. The Directives are not private law but public law, because Directives are addressed to governments, not private individuals. The Directives do not supply the building blocks of a civil code or even fragments of a code, but rather prescribe the outcomes that must be achieved by national contract law.

Moreover, these EU Directives tend only to address the most significant issues from the point of view of their policy focus, such as consumer protection or worker health and safety. They leave many questions that may arise in legal disputes unanswered in the express words of the Directive. Consider, for instance, the questions that have arisen in connection with Article 3 of the Consumer Sales Directive, under which the consumer has the right to the replacement or the repair of non-conforming goods 'free of charge'.[10] In *Quelle*,[11] the consumer had been able to use the kitchen stove that had been supplied for more than a year before it was replaced for non-conformity. On a preliminary reference from the national court,[12] the Court of Justice of the European Union (CJEU) concluded

---

9 H. Collins, 'The Revolutionary Trajectory of EU Contract Law towards Post-national Law' in S. Worthington, A. Robertson and G. Virgo (eds.), *Revolution and Evolution in Private Law*, Hart Publishing, Oxford 2018, p. 315, esp. p. 317.

10 Directive 1999/44/EC of 25 May 1999 on certain aspects of the sale of consumer goods and associated guarantees [1999] OJ L171/12, Article 3(3): 'In the first place, the consumer may require the seller to repair the goods or he may require the seller to replace them, in either case free of charge, unless this is impossible or disproportionate. A remedy shall be deemed to be disproportionate if it imposes costs on the seller which, in comparison with the alternative remedy, are unreasonable, taking into account: the value the goods would have if there were no lack of conformity, the significance of the lack of conformity, and whether the alternative remedy could be completed without significant inconvenience to the consumer.'

11 Case C-404/06, *Quelle AG v. Bundesverband der Verbraucherzentralen und Verbraucherverbände* [2008] ECR I-2685 (CJEU); discussed by K. Lilleholt (2010) 2 *European Review of Contract Law* 192.

12 Treaty on the Functioning of the European Union [2012] OJ C326/47 (TFEU), Article 267.

that the Directive's explicit and specific requirement in Article 3 that replacement of non-conforming goods should be 'free of charge' in order to serve the goal of consumer protection must preclude any charge for the benefit received from the rejected defective goods. In *Putz*, a new dishwasher was delivered and the consumer arranged for it to be installed. When the dishwasher proved defective, the supplier agreed to provide a replacement, but, in accordance with German law, was unwilling to remove the old dishwasher and to install the replacement free of charge. The CJEU held that the duty of 'replacement', properly interpreted, included the duty to remove the non-conforming goods and to install the new dishwasher free of charge, even though installation was not part of the original contract. Finally, in *Wittmer*,[13] the seller of floor tiles argued for the right to refuse replacement, because the costs of removing the old slightly defective tiles and installing new floor tiles would be disproportionate in comparison with the minor significance of the defect. The CJEU stated that the Directive did not permit a refusal to replace the defective tiles on the ground that the cost would be disproportionate. Nevertheless the supplier could ask for a contribution to the cost of replacement if it exceeded the value of the conforming goods. If that contribution deterred the consumer from demanding a replacement, the consumer could alternatively ask for a diminution of the price to reflect the reduction in value of the non-conforming goods. Although these decisions are presented by the CJEU as mere interpretations of the Consumer Sales Directive, it is evident that the Court is elaborating rules of EU private law that try to balance the interests of the parties. Although the purpose of the Directive and the phrase 'free of charge' provides the Court with useful guidance on how the rules should be formulated, in order to fill the many gaps in the rules provided by the Directive, particularly in the case of *Wittmer*, the Court appears to be creating its own rules that balance the financial interests of suppliers against the goal of strong consumer protection. In the absence of explicit rules in the Directive or other EU legislation, it is unclear what the source of these rules can be.

What is especially remarkable about this process of gap-filling carried out by the CJEU is that it involves a transition from what was described earlier as 'meta-law' to the construction of private law rules that directly regulate the relation between the parties. National contract law has traditionally been concerned with both the question of what would be fair and just as between the contracting parties and the broader issue of what would be in the public interest, which in this context of contracts is usually understood as the promotion of trade through freely chosen contractual undertakings. In contrast, EU Directives focus on a relatively narrow set of policy objectives and those objectives are emphasised almost to the exclusion of the traditional private law's concerns

---

13 Joined Cases C-65/09, *Gebrüder Weber GmbH v. Jürgen Wittmer* and C-87/09, *Ingrid Putz v. Medianess Electronics GmbH* [2011] ECR I-5257.

regarding corrective justice between the parties and doctrinal coherence.[14] For instance, Directives seek to cleanse consumer markets of unfair terms in standard form contracts and of unfair commercial practices.[15] Driven by such policy considerations, these Directives typically use what is regarded as the most effective approach to this kind of regulation, which might involve, for instance, the availability of injunctions against unfair terms being used in consumer standard form contracts and criminal sanctions against unfair commercial practices. Although Directives that serve these instrumental purposes necessarily engage with what is normally regulated primarily by national contract law, they need not create any EU contract law in order to secure their goals. Indeed, the Directive on unfair terms includes private law almost as an afterthought by invaliding unfair terms as well as providing for administrative injunctions, and the Unfair Commercial Practices Directive states laconically in Article 3(2) that it 'is without prejudice to contract law and, in particular, to the rules on the validity, formation or effect of a contract.' As instrumental regulation, EU Directives on contract law focus on particular internal market objectives such as facilitating online shopping by consumers, so that their private law effects are often tangential to their purposes and sometimes treated as irrelevant. As a consequence, the traditional dimension of private law of balancing the interests and rights of the parties to the transaction by providing a system of corrective remedies typically plays a subsidiary role in the EU Directives and in some it may be omitted altogether. What is striking, therefore, about the decisions of the CJEU described above in connection with the replacement of defective goods is how the Court interprets the EU's instrumental regulation of national law to produce the rather different type of rule found in private law that directly allocates rights and obligations between the parties to a contract in order to secure corrective justice between them.

In theory it might be possible for the CJEU to respond in such cases where the Directive does not provide a determinate answer by saying that there is no EU law on the question raised by the preliminary reference, so that it can offer no advice. But such a response would undermine the purpose of promoting a single market by developing harmonised laws. It is often stated in EU Commission documents that divergence between national contract laws itself creates an

14 Cf. R. Michaels, 'Of Islands and the Ocean: The Two Rationalities of European Private Law' in R. Brownsword, H.-W. Micklitz, L. Niglia and S. Weatherill (eds.), *The Foundations of European Private Law*, Hart Publishing, Oxford 2011, p. 139; H. Collins, 'The Hybrid Quality of European Private Law' in ibid., p. 453; C.U. Schmid, 'The Instrumentalist Conception of the Acquis Communautaire in Consumer Law and its Implications on a European Contract Law Code' (2005) 1 *European Review of Contract Law* 210.

15 Directive 93/13/EEC on unfair terms in consumer contracts [1993] OJ L95/29; Directive 2005/29/EC concerning unfair business-to-consumer commercial practices in the internal market [2005] OJ L149/22.

impediment to or at least a deterrent to cross-border trade.[16] Assuming that view is correct, the CJEU is strongly motivated to find a solution to the question of law posed in the preliminary reference by constructing novel elements of an EU private law system. Moreover, if a national court has formed the view that an interpretation of EU law is necessary in order for it to determine the outcome of a private law dispute, the CJEU will not want to rebuff the national court by refusing to offer an interpretation of the Directive that appears to be relevant. In practice, therefore, the CJEU cannot avoid creating new private law rules as part of its role in providing authoritative interpretations of EU law.

For the most part, to carry out this task of creating new rules of private law but under camouflage, the CJEU clings ostensibly to an examination of the words in the text of the Directive, as in its elaborate definition of the word 'replacement' in *Putz*. But that textual approach was not convincing in the other two cases mentioned above, where the 'free of charge' phrase was used to deny damages in one case, but was circumvented in the other to avoid a disproportionate remedy. The source of the rules in those cases seems to be little more than a rough estimate by the Court of what degree of consumer protection is required to enable the single market to function successfully, whilst at the same time not severely damaging and alienating the business interests that provide the driving force of the market economy.

This policy guesswork by judges is not always an ideal basis for developing private law rules. It has to be observed, however, that it has been the lifeblood of the common law with its judge-made contract law. Similar to the predicament of judges in the common law, in EU law, in the absence of a civil code or a comprehensive system of private law, the raw materials for answers to questions of private law are thin on the ground. There is no civil code or a common law tradition of precedents to draw upon. Although the body of Directives that affects contracts is described as an *acquis communautaire*, any implication that these regulatory instruments provide a coherent body of principles for the determination of disputes is false, for each Directive focuses on a specific field of regulation. The question posed in this chapter is whether the Charter rights can and should provide a source for rules of private law that will meet the perceived need for EU doctrines of private law that serve the function of helping to complete the internal market.

The issue of whether the CFREU should be used for the purpose of developing rules and principles of private law raises a number of questions. Perhaps the most important legal issue is whether the path of legal reasoning that employs the CFREU to fill gaps in relation to private law in the EU legal order is permitted under the Treaties, or is it beyond the competences or powers of the institutions

---

16 E.g. Communication from the Commission to the European Parliament and the Council, *A More Coherent European Contract Law: An Action Plan*, 12.02.2003, COM (2003) 68 final.

of the EU, including the CJEU, to employ the Charter for that purpose? In other words, would the use of Charter rights to develop private law amount to a breach of the Rule of Law by ignoring the limits placed on the use of the Charter and the competencies of the EU with regard to private law?

In addition, the question of whether the CFREU can and should be used for the purpose of developing rules and principles of private law raises similar issues to those that have been debated in national private law systems. Broadly speaking, the puzzle is whether a set of fundamental rights that were developed primarily in order to empower and protect citizens against the state can be transplanted into private law. The statement of human rights and fundamental principles in the CFREU is derived mostly from the international conventions promulgated by the Council of Europe, including both the European Convention on Human Rights and the European Social Charter.[17] These documents place duties on contracting states to conform to these standards. The puzzle is how this material could provide the source of private law norms that are needed to fill in the gaps left in Directives. In short, how do we turn public law norms about fundamental and human rights into rules about contracts and delict?

Since public law rights and principles are usually stated at a high level of abstraction, it is not difficult to draw on them as a source of inspiration for the creation of private law in the EU. For instance, Article 7 CFREU describes a fundamental freedom: 'Everyone has the right to respect for his or her private and family life, home and communications'. This broad phrase can certainly guide legal reasoning in all sorts of private law contexts, such as an eviction from a home for failure to repay a loan secured on the property.[18] The question then arises whether this source composed of abstract fundamental rights is sufficiently precise in its content to provide a coherent justification for the development of private law rules in EU law. Because legal certainty arising from clear rules laid down in advance is usually perceived to be a key ingredient of the ideal of the Rule of Law, this vagueness and uncertainty in the meaning of fundamental rights appears to present a challenge to the ideal.

Having considered those questions about the propriety and feasibility of using the Charter of Fundamental Rights to resolve issues concerning gaps in the regulations governing the internal market, it will then be suggested that using the Charter as a source of private law can only be properly justified if we reconsider the nature of the ideal of the Rule of Law. Drawing on the theoretical work of Ronald Dworkin, it will be suggested that the advent of the Charter of Fundamental Rights in 2000 changed the nature of the EU legal order, not only because it provided a mechanism for holding EU institutions accountable by reference to a modern statement of human and fundamental rights, but also

---

[17] Council of Europe, Convention for the Protection of Human Rights and Fundamental Freedoms, Rome, 04.11.1950; European Social Charter, revised 1996.

[18] Case C-34/13, *Kušionová v. SMART Capital a.s.*, ECLI:EU:C:2014:2189, para. 65.

because it shifted the implicit notion of the Rule of Law on which the EU legal order is based from a rule-based to a rights-based conception of the Rule of Law. Under this rights-based conception of the Rule of Law, it will be argued that not only is the use of the CFREU as a source of private law consistent with the Rule of Law, but also the Charter is a sound source for private law because it is not properly regarded as being exclusively part of a separate sphere of public law.

2. THE RULE OF LAW

We turn first to the question of whether the use of the Charter of Fundamental Rights for the purpose of developing rules of private law is contrary to the ideal of the Rule of Law. The EU is founded on many core liberal values, including the ideal of the Rule of Law. Article 2 TEU states:

> The Union is founded on the values of respect for human dignity, freedom, democracy, equality, the rule of law and respect for human rights …[19]

Although the TEU does not define the Rule of Law, we can reasonably suppose that at least part of its meaning will be the principle that all political and military power should be constrained by clear rules laid down in advance. In accordance with that meaning of the Rule of Law, Article 5 TEU insists that the institutions of the EU should always act in accordance with the law and the powers conferred on the EU.

> The limits of Union competences are governed by the principle of conferral …
>
> Under the principle of conferral, the Union shall act only within the limits of the competences conferred upon it by the Member States in the Treaties to attain the objectives set out therein …[20]

The Treaties also uphold fundamental rights, though, according to Article 6 TEU, only within the competences of the EU.

> The Union recognises the rights, freedoms and principles set out in the Charter of Fundamental Rights of the European Union …, which shall have the same legal value as the treaties.
>
> The Provisions of the Charter shall not extend in any way the competences of the Union as defined in the Treaties …[21]

---

19 Article 2 TEU.

20 Article 5(1) and (2) TEU.

21 Article 6(1) TEU.

These provisions seem to argue against the use of the CFREU as a source of private law.

That provisional conclusion is based in the first place on the assertion in the Treaty of European Union that the Charter does not extend the competences of the EU 'in any way'. The EU has not had the power to create private law conferred on it by the Treaties. The power is more limited: to remove obstacles to the flourishing of the internal market. Unless we suppose that the creation of EU private law is needed for the purpose of regulating the internal market, the EU lacks the competence to make private law in general. If so, the use of the Charter for such a purpose would be impermissible under the TEU. Indeed, it would be a breach of the principle of the Rule of Law. If the proposal is to create private law rules and principles derived from the Charter, that project appears to be a mechanism for extending the competences of the EU into the field of private law.

It may be responded to this objection that the CJEU is not making private law in its references to the Charter in contractual disputes. Under the preliminary reference procedure,[22] the CJEU must elucidate the meaning of the Directives that have legitimately been enacted as part of the competence related to the internal market. This elucidation, it may be claimed, is merely an act of interpretation as permitted under the Treaty, and does not involve the creation of new norms of private law. But that response seems to fly in the face of the examples given earlier of the CJEU filling the gaps in the rules governing replacement of goods under the Sales Directive. Whilst it may be possible to resolve some issues by relying on definitions of terms used in Directives, thereby avoiding any obvious tension with the ideal of the Rule of Law, the CJEU is required to go much further and to attempt to create a coherent normative framework of rights and obligations to surround the bare bones of the Directive.

Another response to the argument that the CJEU regularly deviates from the ideal of the Rule of Law when it makes rules of private law might be to claim that despite occasional breaches of the formal rules, eventually the system will restore conformity with the ideal through its self-corrective mechanisms. In other words, eventually any unlawful law-making by the judges will eventually be curtailed or invalidated by the legal system itself. Although that claim is true in general, the problem in this particular instance is that under the Treaties it is the function of the CJEU to police compliance with the Rule of Law in the EU. It has the power to review the legality of both legislative and executive acts. For that purpose, it has jurisdiction to hear actions brought by Member States, the Council, the Commission, and the EU Parliament that there has been an infringement of the rules regarding competence, procedures, substantive rules of law, or a misuse of power.[23] But if the CJEU oversteps its powers of preliminary

22 Article 267 TFEU.
23 Article 263 TFEU.

interpretation, *quis custodiet ipsos custodes*? In other words, if the CJEU does begin to construct EU private law rules, there is no institution that can supervise or test the legality of this development.

It is perhaps worth reminding ourselves that, in connection with private law, the ideal of the Rule of Law has typically been associated with strict compliance with the rules laid down in civil codes and precedents. Private lawyers often evince a distrust of any broad ranging judicial discretion both as an issue of principle and also for pragmatic reasons. They often stress the importance of the certainty of the rights and duties of ordinary citizens with regard to each other. That certainty can be achieved, it is believed, by adopting a formalist approach to private law. This formalist approach requires judges to stick to the plain meaning of the established rules of private law to be found in codes and precedents. On this traditional view, heavy reliance on considerations of policy is regarded suspiciously because it introduces an element of unpredictable discretion into the judicial decision. The formalism of private law is in truth also a policy as well, because it is widely assumed that certainty and predictability in the application of private law is good for doing business and making trading links. The policy of fashioning a law that is good for business and the market order therefore points to formalism in legal reasoning as the best approach. Any kind of disruption to established legal doctrines is therefore regarded with hostility both because it threatens to undermine the ideal of the Rule of Law and because it may disrupt the market and therefore hamper economic growth and efficiency. The idea that the creation of private law rules might be left to judicial discretion without constraints other than policy considerations would be regarded by many private lawyers as an anathema to the Rule of Law and the nature of private law itself.

On this account of the ideal of the Rule of Law in EU law, a major problem of legality may arise when the CJEU provides answers to preliminary references in connection with private contractual disputes. In the first place, if the CJEU is making private law rules, that seems to be law-making outside of the competences of the EU. In the second place, if the CJEU can plausibly justify its rulings on the ground that they remain interpretations of Directives and not the creation of new private law, there is still a tension with the ideal of the Rule of Law, because the Court seems to be able to determine the applicable rules by forming its own views about how to balance the various policy considerations that probably informed the Directive. This predicament arises because of the absence of any body of rules and principles that the CJEU could draw upon as default rules. It is in this context of filling gaps without obviously having a legal basis for its rulings that the CJEU sometimes chooses to make references to the Charter of Fundamental Rights. Although the Charter cannot extend the competences of the CJEU, at least it can be presented as a valid source of interpretive principles of law within the EU legal order that may assist in answering preliminary references regarding Directives.

3. THE USES OF CHARTER RIGHTS IN EU PRIVATE LAW

How far has the CJEU taken up the possibility of using Charter Rights to help to resolve private law disputes? It is suggested that two distinct uses of Charter rights have emerged so far. The first use builds on the point that in a private law dispute both parties have fundamental rights. By weighing up these competing rights, the CJEU can try to forge an applicable EU law that takes into account and balances the interests of both parties. The second use of Charter rights has been to create additional legal obligations in national law that are calculated to enhance the effectiveness of an applicable EU Directive. We should examine these two uses of the Charter in private law in turn.

3.1. BALANCING OF INTERESTS

It was suggested above that the regulatory law emanating from the EU tends to be focused on the achievement of policy goals such as consumer protection by elimination of unfair practices in markets. In so doing, it does not view the issues from the normal perspective of private law, which is likely to try to balance the competing interests of the parties to a contract. The Charter of Fundamental Rights can, however, be used to reframe issues in a way that is congenial to the private law perspective. It can do so by requiring courts that are interpreting and applying Directives to have regard to the interests or fundamental rights of both parties. In other words, the fundamental rights of the party whose conduct the Directive is designed to control can be invoked to force a court to engage in a balancing of interests. Given that the Directives that affect contracts typically protect consumers and workers, the role of fundamental rights in this context is likely to favour and protect the interests of traders, suppliers, and employers.

This process of using the Charter to balance the interests of the parties can be illustrated by a reading of *Alemo-Herron v. Parkside Leisure*.[24] The EU Directive, known as the Acquired Rights Directive,[25] creates the rule that when a business is sold to a new owner, the existing employees should keep their jobs and their existing contracts of employment. In the *Alemo-Herron* case, the terms of the workers' contracts, which they were entitled to keep after the transfer of the undertaking from a public authority to a new private corporate owner, provided that their wages would be set by a collective agreement made from time to time between a union and a group of public authorities. Following the transfer of the undertaking to the new private owner, the employer realised that

[24] Case C-426/11, *Alemo-Herron v. Parkwood Leisure Ltd*, ECLI:EU:C:2013:521.

[25] Directive 2001/23/EC on safeguarding employees' rights in the event of transfers of undertakings, formerly Directive 77/187/EEC. The provisions in the earlier and later revised Directive that are relevant to *Alemo-Herron* are identical.

it was apparently bound to pay wage increases set by the public sector collective agreement to which it was not and could not be a party. That restriction would have blocked its probable business plan of reducing wage costs by escaping the governing public sector collective agreement. Apparently sympathising with the employer's plight, the UK Supreme Court referred the case to the CJEU, which upheld the transferee employer's right to ignore the terms set by the new public sector collective agreement. The CJEU did so on the ground that binding the employer to the terms set by a collective agreement to which it could not be a party was an interference with the employer's freedom of contract, a freedom it claimed was protected within the essence of the freedom to conduct a business in Article 16 of the Charter.

The reasoning of the CJEU is explicit that it is using the Charter to balance the interests of the parties. It claims first that the Directive does not aim solely to safeguard the interests of employees, but seeks to ensure a fair balance of interests between employees and the transferee employer.[26] That interpretation of the Directive is controversial, since the only stated purpose of the Directive is to restrict the transferee's powers to impose new terms on transferred employees or to dismiss them. There is no reference in the preamble to the Directive to the need to balance interests of the employer and the employee. The CJEU then observed that the transferred term in the contracts of employment regarding the future binding effect of new collective agreements was 'liable to undermine the fair balance of interests' of the transferee and the employees, because it would limit considerably the room for manoeuvre necessary for a private transferee to make necessary adjustments and changes.[27] This observation highlights the importance that the Court attached to the private law perspective of balancing of interests. That interpretation of the national law regarding a fair balance of interests is, however, slightly misleading. Having given reasonable notice to terminate the existing contracts of employment, the employer could have insisted upon the imposition of new terms of employment that excluded the collective agreement, so the employer's room for manoeuvre still existed, though perhaps only after some delays and the risk that employees would complain about constructive unfair dismissal.[28] The CJEU then invoked Article 16 of the Charter to assert that by reason of the freedom to conduct a business, the transferee must be able to assert its interests in a contractual process to which it is a party and to negotiate the aspects of determining changes in the working conditions of its employees

---

26 *Alemo-Herron*, above n. 24, para. 25.

27 Ibid., paras. 28–29.

28 Transfer of Undertakings (Protection of Employment) Regulations 2006, SI 2006/246, esp. regulation 4(5); this replaces the Transfer of Undertakings (Protection of Employment) Regulations 1981, SI 1981/1794, which were applicable in *Alemo-Herron*. Variations in terms were permitted for business or organisational reasons in *Wilson v. St Helens Borough Council* [1998] ICR 1141 (HL).

with a view to its future economic activity.[29] It was claimed that Article 16 was relevant because the case involved an interpretation of the Directive. Yet the Directive appears to state clearly enough to avoid any ambiguity that the terms of the contract of employment shall be automatically transferred to the new contract between the transferee undertaking and the employees. Article 16 does not appear to assist in understanding this perfectly clear provision. Instead, what Article 16 does in this case is to create an exception to this provision. The exception prevents the transfer of terms of contracts of employment that provide for the continuation of the binding effect of new collective agreements after the transfer has taken place. Where Article 16 is crucial in this legal reasoning is with respect to the provision in the Directive that enables Member States to adopt provisions that are more favourable to employees.[30] The CJEU uses Article 16 to say that this kind of favourable provision that preserves the effect of successive collective agreements after the transfer is not permitted by the Directive. Notice that what is happening here is that a perfectly lawful and effective clause in a contract of employment regarding the effect of collective agreements under English law is invalidated by reference to Article 16 CFREU. What is presented as an interpretation of the Directive is essentially the use of Article 16 to avoid a lawful term in a contract of employment. And ironically, the ground put forward for invalidating this term of the contract was an appeal to 'freedom of contract'. The justification for striking the balance in this way given by the CJEU was that otherwise the transferee undertaking would be deprived of the 'very essence of its freedom to conduct a business'.[31]

My central point is that there is a parallel between the reasoning in *Alemo-Herron* and the cases discussed earlier regarding the replacement of non-conforming goods for the consumer. Although the Charter right was not invoked in the cases concerning replacement of goods, in both instances the CJEU interpreted the applicable Directive and its effects so that it balanced the interests of the parties to the contract in the way that would be expected in private law. One can only speculate why the Charter was invoked in one case but not the other. Perhaps the difference is that the CJEU believed that it could interpret the Directive to achieve a suitable balance of interests in the replacement of defective goods cases, whereas the plain meaning of the Directive in the transfer of undertakings example had to be overridden to create an exception in this instance when the CJEU thought that the transferred employees were protected too well, so the appeal to a higher law, the Charter, may have been attractive as a tool for legitimating that revision of the Directive. In applying the Charter, of course, the court overrides the interests of the workforce, who would presumably rather keep their higher wages set by

29 *Alemo-Herron*, above n. 24, para. 33.

30 M. Bartl and C. Leone, 'Minimum Harmonisation and Article 16 of the CFREU: Difficult Times Ahead for Social Legislation' in H. Collins (ed.), above n. 4, p. 113.

31 *Alemo-Herron*, above n. 24, paras. 35 and 36.

the public sector collective agreement. That result may have been consistent with the ultimate aim of the Directive, however, for it achieved a level playing field for sales of businesses and the capital market in Europe, rather than making the protections for workers stronger in the UK than in Germany.[32]

3.2. ENHANCED PROTECTION OF RIGHTS UNDER DIRECTIVES

The second purpose of invoking the EU Charter of Fundamental Rights in cases concerning EU contract law is to find a means for making the Directive more effective by demanding that national obstructions to the implementation of EU law should be struck down, not, as previously in the internal market deregulatory agenda on the ground of the supremacy of EU law, but now because the Charter rights must be upheld. The principal Article of the Charter used in this context is Article 47:

> Everyone whose rights and freedoms guaranteed by the law of the Union are violated has the right to an effective remedy before a tribunal in compliance with the conditions laid down in this Article.

Article 47 can be combined with other articles of the CFREU in order to interpret a Directive in a way that provides not only an effective remedy for breach of the Directive, but also a robust defence of a fundamental right laid down in the Charter. In these cases, the use of the Charter is designed to favour the intended beneficiaries of the Directive, such as consumers and employees, by overcoming obstacles to the full enjoyment of their rights under national private law.

This second purpose of judicial invocations of Charter rights to decide contractual disputes can be illustrated by another group of well-known cases concerning the application of the unfair terms in consumer contracts Directive to consumer credit transactions, in which a consumer's home is at risk for failure to repay instalments on a loan by the due dates. In such cases, the CJEU has often had to consider whether procedural obstacles in national law that appear to prevent a consumer from receiving the full protection of the Directive can be overcome by a more expansive interpretation of EU law. The Charter right to an effective remedy in Article 47 appears to provide a general instrument for arguing that, to the extent that national law makes it virtually impossible for the intended effects of the Directive to be achieved, national law has to be modified. Where the failure of a national court to provide an adequate or fair opportunity to argue for the invalidity of a term in a credit agreement also has the effect of depriving a person of her home, the Convention right to respect for private life

[32] Case C-499/04, *Werhof v. Freeway Traffic Systems GmbH & Co. KG* [2006] ECR I-2397.

can be invoked as a further reason for ensuring that national procedures should be amended to comply with the high standard of consumer protection in the Directive. In *Kušionová v. SMART Capital* the CJEU stated: 'Under EU law, the right to accommodation is a fundamental right guaranteed under Article 7 of the Charter that the referring court must take into account when implementing [a Directive]'.[33] The Directive on unfair terms in consumer contracts only sets minimum standards and says nothing about civil procedure and very little about remedies. The invocation of Charter rights during preliminary references regarding the meaning of the Directive permits the CJEU to claim that for the sake of making the Directive effective, it must expand its scope to include elements of civil procedure at least to the extent of making sure that the procedure does not effectively block the protection afforded by the Directive. This consumer protection Directive therefore receives a boost by an expansion of its effectiveness as a result of arguments about fundamental rights.

Article 47 has also been used in connection with Directives that provide protections for workers. Directives concerning employment usually leave the choice of enforcement mechanism to national legal orders, since there are often significant differences between the Member States in the institutions and legal mechanisms that they use to regulate labour markets and employment relations. Article 47 can be invoked as a reason for insisting upon a change in national private law. For instance, in *King v. Sash Window Workshop*,[34] the claimant, who was engaged as a sales representative on the basis of a self-employed, payment-by-commission contract, was told by his employer that any leave he might take would be unpaid. On the termination of the contractual relationship, he brought a claim under the national regulations[35] that implemented the Working Time Directive[36] to recover payments for periods of annual leave, whether taken or not, for the entire period of his engagement between 1999 and 2012. Article 7(1) of the Directive provides:

> Member states shall take the measures necessary to ensure that every worker is entitled to paid annual leave of at least four weeks in accordance with the conditions for entitlement to, and granting of, such leave laid down by national legislation and/or practice.

UK law prevented workers from carrying over leave from one year to the next, so it appeared from a literal reading of the national regulations that the worker could not claim back-payments for more than a year. A preliminary reference asked the CJEU whether this result was consistent with the Directive, especially

---

33 *Kušionová*, above n. 18, para. 65.

34 Case C-214/16, *King v. Sash Window Workshop*, ECLI:EU:C:2017:914.

35 Working Time Regulations 1998, SI 1998/1833.

36 Directive 2003/88/EC concerning certain aspects of the organisation of working time [2003] OJ L229/9.

since the reason why the worker had not taken leave was his uncertainty about whether it would be paid.

The CJEU conceded that the Directive contained no provisions on judicial remedies available to the worker. Nevertheless, it held that a national law that only permitted the claim for payment after leave had been taken was incompatible with the Directive, because the uncertainty about payment would deter the worker from taking leave and would prevent the leave from being restful. The worker was entitled to an effective remedy under Article 47 of the Charter, which precluded a requirement that the worker should take unpaid leave before claiming payment. The CJEU then acknowledged the legitimacy of rules that restricted the right to carry over paid leave in some circumstances, though those rules prescribing periods of limitation should only permit strictly necessary derogations in view of the point that the right to paid leave is protected in Article 31(2) of the CFREU.[37] Where the employer had denied any liability to paid leave, it would undermine the purpose of the Directive and amount to unjust enrichment of the employer if the worker were prevented from claiming back-pay for all the years when no paid leave was granted. The result of the preliminary reference was therefore to require the national court to permit the claim for arrears of holiday pay for the whole period of the contract.

These decisions of the CJEU have several elements in common. They use Article 47 of the Charter to favour remedial arrangements and processes in national private law that are likely to produce sanctions and remedies that should serve better the purposes of the Directive. In order to overcome the reluctance to override the normal national laws on remedies, the CJEU invokes other selected Charter rights to bolster its interpretation of the relevant Directive as requiring a particular remedial outcome. The slender original provision of the Directive is therefore invested with additional rules about effective remedies that are guided by the desire not only to make the Directive effective but also to prevent unjust enrichment of one of the parties.

3.3. LAW-MAKING?

These illustrations of the two uses that the CJEU has constructed for the CFREU in the context of contract law demonstrate that the Charter is employed in a rather more ambitious role than merely providing an aid to the interpretation of unclear provisions in Directives. In the first group of cases, the Charter is used to create exceptions to the purposes and apparently clear terms of a Directive; and in the second group, the Charter is used to buttress the aims of a Directive

---

[37] 'Every worker has the right to limitation of maximum working hours, to daily and weekly rest periods and to an annual period of paid leave.'

by requiring a reconfiguration of national contract law and civil procedure to ensure its effectiveness. Are these uses of the Charter compatible with the Rule of Law? Does the CJEU occasionally stray outside its assigned task of merely applying EU law in accordance with rules laid down in legislation by apparently exercising a general 'dispensing power' (as absolute monarchs once did), in order to expand and narrow the coverage and effect of EU law in contract law? To answer those questions properly, we need to reflect further on the nature of the Rule of Law and the duty of the CJEU to uphold EU law. The concept of the Rule of Law is itself open to different interpretations.

4. A RIGHTS-BASED CONCEPTION OF THE RULE OF LAW

In the opening chapter of his book *A Matter of Principle*, Ronald Dworkin advances the thesis that there are two possible conceptions of the Rule of Law.[38] He draws a distinction between the rule-book version of the Rule of Law and a rights-based version of the Rule of Law. He draws this distinction for the purpose of arguing that judges are not necessarily engaging in inappropriate political activity when being activist and not following the rules of law strictly according to their literal meaning, provided that they are upholding the rights of individuals. Whatever the merits of that broader argument about the appropriate role of judges, for my purpose what is crucial is to appreciate the dichotomy between a rule-based conception of the Rule of Law and a rights-based version, for it is the switch from the former to the latter that I shall argue represents the best interpretation of how the Charter of Fundamental Rights of the EU is being used. To the extent that this interpretation is correct, it demonstrates that at least some of the concerns about the use of the Charter to decide private law cases are misplaced. Indeed, it is possible to argue that appeals to Charter rights in the course of deliberations about the meaning and content of EU Directives are exactly what is required by the Rule of Law if it is understood in terms of the rights conception.

According to Dworkin, the rule-book conception of the Rule of Law

> insists that, so far as is possible, the power of the state should never be exercised against individual citizens except in accordance with rules explicitly set out in a public rule book available to all. The government as well as ordinary citizens must play by these public rules until they are changed, in accordance with further rules about how they are to be changed, which are also set out in the rule book.[39]

---

38 R. Dworkin, 'Political Judges and the Rule of Law' in R. Dworkin, *A Matter of Principle*, Clarendon Press, Oxford 1986, p. 9.

39 Ibid., p. 11.

The rule-book conception of the Rule of Law is obviously indebted to the work of H.L.A. Hart and his theory of how a rule of recognition confers and limits all legal powers.[40] In its expression of the importance of freedom from arbitrary power, the rule-book conception of the Rule of Law is also plainly closely affiliated to what has become known as the republican conception of liberty.[41]

In Dworkin's second conception of the Rule of Law, the rights conception that he favours, citizens are regarded as having moral and political rights, which must be respected by positive law. Courts must therefore uphold those rights so far as is practicable. 'The Rule of Law on this conception is the ideal of rule by an accurate public conception of individual rights'.[42] Dworkin explains further that under this rights conception of the Rule of Law, judges should in general follow the positive rules of law that have been laid down in advance, for otherwise judges would be likely to be acting unfairly, unjustly, and in a way that defeats existing rights. Like the rule-book conception, the rights conception of the Rule of Law requires judges normally to enforce the law according to its plain meaning, because those transparent rules usually express an accurate public conception of individual rights. But there will be cases, known as hard cases, where it will be necessary to depart from existing rules of law, even though those rules contain prima facie evidence of what rights people have, in order to uphold properly and accurately the true interpretation of the legal rights of citizens. In his subsequent book, *Law's Empire*,[43] Dworkin explains how a hypothetical and super-human judge known as Hercules should carry out this task of ensuring that he always reaches the right answer to questions of law by producing in his interpretation of the law an accurate conception of the rights of citizens.

It is my contention here that the cases that I have used to illustrate how Charter rights have steered interpretations of EU law and consequently the effect of national contract law have in practice used the rights-based conception of the Rule of Law. In the past, in the absence of a constitution or bill of rights, the EU stuck closely to the carefully negotiated terms of the treaties and the ideal of the Rule of Law was understood from a formalist perspective as requiring fidelity to the literal meaning of the rule of EU law. The ECJ committed itself regularly to a rule-book conception of the Rule of Law, though it insisted that EU rules had a hierarchical relationship to national law, so that in cases of conflict EU law always overrode national law. That doctrine of supremacy of EU law made sense within the framework and legislative agenda of completing the internal market by the dismantling of obstructions to trade presented by national law. The formalism

40 H.L.A. Hart, *The Concept of Law*, Clarendon Press, Oxford 1961.

41 P. Pettit, *Republicanism: A Theory of Freedom and Government*, Oxford University Press, Oxford 1997; Q. Skinner, 'Freedom as the Absence of Arbitrary Power' in C. Laborde and J. Maynor (eds.), *Republicanism and Political Theory*, Blackwell, Oxford 2008.

42 R. Dworkin, above n. 38, p. 11.

43 R. Dworkin, *Law's Empire*, Fontana, London 1986.

of the rule-book approach to the Rule of Law meets other needs, such as giving apparent respect for the division of competences between EU law and national law established in the Treaties whilst preserving the assertion of the superiority of EU law. But since about 2000 and the declaration at Nice of the Charter of Fundamental Rights, we have been witnessing a shift in how the EU institutions present their allegiance to the Rule of Law. Although compliance with the complexities of the Treaty provisions is still held up as a major legitimating tool for EU institutional actions, now, increasingly, justifications for the positions of EU institutions are discovered in Charter rights and more broadly in respect for the European Convention on Human Rights.

This rights-based conception of the Rule of Law is, of course, not unfamiliar in national legal systems. What is striking about this EU approach to a rights-based conception of the Rule of Law is the way it is not governed by the normal 'state-action' doctrine that says it is the institutions of the state that must comply with fundamental rights, not private individuals. Although the EU can avoid a clash with this 'state-action' doctrine by denying that it ever gives Charter rights direct horizontal effect, this denial is surely unconvincing. The project of creating a single market is necessarily about regulating relations between private individuals as well as regulating how states control their borders and their markets. Once the Charter rights become applicable to the interpretation of Directives, they must have effects on private individuals such as consumers and businesses. It is true that the effects can be described as indirect, for in theory all that the CJEU provides is an interpretation of the meaning of a Directive, yet in practice its interpretation will govern the relation between the private parties. In *Alemo-Herron* the employer was given a green light to abandon the collective agreement and to impose its own terms; in *Kušionová v. SMART Capital* the consumer had to be afforded more procedural opportunities to challenge the unfairness of the terms of the credit agreement, the likely effects of which would be to block foreclosure and repossession, at least for the time being. The Charter rights are therefore re-regulating the legal rights between the parties to the contract. This use of fundamental rights in private law may not occur frequently in most national legal systems, but it is becoming routine in the CJEU as it revises the Rule of Recognition towards a rights-based conception of the Rule of Law.

The rights-based conception of the Rule of Law is especially attractive in the context of a legal regime that is radically incomplete. As we have observed, EU Directives rarely address the necessary private law details that will be required to bring their policy aims into fruition in national legal systems. In order to fill out the details of these Directives, the CJEU can adopt a purposive approach and claim that further rules and restrictions are necessarily implied by the broad statements of principle contained in the Directive. Yet the purposive approach is unlikely to be convincing when either the claim is to block the main purpose of the Directive, as in *Alemo-Herron*, or to include matters in the scope of the

Directive that were clearly left to national law on the ground that additional rules will make the Directive a bit more effective, as in *Kušionová v. SMART Capital* and *King v. Sash Window*. In such cases, appeals to Charter rights serve the purpose of providing legitimacy for the judicial rewriting of the terms of the Directive. The CJEU can claim that the Directive must be interpreted or even rewritten at the margins in order to ensure that it is compatible with Charter rights. In this way, Charter rights provide a source of law for the development of EU regulation of contract law. As Dan Wielsch observes, this reliance on Charter rights in the context of EU contract law may fit into a broader agenda in which the construction of an internal market, including its deregulatory aspects, gives legitimacy to what might otherwise be regarded as a single-minded neo-liberal free market agenda. He argues that the EU's promotion of 'market rationality', by which he means the construction of the internal market throughout Europe, requires the EU to 'constitutionalise the very institution it has set free'.[44]

Moreover, the CJEU follows precisely the route that Dworkin proposed in his Herculean model of legal reasoning as required by the rights conception of the Rule of Law. In *Alemo-Herron*, for instance, although the plain meaning of the law was reasonably clear and defensible as fitting into the Directive's purpose of protecting the interests of employees who are being transferred to a new employer, in accordance with the rights-based conception of the Rule of Law, the judges may have provided an accurate interpretation of the rights of the parties. In this case, the CJEU found that the Directive failed to respect sufficiently the transferee employer's Charter right to conduct a business freely and to enjoy freedom of contract. Accordingly, applying the rights-based conception of the Rule of Law, the Court interpreted the Directive to protect the employer's freedom of contract. The Directive was fitted into a coherent account of the rights of the parties that secured employees considerable protection in the event of the sale of their employer's business, but which nevertheless preserved the purchaser's right to develop the business, including necessary adjustments to terms and conditions of employment. Similarly, in the other group of cases involving enhancements to the effectiveness of EU Directives, it is possible to detect a rights-based conception of the Rule of Law in operation in such decisions. The CJEU is willing to trespass into the fields of civil procedure and remedies, hitherto reserved for national law, in order to ensure that its view of the scope of a consumer's rights under EU law is fully respected. To justify this activist approach, it invokes the fundamental rights of the consumer to an effective remedy as laid out in Article 47 CFREU. Those rights are then said to require an interpretation of the Directive which plainly fits uncomfortably

---

44 D. Wielsch, 'Responsible Contracting – The Requirement of EU Fundamental Rights on Private Law Regimes' in H. Collins (ed.), above n. 4, p. 257; D. Wielsch, 'The Function of Fundamental Rights in EU Private Law – Perspectives from a Common European Sales Law' (2014) 10 *European Review of Contract Law* 365.

with the plain text of the Directive and the intended division of competences between the Directive and national private law. It is unclear whether the interpretation presented in *Kušionová v. SMART Capital* and similar cases concerning consumer mortgages, such as *Aziz*,[45] fits with the original purpose of the Directive, but perhaps the Court has felt the need to adapt it and apply it in the field of consumer credit in response to the chaos in the financial markets starting in 2008.[46]

5. CONCLUSION

This chapter has posed the question whether the Charter of Fundamental Rights of the European Union can and should provide a source for rules of contract law in the legal order of the European Union. It was argued that the Charter is needed to fill gaps in the radically incomplete rules of EU contract law. At the same time, it was recognised that it could not be a straightforward task to translate the public law norms that protect fundamental rights in the Charter into rules and principles suitable for contract law. Referring to decisions of the Court of Justice of the European Union, it was contended that the Charter has been used so far for two purposes. The first use is illustrated by the decision of the CJEU in *Alemo-Herron v. Parkside Leisure*.[47] Despite the fact that Directives are instrumental policy-oriented regulations, which are designed to regulate national legal systems rather than contractual rights and obligations directly, in such a case the CJEU's interpretations of EU Directives by reference to Charter rights helps a national legal system to accommodate those rules, by facilitating the amendment of rules laid down by Directives into the normal private law process found in the national legal system of the balancing of the interests of the parties to a contract. As both parties enjoy fundamental rights under the Charter, it provides a vehicle for modifying the Directive to ensure that, in the view of the CJEU, it strikes a fair balance between the interests of the parties. The second use of the Charter has been to extend the reach of EU Directives to ensure that the rights conferred by Directives, such as consumer rights and workers' rights, are properly effective in national contract law and civil procedure. The decisions of the CJEU in *Kušionová v. SMART Capital*,[48] and *King v. Sash Window Workshop*,[49] illustrate how the CJEU uses the Charter to insist on significant changes to national private law, including its civil procedure.

45 Case C-415/11, *Aziz v. Caixa d'Estalvis de Catalunya, Tarragona i Manresa*, ECLI:EU:C:2013:164.
46 J. Rutgers, 'The Right to Housing (Article 7 of the Charter) and Unfair Terms in General Conditions' in H. Collins (ed.), above n. 4, p. 125.
47 *Alemo-Herron*, above n. 24.
48 *Kušionová*, above n. 18, para. 65.
49 *King*, above n. 34.

These uses of the Charter may appear to deviate from the duty of the CJEU to conform to the written laws of the EU and uphold the value of the Rule of Law, because the CJEU appears to be making laws rather than interpreting them, or interpreting them to mean the opposite of what their plain meaning appears to be. It was argued here, on the contrary, that under a 'rights-based' conception of the Rule of Law, as described by Ronald Dworkin, this use of the Charter is legitimate and conforms to the ideal of the Rule of Law. By upholding the fundamental rights of EU citizens in the Charter in hard cases, the CJEU achieves fidelity to the law and upholds the EU legal order.

THE POLISH CIVIL LAW CODIFICATION COMMISSION WORKING ON THE DRAFT OF THE NEW CIVIL CODE

Jerzy Pisuliński

1. POLISH CODIFICATION OF CIVIL LAW

Polish civil law was unified on 1 January 1947. Until then, several legal systems were in force on the territory of Poland: German law in the west, Austrian and partly also Hungarian law in the south, French and partly Russian law in the central part, and Russian law in the east. The task of preparing drafts to unify the whole of civil law was entrusted to the Codification Commission established in 1919. As a result of its work, it was possible to prepare and adopt a Code of Obligations and a Commercial Code, which came into force on 1 July 1934.[1] The Code of Obligations was created following a legal analysis of the three existing civil codes which were in force at the time (Austrian, French and German). It also partly derived its solutions from the Swiss Code of Obligations. On the other hand, the Commercial Code, following the example of the German Commercial Code, governed not only the activities of companies governed by commercial law, but also commercial transactions (transactions between merchants). The provisions of the Commercial Code governing commercial transactions constituted specific law in relation to the provisions of the Code

1 Both codes were adopted by way of a decree of the President of the Republic of Poland: Decree of the President of the Republic of Poland of 27 October 1933 – the Code of Obligations (Journal of Laws No. 82, item 598, as amended) and Decree of the President of the Republic of Poland of 27 June 1934 – the Commercial Code (Journal of Laws No. 57, item 502, as amended).

of Obligations. However, the legislators did not manage to enact the property, family and inheritance law before 1939. Still, the drafts prepared by the Codification Commission provided the basis for the decrees issued in 1945 and 1946 that provided for uniform regulation of property law, the land and mortgage registers, marital law, guardianship law and the law of succession.[2]

As soon as these decrees were adopted, work began on the draft Civil Code, which continued, with a few years' break, until 1962. At that time, several versions of the draft Civil Code were presented (the drafts from 1948, 1954, 1955, 1960, 1961 and 1962). Finally, the Polish Civil Code, which is even now still in force, was adopted on 23 April 1964.[3] A little earlier, on 25 February 1964, the Family and Guardianship Code was enacted.[4] The decision to separate family law from the draft Civil Code was made towards the end of the legislative process and was motivated primarily by political and ideological considerations.

The Civil Code of 1964 is based on a monistic concept. The provisions of the Civil Code refer to all dealings, including relations between entrepreneurs. Therefore, the act implementing the Civil Code repealed the provisions of the Commercial Code.[5] However, many of the Commercial Code's provisions concerning commercial transactions were, with some changes, incorporated into the Civil Code (e.g. the provisions governing commercial sales contracts, contracts regarding agency or commissions, forwarding and carriage contracts, and, partly, storage contracts).[6] In 2003, the provisions on commercial proxy (*prokura*) were also added to the Civil Code (Arts. 109^1–109^9), modelled on the provisions of the Commercial Code.[7] In addition, the Civil Code contains many provisions, sometimes with minor modifications, contained in the Code of Obligations and decrees on substantive and inheritance law. Therefore, it can

---

2 These were the following decrees: of 12 November 1946 – general provisions of civil law (Journal of Laws No. 67, item 369); of 11 October 1946 – property law (Journal of Laws No. 57, item 319); of 11 October 1946 – land and mortgage registers law (Journal of Laws No. 57, item 320); of 25 September 1945 – marital law (Journal of Laws No. 48, item 270); of 29 May 1946 – marital property law (Journal of Laws No. 31, item 196); of 22 January 1946 – family law (Journal of Laws No. 6, item 52); of 14 May 1946 – guardianship law (Journal of Laws No. 20, item 135); of 8 October 1946 – the law of succession (Journal of Laws No. 60, item 328).

3 Journal of Laws No. 16, item 93, as amended. See consolidated text of the Journal of Laws of 2020, item 1740.

4 Journal of Laws No. 9, item 59, as amended. See consolidated text of the Journal of Laws of 2020, item 1359, as amended.

5 Cf. Art. VI of the Act of 23 April 1964 (Journal of Laws No. 16, item 94, as amended). However, the provisions of the Commercial Code on the companies and commercial proxy remained applicable for longer (until the end of 2000 when a Code on Commercial Companies of 2000 was adopted, and until 2003 when the Civil Code was amended).

6 See J. Pisuliński, 'Die Evolution des polnischen Vertragsrechts. Aktuelle Lage und Zukunft' (2010) 6(3) *European Review of Contract Law* 320–21.

7 See J. Pisuliński, 'Die Handlungsvollmacht nach polnischem Recht' in C. Baldus and W. Dajczak (eds.), *Der Allgemeine Teil des Privatrechts. Erfahrungen und Perspektiven zwischen Deutschland, Polen und den lusitanischen Rechten*, Peter Lang, Frankfurt am Main 2013, pp. 385–401.

be concluded that the Civil Code was largely a continuation of the solutions developed by the Codification Commission before the Second World War, based, as has already been mentioned, on the solutions adopted in the major European codification processes. It certainly distinguished the Polish Civil Code from other civil codes of socialist countries adopted at that time. Fortunately, the influence of the ideology of those times on the Civil Code was (in the normative level) not significant. It manifested itself primarily in the specific regulation of contractual relations between the so-called social economy entities (mainly between state-owned enterprises and cooperatives)[8] and in the concept of uniform state ownership[9] and the typology of ownership (social ownership, individual and personal ownership) as adopted in the property law. Social property was in particular protected (e.g. acquisitive prescription (usucaption) of state-owned property was forbidden).[10] These provisions were repealed following the amendment of the Civil Code by the Act of 28 July 1990.[11]

2. WHY THE WORK ON THE NEW CODIFICATION WAS INITIATED

The reasons for the codification efforts focused on Polish civil law after the First and Second World Wars were similar to a certain extent. First of all, it was about unifying civil law throughout the country, and after 1947 – when civil law had already been effectively unified – the aim was to codify provisions which were scattered across various legal acts (the Code of Obligations, the Family Code,[12] and the decrees on substantive law, inheritance law and matrimonial and guardianship matters) in a single act. In the case of the 1964 codification, it was, naturally, also a matter of adapting the regulation of civil law to the new social relations and, in particular, to the new socialist ideology.[13] The changes dictated

---

8 Cf. Arts. 397–404 of the Civil Code. However, these relations were governed primarily in the non-code instruments, mainly the so-called general terms and conditions (of normative nature), issued on the basis of Arts. 2 and 384 of the Civil Code (as originally worded).

9 According to Art. 128(1) of the Civil Code, socialist national (state) property was in the hands of the state. This meant that state-owned legal entities did not own the national assets allocated to them; instead, they held the so-called management right (they exercised the rights arising from state ownership on their own behalf). However, the nature of that right was not clear.

10 Cf. Art. 177 of the Civil Code.

11 Journal of Laws No. 55, item 321. Its provisions came into force on 1 October 1990. Earlier, on 1 February 1989, the aforementioned Art. 128 of the Civil Code was repealed.

12 The Family Code of 27 June 1950 (Journal of Laws No. 34, item 308) was replaced by the Family and Guardianship Code.

13 The changes that were introduced into family law under the influence of this ideology – equal rights and obligations of spouses and equal rights of children born in and out of wedlock – should be regarded as positive. In this respect, the Polish family law overtook many Western European codes in which similar changes (albeit for other reasons – mainly under the

by the socialist ideology were not profound and were eliminated relatively quickly after the political breakthrough in 1989.

The Civil Code has been amended more than 70 times since 1990.[14] Changes in the Civil Code were only partly caused by the need to adapt Polish law to European law with Poland's accession to the European Union (only three Directives were fully implemented in the Civil Code: Directive 86/653 on self-employed commercial agents, Directive 85/374 on liability for defective products and Directive 93/13 on unfair terms in consumer contracts; other important Directives in the field of civil law, including Directive 1999/44 on the sale of consumer goods and associated guarantees, were implemented in non-Code acts).[15] Many amendments to the Civil Code were caused by the adjustment of civil law provisions to the changed socio-economic conditions, especially as the country moved away from a planned economy and private entrepreneurship developed. This may explain, for example, the introduction of provisions concerning lease agreements (*leasing*) into the Civil Code (Arts. 709^1–709^{18}), the amendment of the contracting provisions (e.g. the introduction of provisions on tender procedures,[16] offer cancellation and acceptance modifying an offer)[17] or the introduction of a new type of transmission easement[18] (Arts. 305^1–305^4). The introduction of legacy 'by vindication' (*zapis windykacyjny*) in the law of succession (Arts. 981^1–981^6 Civil Code) served to extend party autonomy in this area of law. In order to comply with the requirements of the Constitution of 1997, the provisions on liability for damage caused in the exercise of public authority were amended.[19] However, not all amendments to the Civil Code were justified or well thought out.

In 2006, the Civil Law Codification Commission (CLCC), attached to the Ministry of Justice,[20] began to work on a draft for a new Civil Code by

influence of human rights and feminist movements) were introduced as late as the 1970s and sometimes even later.

14 Until 1990 the Civil Code was amended only six times (in 1971, 1976, 1982, 1984, 1985 and 1989).

15 In 2014, in connection with the implementation of Directive 2011/83/EU on consumer rights into Polish law, the provisions implementing Directive 1999/44/EC were incorporated into the Civil Code provisions on sales.

16 Cf. Arts. 70^1–70^5 added by the Act of 23 August 1996 (Journal of Laws No. 114, item 542). These provisions were amended in 2003.

17 Cf. Arts. 66^2 and 68^1 of the Civil Code, added by the Act of 14 February 2003 (Journal of Laws No. 49, item 408).

18 This is a reference to transmission easement, which enables entrepreneurs to use real property to install and operate equipment for the transmission of water, energy and gas. These provisions were introduced into the Civil Code by the Act of 30 May 2008 (Journal of Laws No. 116, item 731).

19 See Arts. 417–417^2 of the Civil Code introduced by the Act of 17 June 2004 (Journal of Laws No. 162, item 1692).

20 The activities of the CLCC were governed by the Regulation of the Council of Ministers of 22 April 2002 on the establishment, organisation and operation of the Civil Law Codification Commission (Journal of Laws No. 55, item 476, as amended). See consolidated text of the Journal of Laws of 2016, item 1741. The tasks of the CLCC were defined in §8(1) of the

presenting a Green Paper.[21] In this Green Paper, the CLCC analysed legislation in the field of civil law, including in particular the Civil Code and the Family and Guardianship Code. It made many suggestions in the Green Paper for far-reaching amendments to the two codes. The Green Paper was also to spur a discussion on the shape and role of the Civil Code in the legal system of the Republic of Poland. It did not prejudge whether a new Civil Code should be adopted or whether the two existing codes should instead be broadly revised. Contrary to what its subtitle implied, the Green Paper did not present how the then CLCC imagined a possible new Civil Code. Nor did the Green Paper include any legislative objectives for possible future codification.

The direct reason for the CLCC undertaking its work on the draft of the new Civil Code was a report prepared at the end of 2005 by the Prime Minister's Legislative Council, in which the Council stated that the existing Civil Code was outdated and changes triggered the process of decodification. Therefore, the Legislative Council considered it urgent to develop a new Civil Code.

This opinion on the Civil Code cannot be shared fully. However, it is a fact that the process of decodifying civil law is in progress as a result of the enactment of numerous new laws that are often inconsistent with the provisions of the Civil Code. This hinders the application of civil law rules and leads to legal uncertainty. It should also be stressed that, due to its pandectic structure, it is difficult to introduce provisions implementing European Directives into the Civil Code. The Directives regulate contracts on the basis of a specific marketing method (e.g. distance or off-premises contracts) or a specific risk incurred by the weaker party to the contract, usually the consumer (e.g. timeshare, travel or consumer credit contracts). The legal classification of these contracts is irrelevant – from the point of view of national law, these may be both nominate and innominate contracts. Shortcomings in the Civil Code, which does not govern many aspects of contractual relations in a complete way, also contribute to difficulties in its application. The Civil Code does not sufficiently regulate service contracts, which now play an increasingly important role in the economy. The best example is a construction contract; the provisions regulating such a contract in the Civil Code fail to meet the needs of modern standards of construction. Many contracts concluded in practice are not regulated at all by the Civil Code, or their regulation is outdated. Finally, the Civil Code should be open to new technologies. The existing amendments to the Civil Code, which were aimed at adapting its provisions to new ways

---

Regulation (preparing objectives and general directions for changes in civil law, family law and private commercial law, and preparing objectives and drafts of fundamental importance for the system of civil law, family law and private commercial law, taking into account the tasks resulting from the need for harmonisation of Polish law with European law).

21 Z. Radwański (ed.), *Green Paper: Optimal Vision of the Civil Code in the Republic of Poland*, Warsaw 2006.The text is also available at: https://arch-bip.ms.gov.pl/pl/dzialalnosc/komisje-kodyfikacyjne/komisja-kodyfikacyjna-prawa-cywilnego/.

of communicating, are not sufficient and, at the same time, cause various interpretation problems. For all these reasons, it is indeed necessary to work on the draft Civil Code. However, this does not prejudge how changes should be made, whether gradually, for example by replacing existing provisions with new ones, or comprehensively, by repealing and replacing the existing Civil Code, as has been done, for example, in Hungary and the Czech Republic.

3. OUTCOME OF THE WORK ON THE NEW CIVIL CODE

Work on the draft Civil Code had continued for the following nine years from 2006 until 17 December 2015 (during the CLCC's third and fourth terms and partly also during its incomplete fifth term), i.e. until the date on which the CLCC's Chair, Vice-Chair and all its members were dismissed. This work resulted in the following drafts.[22]

Draft of Book One (General Part) – The first version of the draft of Book One of the Civil Code was adopted and announced by the CLCC in 2008.[23] A revised draft of the General Part, substantially changed compared to the draft of 2008, was adopted at the CLCC's last session on 22–23 January 2015 during its fourth term.[24] The draft does not include provisions on legal incapacitation, as the CLCC undertook work to replace incapacitation with new provisions that would be in line with the UN Convention on the Rights of Persons with Disabilities adopted by the General Assembly of the United Nations on 13 December 2006.[25] The objectives for the proposed regulation and draft provisions amending the existing Civil Code were prepared.[26] The draft was to be discussed at the CLCC's plenary session on 17 December 2015.

Draft of Book Two (Law of Obligations) – Draft provisions for the general part on obligations were prepared by the CLCC in the period 2006–2010, with the CLCC continuing its work on the project in 2011–2015. During the process, many changes were made to the earlier draft. In 2015, work was under way on including provisions on pre-contractual information obligations and on concluding off-premises and distance contracts in the draft. The CLCC also started its discussions on the draft. The draft had not been completed by December 2015.

---

22 These drafts were presented in detail in *Kwartalnik Prawa Prywatnego* (*Private Law Quarterly*) 2016/2, 454–57.

23 The draft is also available at: https://arch-bip.ms.gov.pl/pl/dzialalnosc/komisje-kodyfikacyjne/komisja-kodyfikacyjna-prawa-cywilnego/.

24 The draft was announced in print, see P. Machnikowski (ed.), *Civil Code. Book One. General Part. The draft of the Civil Law Codification Commission adopted in 2015 with comments from members of the CLCC task force*, Warsaw 2017.

25 Journal of Laws of 2012, item 1169.

26 The latest version of these provisions dates back to 3 December 2015.

While working on a specific part of the law of obligation, the following partial drafts were prepared (none of which was adopted by CLCC): on loan agreements,[27] on pension and life annuity agreements, on the use of someone else's property or rights,[28] on surety and guarantee agreements. Work was also carried out on the regulation of service agreements[29] and insurance[30] contracts.

The Codification Committee also held a discussion on the structure of the specific part of the law of obligation.[31] However, no decision was made on that structure as it was postponed until all the drafts regulating individual groups of nominate contracts had been prepared.

Draft of Book Three (Property Law) – In the years 2006–2010, two teams from the CLCC were working on draft general provisions of property law, provisions on ownership and provisions concerning limited rights *in rem*. During the CLCC's next term, the property law draft was discussed three times in plenary sessions by the Commission. At the session on 25–26 July 2013, a decision was made to exclude the provisions on pledging rights (on pledges and mortgages) from the provisions of the draft property law and to include them in the new book on security interests for receivables (at that time, a preliminary draft structure of that book was adopted). However, work on the draft of the book on securities for receivables did not commence. In later years, the work on the draft property law was not continued.

---

27 The draft governed loan agreements and credit facility agreements (now regulated separately in the banking law).

28 The draft covered hire (*najem*), tenancy (*dzierżawa*), lease (*leasing*) and agreements on provision for use. The draft also contained general provisions applicable to all these contracts.

29 The draft version of 10 February 2015 was published in *Transformacje Prawa Prywatnego (TPP)* (*Transformation of Private Law*) 2014/4, 75 et seq. A discussion of the draft's objectives by M. Pecyna and F. Zoll was published in *TPP* 2014/4, 71 et seq.

30 The CLCC also adopted a draft amendment to the provisions of the Civil Code in force which introduced provisions on contracts of group insurance for third parties. The draft version, dated 28 November 2014, is available, together with a statement of grounds, at the following address: https://arch-bip.ms.gov.pl/pl/dzialalnosc/komisje-kodyfikacyjne/komisja-kodyfikacyjna-prawa-cywilnego/.

31 See papers by Z. Radwański ('Wstępny projekt systematyzacji tak zwanej części szczegółowej prawa zobowiązań' (Preliminary draft for systematisation of the so-called detailed part of the contract law)), J. Pisuliński ('W sprawie systematyki części szczegółowej prawa zobowiązań (głos w dyskusji)' (On the systematisation of the detailed part of the contract law (a voice in the discussion))), M. Pecyna and F. Zoll ('Założenia projektu struktury części szczegółowej zobowiązań. W poszukiwaniu nowego modelu' (Assumptions of the draft structure of the detailed part of the contract law. In search of a new model)) and R. Szostak ('Problem systematyki umów obligacyjnych w nowym kodeksie cywilnym' (The problem of classification of obligation contracts in the new civil code)), published in *TPP* 2012/1. For the regulation of intermediation contracts, see also E. Rott-Pietrzyk, 'Systematyka części szczegółowej zobowiązań a miejsce umów o pośrednictwo sensu largo (głos w dyskusji)' (The classification of the detailed part of the contract law and the place for intermediation contracts in the broad sense (a voice in the discussion)), *TPP* 2013/1, 41 et seq. E. Rott-Pietrzyk, M. Grochowski, 'Umowy pośrednictwa w obrocie towarami lub usługami: Część ogólna i umowa agencyjna (projekt reformy)' (Intermediary Contracts Concerning Goods And Services: General Part and Commercial Agency Contract (Reform Project)), *TPP* 2020/1, 53 et seq.

In its 2006–2010 and 2011–2015 terms, the CLCC also worked on draft provisions for the book on the law of succession. The work did not end with the preparation of a comprehensive draft of the law of succession; only partial drafts were prepared, including draft provisions on legacy 'by vindication', which were introduced into the Civil Code.

The CLCC did not carry out any work on the draft of the family law.[32] This was partly due to the composition of the Commission, which lacked experts in family law, and partly due to the fact that the Family and Guardianship Code was subject to two major amendments in 2004 (as regards matrimonial property regimes) and 2008 (with respect to parent-child relationships). The Commission asked the Institute of Justice to conduct a study on the practical application of some of the new provisions (e.g. concerning contact with children, ruling on alternating custody in divorce judgments)[33] in order to use them to prepare proposed amendments for the purposes of the new codification. The Commission also held, inter alia, a meeting on 18 June 2013 with family law scholars and family court judges to discuss the proposed changes to family law.[34]

4. FURTHER WORK ON THE NEW CODIFICATION: ACADEMIC DRAFT OF THE CIVIL CODE

Following the dissolution of the CLCC, heads of civil law departments of Polish universities decided at a meeting in January 2016 in Warsaw to continue the work on the CLCC's drafts as part of the so-called academic draft of the Civil Code.[35] Several task forces were formed. Every six months, conferences are held at which the outcomes of the task forces' work are presented and discussed in public.[36] The work on draft provisions on intermediation and service contracts is currently the most advanced.[37] The structure of the general part of the law of

---

32 The CLCC assumed in the Green Paper that family law would be governed by the Civil Code.

33 See https://iws.gov.pl/analizy-i-raporty/raporty/.

34 See the report in *Rodzina i Prawo* (*Family and Law*) 2013/26–27, 140 et seq.

35 For more information, see http://www.projektkc.uj.edu.pl/.

36 So far, such conferences have been held in Warsaw (29 April 2016), Wrocław (14 October 2016), Kraków (25–26 May 2017), Katowice (13 October 2017), Lublin (10–11 May 2018), Wrocław (25–26 October 2018) and Gdańsk (23–24 May 2019). Reports on these conferences are published in the *Państwo i Prawo (PiP)* (*State and Law*) journal (reports on the conferences in Warsaw – *PiP* 2017/1, 123–125; Wrocław – *PiP* 2017/4, 134–135; Kraków – *PiP* 2018/2, 121–123, Katowice – *PiP* 2019/1, 140–142, Gdańsk – *PiP* 2020/8, 146–147).

37 See more E. Rott-Pietrzyk, M. Grochowski, „Struktura regulacji umów o pośrednictwo handlowe (wnioski prawnoporównawcze i propozycje legislacyjne) [The structure of regulations governing the contracts relating to commercial intermediation (Outcome from the comparative analyse and legislative proposals)], STPP 2018/1, 3 et seq.

obligation and specific part of the law of obligation has also been discussed.[38] Unfortunately, the work has not been very intense due to a lack of funding and the amount of time that members of these task forces are able to devote – on top of their normal professional responsibilities – to preparing and editing drafts.

---

38 For the structure of the general part of contract law, see J. Pisuliński, 'Struktura części ogólnej prawa zobowiązań (wprowadzenie do dyskusji)' (The structure of the General Part of the Contract Law (introduction to the discussion), *TPP* 2017/2, 37–50; for the structure of the detailed part of the contract law, see W.J. Kocot, 'Systematyka prawa zobowiązań umownych w przyszłym kodeksie cywilnym' (The classification of the contract law in the future civil code), *PiP* 2018/3, 82–109.

PART III

PARTY AUTONOMY AND SELECTION OF NORMS

TYPES OF CONTRACTS AND LAW'S AUTONOMY-ENHANCING ROLE

Hanoch DAGAN*

1. INTRODUCTION

In *The Choice Theory of Contracts*[1] Michael Heller and I offer a way to understand contract which departs from two entrenched tenets of contract theory. First, we argue that contract theory should move beyond the universalising tendency advocated by the Willistonian project and shift at least some of its emphasis from 'general' contract law to (or rather back to) particular contract types. Whereas contract is an important category for thinking, the various contract types – including the residual type of 'freestanding contracting' – are the proper categories for deciding. In other words, while the Willistonian tradition emphasises contract's uniformity, choice theory highlights its *multiplicity*.

We are not the first to warn against the flattening effects of contract monism and the unprincipled multiplicity of the common law (and European civil law) that Williston hoped to systematise. But unlike other critiques, choice theory offers a *principled* account of contract's multiplicity. The principle that stands at the foundation of contract law is autonomy. At this point we again part ways with existing theories. Liberal theories of contract typically aim at distilling an autonomy-based account purged of any teleological foundation. Our account is diametrically different, since choice theory embraces autonomy's

* Thanks to Hugh Collins, Stefan Grundmann, Przemyslaw Palka, Daniel Markovits, and Magda Raczynska for their helpful comments.

1 See H. DAGAN and M.A. HELLER, *The Choice Theory of Contracts*, Cambridge University Press, New York 2017.

role as contract's *telos*. Contract, we argue, is a valuable convention – indeed, a convention that any liberal polity must enact – because and to the extent that it proactively enhances individual autonomy, namely people's self-determination or self-authorship; our right to write and re-write the story of our lives.

One important takeaway of choice theory lies at the juncture of these two proposed shifts. A *teleological* theory of contract, which celebrates its autonomy-enhancing function, offers the key for understanding contract's multiplicity and appreciating its role in a liberal polity. Indeed, a proper understanding of contract as an essentially power-conferring (as opposed to duty-imposing) institution implies that its most fundamental contribution to liberal societies is in expanding our options. Thus, by ensuring the multiplicity of contract types – more specifically, the availability of diverse, normatively attractive contract types in each important sphere of human interaction – contract law complies with autonomy's fundamental imperative of enabling people to make their lives meaningfully their own by legitimately enlisting others to their most important projects.

Providing a rich inventory of contract types is important for people's autonomy because bargaining for terms is not the dominant mode of contracting. The mainstay of present-day contracting is not one of designing deals from scratch, but rather choosing from among the available range of off-the-shelf contract types and only then making a few contextual adjustments within the deal. Each contract type uses distinctive doctrinal features embedded in the law to embody a set of normative concerns (the type's DNA, if you will) and stabilise its shared cultural meaning, thus making it more available to contracting parties.[2]

In this chapter I hope to recruit an unsuspecting ally: Robert Nozick. Choosing Nozick as a fellow-traveller seems suspicious. After all, his *Anarchy, State, and Utopia*[3] is the most renowned *libertarian* manifesto of recent times. Nozick's entitlement theory, which underlies his account of justice in holdings, is rightly considered a prime example of a blueprint advocating a monist understanding of property along the lines of its Blackstonian rendition as sole and despotic dominion.[4] More importantly for the purposes of this chapter, entitlement theory is also the foundation of the most outspoken libertarian account of contract law: Randy Barnett's consent theory of contract. The main function of contract law in this account is to prescribe the transfer rules of law in line with the rightsholders' consent, in order to delineate the boundaries of protected domains.[5]

---

2 As the text clarifies, contract types are not standard form contracts or boilerplate terms as such. Standard forms are particular instances of contract types.

3 See R. Nozick, *Anarchy, State, and Utopia*, Basic Books, New York 1974, p. 153.

4 See G.S. Alexander and H. Dagan, *Properties of Property*, Wolters Kluwer/Aspen, New York 2012, ch. 3.

5 See R.E. Barnett, 'A Consent Theory of Contract' (1986) 86 *Colum. L. Rev. (Columbia Law Review)* 269, 270, 302.

Nozick's libertarianism has been the target of an intense, convincing, and familiar critique that I will not repeat here.[6] But *Anarchy, State, and Utopia* also offers another and less familiar – indeed somewhat neglected – argument on behalf of the minimal state: an account of utopia as a framework for utopias. This ideal of a framework for utopias is captivating. It takes differences between people seriously, insisting that all individuals deserve respectful treatment of their own autonomy. Unlike the conception of negative liberty (or independence) typically associated with libertarian authors,[7] obviously including Nozick, this ideal builds on, or at least acknowledges, a richer understanding of autonomy as a form of self-authorship (or self-determination) requiring diverse options.

But while Nozick's account of utopia is inviting, his assertion that the minimal state, and only the minimal state, can bring about this utopia is, I argue, wrong and misleading. This means that if we agree with Nozick that the liberal state as a framework for utopias is an inspiring notion, we need to discard the libertarian credo of the minimal state and the conventional conceptions of private law's building blocks resonating in it. More specifically, if contract law is to be guided by this autonomy-enhancing utopian promise, it must not follow Barnett's consent theory, but rather subscribe to choice theory. A genuinely utopian contract law requires a robust legal edifice of a sufficiently varied inventory of contract types for each sphere of social life.[8]

Inviting utopian students of Nozick to embrace choice theory, this chapter explains why adherence to its autonomy-based *telos* requires contract law to be both proactive and pluralist. In order to facilitate people's autonomy, contract law should, as it to a significant extent already does, proactively enhance choice, rather than merely vindicating people's gatekeeping authority. Contract law's embrace of the objective approach and its extensive gap-filling apparatus are familiar means for pursuing this mission. No less important is the heterogeneity among contract types, especially where it generates an adequate range of options within major spheres of contracting. Complying with this injunction of intra-sphere multiplicity admittedly is a complex task, involving both substantive and institutional challenges, but neither seems overwhelming. The effort is worth our while, since only by focusing on this task will we push contract law to live up to its own (implicit) autonomy-enhancing ideals.

---

6 For a poignant criticism by a particularly competent commentator, see R. Nozick, *The Examined Life: Philosophical Meditations*, Simon & Schuster, New York 1989, p. 286.

7 As well as with Kantians. See A. Ripstein, *Force and Freedom: Kant's Legal and Political Philosophy*, Harvard University Press, Cambridge 2009, pp. 14, 34, 45.

8 It also implies that contract law should take seriously the autonomy of the parties' future self and that relational justice must serve as the floor of legitimate contractual interactions eligible for law's support. See H. Dagan and M. Heller, 'Freedom, Choice, and Contract' (2019) 20 *Theoretical Inquiries L. (Theoretical Inquiries in Law)* 595, 606.

2. FRAMEWORK FOR UTOPIAS

Nozick's great insight is that utopia must be conceptualised as 'a framework for utopias, a place where people are at liberty to join together voluntarily to pursue and attempt to realise their own vision of the good life.' In treating us all 'with respect by respecting our rights' and in allowing us, 'individually or with whom we choose, to choose our life and to realize our ends and our conception of ourselves, insofar as we can, aided by the voluntary cooperation of other individuals possessing the same dignity', this framework for utopias 'best realizes the utopian aspirations of untold dreamers and visionaries'.[9]

To secure these happy effects, Nozick argues, utopia's law must reject the temptation of 'planning in detail, in advance, one [utopian] community in which everyone is to live'. Instead, it should operate as a 'libertarian and laissez-faire' framework, which facilitates 'a diverse range of communities', many (maybe most, or even all) of which would be neither libertarian nor laissez-faire, in order to enable 'more persons … to come closer to how they wish to live, than if there is only one kind of community'. By facilitating 'voluntary utopian experimentation' and 'provid[ing] it with the background in which it can flower', this utopian state invites 'many persons' particular visions', enabling us 'to get the best of all possible worlds'.[10]

Indeed, because Nozick believes that his account of utopia provides independent support to the minimal state, he concludes that his libertarian theory of the state is both right and inspiring. But this conclusion is wrong. Nozick's exciting vision of utopia defies rather than supports libertarianism. To see why, we need to appreciate the robustness of the ideal of a framework for utopias and realise its profound dependence on law or law-like conventions. While the former step can and should be read as a friendly extension of Nozick's utopian vision, the latter implies that this vision must rely on an unambiguously non-libertarian conception of private law and thus must repudiate the consent theory of contract.[11]

Nozick envisages a diverse menu of comprehensive lifestyle options, in which '[d]ifferent communities, each with slightly different mix, … provide a range from which each individual can choose that community which best approximates *his* balance among competing values'.[12] But a viable framework for utopias offering

---

9 R. Nozick, above n. 3, pp. 312, 332–33.

10 Ibid., pp. 309, 320, 332–33.

11 On its face, the text overstates the conclusions of the discussion that follows because my argument refers to law *or law-like conventions*, which implies that the infrastructure required for a framework of utopias need not necessarily emanate from state law. But for these non-statist sources to function like law they do indeed have to be law-like, namely normative coercive institutions. Cf. H. Dagan, *Reconstructing American Legal Realism & Rethinking Private Law Theory*, Oxford University Press, New York 2013, ch. 2.

12 R. Nozick, above n. 3, p. 312.

people a diverse menu of options for interpersonal interaction from which to choose when pursuing their conception of the good surely requires more than a variety of all-encompassing communities. Part of modernity's promise, which Nozick undoubtedly embraces, is the option of multiple group affiliations. This means that people should be able to choose their associations in their various, and possibly incongruent or even conflicting, capacities.[13]

Moreover, and more importantly for my purposes, self-determining individuals should be able to choose from not only a range of comprehensive options dealing with lifestyles and conceptions of the good. Rather, choice should also be available for many other and more specific decisions they face in various spheres of life. These decisions may be less dramatic, but they are still significant and, again, disconnected and potentially incompatible components of their life story. Self-authorship implies not only choosing between life in a 'capitalist' community and a *kibbutz*, as Nozick insists,[14] but also, and just as importantly, choosing whether we want to live in a fee simple absolute or a common interest community; to work as an employee or an independent contractor; to do business in a partnership, a close corporation, or a publicly held corporation; and whether to form an intimate bond of marriage, or rather cohabit.

The liberal commitment to individual self-authorship, which makes Nozick's conception of utopia as a framework for utopias so appealing, requires a sufficiently diverse set of viable options for all these and many other discrete yet significant decisions regarding our interpersonal interactions, in addition to the more comprehensive options that Nozick emphasised. As Joseph Raz explains, autonomy requires not only appropriate mental abilities and independence, but also 'an adequate range of options'. Therefore, autonomy 'cannot be obtained within societies which support social forms which do not leave enough room for individual choice'; for choice to be effective, for autonomy to be meaningful, we require, other things being equal, 'more valuable options than can be chosen, and they must be significantly different', so that choices involve 'trade-offs, which require relinquishing one good for the sake of another'.[15]

So far so good. Nozick the libertarian need not object to any of these observations. But can all these options at all these levels indeed be instantiated in the minimal state? Does the freedom to initiate cooperative arrangements, which Nozick the libertarian relies upon, suffice for the task of securing the diversity of the menu, which Nozick the utopian considers crucial?

Nozick seems to believe that this is indeed the case. Although conceding that his system 'does not require' people 'to innovate' and that they may 'stagnate if

---

13 See e.g. G. Simmel, *Conflict and The Web of Group Affiliations*, The Free Press, New York 1955, pp. 130, 150–54; S. Stern, *Taking Community Seriously: Toward a Reform in Takings Law*, unpublished manuscript.

14 See R. Nozick, above n. 3, p. 321.

15 J. Raz, *The Morality of Freedom*, Oxford University Press, New York 1986, pp. 372, 395, 398.

they wish', Nozick is not alarmed by this problem as long as his framework provides the 'liberty to experimentation of varied sorts'.[16] This is exactly what private law does and should do according to some conventional accounts of property and contracts. As long as property is understood as 'sole and despotic dominion' and contract conceptualised around people's consent, so the argument goes, free individuals can use these fundamental building blocks of private law and tailor their interpersonal arrangements so that they best serve their own utilitarian, communitarian, or other purposes.[17] But would this minimalist conception of private law indeed suffice? Can we trust it to do the job of securing Nozick's utopia?

No, we cannot. The state's obligation to foster diversity and multiplicity, as Raz noted, cannot be properly accomplished through a hands-off or passive approach by the law. Why? Because such an attitude 'would undermine the chances of survival of many cherished aspects of our culture'.[18] Appreciating the indispensable roles – both material and expressive – of private law (or any parallel law-like convention, for that matter) in facilitating interpersonal arrangements[19] implies that a commitment to personal autonomy requires that a liberal state, through its laws, work more actively to 'enable individuals to pursue valid conceptions of the good' by providing them a multiplicity of options.[20]

Economic analysis of private law, which investigates its incentive effects, forcefully demonstrates how many of our existing practices rely on legal devices that help overcome numerous types of transaction costs – information costs (symmetric and asymmetric), bilateral monopolies, cognitive biases, and heightened risks of opportunistic behaviour – that generate the participants' endemic vulnerabilities in most cooperative interpersonal interactions.[21] Merely enforcing the parties' expressed intentions would not be sufficient to overcome the inherent risks of such endeavours. If many (if not most) of them are to be viable alternatives, law must provide the background reassurances that help to ensure the trust so crucial for success. Even where parties are guided by their own social norms, law often plays an important role in providing them background

---

16 R. Nozick, above n. 3, p. 329. Nozick mentions a few other difficulties in implementing his ideal of utopia in the actual world. See ibid., p. 307.

17 See T.W. Merrill, 'Property as Modularity' (2012) 125 *Harv. L. Rev. Forum (Harvard Law Review Forum)* 151, 157–58.

18 J. Raz, above n. 15, p. 162.

19 For more detailed analyses on which the remainder of this Part draws, H. Dagan and M.A. Heller, above n. 1, ch 7.

20 J. Raz, above n. 15, pp. 133, 265.

21 See e.g. I. Ayres and R. Gertner, 'Filling Gaps in Incomplete Contracts: An Economic Theory of Default Rules' (1989) 99 *Yale L.J. (Yale Law Review)* 87; R.B. Korobkin and T.S. Ulen, 'Law and Behavioral Science: Removing the Rationality Assumption from Law and Economics' (2000) 88 *Cal. L. Rev. (California Law Review)* 1051. On top of these transaction costs, there are certain features of cooperative endeavours – notably affirmative asset partitioning – that are (almost literally) impossible to achieve without legal intervention. See H. Hansmann and R. Kraakman, 'The Essential Role of Organizational Law' (2000) 110 *Harv. L. Rev. (Harvard Law Review)* 387.

safeguards, a safety net for a rainy day that can help to establish trust in their routine, happier interactions.[22]

But law's effects are not only material. Because contract law tends to blend into our natural environment, its categories play a crucial role in structuring our daily interactions.[23] Thus, alongside these material effects, many of our conventions – including many social practices we take for granted as the options we currently have (think bailment, suretyship, or fiduciary) – become available to us only due to cultural conventions that are often legally constructed.[24] This is especially true in modern times. Hence, if these notions were not legally coined, people would not only have to consider the transaction costs of constructing these arrangements from scratch: they would also face 'obstacles of the imagination' just coming up with the options in the first place. Indeed, the contract types law establishes play an important cultural role. Like other social conventions, they serve a crucial function in consolidating people's expectations and in expressing normative ideals regarding the core categories of interpersonal relationships they participate in constructing.

Both the material and the expressive functions of contract imply that freedom of contract, though significant, cannot possibly replace active legal facilitation. Lack of legal support is often tantamount to undermining – maybe even obliterating – many cooperative types of interpersonal relationships and thus people's ability to seek their own conception of the good. This gap between the libertarian blueprint and Nozick's utopian ideal admittedly relies on people's fallibility, notably their cognitive failures and the way they tend to prefer their self-interest to the interests of others. But these imperfections cannot be dismissed as contingent features that need not bother Nozick the utopian. While their significance may vary from one empirical context to another, these human features are sufficiently ingrained to render irrelevant if not self-defeating any purportedly utopian theory that ignores them.[25]

3. FROM CONSENT TO CHOICE

The very same gap that explains why Nozick's libertarian blueprint cannot plausibly serve as the foundation of a Nozickian framework for utopias also

---

22 Cf. H. Dagan and M.A. Heller, 'The Liberal Commons' (2001) 110 *Yale L.J.* 549, 578–79; R.J. Gilson, C.F. Sabel and R.E. Scott, 'Braiding: The Interaction of Formal and Informal Contracting in Theory, Practice, and Doctrine' (2010) 110 *Colum. L. Rev.* 1137.

23 See e.g. R.W. Gordon, 'Unfreezing Legal Reality: Critical Approaches to Law' (1987) 15 *Fla. St. U.L. Rev. (Florida State University Law Review)* 195, 212–14.

24 See e.g. I. Ayres, 'Menus Matter' (2006) 73 *U. Chi. L. Rev. (University of Chicago Law Review)* 3, 8.

25 I do not deny that a theoretical account of contract could start from an ideal world in which no such imperfections exist. But at some point, these *systematic* imperfections would have to be addressed if a contract theory aims to provide any guidance for, or justification of, the law.

shows why a contract law that would rely on Barnett's consent theory is likely to frustrate – rather than support – such a Nozickian utopia.

Contract law for Barnett is 'that part of a system of entitlements that identifies those circumstances in which entitlements are validly transferred from person to person by their consent.' The function of contract law's rules and principles 'is to identify the rights of individuals engaged in transferring entitlements, and thereby indicate when physical or legal force may legitimately be used', and then 'to rectify any unjust interference with the transfer process'. The (one and only) animating principle of these rules is consent: 'the consent of the rights holder to be legally obligated … distinguishes valid from invalid transfers of alienable rights in a system of entitlements'. This pivotal role of consent is justified because only by requiring that 'others take the interests of the rights holder into account when seeking to obtain the rights she possesses' can contract law properly 'facilitate freedom of human action and interaction'.[26]

Indeed, for Barnett, contract law – like its sister doctrines of private law that participate in setting up our system of entitlements – 'demands that the boundaries of protected domains be ascertainable, not only by judges who must resolve disputes that have arisen, but, perhaps more importantly, by the affected persons themselves before any dispute occurs.' The crucial significance of this 'boundary-defining' requirement relies on Barnett's libertarian premise in which individual rights require that 'the boundaries within which individuals may live, act, and pursue happiness [are] free of the forcible interference of others'. This premise also renders the '"strict liability" theory of contract', in which 'objective consent generally takes precedence over subjective assent', appealing because '[o]nly a general reliance on objectively ascertainable assertive conduct will enable a system of entitlements to perform its allotted boundary-defining function.'[27]

Barnett's theory of contract, which is both reactive (in the sense that it perceives law's task merely in terms of providing parties with enforcement services) and uniform across contract types, can be appealing to libertarian students of *Anarchy, State, and Utopia*, who are concerned only with setting clear interpersonal boundaries and defending people's independence. But it must be rejected by utopian ones, because – as we have just seen – the state's obligation to enhance autonomy by fostering diversity and multiplicity, which is the impetus of Nozick's conception of utopia, cannot be properly fulfilled through a hands-off attitude. A genuinely liberal contract law must take seriously the commitment to our self-authorship. It must adhere to the unique responsibility of private law to proactively enhance people's autonomy and thus offer a sufficiently diverse repertoire of contract types for each contracting sphere – commerce, work, intimacy, and home – so as to offer people meaningful choice for these important spheres of social activity and interaction.

---

26 R.E. Barnett, above n. 5, pp. 270, 295, 297–99.

27 Ibid., pp. 291, 302–03, 306.

Admittedly, one implication of the choice theory of contracts converges with its consent counterpart. Like consent theory (as well as many others), choice theory supports the objective theory of contract, in which 'the making of a contract depends not on the agreement of two minds in one intention, but on the agreement of two sets of external signs.'[28] But choice theory provides to the objective approach a much more secure justification. Whereas a consent-based contract law should, in fact, settle for protecting the reliance interest of misled promisees,[29] a contract law devoted to autonomy-*enhancement* must not.

As Jody Kraus claims, 'making subjective intent a necessary condition for making a promise' would have severely limited the role of promising only to 'individuals who make promises to people who already trust them'. Kraus does acknowledge the downside of objective theory to personal autonomy: it undermines 'the negative right of individuals (merely objective promisors) to be free from subjectively unintended obligations'. But as he asserts, the law justifiably follows the prescriptions of 'personal sovereignty' – the conception of individual autonomy on which promissory morality relies – to 'give priority to respect for the positive liberty of faultless individuals' who 'choose to undertake objectively binding promises', over the 'negative liberty of blameworthy individuals'.[30]

The widespread endorsement in modern contract law of the objective theory of contract[31] is only the first doctrinal implication of taking seriously contract's autonomy-enhancing *telos* as choice theory prescribes. Logically following it is the transition from strict adherence to the indefiniteness doctrine to the prevailing gap-filling apparatus. Whereas the traditional common law of contracts was very hesitant to enforce incomplete agreements, modern law takes a diametrically opposite attitude.[32] Contemporary contract law is no longer satisfied with providing enforcement services to parties who fully specify the terms of their engagement. To be sure, where commercial parties 'intentionally and deliberately' do not 'incorporate in their agreements readily available, verifiable measures of performance', courts correctly infer that they do not intend legal enforcement.[33] But beyond this category, current law – both the Uniform Commercial Code and the Restatement (Second) of Contracts[34] – goes

---

28 O.W. Holmes, 'The Path of the Law' (1897) 10 *Harv. L. Rev.* 457, 464.

29 See L.M. Solan, 'Contract as Agreement' (2008) 83 *Notre Dame. L. Rev. (Notre Dame Law Review)* 353.

30 J.S. Kraus, 'The Correspondence of Contract and Promise' (2009) 109 *Colum. L. Rev.* 1603, 1609, 1620–21, 1624. Cf. W. Barnes, 'The Objective Theory of Contracts' (2008) 76 *U. Cinn. L. Rev. (University of Cincinnati Law Review)* 1121, 1129–31.

31 The exception to this rule is arguably France, but its deviation from it seem quite nominal. See W. Barnes, 'The French Subjective Theory of Contract: Separating Rhetoric from Reality' (2008) 83 *Tulane L. Rev. (Tulane Law Review)* 359.

32 See E.A. Farnsworth, *Contracts*, 4th ed., Aspen, New York 2004, pp. 120–21.

33 R.E. Scott, 'A Theory of Self-Enforcing Indefinite Agreements' (2003) 103 *Colum. L. Rev.* 1641, 1657, 1659.

34 See UCC (Uniform Commercial Code) §2-204(3).

out of its way to facilitate transactions by offering defaults that can fill gaps, even regarding quite crucial aspects of a transaction (like price[35]).[36]

Barnett is of course aware of this dominant feature of our law, and he also appreciates (at least implicitly) the important difference between implied terms, which are implicit in the facts of the parties' specific interaction, and default rules, which are not. But he insists that contract's gap-filling apparatus is nonetheless compatible with consent theory. As long as contract law's gap-filling apparatus, which is entailed by 'the inevitability of incompleteness', is understood in terms of supplying *defaults*, he argues, it does not defy consent theory. The key for this reconciliation lies in consent theory's blueprint for the choice of defaults: a consent-based contract law recommends 'conventionalist default rules', namely 'default rules that reflect the commonsense expectations of persons in the relevant community of discourse', and there are good reasons to assume that 'such terms can be and often are indirectly consented to by parties who could have contracted around them – but did not.'[37]

Others have doubted the competence of the various legal actors who are responsible for supplying defaults to credibly identify these conventionalist or common-sense expectations.[38] The more pertinent difficulty with Barnett's account of gap-filling for our purposes is that it does not explain the breadth and depth of this core function of current law. If law's ultimate loyalty would have been to the parties' consent and its foundational commitment was to ensure the ideal of clearly delineated interpersonal boundaries, it should have adhered to the traditional common law approach, because this approach induces parties to spell out the main terms of their interaction and thus reduces the divergence between their actual intent and the norms that govern their agreements. By contrast, opting for contemporary law's more capacious gap-filling apparatus is a clear entailment of choice theory's most fundamental prescription of *expanding* the scope of people's voluntary obligations in order to empower their self-determination.[39] The robust gap-filling apparatus of modern contract law,

---

35 See UCC §2-305, and see Restatement (Second) of Contracts §33 (Am. Law Inst. 1981).

36 See e.g. 1 A. Corbin, *Corbin on Contracts §95*, LexisNexis, New Providence, 1963, pp. 400–01.

37 R.E. Barnett, 'The Sounds of Silence: Default Rules and Contractual Consent' (1986) 78 *Va. L. Rev. (Virginia Law Review)* 821, 821, 826, 875, 906.

38 See A. Schwartz and R.E. Scott, 'Contract Theory and the Limits of Contract Law' (2003) 113 *Yale L.J.* 541, 594–609.

39 I do not ignore the difficulty that inhere in this prescription. As law's gap-filling apparatus becomes increasingly elaborate, the risk that its coverage will be *over*-inclusive – that it will apply not only to fully *voluntary* obligations – becomes increasingly real. See R. Kreitner, 'Fear of Contract' (2003) *Wisc. L. Rev. (Wisconsin Law Review)* 429, 430. Involuntariness is a problem that an autonomy-enhancing contract law must take seriously. To some extent, this risk of over-inclusiveness can be reduced by making the convention prevalent. But an autonomy-enhancing contract law should not be content with this partial safeguard to the risk of involuntariness. Two features of contract law can confront this risk: the familiar doctrines – notably duress and fraud – that delimit the scope of enforceable promises to those that are not the product of the promisee's manipulation of the promisor's free will, and the reliance on legal formalities.

which seems indefensible for a contractual regime based on an ideal of reciprocal respect for independence, nicely fits choice theory's understanding of private law as the domain of reciprocal respect for self-determination.

Making gap-filling a core function of contract law quickly necessitates another feature choice theory celebrates, namely the significant variation among contract types. In other words, expanding the facilitative ambition of contract law requires it to adjust the means with which it can identify mutually beneficial interactions worthy of its support, as well as the rules that can best support them. This devotion to contract's autonomy-enhancement *telos* can explain and justify the development of promissory estoppel and of the material benefit rule as contract's additional gatekeeping doctrines alongside the traditional consideration doctrine.[40] It likewise accounts for the gradual recognition that other rules which are at times presented as part of contract law's signature – like the mirror-image rule for offer and acceptance, the standard of performance of perfect tender, the promisor's strict liability, or the dominance of expectation damages – all in fact prevail only in certain contract types, and not in others.[41]

These three features of our contract law – the dominance of its objective approach, the robustness of its gap-filling apparatus, and the significant differences among the contract types it facilitates – naturally lead to the fourth feature of a liberal contract law, which takes seriously the commitment to proactively facilitate contract's autonomy-enhancing potential, namely its commitment to secure intra-sphere multiplicity. To be sure, in some contexts – notably in the commercial sphere – there are powerful economic forces catalysing demand for options, so the task of contract law can and by and large should be mostly reactive. But in the other contractual spheres – think work, intimacy, or home – where collective action problems or other (say, cognitive) difficulties inhibit the translation of people's preferences for new contract types into a market-based demand, market demand cannot delimit the state's obligation. The liberal commitment to personal autonomy as self-authorship requires the state, through its laws, to enable individuals to pursue their own conceptions of the good by *proactively* providing a multiplicity of options for interpersonal interaction.

Choice theory claims that, other things being equal, multiplicity of types is conducive to autonomy. But it acknowledges of course that at times more choice may be autonomy-reducing, and therefore concludes that 'an unqualified call for multiplicity should be rejected'. Indeed, Heller and I point out four main concerns that may require limiting multiplicity: (1) people's cognitive constraints imply that if there are too many distinct types, multiplicity might curtail their effective choice; (2) multiplicity may trigger boundary disputes arising from

---

40 See R.E. Scott and J.S. Kraus, *Contract Law and Theory*, 5th ed., LexisNexis, New Providence, 2013, pp. 184–86.

41 See H. Dagan and M.A. Heller, *The Canon of Contract Law* (unpublished manuscript).

ex post opportunistic manoeuvring; (3) in some market structures – notably, markets for unskilled workers in times of non-negligible unemployment – multiplicity might undermine the autonomy of weak parties rather than, as usual, augmenting it; and (4) certain contract types may be particularly vulnerable to the risk of interest group rent seeking, which might yield autonomy-reducing consequences. These concerns are important and require refinements of choice theory's broad multiplicity injunction, but there is no reason to suspect that they are all-encompassing in a way that would have overwhelmed its normative significance.[42] Therefore, in sharp contrast to the reactive and monist prescriptions of consent theory, a contract law that adheres to Nozick's vision of utopia must adopt the proactive and pluralist injunctions of choice theory.

In *The Choice Theory of Contracts*, Heller and I sketch the contours of a legal regime which takes this responsibility seriously. The gist of our claim is that a liberal contract law should support choice within each familiar category of human activity, such that within each sphere law provides enough and sufficiently distinctive contract types. Defining what constitutes an 'adequate range of options' within any given contracting sphere – namely what is the optimal number of contract types and what is the optimal variance among them – is a complex task, which should rely, at least to an extent, on empirical facts regarding people's choice mechanisms. But the core guideline is normative: for contract types to be autonomy-enhancing they need to be *partial functional substitutes* for each other. 'They need to be substitutes because choice is not enhanced with alternatives that are orthogonal to each other; and their substitutability should not be too complete because types that are too similar also do not offer meaningful choice'.[43]

This means that although the distinction between different terms and different types is imprecise,[44] changes in terms create a new contract type only once they imply the addition of a significant alternative category of interpersonal interaction structured around a distinct (and robust) animating principle.[45] A proper taxonomy of contract types, in turn, implies that 'the classification of the contract as a particular type generates a set of abstract expectations as to what is central to that contract'.[46] Finally, a particularly attractive strategy for

---

42 H. Dagan and M.A. Heller, above n. 1, pp. 127–30.

43 H. Dagan and M.A. Heller, above n. 1, pp. 97, 106–07. Conceptualising contract types along these lines answers Hugh Collins' concern regarding the legitimacy of a contract law, which (appropriately, in his view) resists 'the universalizing tendency of formal logical rationality to apply the same rules to every type of transaction' and sets up different rules 'according to the category of contract'. H. Collins, *Regulating Contracts*, Oxford University Press, New York 1999, pp. 78, 181.

44 See O. Bar-Gill and C.P. Gillette, 'On the Optimal Number of Contract Types' (2019) 20 *Theoretical Inquiries L.* 487, 490.

45 H. Dagan and M.A. Heller, above n. 1, pp. 98–99.

46 C. McCrudden, *Buying Social Justice: Equality, Government Procurement, & Legal Change*, Oxford University Press, New York 2007, p. 529.

enriching the existing contract types repertoire of a given sphere is to 'proactively look out for innovations – such as those based on minority views and utopian theories – that have some traction but would fail if left to people's own devices'.[47]

Indeed, implementing choice theory is not a straightforward matter. Quite the contrary; it raises complicated challenges.[48] I briefly mentioned two substantive challenges: choice theory requires both to address the reasons that may make additional contract types autonomy-reducing, rather than autonomy-enhancing, and to (roughly) figure out how many contract types would work best for each sphere and what should their variance be. Another set of challenges, to which I now turn, relates to the institutional allocation of labour regarding the creation of contract types.

4. THE INSTITUTIONAL CHALLENGE

The Choice Theory of Contracts addresses both the substantive and the institutional challenges. But because Oren Bar-Gill and Clayton Gillette's recent critique of our book significantly enriches the institutional analysis, it is advisable to elaborate a bit more on this front. Doing so in this chapter, which is dedicated to enlisting students of Nozick's vision of utopia, is particularly called for given the suspicion of Nozick's followers towards state institutions.

The institutional question Heller and I posed in our book was triggered by familiar concerns about the capacities of legal institutions – notably generalist courts – to create good rules for sophisticated commercial parties.[49] We did not doubt that such parties are more competent for the task than are competing legal institutions. We argued, however, that there is no reason to extrapolate from the commercial context more devastating conclusions, implying that no legal institutions are sufficiently competent to implement choice theory. Rather, 'implementing choice theory is a matter of comparative institutional

---

47 H. Dagan and M.A. Heller, above n. 1, p. 116.

48 For the purposes of this chapter, I limit the discussion to the implementation difficulties of choice theory's prescription of intra-sphere multiplicity. Other challenges of this autonomy-based account of contract – notably identifying the proper ways of addressing possible detrimental implications of contract law for the autonomy of the parties' future self, and of limiting the use of contract law's coercive power to interactions that comply with its ultimate justification of reciprocal respect to self-determination – must wait for another occasion. See H. Dagan and M. Heller, 'Specific Performance', available at https://papers.ssrn.com/sol3/papers.cfm?abstract_id=3647336; H. Dagan and O. Somech, 'When Contract's Basic Assumptions Fail: From Rose 2d to COVID-19', (2011) *Can. J.L. & Juris. (Canadian Journal of Law and Jurisprudence)*; H. Dagan and A. Dorfman, 'Justice for Contracts', available at https://papers.ssrn.com/sol3/papers.cfm?abstract_id=3435781.

49 See A. Schwartz and R.E. Scott, 'The Political Economy of Private Legislatures' (1995) 143 *U. Pa. L. R. (University of Pennsylvania Law Review)* 559; A. Schwartz and R.E. Scott, 'The Common Law of Contract and the Default Rule Project' (2016) 102 *Va. L. Rev.* 1523.

competence', so that while 'in the commercial sphere ... private parties [are likely] to dominate contract type creation ... in the family and employment spheres, other, more public actors, may take the lead.' Even in these spheres, legal institutions are surely not perfect for the task. But they are, or at least likely to be, better suited than the contracting parties.[50]

The Choice Theory of Contracts offers some preliminary thoughts on possible strategies for coping with concerns of institutional competence – referring to what we called the comparative, the experimental, and the incremental strategies – alongside some examples, such as the judicial recognition of cohabitation,[51] which show 'the significant compliance (though imperfect and insufficient) of evolving contract law with the obligation to support multiplicity.' We acknowledged that much more work needs to be done on this front, noting that 'full answers will inevitably be linked to a particular contract type or a specific state or national institutional design.'[52]

Bar-Gill and Gillette add to this institutional analysis an important dimension by focusing on considerations of political economy.[53] They are justifiably concerned with the 'traditional rosy story of government', which 'treats government actors as cognizant of and motivated by (1) a widely shared view of the public interest, (2) the extent to which market failures inhibit achievement of that public interest, and (3) the tools and political will necessary to implement policies that align with that interest.' Bar-Gill and Gillette conclude that 'Dagan and Heller's faith in governmental processes to develop contract types is overstated', since we are not sufficiently sensitive to 'the public good nature of governance', which implies the endemic collective action problems of government intervention.[54]

At times, these problems imply that government might undersupply contract types by either 'affirmatively suppressing contract types that the market would create' or failing 'to produce a contract type that the market fails to generate, and that government is uniquely positioned to produce.' A parallel, and for Bar-Gill and Gillette 'greater concern', is one of oversupply of contract types,

---

50 H. Dagan and M.A. Heller, above n. 1, pp. 128, 131.

51 There are quite a few other examples of contract-type innovations, which are by now part of the contract canon, that we have not addressed in our book, such as outputs and requirement contracts. See UCC §2-306; see also S. Smith, 'A New Approach to the Identification and Enforcement of Open Quality Contracts: Reforming the Law of Exclusivity and Good Faith' (2009) *Val. U.L. Rev. (Valparaiso University Law Review)* 871, 879–933.

52 H. Dagan and M.A. Heller, above n. 1, pp. 15, 132.

53 Bar-Gill and Gillette also address the issue of competence, arguing that 'government would generally lack the access to information necessary to identify the optimal number of contract types.' O. Bar-Gill and C.P. Gillette, above n. 44, p. 487. I do not underestimate the significance of this task – see text accompanying n. 43 – but the evident undersupply of contract types in the non-commercial spheres of contracting on which choice theory's prescription focuses makes this concern premature.

54 O. Bar-Gill and C.P. Gillette, above n. 44, p. 487.

either 'because interest groups with disproportionate access to the [pertinent] agency ... lobby for an excessive number of types' or because 'individuals in those agencies have incentives to create them in order to demonstrate to clients (congressmen, interest groups) or to superiors within the agency that they are performing their assigned function.' (Bar-Gill and Gillette are worried about oversupply because an 'excessively large number of contract types' is inefficient as it tends to reduce the positive externality of comparison-shopping and thus to dilute the forces of competition;[55] oversupply may also, as I have noted,[56] undermine autonomy given people's cognitive constraints.) Finally, even if government actors may produce contract types optimal in quantity, 'government intervention could cause suboptimal terms to be part of a contract type'.[57]

Bar-Gill and Gillette do not ignore that institutional inquiries are always comparative. They fully realise that the alternative to government involvement is leaving the task to the market and that this alternative is also far from being perfect. Indeed, Bar-Gill and Gillette agree with choice theory's premise[58] that 'standard market failures might cause markets to produce a suboptimal number of contract types', although they also show that these failures at times may push in the opposite direction, resulting in the provision of too many contract types. But Bar-Gill and Gillette are still worried that the political economy consideration they highlight may suggest that government involvement 'might do more harm than good'. Thus, they conclude that whereas the lack of an 'ideal mechanism' for implementing choice theory 'does not deny [its] efficacy', we need to be careful not to replace 'market failure with government failure' that 'replicate[s], rather than cure[s], the shortcomings of markets'.[59]

Point well taken. Adding political economy considerations to the comparative analysis of the expected performance of the pertinent institutions is surely important and there may well be contexts in which the expected shortcomings of government agencies would imply that we may be better off leaving the task to the market, notwithstanding its deficiencies. This conclusion justifies Bar-Gill and Gillette's 'cautionary note'.[60] But nothing in this note is different from parallel concerns of 'government failure' regarding the numerous other contexts in which agencies are currently involved. And yet, the least controversial set of justifications for regulation by governmental agencies includes various types of market failures, that is, cases in which for reasons like monopolies or anti-competitive behaviour, externalities or public goods, or informational inadequacies, an 'uncontrolled marketplace' is likely to 'fail to produce

55 Ibid., p. 492.
56 See above text accompanying n. 42.
57 O. Bar-Gill and C.P. Gillette, above n. 44, p. 487.
58 H. Dagan and M.A. Heller, above n. 1, p. 115.
59 O. Bar-Gill and C.P. Gillette, above n. 44, p. 487.
60 Ibid., p. 487.

behaviour or results in accordance with the public interest'.[61] Whereas the rosy story of government[62] must indeed be rejected, I see no reason for substituting it with a particularly gloomy story, in general, and certainly not in the context of supplying contract types.[63]

Furthermore, when Heller and I refer to the responsibility of legal institutions to contract's autonomy-enhancing *telos*, we do not limit our account to agencies. Quite the contrary, we mentioned a long list of pertinent legal actors, highlighting 'courts or legislatures – the ordinary contract lawmakers in liberal societies'. One (relatively) happy story of choice theory manifestation we discussed is the judicial creation of the law of cohabitation that structures 'a distinct contract type which helps stabilise relationships of long-term informal intimacy between marriage and, say, roommates'. Courts' responsiveness to 'an emerging – albeit minoritarian – innovation', we argued, is laudable from an autonomy-enhancing perspective especially given the 'failure of cohabitants to gain legislative recognition', which 'may be best explained by a collective action and political economy story'.[64]

The case of cohabitation may suggest a seemingly surprising but potentially important conclusion. Recall that the engagement of *The Choice Theory of Contracts* with the institutional question was aimed at delimiting the incompetence critique of legal actors – in particular judges – to the commercial context.[65] Bar-Gill and Gillette's focus on political economy implies that, at least in contexts where generalist judges do not suffer from this difficulty – namely the three contracting spheres to which choice theory's injunction of proactively facilitating multiplicity is particularly significant: work, housing, and intimacy[66] – courts should play a particularly important role in implementing choice theory.[67] This conclusion nicely fits the common law tradition in which much of private law is the result of continuous law-making judicial activity.[68] It also fortifies the claim that, notwithstanding Bar-Gill and Gillette's important cautionary note,

61 R. Baldwin et al., *Understanding Regulation: Theory, Strategy, and Practice*, 2nd ed., Oxford University Press, New York 2012, p. 15. For other justifications, see H. Dagan and R. Kreitner, 'The Other Half of Regulatory Theory' (2020) 52 *Conn. L. Rev. (Connecticut Law Review)* 605.

62 See above text accompanying n. 54.

63 See S.P. Croley, *Regulation and Public Interests: The Possibility of Good Regulatory Government*, Princeton University Press, Princeton 2007.

64 H. Dagan and M.A. Heller, above n. 1, pp. 130, 132.

65 See above text accompanying n. 49.

66 H. Dagan and M.A. Heller, above n. 1, ch.11.

67 I do not deny that even in these spheres the private law of contract types may require regulatory support. See H. Dagan and M.A. Heller, above n. 1, pp. 76–78.

68 See e.g. M.A. Eisenberg, 'Principles of Legal Reasoning in the Common Law' in D.E. Edlin (ed.), *Common Law Theory*, Cambridge University Press, New York 2007, pp. 81, 82. I defend in some detail the role of judges in the development of private law elsewhere. See H. Dagan, 'Judges and Property' in S. Balganesh (ed.), *Intellectual Property and the Common Law*, Cambridge University Press, New York 2013, p. 17.

'[t]here is room to implement choice theory such that contract law does a better job than the status quo in enhancing people's self-determination'.[69]

5. CONCLUDING REMARKS

Liberals, especially of the Nozickian stripe, are accustomed to think about the ideal contract law as both reactive and minimalist. The best way contract law can serve freedom, they assume, is by following the parties' consent, that is, enforce whatever private deals they agree to and otherwise get out of the way. Drawing on Nozick's vision of utopia as a framework of utopias, this chapter argues that this view, in which contract law should adopt such a hands-off stance, is misguided and accordingly that the consent theory of contracts should be rejected. In its stead, liberals should opt for choice theory, which focuses on how contract law can, should, and to some extent already does facilitate people's autonomy. I do not underestimate the challenges, both substantive and institutional, choice theory must face. But there is no reason to think that these challenges are insurmountable; and facing them is worthwhile once we appreciate contract's moral significance of giving free individuals 'a facility for extending their reach by enlisting the reliable collaboration of other free persons'.[70]

---

69 H. Dagan and M.A. Heller, above n. 1, p. 15.

70 C. Fried, 'The Ambitions of Contract as Promise' in G. Klass, G. Letsas and P. Saprai (eds.), *Philosophical Foundations of Contract*, Oxford University Press, New York 2014, pp. 17, 20. Recently, Fried embraced choice theory's prescription of facilitating contract types. See C. Fried, 'Contract as Promise: Lessons Learned' (2019) 20 *Theoretical Inquiries L.* 367.

LEGISLATIVE OPTIONS FOR REGULATING OPTIONAL RULES

Lorenz KAEHLER

1. OPTIONS CREATED BY DEFAULT RULES

Every default rule creates an option for both parties that negotiate a contract. They can either stick to the default rule or choose an alternative one. Which rights and duties they have depends in this respect exclusively upon them. This opportunity to choose constitutes an option which the parties can exercise. Without the default, the situation would be different. There would be either a mandatory rule that applies in any case or a gap which still has to be filled. The parties' choice would in any event not matter. In contrast, with a default rule they have at least two opportunities from which they can choose according to their interests.

With the help of default rules the parties do not need to negotiate their agreement in detail. Instead, they can formulate an agreement, even about a huge construction project, on one DIN A4 page without risking it being invalid due to indeterminacy. This was, at least in Germany, for many years a widespread practice and is occasionally even practised nowadays.[1] Without default rules in the background, this would be impossible and the parties would have to make detailed agreements to avoid indeterminacy and the risk of major contingencies

---

1 For the growth of contracts in Germany see G. LANGENFELD, *Vertragsgestaltung*, Beck, Munich 2004, p. 80; for the common law see T. LUNDMARK, 'Verbose Contracts' (2001) 49 *American Journal of Comparative Law* 121, 130; C. HILL and C. KING, 'How Do German Contracts Do As Much with Fewer Words?' (2004) 79 *Chicago-Kent Law Review* 889.

not being provided for. The opportunity to conclude a contract without a thorough negotiation of the details hence rests on default rules. Such rules give the parties an option to either make their own determination or to rely on the default. This option is even important when the parties opt out of the default and choose their own rules. For the proposal to opt out might reveal valuable information to the other or a third party.[2]

Accordingly, by making a certain rule mandatory the legislator abolishes an option. The parties can no longer choose between various states of affairs but have to stick to the predetermined rule. Nevertheless, mandatory rules can also create an option by giving one of the parties the right to choose between different predetermined states of affairs. Various EU Directives, for instance, foresee a mandatory right of withdrawal[3] for the consumer within two weeks of the conclusion of a contract. The consumer thus gets an option to withdraw, no matter what the parties agreed to. Therefore, the choice between mandatory and default rules is not identical with the choice between optional and non-optional rules. But mandatory rules in any case limit the options the parties would otherwise have. Once a rule becomes mandatory, the parties are unable to make an alternative rule part of their contract.

This consequence is crucial for understanding the justificatory burden of a mandatory rule. Because a mandatory rule constrains freedom of contract, for it to be legitimate it is not enough to demonstrate that it fairly and efficiently distributes rights and duties. For even if such a distribution is achieved, the question remains why it should be forced upon the parties and why the parties shall not have the right to choose a suboptimal rule. Moreover, it is already questionable whether a certain mandatory rule can contain the best distribution of rights and duties for all circumstances such that it would lead in all situations to the best possible outcome. For a mandatory rule excludes not only some but all possible alternative rules, and it does so not only for some but for all situations. Therefore, for it to be legitimate one has to show that either there is no conceivable situation in which an alternative rule would be superior or that one could not allow the parties to choose such a rule because of a possible abuse of this right in other situations.

The former condition that there is no rule preferable in at least one situation is difficult to fulfil because one can hardly show that a certain rule is ideal for all constellations, such that its mandatory character would never prevent one from finding a better one. One cannot know in advance the manifold situations

---

2 I. Ayres and R. Gertner, 'Filling Gaps in Incomplete Contracts: an Economic Theory of Default Rules' (1989) 99 *Yale Law Journal (Yale LJ)* 87, 107.

3 Art. 6 of Directive 2002/65/EC of the European Parliament and of the Council of 23 September 2002 concerning the distance marketing of consumer financial services [2002] OJ L271/16; Art. 9 of Directive 2011/83/EU of the European Parliament and of the Council of 25 October 2011 on consumer rights [2011] OJ L304/64.

in which private law applies and estimate the interests involved that are crucial for determining whether a rule is best. This is especially true of abstract contract rules that apply in very different environments and areas, from the purchase of a takeaway coffee to the purchase of a whole company. The analysis of typical interests and of typical bargaining power does not help in this regard either, because it is confined to typical situations and does not deal with all situations. So it is almost impossible to prove that a certain contract rule is ideal in all situations and that no alternative rule is ever preferable. The legislator is hence confronted with a high threshold before adopting a mandatory rule. By prohibiting an opt-out completely, he excludes any other rule that the parties could choose, even though this rule might turn out to be optimal for some situations.

A mandatory rule can thus hardly be justified by the idealness of its content. Instead one has to justify it with the potential abuse of the freedom to opt out from it. Then the argument is not that the predetermined rule is always superior, but that the possibility to opt out from it would in many situations lead to a worse result, so that it is on balance better to prevent an opt-out completely. One trades the possible advantage of an opt-out in some situations against the possible disadvantage in other situations. The latter situation might occur especially if one of the parties does not completely realise the impact of the opt-out or if the other side has the greater bargaining power and can force the rule preferred by him upon his counterparty. Then the weaker party has to accept the opt-out or be denied the conclusion of the contract completely. At first glance, an imbalance of bargaining power and the aim of protecting consumers seems thus to justify the mandatoriness of private law rules. At least, various EU Directives and Regulations for the protection of the consumer follow this line of justification.[4]

However, the argument presented is far from conclusive because it is, at least in some cases, possible to protect consumers by designing protective default rules. Such rules might shape expectations that are difficult to overcome and thus influence standards like good faith, imbalance of rights and duties, and immorality. Moreover, default rules might be accompanied by the duty to inform the consumer about his rights and duties, such that the lack of information is no longer a reason to prohibit an opt-out. So the necessity alone to protect one of the parties does not always suffice to justify a mandatory rule. Instead, one has to analyse the particular rule and balance the pros and cons of designing it as a default or a mandatory one. This has been extensively discussed elsewhere.[5] Less attention has been paid to the fact that the legislator is not confronted with the simple choice to either make a certain rule mandatory or not.

4 Recital 32 of Directive 2002/65/EC, above n. 3; recital 6 of Directive 2011/83/EU, above n. 3.

5 See references in L. Kähler, *Begriff und Rechtfertigung abdingbaren Rechts*, Mohr Siebeck, Tübingen 2012, pp. 360–437.

Such a choice and the discussion about it misleadingly suggest that no other choice could be made when designing default rules.

Yet such a choice does exist. In the regulation of private law it is not only important whether a certain rule shall be mandatory or not, but what content the rule shall have in the first place. In this regard, a much greater variety of rules that could be adopted frequently exist than the mere choice between one mandatory and one default rule. Most of the time, there are various mandatory and default rules, as well as their combinations, which the legislator could adopt to regulate a certain question. His choice is hence much broader. He can adopt the rule that the parties would have agreed to,[6] the rule that would be market-mimicking[7] or fair, or the rule that best accounts for the plurality of aims[8] underlying private law.

In addition, the legislator can also regulate the way an opt-out is carried out and the possible alternatives the parties can choose. The legislator is hence not forced to either recognise an unlimited freedom of contract or to reduce the various contractual agreements to only one. Instead, he can also limit and shape the parties' choices without abolishing them completely. In order to shed more light on this question, the following chapter shall sketch out four different opportunities for such regulations. They all enhance the choices the legislator has and help to preserve the freedom of contract to some degree, while at the same time also helping to protect the interests of both parties by excluding some agreements.

All of this is not to support the suggestion sometimes made that between mandatory and default rules there are other categories of semi-default, half- or 'three-quarters-mandatory' rules, etc.[9] In whatever way the opt-out procedure and the possible default rules are shaped, one can always decide whether the parties have, at least under some conditions and to some degree, the freedom to opt out of a certain rule. If this is the case, the rule is a default one; if this is not the case, it is a mandatory one. Therefore, it is possible to categorise rules as either mandatory or default. But this should not lead to the assumption that one can only choose between the mandatoriness of a certain rule and its default character. The classification of rules by a binary conceptual scheme does not exclude the possibility that within a certain category like 'default rule' a lot of subcategories exist. Moreover, the legislator can adapt as well as combine various rules. In particular, instead of making a certain default rule mandatory, he can also regulate the option created by it.

---

6 F. Easterbrook and D. Fischel, 'The Corporate Contract' (1989) 89 *Columbia Law Review* 1416, 1445.

7 R. Korobkin, 'The Status Quo Bias and Contract Default Rules' (1998) 83 *Cornell Law Review* 608, 669.

8 L. Kähler, above n. 5, p. 305.

9 I. Ayres and R. Gertner, 'Strategic Contractual Inefficiency and the Optimal Choice of Legal Rules' (1992) 101 *Yale LJ* 729, 743; M. Hesselink, 'Non-Mandatory Rules in European Contract Law' (2005) 1 *European Review of Contract Law* 44, 60.

For this reason, it is important to understand the options the legislator has when regulating private law. Only when the picture of possible choices is complete can he make a rational decision which rule to adopt. Otherwise the danger prevails of prematurely making a certain rule mandatory only because of the potential for abuse in some situations. The legislator should also consider protecting the interests of the weaker party by restricting the opt-out only to cases where such an abuse occurs. If this is possible, the potential abuse no longer justifies excluding an opt-out completely.

This is important not only for the legislator but also for judges in the event that they have to decide whether a certain rule is a mandatory or a default one. When this question is left open in a certain statute, the judge has to have resort to general considerations similar to the ones of the legislator. He or she also then needs a complete picture of the regulatory options in order to rationally decide which alternative fits best with the general principles of contract law of the particular legal system. For instance, instead of declaring a certain rule non-mandatory, a judge can also set out conditions for the opt-out or an opt-in. It is thus worthwhile having a closer look at the possible regulations of default rules. In the following I will first consider the conditions of the opt-out in more detail (sections 2–3), before turning to the regulation of the opt-in rules (sections 4–5).

2. OPT-OUT CONDITIONS

Opt-out conditions set out the circumstances in which the parties to a contract can deviate from the default. Apart from the minimal condition that an agreement about a certain question has been reached, there can be various other conditions that must be met before an opt-out is accepted.

Ayres and others have called such conditions 'altering rules',[10] which suggests that these rules are different from the altered rule. Opt-out conditions could indeed be constructed as separate rules, if one distinguishes between the primary rule about the subject matter and the secondary rule about the applicability of the primary rule. The secondary rule can either be formulated in the antecedents of the primary rule ('Unless otherwise agreed, …') or as an independent rule ('The previous rule applies only if …').[11] But this concerns just its formulation, not its conceptual distinction from the primary rule.

---

[10] I. Ayres, 'Regulating Opt-Out: An Economic Theory of Altering Rules' (2012) 121 *Yale LJ* 2032, 2036; L. Willis, 'When Nudges Fail: Slippery Defaults' (2013) 80 *University of Chicago Law Review (U. Chi. L. Rev.)* 1155, 1213.

[11] L. Kähler, above n. 5, p. 19.

For instance, the primary rule that the buyer can claim a reduction of the price if the purchased good is defective and cannot be improved[12] sets out conditions (purchase, defectiveness, lacking improvability) as well as a legal consequence (price reduction), none of which concerns the question whether the parties can opt out of this rule. For this purpose, one needs a secondary rule stating under which conditions a deviating agreement is valid and supersedes the primary rule.

The separation between primary and secondary rules shows that the default rule is not altered by an opt-out. It merely excludes the applicability of the primary rule for one contract. In particular, an opt-out does not change the legal consequences of the default. In a future case, the rule applies unaltered so that the same legal consequences come about, unless the parties again opt out of it. The name 'altering rule' is in this respect misleading.[13] According to the secondary rule, these consequences are confined to the situation where the parties did not opt out of it. Hence, the parties do not alter the rule by an opt-out, as they merely use an opportunity the legislator has provided them. This is an important point because it indicates that an opt-out neither changes the law nor questions the authority of the legislator.

Consider, for instance, a rule for the lease of a residential space according to which the lease agreement applies for an indefinite period of time, unless the parties have agreed on another period in written form.[14] This rule does not prohibit the parties from concluding an oral contract or from foreseeing a limited lease period. But it does set out the additional condition of a written form, without which the time limit will not be valid. It thereby protects not only the tenant, who is warned by a written declaration of the time limit, but also third parties who later acquire the property and are then bound by the lease agreement even though they did not negotiate it. These third parties can then rely on a written text and thus better estimate how long they will be bound.[15] So instead of making the unlimited period of time for a lease agreement mandatory, the legislator can protect the interests of tenants and third parties by requiring that certain conditions for an opt-out are fulfilled.

More generally, opt-out conditions do not create obligations the parties have to fulfil. No party can require the other to comply with these conditions. But in order to deviate from the default, they have to meet these conditions. The force

---

12 Cf. Art. 3(2) of Directive 1999/44/EC of the European Parliament and of the Council of 25 May 1999 on certain aspects of the sale of consumer goods and associated guarantees [1999] OJ L171/12.

13 Cf. I. Ayres, above n. 10, p. 2036, mentioning that he was 'almost convinced' to change the name to 'displacing' rule.

14 This is a simplified version of §550 German Civil Code (BGB).

15 §566 BGB.

created by the conditions is therefore an indirect one and the rule is in this sense 'soft law'. But it is at the same time part of the binding law and entails a clear sanction: unless the conditions are met, the opt-out is not recognised and any alternative rules chosen by the parties remain invalid. In this sense, opt-out conditions are not merely soft law in the sense of recommendations or a nudge,[16] but rather 'hard law'.

Opt-out conditions impose a cost for the parties who wish to use an alternative rule. Not just any agreement will suffice because the conditions have to be met. For instance, formulating an exact time for the end of the lease in a written agreement is more cumbersome than mentioning it orally. The opt-out costs could be offset by higher costs that arise under the default rule for the implementation of the contract. For instance, it might be easier for judges and third parties to recognise the parties' will in a written document rather than in an oral agreement in order that fewer mistakes in its recognition will be made. But opt-out conditions might also lead to greater costs, especially if the parties fail to comply with them. Then a default rule applies which does not fit the parties' interests.

Opt-out conditions might in some situations also be justified by the prevention of externalities to third parties. In such a situation, the parties have to bear the costs in order to save expenses for a third party. In the example of the form-clause for limited lease agreements above, the landlord and the tenant have to make the effort to put their agreement in writing in order that future owners of the property can better understand their rights and duties. The justification for this then depends on the difficult estimation of which costs are higher overall: the costs of meeting the opt-out conditions or the costs saved after meeting these conditions. Even more controversial is the justification for opt-out conditions when it consists in preventing the parties from choosing the wrong rule.[17] In this case, the legislator creates a hurdle for opting out because he distrusts the parties' choice and paternalistically assumes that he knows better than the parties which rule would be optimal for their particular contract.

Due to opt-out conditions, default rules become more sticky than they already are.[18] Compared with a situation in which any alternative agreement suffices for an opt-out, it becomes more difficult under such conditions to deviate from the standard set by the legislator. The degree to which the stickiness is increased depends on the particular conditions of the default rule. They can vary considerably, from easy-to-fulfil conditions, like the usage of a certain

---

16 Contrary to that, C. Sunstein, 'Deciding by Default' (2013) 162 *University of Pennsylvania Law Review* 1, 5 regards default rules as 'canonical nudges'.

17 I. Ayres, above n. 10, pp. 2084–2088.

18 There are several explanations for the stickiness: see C. Sunstein, above n. 16, p. 17; for mechanisms to inhibit the stickiness see L. Willis, above n. 10, p. 1174.

expression[19] or presenting it in a certain frame,[20] to conditions that are very costly, like notarisation.

Due to the hurdle created by opt-out conditions, a default rule can have considerable influence. The legislator can use it as an instrument for his purposes, as he can make sure that the opt-out is valid only rarely. Consequently, his decision to establish it in one way or another has to be taken seriously. It is not trivial, although the parties can deviate from it. Against this background, the position of the ECJ to give only binding provisions an indicative value for a principle of Community law becomes questionable.[21] For this suggests that defaults are made erratically so that no principles can be derived from them, which can hardly be assumed, given the great significance they have. Moreover, this position overlooks the fact that traditional contract law mainly consists in default rules and can nevertheless entail principles like 'no duty to pay damages caused without fault'.

Opt-out conditions can be of various kinds. They can, for instance, require certain information without which an opt-out is not accepted. So they might require notifying the other party that the liability foreseen deviates from the statutory standard.[22] In this case, the other party gets the valuable information that the legislator considers another form of liability adequate, meaning that this party thus has a reason to investigate whether the risk is acceptable. If this information is insufficient for the intended protection of interests, it might in addition be required that the other party also has to be informed about the possibility of obtaining insurance.[23] In this way, the party knows not only that the agreement differs from the default, but also what has to be done to reach a similar result. Interestingly, no minimal content of the agreed-upon rule is required in this case and it is merely an information condition that has to be fulfilled.

If a certain minimum content of the default rule has to be preserved, the opt-out conditions can be made even stricter. One might create the additional condition that an opt-out will only be accepted if it stays within a certain range of rules, for example a corridor of liability[24] limitations. In this way, one can ensure that a certain liability prevails even though no particular liability rule is prescribed. By making such opt-out conditions stricter, the legislator can gradually increase

19 See for the branding of opt-in rules, S. Pellegrino, 'Branding Pro-Consumer Contracts: Developing a New Consumer Protection Technique in Light of the CESL Proposal' [2015] *Journal of European Consumer and Market Law* 3, 8.

20 L. Willis, above n. 10, p. 1173.

21 Case C-101/08, *Audiolux v. Groupe Bruxelles Lambert, Bertelsmann and Others*, ECLI:EU:C:2009:626, para. 34. Such a view accords with U. Mattei, 'Hard Code Now!' (2002) 2(1) *Global Jurist Frontiers,* article 1.

22 E.g. §451h(2) sentence 2 of the German Commercial Code (HGB).

23 This comes close to the conditions of §451g number 1 HGB.

24 Cf. §449(2) number 1 HGB.

the impact of the underlying default rule.[25] These conditions can range from minimal conditions like the comprehensibility of the chosen rule up to severe requirements like notarisation.

Opt-out conditions are especially important in the context of European contract law, which pursues aims that sometimes contradict each other. On the one hand, European contract law furthers the single market with the free movement of goods and services (Art. 3(3) TEU). For this purpose, it is best if the sellers of goods can rely on the contract law of their home country, without having to comply with the law of the other Member States. After all, it is a considerable hurdle to adapt one's terms to 27 different legal orders. This would be an argument for allowing easy opt-outs from otherwise applicable rules. On the other hand, the EU also wants to promote the interests of consumers and to ensure a high level of consumer protection (Art. 168(1) TFEU). This purpose requires the consumer to be able to rely on the law of his home country and not to have to study foreign law in order to buy a product from a seller in another Member State. So for the consumer it seems necessary that the seller should adapt to the conditions of the state where the consumer lives.

The dominant approach of European law to this tension between a single market and the protection of consumers has so far been to create mandatory rules that apply throughout the EU, at the strongest in case of full harmonisation in which the Member States can in no way modify or supplement the adopted rule.[26] In this case, not only are Member States not allowed to create their own default rules in the regulated area, but also private parties cannot opt out of them. Mandatory uniform rules of this type have been introduced by the Doorstep Selling Directive 85/577/EEC, the Distance Selling Directive 97/7/EC and, most importantly, the Sale of Consumer Goods and Associated Guarantees Directive 99/44/EC. In each case, mandatory rules were promoted in order to create a single market and protect consumers.

Unfortunately, as a result the parties have in many areas hardly been left any freedom to adapt their contract to their specific needs. For instance, when one party buys vegetables on the street from another party, without any documentation of the transaction, and where the parties only encounter each other accidently, the buyer can still, under current EU law, even one and a half years after the conclusion of the contract demand new vegetables if some of the vegetables he or she bought were mouldy at the time of the sale.[27] There is currently no way to opt out of this rule (although this was possible before the Consumer Goods Directive was implemented). Today, the parties cannot reach any other valid agreement on a shorter period because the consumer rights in this field are mandatory.[28]

---

25 I. Ayres, above n. 10, p. 2087.

26 For an endorsement of this movement see U. Mattei, above 21.

27 Art. 5(1) of Directive 1999/44/EC, above 12.

28 Art. 7(1) of Directive 1999/44/EC, above 12.

With opt-out conditions, the situation would be different. These conditions could ensure that the interests of the consumer are preserved even though an opt-out takes place. For instance, it would be possible to create a condition where the parties could opt out of the two-year limitation period only if they agree upon a limitation period that is not shorter than the lifecycle of the goods being sold. It would then be possible to alter the two-year limitation period in relation to vegetables, whereas it would remain intact in relation to cars.

Even the tension between the creation of the single market and the protection of consumers could be eased by opt-out conditions. One could, for instance, allow the parties to opt out of the remedies for lack of conformity of the goods sold, if the buyer receives sufficient compensation. Such compensation could, for instance, consist in a standardised European guarantee that gives the buyer a right against a third party in the event that the good is damaged. In this case, the consumer who buys a certain good can rely on the guarantee, which, due to standardisation, would have the same content throughout Europe. The seller, however, after acquiring the guarantee from the third party, could modify the remedies in the contract and adapt them to his business model, which could include the possible reliance on the law of his Member State. Then the consumer's uncertainty as to the rights he has against the seller would be compensated for by the guarantee against the third party, which would have to meet minimum requirements like a certain degree of solvency. In this respect, the guarantee resembles a form of insurance against damages. So instead of making consumer sales law mandatory and curbing innovation of new sales terms, the opt-in condition of a European guarantee could ensure the necessary protection of consumer interests.

A European guarantee would, of course, increase the costs of the sale and many sellers would prefer to stick to the default rules rather than make a modified offer that includes such a guarantee. But because the parties are not obliged to offer a guarantee, these additional costs do not necessarily burden the parties. On the contrary, compared to mandatory rules, such an option, at least in some situations, saves costs. This is the case when the guarantee is cheaper for the seller than the fulfilment and handling of the remedies. Such situation arises especially if the guarantor, but not the seller, deals with a high number of complaints, so that it is efficient for the guarantor, unlike the seller, to create the infrastructure to handle them.

Opt-out conditions might in this way replace secondary rules that make contract rules mandatory.

3. OPTION OFFERS

An especially interesting form of opt-out condition is an option offer made by one party. The other party can decline it, accept it without modification, or accept it with the modification that a certain default rule is chosen. As far as the default is concerned, it is totally up to the other party to determine the contract's content. Therefore, this party will be called in the following the 'choosing party' and distinguished from the 'offering party'. Usually, a modified acceptance does not suffice for the conclusion of a contract, because the offering party has to consent to the modification. Therefore, in modifying an offer a party takes the risk that no contract will be concluded if the offering party does not accept the modification. But if the law provides for an option offer in the case of a proposed opt-out, the situation is different. Then the offer and its modification suffice for the conclusion of the contract. It is merely the decision of the choosing party whether an opt-out occurs.

With an option offer, the choosing party has three possibilities: he or she can decline the offer that includes an opt-out from a particular default rule, accept the offer with the opt-out, or accept the offer but stick to the default. Thus, the choosing party is not forced to accept the opt-out. Instead, he or she has the option to decline it and nevertheless conclude the contract. To provide an option offer, the law has to declare sufficient an acceptance in which the choosing party modifies the offer by returning to a certain default. An alternative way to construe it is to understand the option offer as a consent with two versions of a certain contract. The law might make the acceptance of a particular opt-out conditional on such an option offer.

With an option offer, the parties can find alternative rules that fit their purposes better than the default rule, without neglecting the interests of the choosing party. For this party is not forced to accept the opt-out. The offering party can propose a whole menu of possible rules, as long as the default rule is one of them. Like other menus of rules,[29] this enhances opportunities. The opportunity to choose the statutory default signals to the choosing party the importance and the legislator's endorsement[30] of this rule and thus indicates that opting out from it is risky.

The offering party might attach different prices to the menus of rules from which the other party can choose. Thus, the costs associated with each rule become transparent. If the default rule is combined with a higher price, whereas the contract with an alternative rule is cheaper, the choosing party has an incentive to opt out. This is especially relevant in cases in which the default rule causes high costs such that the parties should have the opportunity to find an alternative arrangement, instead of being forced into an inefficient contract. Option offers are among the arrangements in which one party decides on the alternatives and the other party chooses from among them. Such dual-choice

---

29 I. Ayres, 'Menus Matter' (2006) 73 *U. Chi. L. Rev.* 3; O. Bar-Gill and O. Ben-Shahar, 'Optimal defaults in consumer markets' (2016) 45 *Journal of Legal Studies* S137, S140.

30 For the endorsement of defaults see C. Sunstein, above n. 16, p. 20; L. Willis, above n. 10, pp. 1168–1169.

arrangements help to adapt the contract to the interests of both parties without forcing one side to submit to the stronger bargaining position of the other.

Such an arrangement would, for instance, be sensible for the right of withdrawal within two weeks which consumers have under European law in relation to the long-distance sale of goods.[31] They can exercise this right even if the purpose of the acquired goods is, like in the case of Christmas decorations, limited to a short period. They can thus withdraw from the contract after having used the goods, pay no or low[32] fees for the usage and thereby practically freeride on the sales of goods, which will be ultimately paid for by third parties. To avoid this kind of abuse, it would be reasonable for one party to be able to make the other an offer either to buy such seasonal goods for a lower price with a reduced withdrawal period of two days, or to keep the two-week withdrawal period for a higher price. This leads to the separation of consumers who are willing to keep the goods from those who either want to return the goods or who are uncertain about them. Consequently, the first group of consumers can be offered a lower price and is no longer forced to subsidise the other group. By including additional requirements, one can make sure that this choice is real. So one might require, for example, that the costs of sticking to the default do not grossly exceed the real costs connected with it and do thus not become prohibitive.

Thanks to option offers, the greater bargaining power of the stronger party does not necessitate the creation of mandatory rules. To avoid the abuse of this power it is enough to shift the choice of rules to the weaker party by letting that party decide whether or not to opt out. This strengthens the latter's position and enhances his or her autonomy because he or she thereby has the choice to accept an opt-out without being forced to do so. Only if this party is unable to make a decision could a mandatory rule excluding such a choice be justified.

An option offer differs from an ordinary default rule even though both include the opportunity for opting out. In the case of an ordinary default rule, one party can make a take-it-or-leave-it offer deviating from the default, so that the other party must accept the opt-out if he or she wants to conclude the contract at all. With an option offer, such a take-it-or-leave-it offer is possible only where the offeree sticks to the default. If he or she wants to deviate from the default, he or she must offer the other party at least two choices, i.e. the default and an alternative to it, so that a take-it-or-leave-it offer is excluded. The parties' unequal bargaining power is thereby compensated for by making the weaker party choose the rules.

Option offers should not be confused with options that give one of the parties a right to choose between two states of affairs once a contract is made. For instance, the already mentioned right of withdrawal in European consumer law[33] is an option to either cancel the contract or to keep it. In contrast, an

[31] Art. 6 of Directive 2002/65/EC, above n. 3.
[32] Art. 7 of Directive 2002/65/EC, above n. 3.
[33] Above n. 3.

option offer expires once the contract is made. It merely gives the choosing party a choice that has to be made at the conclusion of the contract. However, this does not exclude designing the option offer in such a way that an option arises that expires long after the contract is concluded. One might, for instance, give the choosing party the right to decide whether to opt out within a certain period after the conclusion of the contract. The consumer might, for instance, be able to opt for a certain warranty within one month of the conclusion of the contract, but thereby lose a price reduction that was combined with the waiver of the warranty.

Option offers belong to default rules. They always allow, at least under some circumstances, opting out of default rules. The condition that only one of the parties can decide about the opt-out limits the choices, but does not totally abolish them. Option offers are, like other opt-out conditions, a compromise between an unconditional mandatory rule and an unconditional default rule. An autonomy-minded legislator should consider to introduce option offers before declaring a rule mandatory.

4. RESPONSE RULES

One of the most interesting possibilities for regulating contract law concerns response rules. Under these rules, the law accepts an opt-out from a certain default, but at the same time alters its legal consequences. One might construe it as a contract law rule that applies in the event that the parties choose a certain rule. The legislator thereby reacts to the choices of the parties instead of making his own rule obligatory. The advantage of such a response is that he can react in different ways to different opt-outs instead of creating a uniform rule applying in all cases. In this way, the regulation of contracts can be fine-tuned to the particular choices the parties make. In an extreme version, contract law could be personalised in this regard, which would mean that for each party and each situation a different response could be foreseen.[34] It becomes more flexible, as it can adapt to manifold opt-outs without having to create a mandatory rule which uniformly applies. Intriguingly, response rules could also be more flexible than default rules. For the content of an ordinary default rule is stable and does not depend on the parties' choice. It applies uniformly to all contracts and impacts the negotiation. The only question is whether the parties opted out from it. In contrast, response rules can depend upon the choice the parties made.

Take for instance the already mentioned case of a lease agreement for a flat. As a default, it is concluded for an unlimited period of time. If the parties deviate from the default and choose a certain period, like two or three years,

[34] See C. SUNSTEIN, above n. 16, p. 48.

termination is allowed under German law at the earliest one year after the use of the residential space has been permitted.[35] The legislator thereby prevents a situation where a limited lease is shortened even after the conclusion of the contract to less than one year. He does not require that such a termination period of one year has to be observed in all cases. If the lease is for an unlimited time, the contract could be terminated even earlier than one year after the flat has been handed over. Instead, the rule is confined to the situation where the parties initially agreed on a limited lease period. The rationale for such a rule seems to be that if the tenant has, due to the limited lease period, made arrangements in advance, like renting an alternative flat, he or she should not be forced to rearrange them again. The legislator thus merely reacts to what the parties have chosen instead of prescribing the lease period completely.

It is usually easier to design a default that uniformly applies unless the parties have made another choice than one that responds to an unknown choice that the parties have still to make. While the default rule is singular and the opt-out conditions are limited, the opportunities for alternative rules chosen by the parties are virtually unlimited. Accordingly, the reactions to them might vary considerably. There are manifold ways in which an opt-out can be complemented. The regulator can declare part of the opt-in void or merely supplement the legal consequences foreseen by the parties. He might also not react at all to certain choices.

This opportunity to react in different ways explains why response rules are rare, but it does not indicate that they should not be used at all. In comparison to a mandatory rule, they preserve the parties' freedom to choose their own rules, while still protecting the interests of the weaker party by responding in a particular way. Although the possible responses are unlimited, the legislator can confine himself to a few of them or use standards or general conditions to describe a necessary response. Conditions like 'a significant abbreviation of a certain right' are, for instance, standard-like and can cover many situations. Despite the large number of possible opt-outs, one hence does not need an equally large number of response rules in order to regulate contracts.

Response rules might have the advantage, in comparison to opt-out conditions, that they apply even if the parties did not foresee them in the opt-out. The parties do not have to meet certain conditions because their choice is accepted at the first stage, whatever its content is, and only modified at the second stage. Unlike with default rules, the parties are not pushed towards a particular choice against their will. Response rules are thus not necessarily a case of 'libertarian paternalism'.[36] Nevertheless, they ensure that certain interests

---

35 §550 sentence 2 BGB.

36 For this idea see C. Sunstein and R. Thaler, 'Libertarian Paternalism Is Not an Oxymoron' (2003) 70 *U. Chi. L. Rev.* 1159.

are protected. They do not annihilate the parties' choice, as would be the case for a mandatory rule that applies independently of the parties' choice. This is especially important because parties frequently make agreements without knowing in detail the contract law that is relevant for them. Therefore, they might miss the opt-out conditions without intending to do so. In this case, a rule would apply that they did not want and their own choice would be neglected. A response rule can instead preserve as much of their original agreement as possible, while still protecting the interests of the weaker party.

For these reasons, it is important not to limit one's attention to the much-discussed questions of whether rules should be mandatory or not, what the content of the default should be and under what conditions the parties shall be allowed to opt out.[37] These questions lead to wrong alternatives. In particular, the question is not simply whether one should accept the parties' choice or overturn it. The question rather is whether one should accept it, overturn it or respond to it in another way. This might include a partial overturn, but can also be limited to a supplement. In the case of the above-mentioned termination rule, a partial overturn would consist in the rule that the parties are not allowed to agree on a shorter termination period once they have limited the lease period. A supplement would consist in the rule that the termination period shall be at least one year.

The decision whether the legislator should respond to the parties' choice or influence it by default or mandatory rules depends on a plurality of factors that vary with the type of contracts and situations being regulated. In some cases, it might be necessary not to allow a certain opt-out, for instance if risks to the life and body of the parties are concerned. But this does not exclude the fact that in other cases it suffices to modify and supplement the rules chosen by the parties in a certain way. This is especially the case when one cannot expect the parties to know in advance the rules that apply. The rules about interpreting contracts are an example in this regard. They construe the will of the parties by responding to the particular agreement. Hardly anybody knows precisely which rules apply, but everybody can rely on the fact that his or her will shall be taken seriously, unless the legislator interferes for political reasons.[38] Therefore, these rules are better understood as response rules to a certain agreement rather than a default from which the parties have to opt out. The legislator hence has more choices than designing a default that always applies unless the parties have opted out of it, or prescribing a mandatory rule that applies independently of the parties' choice. Thanks to response rules, the legislator can react in manifold ways tailored to the particular rules the parties made.

---

37 According to I. Ayres, above n. 10, p. 2034, this history of modern contract law could be seen as a sequential treatment of these questions.

38 For this intervention via interpretation see L. Kähler, 'Policy Interventions via Contract Interpretation' (2014) 22(5) *European Review of Private Law* 641.

Interestingly, the already mentioned European guarantee that applies in the case of an opt-out from the ordinary contractual remedies for sold goods could also be designed as a response rule. Instead of prohibiting such an opt-out, the legislator could accept it under certain conditions and supplement the opt-out with a guarantee against certain certified guarantors. These guarantors would in turn have a claim against the seller. The advantage of such a response is that the seller can avoid having to establish its own system for handling defective goods. This would be especially helpful for small businesses that want to trade throughout Europe but do not want to communicate in 24 languages with consumers in the various European countries. With an appropriate response rule, they would merely have to compensate a third party against whom the consumer could enforce the guarantee. These third parties can specialise in handling complaints and use the economy of scale for this purpose.

The response of contract law to the parties' choice might surprise them and distort their agreement. When deciding about a response rule, one has, therefore, to balance the advantage of opt-outs being accepted with the disadvantage of the contract being, unknown to the parties, modified. But one should bear in mind that these disadvantages also occur with mandatory rules which also apply independently of whether the parties knew about them. A response rule is normally milder than a complete prohibition.

Response rules could, theoretically, be higher-order defaults from which the parties can opt out. This is the case if the parties can, at least under certain conditions, modify the response rule. However, response rules have to be mandatory in many cases in order to protect certain interests. If a reaction to a particular choice of rules is necessary at all, it will most of the time be a mandatory reaction. Otherwise, one could refrain from intervening in the contractual content altogether. In this respect, a response rule resembles private international law, which accepts the parties' choice of law, but reacts by giving way to overriding mandatory provisions (e.g. Art. 9(2) Rome I Regulation 593/2008).

Especially for European private law, response rules are an attractive tool. They allow the parties to design their contract in a way that is influenced by the various traditions of the Member States and thus enable a plurality of contractual arrangements. Nevertheless, European contract law can at the same time ensure a minimum protection of consumers by preventing an uncompensated opt-out. Depending on the specific choice the parties made, the response of the legislator can thus be tailored. He does not have to become as specific as to create personalised responses, similar to personalised[39] default rules. But the choice can be significantly enhanced. For instance, while completely opting out from the withdrawal right in consumer contracts might prompt the reaction of a guarantee against a third party, making the withdrawal period shorter might be

39 C. Sunstein, above n. 16, p. 48.

compensated for by a longer limitation period. In such a way, the protection of consumers can be realised without curtailing the freedom of contract altogether and without levelling the variety of European contract law to only one set of rules. At the same time, the uniformity of European private law as regards certain questions could be preserved, as the response rules could be the same throughout Europe and guarantee in particular a minimum level of consumer protection.

An area of European consumer law in which response rules might play an especially important role is the right of withdrawal which exists for distance or doorstep sales, as well as for certain forms of consumer credit.[40] If the information the trader provides for the consumer about how to withdraw from the agreement is incorrect, the period for which the withdrawal can be exercised is extended under current law.[41] To do so, the consumer does not even have to show that he could not exercise his right due to the mistake in the instruction. The trader's mistake does not have to be causal for the consumer's late withdrawal from the agreement. Even small and harmless mistakes can therefore have severe consequences. The rationale for this harsh sanction seems to be to incentivise the trader to provide exact instructions about the withdrawal.

With a response rule, however, the sanction could be tailored much better to the particular mistake while still preserving the incentive to provide correct instructions. A response rule could, for instance, give the trader the choice either to accept a late withdrawal or to pay the consumer a certain penalty for the incorrect instructions. Thereby, one prevents the withdrawal right from being exercised simply because the consumer changed his mind, independently of the mistake in the instructions, but still keeps the incentive to comply with European standards. One might also distinguish between a complete failure to give instructions and a mistake in giving these instructions, and only in the latter case restrict the withdrawal by giving the trader the right to opt out of the information requirement by paying a certain sum. Once again, the legislator's possible responses are unlimited. Not all of them can be realised, but it is important to bear in mind that such choices exist. The legislator does not have to choose between making a particular rule a default or mandatory one because he can also adopt response rules.

5. OPT-IN RULES

A final instrument that is important for enhancing regulatory choice within private law is an opt-in rule. Such a rule applies only if the parties choose it. In contrast

40 Above n. 3.

41 Art. 6(1) of Directive 2002/65/EC, above n. 3.

to alternative rules formulated by the parties, opt-in rules are part of the law and their validity therefore unquestionable, save for possible unconstitutionality. So by creating an opt-in rule the legislator gives the parties the choice to adopt a certain rule without worrying about their choice being invalid because it infringes some statutory norm. This is a huge advantage of opt-in rules over opt-out rules, due to the vague standards about the permissibility of opt-outs, which make it difficult to predict, especially for standard terms,[42] whether or not an opt-out will be accepted. Once an opt-in rule is part of statutory law, the parties no longer have to worry about the validity of their choice.

In addition, statutory opt-in rules signal to the parties that the legislator regards a certain arrangement as fair even though he has not prescribed it as a default or as a mandatory rule. His endorsement[43] might thus impact the parties' choice. Opt-in rules can serve as a focal point which parties agree to in the event that they want to deviate from the default, but hesitate to accept terms formulated by only one side. Parties that have only a limited knowledge of contract law and are uncertain as to the effect of a particular clause might thus have resort to an opt-in rule and rely on it having been designed by the legislator. This might work particularly well if the opt-in rules contain mandatory rules[44] that cannot be changed once an opt-in has occurred. For then consumers can rely on the opt-in rules without fearing that they could be modified against their interests.

This reliance by the parties could even be increased if the legislator at the same time limits the opt-out choices by creating a mandatory opt-in menu. In this case, he does not totally prescribe for the parties the rules governing their contract but instead limits their choice. The menu is all they can choose from. In this case, there is no legally valid possibility to design an alternative rule. Although such a restriction makes the difficult presupposition that there is no superior rule, it still preserves more freedom of contract than a mandatory rule prohibiting any deviation from the prescribed rule.

Opt-in rules are also important for generating principles of law. When the law consists merely of default and mandatory rules, it leaves open the alternative arrangements that the parties can choose. Principles made on the basis of the existing law are then based only on prohibitions and prescriptions. One thus ignores the fact that the law also accepts alternative arrangements to a certain default. This is not the case when opt-in rules complement the picture. They help to better understand how competing principles like freedom of contract, on the one hand, and the protection of consumers, on the other hand, should be balanced. Opt-in rules create examples of how alternative arrangements could

---

42 See Art. 3(1) Unfair Terms Directive 93/13/EEC of 5 April 1993 on unfair terms in consumer contracts [1993] OJ L 95.

43 C. Sunstein, above n. 16, p. 20.

44 For this 'consumer protection technique' see S. Pellegrino, above n. 19, p. 8.

be made. This is most important in an environment in which alternatives to the default are likely to be treated as invalid and examples of admissible rules helpful. They might then function as an exception to a prohibition in demonstrating which deviating arrangement would be accepted.

Consider, for instance, statutory rules about the continuation of a commercial partnership after the death of one of its partners. These rules might entail the right of the heir to limit his or her liability and give the remaining partners in return the option to reduce the heir's share of the profit.[45] In this way, the risks of liability and the chances to participate in the profit are rebalanced. If statutory law explicitly foresees such an opt-in rule, it erases any doubt that a reduction of the heir's profit complies with statutory law. Otherwise doubts would remain whether such a reaction would excessively curtail the heir's right to limit his or her liability. A statutory opt-in rule would signify that a certain opt-out is accepted. It hence makes sense, especially in the context of prohibitions the range of which would otherwise remain questionable.

This recalls Hegel's remark that the law only contains prohibitions and that permissions are in the final instance based on them.[46] Taken literally, this does not hold for an opt-in rule because it is neither a prohibition nor can it be constructed by one. An opt-in rule's content is not exhausted by the assumption that everything which is not prohibited is allowed. Its permission is, unlike other permissions, explicit. But Hegel's analysis holds insofar as opt-in rules would be superfluous if there was no doubt about the validity of an agreed-on rule. Therefore, it is no accident that the rise of mandatory rules and the prohibitions underlying them has been accompanied by the rise of opt-in rules.

Most important for opt-in rules seem to be whitelists of standard terms that could be accepted once the parties have opted out of a default. Without such lists, there is frequently considerable uncertainty about the validity of standard terms, due to the vague and extensive general clauses controlling them. It is especially difficult to predict whether courts will regard a term as unfair because it causes a significant imbalance in the parties' rights and obligations arising under the contract, according to Article 3(1) of the Unfair Terms Directive 93/13/EEC. In particular, German courts interpret the law implementing these requirements so strictly that it is almost impossible to limit the liability by standard terms to a significant degree. The general clause restricting certain standard terms hence has far-reaching effects.

To enhance party autonomy and to better illustrate in which cases an opt-out is acceptable, whitelists of standard terms could be adopted as part of the European Directives and Regulations. They would supplement the blacklist that already exists, like in Article 3(3) of the Unfair Terms Directive, and would

---

45 Cf. §139 para. 5 HGB.

46 G.W.F. Hegel, *Grundlinien der Philosophie des Rechts*, original 1820, Johannes Hoffmeister ed., Meiner, Hamburg, 1995, §38.

likewise not be exhaustive. Between the white and blacklists a whole grey area would remain in which alternative arrangements could be made, although the parties would take the risk that their arrangement might later be regarded as void, due to the strict requirements for standard terms.

Whitelists of standard terms would contribute to a more balanced approach to the control of standard terms than exists currently. Under the prevailing European law, it is in case of doubt more risky to declare a particular standard term valid than to declare it invalid because European law predominately consists of prohibitions and not permissions. Therefore, in case of doubt it is riskier for a national court to declare a certain clause valid than to declare it invalid, as it can only in the latter case be overturned by the ECJ for not recognising the impact of the Unfair Terms Directive. From this an invalidity bias arises that endangers freedom of contract. Consider, for instance, the ECJ's position that the Annex to the Unfair Terms Directive 93/13/EEC is 'an essential element on which the competent court may base its assessment as to the unfair nature of that term'.[47] So far, this Annex only contains prohibitions and no permissions. It should not come as a surprise that the assessment of the unfair nature of terms heavily leans towards an intervention.

Whitelists of standard terms would help to overcome this bias. For there would then be for courts, as well as for the legislators of the Member States, examples of which alternative arrangements are valid. Whitelisted standard rules are less intrusive than mandatory rules, as they apply only with the consent of both parties. Nevertheless, they can influence the negotiations by providing a resort to which the parties can return in the event that they cannot agree on another arrangement, but are both willing to deviate from the default. Most importantly, whitelists of standard terms can complement the basis of blacklists so that a more balanced picture arises.

Like almost any other rule,[48] opt-in rules change the regulatory environment and are thus not a neutral device. A conscious choice architecture remains necessary.[49] For opt-in rules can become so attractive as to dominate parties' choices and oust other arrangements, especially if they accord with the interests of the party with the stronger bargaining power. Such was the fear, for instance, for the once-proposed Common European Sales Law (CESL)[50] ('the blue button'),

---

47 Case C-488/11, *Brusse, de Man Garabito v. Jahani*, ECLI:EU:C:2013:34, para. 55; C-472/10, *Hatóság v. Invitel*, ECLI:EU:C:2012:242, para. 26.

48 C. Sunstein and R. Thaler, above 35, p. 1161; L. Willis, above n. 10, p. 1223.

49 C. Sunstein, 'The Storrs Lectures: Behavorial Economics and Parternalism' (2013) 122 *Yale LJ* 1826, 1879.

50 Proposal for a Regulation of the European Parliament and of the Council on a Common European Sales Law, COM (2011) 0635 final. For the debate see the overview in S. Pellegrino, above n. 19, p. 5; E.A. Posner, 'The Questionable Basis of the Common European Sales Law: The Role of an Optional Instrument in Jurisdictional Competition' (2013) 50 *Common Market Law Review* 261.

which the parties would have been able to choose instead of the sales law of the Member States.[51] For it might then have happened that many companies would only have offered their contracts under this regime, without giving the other parties the opportunity to choose a different law with which they were more familiar. The dominance of the opt-in rule would not necessarily indicate that its content was superior, as other European private laws could not equally be chosen in all Member States and the mandatory rules of the otherwise applicable law thereby avoided.

Despite these possible drawbacks, opt-in rules are a valuable instrument. They do not have to be exhaustive[52] and privileged like a European sales law. Instead, they could be confined to single issues like the liability of the parties. They would enhance parties' autonomy by giving them a viable option to choose a rule other than the default one. The stricter the limits on freedom of contract become, the more it seems necessary to carve out such islands of remaining choices.

6. CONCLUDING REMARKS

In regulating contract law, the legislator has a plurality of choices. He is not confined to either prescribing a default rule from which the parties can unconditionally opt out or prohibiting all alternative arrangements via a mandatory rule. Instead, he can design the options created by a default rule in various ways. The most important of such options are, first, opt-out conditions, according to which an opt-out is accepted only if certain conditions, like being in writing, are met. Second, one might allow one party to make an option offer to the other party. In this case, the consumer or another weaker party can decide whether the contract shall follow the default rule or deviate from it. The consumer might have a financial incentive to opt out but is not required to do so.

Third, there is the opportunity of response rules which have so far escaped academic attention. These leave the parties' opt-out decision intact but modify or supplement it with additional rules. Unlike ordinary default rules, response rules do not apply unless the parties have made another choice, but only in the event that they have made a particular choice. The law can thus react in manifold ways to the parties' decision. Finally, the legislator can adopt opt-in rules, the application of which depends on the parties' choice. Unlike the rules that the

---

51 For the dispute whether the parties would thereby choose a second national contract regime or European law, see M. Fogt, 'Private International Law Issues in Opt-out and Opt-in Instruments of Harmonization: The CISG and the Proposal for a Common European Sales Law' (2012) 19 *Columbia Journal of European Law* 83, 94.

52 Proposal COM (2011) 0635, above n. 49, recital 25.

parties choose as an alternative to the default, they are unquestionably valid, due to their statutory status. Therefore, they are of special importance in areas like the law of standard terms, in which wide-ranging prohibitions cast into doubt the validity of private arrangements.

If the legislator wants to protect the interests of a certain group and assumes that default rules do not suffice for this purpose, he is thus not forced to adopt a mandatory rule which applies independently of the parties' choice. Instead, he can shape and delimit the options private parties have in a variety of other ways.

A PRIVATE INTERNATIONAL LAW PERSPECTIVE ON THE CREATION OF NORMS AND TRANSNATIONAL GOVERNANCE

Horatia MUIR WATT

1. INTRODUCTION

The topic of norm creation by contract is to a certain extent a mainstay of private international law, at least as applied to markets. It rests on what is arguably the most significant contemporary principle within the discipline, 'party autonomy', or contractual freedom of choice of the governing law. Such a principle fulfils a key function within the political economy of private ordering in today's global context. Indeed, while such a principle emerged as part and parcel of the 'mythology of modern law',[1] it has also worked, less visibly, to destabilise modernity's assumptions about the relationship between law and sovereignty, which are now, in the 'era of the post'[2] at the heart of considerable turmoil. Critical legal scholarship has highlighted the ways in which the principle of party autonomy empowers the fiction of an autonomous private

---

1 See P. FITZPATRICK, *The Mythology of Modern Law*, Routledge, Chapman & Hall, London 1992.

2 M. XIFARAS, 'The Global Turn in Legal Theory', (2016) 29 *Canadian Journal of Law & Jurisprudence* 215–243.

transnational legal order and, by the same token, fits it into the wider debate on the future of law beyond the state.[3]

The potential relevance of this project for an audience of contract lawyers is obviously linked to the fact that contract is the cardinal tool by means of which market players with local affiliations may rise above the constraints and contingencies of restrictive regulation designed for domestic consumption and thereby deploy their activities unhindered in a disembedded 'space' beyond the state. Indeed, the conceptual correlate of this empowerment of private actors to create their own normative space is the existence of an original lawless hinterland beyond the jurisdiction of nation states. According to the received wisdom of the discipline, that hinterland came to be filled up (at various points in history, according to the particular narrative) with the spontaneous self-regulating contractual practices, for the greater benefit of international trade, or the worldwide community of merchants, under the benevolent gaze of territorial sovereigns. Classical historiography locates the genesis of party autonomy in a famous consultation by Charles du Moulin on the conflict of laws in matrimonial property in the early 16th century.[4] Five centuries on, it is still the legal linchpin of some of the most powerful drivers of the global economy. Flows of private trade and investment, the functioning of financial markets, or international arbitration, all depend very largely on a widespread acceptance that parties to international transactions are free to design the legal regime governing their relationship.

The relevant legal regime and its legal-theoretical justifications may require something by way of a preliminary elaboration[5] and we shall attempt to do this below. However, reaching beyond the dogmatics of private international law on the topic of transnational norm creation by contract involves a critical line of enquiry that has more proximity with the political economy of private law than with more classical doctrinal analysis. It aims to understand why and how an astonishingly truncated or petrified version of party autonomy came to be widely accepted as the new form of legal 'common sense' throughout the

---

3 Ibid.
H. Muir Watt, 'Empire through contract: A private international law perspective' in C. Cutler and T. Dietz (eds.), *The Politics of Private Transnational Governance by Contract*, Routledge, London 2017; and 'Party Autonomy in Global Context: Political Economy of a Self-Constitutionalizing Regime' in E. Brousseau, J.M. Glachant and J. Sgard, *Oxford Handbook on International Economic Governance*, forthcoming, which benefited considerably from the interdisciplinary feedback provided by the editors, whose comments were integrated into the draft. I am extremely indebted to them all.

4 Consultation for the de Ganay spouses in 1525.

5 Not that some contract lawyers are not more than aware of these issues. See H. Collins, 'Flipping Wreck: Lex Mercatoria on the Shoals of Ius Cogens' in S. Grundmann, F. Möslein and K. Riesenhuber (eds.), *Contract Governance: Dimensions in Law and Interdisciplinary Research*, Oxford Scholarship Online: September 2015.

(largely) Western world of market economies, at least as far as international transactions were concerned.[6] Therefore, the aim of this contribution can also be seen as contributing to a wider transdisciplinary dialogue, not only between contract law and private international law, but more broadly between law and the social sciences, on a defining paradox underlying the empowerment of private actors through contract.[7] Indeed, a similar pattern seems to recur within various (Western) discourses on modernity, whether the perspective is that of law, philosophy or political economy. In this respect, our attempt here to identify the genealogy of the legal categories that are currently at work in transnational economic governance is also designed to help understand what might be specific to the legal variant of the classic, individualist liberal discourse, as opposed, say, to the social scientific, or the standpoint of political philosophy.

Private international law, then, sees the transnational area as the place where nation state legislators lose any exclusive political legitimacy and any correlative interest in imposing their own views and policies (at least as far as private transactions are concerned) on the conduct of private actors. According to conventional argument, they lack both the authority and the incentive to regulate beyond the limits of their respective territorial jurisdiction and indeed the means to do so. Indeed, it is said, nation states pursue a different set of priorities once the national polity is not engaged or endangered, and actively encourage transnational commerce under more liberal conditions than those which are acceptable within the confines of local territory. The discipline translates this idea by conferring a privilege on transnational economic relations that can be located beyond the thrust of state policies; these do not automatically constrain private parties, who thereby gain freedom to act in their own best interests, and, supposedly, those of cross-border commerce more generally. It is only relatively recently, since the expansion of the regulatory state in the latter part of the last century, that this narrative has been severely challenged by the correlative multiplication of mandatory 'extra-territorial'[8] legislations targeting private transactions.

Indeed, emblematically, since the post-war expansion of international trade in the second half of the last century and the first inklings of contemporary neo-liberal globalisation, the *lex mercatoria* has been represented by private international lawyers and the various practitioners, notably arbitrators,

6 See C. Cutler and T. Dietz, 'Introduction' in id. (eds.), above n. 2.

7 For the awareness of which I reiterate my debt to Eric Brousseau, Jean-Michel Glachant and Jérôme Sgard (see n. 2 above).

8 The concept of extraterritoriality is frequently essentialised by lawyers as if it had a unitary and determinate legal meaning. This is of course a fallacy. However, the important point is that today, private international law, torn between the exigencies of late capitalism and the claims of new domestic regimes, has had to reconceptualise the relationship between law and markets because of the growth of these mandatory economic policies.

produced by this epistemic community[9] as an immemorial form of private governance of shared or common spaces without dominion, such as the high seas.[10] Norms generated by the informal practice of non-state actors are tolerated or encouraged by the surrounding (or earth-bound) national polities. Often, historians describe such processes through the lens of custom, which forms more easily in the spaces where formal regulation does not reach. Political theorists see private sources of global governance as an alternative to institutionalised arrangements, while political economists point to modes of self-regulation by market players, each with their own sets of winners and losers.

In turn, the specifically legal lens through which spontaneous market ordering is envisioned is that of contract. However, two distinct threads appear under this label. Under a first perspective, the channel through which informal cross-border practice becomes normative is the repetition of discrete agreements between private actors that then serve to evidence the existence of shared normative standards. In turn, progressively, these may become the legal regime by default. An explicit example (among many) can be found, for instance, in the way in which the European Union[11] regulates choice-of-forum clauses. Thus, according to Article 25 of the Brussels I Regulation, the clause must either be evidenced in writing, or in a form which 'accords with practices which the parties have established between themselves', or, 'in international trade or commerce, in a form which accords with a usage of which the parties are or ought to have been aware and which in such trade or commerce is widely known to, and regularly observed by, parties to contracts of the type involved in the particular trade or commerce concerned'. Leaving room for informality, the (formal) text lends binding force to standards issuing from the repeated exercise of freedom of contract in a similar direction by multiple actors over time.

But under a second perspective that will form the focus of this contribution, law goes a step further in conceptualising contractual freedom beyond the state as a form of self-governance. In private international law, the principle of party autonomy signals the possibility for non-state actors to carve out a regulatory space in which they can define the rules of the game not only as between themselves but also, to a large extent, in respect of third parties. While the reference to autonomy might evoke – accurately so, in view of its 19th-century

---

9 See M. Schinazi, *The Three Ages of International Commercial Arbitration*; PhD dissertation, Sciences po Paris, publication forthcoming with Cambridge University Press, 2020.

10 On the genealogy and troubled history of dominion (or empire) over the sea, see P.G. Monateri, *Dominus Mundi. Political Sublime and the World Order*, Hart Publishing, Oxford 2018.

11 Regulation (EU) No. 1215/2012 of the European Parliament and of the Council of 12 December 2012 on jurisdiction and the recognition and enforcement of judgments in civil and commercial matters (recast). The short title (used below) is 'Brussels I Regulation'.

pedigree – a political or philosophical ideal of individual liberty, it is understood in private international law as a specific avatar of contractual freedom, empowering private actors to choose both the law (meaning the national system of law, or a set of rules from a given country) which is to govern their contract and the forum (a court of a given country, or an arbitrator) to which disputes will be referred. It signifies that contracting parties may, on the condition that their relationship qualifies as international, set aside the potentially applicable substantive laws of states in favour of rules either of their own making, or of any legal system in the world. The literature on this principle and its justifications is abundant.[12] Its continuing success is testified by the fact that it is enshrined in an astonishing number of national codes worldwide,[13] and is indeed still expanding as a central element of transnational soft law, as illustrated by the recent adoption of the so-called 'Hague Principles' on the choice of law in international contracts.[14] Examples of the use made by private actors of this delegated norm-making ability range from Lloyds' self-regulating insurance market, to the rise of corporate codes of conduct or other norms of corporate social responsibility that are passed along global value chains through successive discrete contracts. Generally, this process of private international law-making through contract is viewed favourably in the literature, as aligned either with efficiency concerns, or the interests of international trade, or sometimes even,

---

12 The literature on this principle, its origins, evolution, current status and limits is too abundant to be cited exhaustively. See among many others: H. Batiffol, 'Subjectivisme et objectivisme en droit international privé des contrats', Mél Maury vol. I, 39; A. Briggs, *Agreements on Jurisdiction and Choice of Law*, Oxford University Press, Oxford 2008; G. Cuniberti, 'Beyond Contract – The Case for Default Arbitration in International Commercial Disputes' (2009) 32 *Fordham International Law Journal (Fordham Int'l LJ)* 417; J. Damman and H. Hansmann, 'Globalizing Commercial Litigation' (2008) 94 *Cornell Law Review* 1; M. Lehmann, 'Liberating the Individual from Battles Between States – Justifying Party Autonomy in Conflict of Laws' (2008) 41 *Vanderbilt Journal of Transnational Law* 381; T. Marzal Yetano, 'The Constitutionalisation of Party Autonomy in European Family Law' (2010) 6 *Journal of Private International Law* 155; H. Muir Watt, 'Aspects économiques de droit international privé (Réflexions sur l'impact de la globalisation économique sur les fondements des conflits de lois et de juridictions)' (2005) 307 *Recueil des cours de l'Académie de Droit International de la Haye (RCADI)* 25–384; J.P. Niboyet, 'La théorie de l'autonomie de la volonté' (1927) 16 *RCADI* 1; P. Nygh, *Autonomy in International Contracts*, Clarendon Press, Oxford 1999; A. von Overbeck, 'L'irrésistible extension de l'autonomie de la volonté en droit international privé' in *Hommage à F. Rigaux*, Bruylant, Brussels 1993, p. 619. The history of the principle has been documented exhaustively in a recent monograph by A. Mills, *Party Autonomy in Private International Law*, Cambridge University Press, Cambridge 2018.

13 See for an impressive panorama, S. Symeonides, *Codifying choice of law around the world. An international comparative analysis*, Oxford University Press, Oxford 2014; and, for example, emblematically, Article 3 of Regulation (EC) No. 593/2008 on the law applicable to contractual obligations (Rome I).

14 Cf. the Hague Principles on the Choice of Law in International Contracts (adopted on 19 March 2015). More on these below.

by reference to the contractualisation of corporate codes of conduct, as a form of fairer governance of delocalised industries.[15]

Nevertheless, for some time now, critical legal scholarship has been shaping an alternative analytical framework that challenges the extensive freedom to rise above national regulation that has been conceded to private enterprise, draws attention to the negative distributional consequences of disembedded norm-generation, or connects unfettered regulatory power to the dictates of neo-liberalism and the financialisation of the global economy.[16] In order to spell out this critique, it seems useful first to set the scene from an interdisciplinary perspective in order to understand the defining, transversal paradox of party autonomy (section 2). The various legal-theoretical representations of contract governance will then be explored (section 3), before analysing the relationship, within the law, between the idea of 'private legislation' and issues of 'merely technical' design (section 4). The latter are at the root of the fundamental reversal of the relationship between law and market that accompanies the move from liberalism to neo-liberalism (section 5). This is why significant distributional effects thereby attach to party autonomy in its specifically global function (section 6).

2. SETTING THE SCENE: AN INTERDISCIPLINARY PERSPECTIVE

Certainly, as far as law is concerned, the profound transformations linked to contemporary globalisation have meant that while state-centred liberalism continues to define contemporary paradigms in legal thinking, it does so according to a curiously abridged version, which in turn affects the shape of the social, political or economic 'reality' that it purports merely to govern (as it were, that it appears to acts upon from the outside).[17] But law is not isolated in this respect. A classic liberal meta-discourse still seems to determine structures of thought right across the social sciences, including law[18] – however descriptively

15 That significant corporate accountability can be achieved under contemporary capitalism is, astonishingly, rarely questioned. See, however, G. Baars, *The Corporation, Law and Capitalism. A Radical Perspective on the Role of Law in the Global Political Economy,* Historical Materialism Book Series vol. 188, Brill, Leiden/Boston 2019.

16 See notably the references cited in n. 2 above.

17 As will be seen below, the ensuing distortion is of very specific relevance in the part of the law – private international law – which provides the (generally invisible) the legal framework and forms of late capitalism, or, in different terms, the informal normative infrastructure of the global economy.

18 But does law qualify as having its place among the latter? For a negative answer from a lawyer's perspective, see S. Geoffrey, 'Taking Methods Seriously (Part One)' (2007) 2(1) *Journal of Comparative Law* 94. The author questions whether those outside law should

inadequate and normatively inappropriate it is understood to be, nevertheless, in relation to our globalised, or post-colonial, or post-political, or technological world. The question to be borne in mind here is that of the nature and content of law's own addition, if any, to this broad script which runs across disciplines and undoubtedly mirrors a shared inability to represent social reality other than through a mid-19th-century intellectual apparatus and vocabulary.

One possible answer is that law's peculiar vision is directly performative. In order better to understand its constitutive role, an important preliminary point is in order. Markets, contracts, corporations, money, property are all legal concepts which shape social, political or economic structures – despite conventional wisdom to the contrary, and indeed more sophisticated accounts within the social sciences, which take such realities to pre-exist in some raw or natural form 'out there' (as the saying goes). As has been astutely observed, it is easy to overlook the fact that '[t]he basic elements of global economic and political life – capital, labour, credit, money and liquidity as well as power and right – are creatures of law. Law not only regulates these things, it creates them'.[19] This observation is quite obviously true in a 'domestic' setting, that is, within the confines of one state, or one local economy, or one municipal legal system. But it is also clearly valid for the institutions of *private* law (contract, property, debt, corporations, etc.)[20] which provide the more invisible backdrop against

take law seriously as an intellectual discipline capable of contributing to the development of epistemological thinking in the natural and social sciences. This is because the governing paradigm in legal studies has always been the 'authority paradigm', which results in law being closer to theology than to the social sciences. 'It is not a science dedicated to enquiring about the nature of the physical world, society or social relations. Its epistemological development remains trapped in the seventeenth and eighteenth centuries: thus, as a discipline, law has little to offer other social sciences'. However, other lawyers have less doubts about the potential contribution of law to the epistemology of the social sciences. See R. Encinas de Munagorri, C. Herrera, S. Hennette-Vauchez and O. Leclerc, *L'analyse juridique de (x)*, Editions Kimé, Paris, 2016, which, like the analysis below, proceeds from the conviction that a specifically legal perspective could shed light on normative phenomena generally considered as non-legal (precisely because they are not captured outside the state-centric liberal paradigm described here).

19 D. Kennedy, *A World of Struggle. How Power, Law, and Expertise Shape Global Political Economy*, Princeton University Press, Princeton 2016, p. 11.

20 The reality, significance and parameters of the distinction between public and private law, while considered one of the linchpins of 'classical legal thought' (that is, more or less, forms of legal thought which coincided with political democratic liberalism and the colonial expansion of capitalism from the late 19th century), are among the most debated topics in legal theoretical literature. D. Kennedy, 'The Stages of the Decline of the Public/Private Distinction' (1982) 130 *University of Pennsylvania Law Review (U. Penn. LR)* 1349; W. Wiecek, *The Lost World of Classical Legal Thought: Law and Ideology in America, 1886–1937*, Oxford University Press, New York 1998; M. Horowitz, 'The History of the Public/Private Distinction!' (1982) 130 *U. Penn. LR* 1423. Here, it suffices to say that private law governs, approximately, horizontal interactions between private actors (such as market relations), whereas public law governs the vertical relationship between the state or government and individuals (as in constitutional law).

which *international* markets and credit, foreign investment and contractual value chains first developed and continue to operate. These categories are the building blocks of 'informal empire'.[21] They frame, as it were, 'the background rules which determine the balance of power between various interests, and have constituted the means through which non-state global power has been asserted and structured'.[22]

Similarly, then, and perhaps less obviously, when capital expands beyond domestic boundaries, it does so by creating legal mechanisms (along with accompanying discourses) which are designed to overcome the various obstacles or sources of resistance produced by the division of the world, whether geo-politically (through frontiers, territorial sovereignty and different legal systems) or culturally (through potentially conflicting ideologies). Thus, when private international law provides the foundations for the cardinal drivers of the global economy (foreign investment, transnational value chains, global finance, multinational firms, etc.), it not only empowers transnational capital in invisible but highly potent ways, but it simultaneously paves the way for the turn from domestic or state-framed liberalism to neo-liberalism.[23] The expression *contrat sans loi* ('lawless contract'), suggesting that private contract rises above the law to which it is ordinarily subordinate, encapsulates the effects of the doctrine of private autonomy in this respect.[24] Coined at the turn of the 20th century, in reaction to moves made by courts to free international transactions from regulatory constraints designed for domestic markets (such as the illegality of the gold standard in domestic contracts), the expression ('lawless contract') suggests

21 M. Koskenniemi, 'Empire and International Law: The Real Spanish Contribution' (2011) 61(1) *University of Toronto Law Journal* 1.

22 A similar public international law perspective would be to say that, while ostensibly designed to ensure equality among (assumedly liberal) states, ideas such as statehood and sovereignty, for example, serve more subtly 'to allocate bargaining power among groups with conflicting projects (religious and secular institutions, majority and minority communities, local elites and foreign economic interests and local populations …)': D. Kennedy, above n. 18.

23 The difference between liberalism and neo-liberalism will be taken here, following Foucault (see, in particular, M. Foucault, *The birth of biopolitics*, Collège de France, 1978–79, ed. M. Senellart, translated by G. Burchell, Palgrave, Basingstoke) as involving a radical break in forms of governmentality, not a mere recurrence. The two strands are in many ways antagonistic rather than separated by a mere difference of degree (see M. Foessel, 'Libéralisme v. Néolibéralisme', *Esprit*, November 2008). From a legal perspective, the neo-liberal turn comes with a reversal of the relationship between public and private law, which is central to the gist of this chapter. This is because, in the place of the liberal state on which liberalism relies to shore up markets and provide a top-down institutional framework for individual relationships, neo-liberalism puts the individual *homo oeconomicus* at its centre, as entrepreneur, who can be reprogrammed in the rationalisation of society and the economy.

24 There were many influential attempts during the 20th century to reformulate the principle of party autonomy so as to make party freedom of choice of law appear subordinate to the requirements of the 'normally' or 'objectively' applicable law (see e.g. H. Batiffol, *Les conflits de lois en matière de contrat*, Paris 1938).

disapproval. Interestingly, the idea of a 'law-free contract' still shocks today, even though the developments in positive private international law discussed below have actually entailed a disactivation of any mandatory legal rules potentially applicable to international contracts.

Indeed, as will be further elaborated below, this has allowed for an inversion in the relationship between the law and private actors, whenever the latter are represented (according to a definition which the law itself constructs) as acting beyond the remit of one single sovereign state which would otherwise have natural jurisdiction to prescribe the conduct to be adopted. In order to understand this inversion, the crucial point is the fact that in a state-centred liberal context, the legal language of freedom of contract was predicated on its being part of a working hierarchy of norms, which was ultimately regulated and enforced by a constitutional state – a *Rechtstaat*. Self-interested social actions were thus both made possible and regulated by a broader normative order that (increasingly) took care of the common good. In a similar manner, international private law was conceptualised within an international space that rested on rules of coordination and mutual recognition between sovereign states.

The international scene was thus organised on the basis of the private/public divide, via the mediation of inter-state arrangements. However, today, this discourse on the freedom to contract, both ideological and instrumental, has entirely lost its constitutional mooring in national polities. Largely as a result of phenomena understood to be linked to contemporary globalisation, it has become 'disembedded' from the institutional framework whence it drew its initial legitimacy. It survived globalisation, as it were, in an abridged or truncated form. Similar distortions are familiar, in the legal field, in instances of legal 'transplants':[25] the truncated version of an institution or concept bears an entirely different meaning out of its initial context and may be all the more powerful for the simplification it produces. In this way, the abridged and truncated version of the discourse of contractual freedom is at work in a most powerful manner in today's global world, without any of the legal mechanisms designed to ensure

[25] The idea of 'legal transplants' was developed in comparative legal theory as a challenge to the idea that law is too closely linked to society (and culture) to make any sense when transposed from one context to another and that a crucial driver of law's development is borrowing from other legal systems (see A. Watson, *Legal Transplants: An Approach to Comparative Law*, University of Georgia Press, Athens 1974). This thesis was in turn hotly contested, to become one of the most significant bones of contention in comparative legal literature (see P. Legrand, 'The impossibility of legal transplants' (1997) 4 *Maastricht Journal of European and Comparative Law* 111). It is certainly very likely that when legal 'borrowing' does take place (whether through colonial or neo-colonial conquest or the will of policy-makers), foreign elements acts as 'irritants' within the receiving system (see G. Teubner, 'Legal Irritants: Good Faith in British Law or How Unifying Law Ends Up in New Differences' (1998) 61 *Modern Law Review* 11; G. Frankenberg, *Order from Transfer. Comparative Constitutional Design and Legal Culture*, Edward Elgar, Cheltenham 2013).

that it is counterbalanced by at least some understanding of the general interest. Not only does the distortion itself go unnoticed and the subsequent imbalance represented as normality, but the liberal tradition is invoked to justify what is essentially a very different, neo-liberal, move: the legal understanding of the relationship between the public and the private is actually reversed, and it is exactly this that becomes 'globalised'.[26]

Thus, a majority of judges, arbitrators, academics, corporate lawyers, or businessmen talk in this abridged language throughout Western economies and see the world through its lenses; they use it to justify, in legal terms, the very stuff of global markets, structures of production, corporate personality or dispute settlement procedures. Of course, economists and political scientists are fighting with similar paradoxes: whether in adhesion or in opposition, classical liberalism is the common ideological home country of the social sciences, even though, at the very same time, it is well known that it is not an appropriate description of the world we live in and leaves us under-equipped to try to imagine how it could be made better. In particular, like the lawyers, economists still see the world as peopled with free and informed individuals who contract from a state of equilibrium and for mutual advantage. Experimental additions to the core framework have been made, under the euphemisms of imperfect competition, disequilibrium economics, or information asymmetries, yet they leave the premise unchanged. It is hoped that what follows might be useful, as it were as a matter of comparative interdisciplinary epistemology, to identify the recurrence of a similar paradox.[27] It may also be that a specifically legal take might potentially enrich the perspective of the social sciences at least as much as, say, economics has, more visibly, left an enduring imprint on contemporary legal doctrine and mindset.

3. LEGAL-THEORETICAL REPRESENTATIONS OF PARTY AUTONOMY

While the historical origins of the idea of party choice of law are certainly much older, it was in the course of the 20th century that the principle of party autonomy emerged specifically as a key methodological concept in private international law. It served the progressive liberalisation of cross-border markets, which broke the frames of protectionist regulatory schemes, emancipating

---

[26] Legal theorists are divided as to what is it exactly, within the law, that is 'globalised'. For the most convincing account, according to which, rather than particular rules or institutions, it is probably a mindset or legal consciousness, see D. KENNEDY, 'Three Globalizations of Law and Legal Thought: 1850–2000' in D.M. TRUBEK and A. SANTOS (eds.), *The New Law and Economic Development. A Critical Appraisal*, Cambridge University Press, Cambridge, 2006.

[27] I owe this point to Eric Brousseau et al. (see n. 2 above).

international flows of capital, goods and services from the claims of territoriality. Through a series of technical moves which will be described below, the law has accredited freedom of choice as the foundation of a whole parallel world of private transnational ordering, complete with its own institutions and governing principles. Indeed, from the resulting representation of the relationship between free choice of law and sovereign authority stems the fiction of an autonomous private transnational legal order, widely accepted as the source of regulation, conceded by the various states, of cross-border relationships between economic actors. From this perspective, party autonomy is to a large extent the expression, within the confines of private international contract law, of a wider political economy which serves the global expansion of the neo-liberal market. As such, it fulfils a significant function in creating an enabling environment for private-sector activity in the context of a globally integrated economy. This role is rarely questioned, any more than the various supporting fictions which have worked to ensure the expansion of the principle within the liberal legal paradigm.

Indeed, under the classical liberal paradigm, party autonomy was designed to be exercised within a political framework which ensured the ultimate primacy of public market regulation. This scheme owes as much to domestic contract theory as to the Westphalian model of the public international legal order, composed (exclusively) of equal and sovereign states. Together, state sovereignty and freedom of contract combined to produce a view of the relationship between law and market in the transnational economic sphere according to which the empowerment of private actors was subject to limits imposed in the name of the general interest.[28] Whether framed in terms of public policy or overriding mandatory rules, such restrictions imposed upon the conduct of private transnational trade are set by a presumptively like-minded community of sovereign states similarly desirous of promoting the reciprocal benefits of international trade.

Within such a scheme, the reasons for which any sovereign state would allow parties to contract out of its own rules and substitute those of a neighbouring community, were to be found both in the purported special needs of cross-border transactions and the dilution of the claim of any one state to regulate them exclusively.[29] This implied in turn that sovereign states were deemed to be unconcerned, or their polities less affected, by transactions which did not directly involve their domestic economy; in a world where market was coextensive

---

28 P. Francescakis, 'Quelques précisions sur les lois d'application immédiate et leurs rapports avec les règles de conflit de lois', *Revue critique de droit internatinal privé (Rev. crit. DIP)* 1966, 1; G.P. Romano, 'Règles internationalement supplétives et règles internationalement disponibles' in *Regards comparatistes sur le phénomène contractuel*, Presses Universitaires d'Aix-Marseille, Aix-en-Provence 2009.

29 See L. Ribstein, 'From Efficiency to Politics in Contractual Choice of Law' (2003) 37 *Georgia Law Review* 363.

with territory, this idea translated methodologically into a presumption of territoriality of national regulation.[30] And indeed, this separation of the two worlds of domestic and international transactions had a functional justification: social and economic policies were non-negotiable in homogeneous cases which fell clearly within their regulatory ambit; on the other hand, such policies were not endangered by contracting-out when the relationship, bearing foreign elements, was not perceived to 'belong' to the local economy.

However, while contractual choice of law might be encouraged in the interests of cross-border commerce, its corollary was the assumption that the community of states – specifically, those which were sufficiently closely connected to the parties to justify the jurisdiction of their courts – would moderate private autonomy to accommodate the requirements of the common good. No unbridled *contrat sans loi*, then, but a regulated freedom to be subject to the sovereign legal order of one's choice. Like international commercial arbitration, whose growth followed on the generalisation of party autonomy as a foundational principle of choice of law, the empowerment of private actors is supposed to cater to the special needs of international economic intercourse.

The notion that party autonomy in the international arena, like freedom of contract in the domestic context, is a measured concession by the liberal state to private ordering,[31] rests on theoretical premises which are also to be found, outside the field of contract, at the heart of multilateral conflicts methodology. Thus, the very representation of the conflict between laws within the continental Savignian tradition[32] presupposes a certain commonality of normative preferences among like-minded (and pre-regulatory) sovereigns. Indeed, private law – of which the province is that of horizontal relationships between non-state actors – is perceived to be largely facilitative of private transactions,[33] so that

30 This notion is far from irrelevant today. See the US Supreme Court's influential ruling on this point in *Morrison v. National Australia Bank*, 561 U.S. 247 (2010).

31 N. Jansen and R. Michaels, 'Private Law Beyond the State? Europeanization, Globalization, Privatization' (2006) 54 *American Journal of Comparative Law (AJCL)* 843.

32 That is, a tradition supposedly inherited from the work of German legal historian Carl von Savigny, whose magnum opus on Roman law included an (eighth) volume on the principles designed to solve the conflicts of laws between German princedoms or city-states. In this context, Savigny claimed that the methods hitherto applied (since the Middle Ages) for determining the scope of statutes (statutism), which consisted in asking whether a given statute was personal (applicable to local subjects including when they are abroad) or territorial (applicable throughout the territory but not beyond), could be reformulated, to identical effect, by assigning to each type of legal relationship a specific 'seat' (for instance, issues pertaining to the person, such as marriage, would be subject to the law of the domicile, whereas questions of tort would be governed by the local law). This second formulation was to become the standard expression of choice-of-law methodology (known as 'multilateralism', as mentioned above, because the seat of the legal relationship could be anywhere, that is, at home or in a foreign country).

33 A. Ogus, 'Competition between National Legal Systems: A Contribution of Economic Analysis to Comparative Law' (1999) 48 *International and Comparative Law Quarterly* 405.

a conflict of laws may be seen essentially as the virtual availability of as many interchangeable sets of rules as there are connections between a given set of facts and different legal systems. Conversely, any given legal system is assumed to provide a set of rules of contract law that can suitably – that is, rationally – be applied in any geographical context.

This double, liberal, representation of the relationship between state and market, law and territorial polity, had however to adjust to the rapid growth (in Europe, largely in the second half of the 20th century) of public economic regulation affecting the market (such as competition, securities, consumership) or society (health, environmental, social protection), as well as the rise of fundamental rights in fields of private law previously considered to be immune from 'constitutionalisation'.[34] Public policy concerns, social rights, or *lois de police* ('overriding mandatory provisions')[35] in the legislation of states with close connections with the relationship in dispute, frequently endowed with 'extraterritorial' scope,[36] narrowed the expanse of private empowerment.

---

34 Lawyers are familiar with the considerable body of legal literature on the topic of the contemporary constitutionalisation of private law. This phenomenon is one of the reasons for the decline of the distinction between public and private law, which was cardinal to classical legal thought. This evolution has taken place because individual fundamental rights (enshrined in a constitutional document or, where relevant, in the European Convention on Human Rights) have been given 'horizontal effect'. This means that these rights can be invoked by citizens against other citizens (and not only against the state) and therefore affect the part of the law (private law) which, traditionally, dealt with interpersonal or horizontal relationships.

35 One definition (borrowed from EU law) is provided in the text below: *lois de police* are 'provisions the respect for which is regarded as crucial by a country for safeguarding its public interests, such as its political, social or economic organisation, to such an extent that they are applicable to any situation falling within their scope, irrespective of the law otherwise applicable to the contract' (Rome I Regulation, Article 9). This definition presupposes that in a given legal system, some provisions are more mandatory (more 'imperative') than others. The idea behind the usual principles of the conflict of laws is that the private laws of like-minded, liberal states are ordinarily interchangeable. This is the essence of 'multilateralism' as described above. It is assumed, then, before a French court, that foreign law can be substituted for French law in a case where a transaction (or other social relationship) has close connections to another economy (or society), without any significant alteration to the pursuit of French public policy objectives (for instance, sufficient information for market transactions). However, this assumption may on occasion turn out to be wrong: the applicable foreign law may induce an outcome which turns out to be inacceptable in policy terms because it is contrary to a specific objective (for instance, the protection of a certain category of market actors such as consumers). In such a case, the court will derogate from the usual 'blind' methodology and apply French 'overriding' or 'super-mandatory' rules instead.

36 Super-mandatory rules (as defined and explained in the preceding footnote) are often considered to claim 'extraterritorial' scope, meaning very simply that they are triggered when a given private conduct has an effect (or a significant effect) on a local market, even when such conduct itself takes place abroad (outside the local territory). Currently, in the United States, there is a trend away from extraterritoriality in respect of public regulatory law, notably in order to discourage so-called F-cubed actions (that is foreign plaintiffs bringing

Importantly, such concerns were relevant both to judicial proceedings within the forum state, or in respect of foreign judgments and awards at the enforcement stage. Thus, in a European setting, first in the Rome Convention (Art. 7) and now in the recast Rome I Regulation (Art. 9),[37] room was made for 'provisions the respect for which is regarded as crucial by a country for safeguarding its public interests, such as its political, social or economic organisation, to such an extent that they are applicable to any situation falling within their scope, irrespective of the law otherwise applicable to the contract'. Such rules may override the otherwise applicable law when a court thinks this makes sense in terms of the policies they express.

Beyond this adjustment, however, private international law did not proceed to revisit the conceptualisation of party autonomy in the light of the intensive growth of market and social regulation in the domestic sphere, with its transformation of the nature and function of private law;[38] nor did its methods appear to evolve in response to the decline of the Westphalian model in international relations and the tectonic upheavals induced by globalisation within both the theory of law and sovereignty and the reality of cross-border trade and investment. Yet within the changed normative, political and economic environment, party autonomy can no longer be represented as a carefully monitored concession of the liberal sovereign state. In other words, there was a shift from obligation to empowerment, which might be framed in more Foucauldian terms as a move to a neo-liberal model of private governance.[39] Technically, it involves what might be called 'methodological slippage'.

---

actions in US courts against foreign defendants over foreign conduct): see the *Morrison* case, above n. 29. In fact, to say that a law or statute is territorial or extraterritorial means very little in technical terms, since the same statute can be said to be one or the other, according to which factual element is used to trigger its application or how its scope is defined. For instance, in the *Morrison* case the US Supreme Court decided that US securities regulation is triggered when the litigious transaction takes place within the United States. The focus of such regulation, we are told, is the transaction itself. It would therefore have been to give extraterritorial (meaning excessive) effect to the relevant provisions on securities fraud to apply them to transactions which took place on the Australian market. But if the scope of these provisions is defined slightly differently – if an emphasis is put on a different policy objective and a different 'focus' or triggering factor is retained – then they can be seen to apply territorially. For instance, here, the initial fraud allegedly took place in the United States. Had the focus of the relevant provisions been defined as relating to the fraud and not the resulting transactions, then the securities regulation could have applied without being made to appear 'extraterritorial'.

37 Regulation (EC) No. 593/2008 of the European Parliament and of the Council of 17 June 2008 on the law applicable to contractual obligations (Rome I).

38 F. Cafaggi and H. Muir Watt (eds.), *The Regulatory Function of European Private Law*, Edgar Elgar, Cheltenham 2009; H.-W. Micklitz, 'The Visible Hand of European Regulatory Private Law – The Transformation of European Private Law from Autonomy to Functionalism in Competition and Regulation' (2009) 28 *Yearbook of European Law* 3.

39 M. Foucault, above n. 22.

4. PRIVATE LEGISLATION AND ISSUES OF 'MERELY TECHNICAL' DESIGN

Unquestioning acceptance of the principle of party freedom in a large number of legal systems (and more to go)[40] points to its status as a foundational myth of private international economic law.[41] Indeed, its success has been surprisingly unimpeded by the fact that significant issues as to its real ambit remain unsettled, as will be shown below. Nor does it seem to matter that despite its Kantian pedigree, its dominant justification is essentially utilitarian, linked to the needs of international trade. Although methodological, political and economic objections do appear from time to time,[42] they remain largely unheeded.[43] Its astonishing success is, most recently, illustrated by the Hague Principles on the Choice of Law in International Contracts (2015), which affirm the general principle of party autonomy with limited exceptions.

The power thus conceded to private actors to harness available state legislation for the needs of their cross-border transaction was, and still is, predicated on the double requirements of the rule of law. The first perceived expression of the latter is a condition of internationality, which is supposed to prevent domestic

---

40 M. Pertegas and B.A. Marshall, 'Harmonization Through the Draft Hague Principles on Choice of Law in International Contracts' (2014) 39 *Brooklyn Journal of International Law* 975.

41 For the 'merely technical' in the subtitle of this paragraph, see D. Kennedy, 'The Political Stakes in "Merely Technical" Issues of Contract Law' (2002) 10(1) *European Review of Private Law* 7.

42 Objections are variously linked to the general transformation of private law and the anachronistic nature of freedom of contract, or to the potential democratic deficit resulting from the permission to contract out of local rules, or to the uncertain economic rationality underlying the apparent indifference of states to free-riding on successful regulatory models (which are made available for free choice by private actors from different constituencies).

43 Across the Atlantic, attempts were certainly made to adjust traditional choice-of-law methodology to the increasingly regulatory function of private law. Although these attempts were not always successful in the long run, the important lesson of the American realist revolution was that 'jurisdiction-selecting' rules (a methodological point which will be explained below) as practiced in the continental European tradition were unworkable in a world where private law is neither purely facilitative nor indeed interchangeable. From a 'functionalist' perspective (or according to the methodology that has come to be known as 'governmental interests analysis'), conflicts of laws arise from the existence of contradictory regulatory interests, identified by sounding out the policies of the states involved. This perspective met with considerable resistance in Europe, often on (legal-theoretical) grounds similar to those which have been opposed more recently to the invasion of law and economics doctrines. See for example, G. Kegel, 'The Crisis of the Conflict of Laws' (1964) 112 *RCADI* 91. Although today such methodology has made considerable inroads, notably in EU private international law (in the form of *lois de police* as will be explained below), it is still considered derogatory. In the United States, the focus of practice and scholarship has turned in recent years away from these methodological concerns to the (territorial/extraterritorial) scope of public economic regulation (as will be explained below), leaving little room for discussion of the legal status of freedom of choice of law in contract.

contracts from circumventing local public policy; the second is the requirement of the public (meaning state) origin of the chosen law, so as to prevent parties from cherry-picking or resorting to wholly private rules. Both conditions are indissociable from a certain type of methodology traditionally practised in private international law in the continental European tradition and, until the (comparatively late) onslaught of legal realism in this field in the 1970s, in the United States. This methodology, unhelpfully called 'multilateralism'[44] leads the court to the (national) legal system (that of one of the sovereign nation states) which must supply the rule of decision in a particular case, whenever there is an 'international element' (but for which, the case would be purely domestic and fall within the remit of the local or 'forum' state). The latter requirement signifies that this choice-of-law methodology is triggered only when there is a potential 'conflict of laws' (that is, a risk that two or more sovereigns would wish to prescribe the outcome of the case). However, neither the requirement that the legal system be one of a sovereign state, nor the condition, of internationality, in the contemporary legal context, fulfils the function of safeguarding the public interest for which it was initially designed. On the contrary, as currently framed, they create a hiatus between the rules and practice of international contracting; hence, a sense of methodological misfit. Furthermore, both serve to perpetuate a vision of the world, including the relationship between regulation and party autonomy, on the foundations of which the myth of autonomous private ordering was constructed.

The first condition restricts the exercise of free choice of law to international contracts – or rather, due to the extraordinary difficulty of defining this cardinal requirement, to contracts of which all the elements relevant to the situation at the time of the choice were not located within one state. In a European setting, the Rome I Regulation introduces, in addition, the idea that a domestic contract is one which is connected solely to Member States' territories as a whole (Art. 3(4)). However, whether the perspective adopted is national or, now, European, it presupposes a bright line separating the closely regulated world

44 Not be confused with the usages of the same term in public international law or international relations. This methodology consists of a set of rules which identify, for each abstract category of legal issues (for instance, contract, tort, etc.), the legal system which, in abstract terms, appears to have the strongest title or reason to govern. The latter is expressed in terms of 'connecting factors', which are usually factual-geographical elements deemed to best express the metaphorical 'centre of gravity' or the 'seat' of each legal relationship within the corresponding category of legal issues: an example would be 'the place where the harm occurs'. Thus, the private international rule for torts would say (and still does, in the European setting): the (national) law (or legal system) applicable to a tort (that is, the system which provides the rule of decision for the court) is the law of the place where the harm occurs (*lex loci delicti*). This methodology is 'jurisdiction-selecting' as it leads the court to a legal system as a whole (French law) and not to any particular rule (we do not know before we set the rule in motion what type of answer French law will bring to the case, nor whether it makes sense in policy terms to apply it to the specific case).

of the domestic (or intra-European) economy, from the area of freedom where, beyond national (or European) frontiers, state policies relax their grip. However, the rise of the regulatory state, entailing the multiplication of overriding mandatory rules or *lois de police* with extraterritorial thrust (as seen above), has made it difficult to maintain the bright line between domestic and international spheres in terms of the respective intensity of state interests. In other words, the idea that sovereign regulatory concerns stop at national borders could not survive either the appearance of new forms of market regulation or the growing interconnectedness of local economies.

Hence the idea (explained above) that some legal provisions are 'hyper-mandatory' or 'overriding', meaning that a court must apply them whatever the normally applicable law, including the law chosen by the parties. However, this methodology is considered strictly derogatory, in the sense that it does not represent the 'normal' way of reasoning in the conflict of laws. Therefore, it does not affect the initial requirement that the contract be international, or non-domestic, for the principle of party choice to come into play as a choice-of-law rule, accrediting in turn the distinctiveness of the world of international transactions. Maintaining this fiction contributes to perpetuating the underlying world-view of a community of states conceding an area of party freedom beyond their frontiers, but over which they retain the ultimate control. This representation of an orderly world in which benign liberal states determine the outer limits of private economic activity is also linked to the second limitation on freedom of choice. Although according to the relevant legal texts parties may choose any law in the world, with no requirement as to geographical linkage to the state whose law is thus chosen and no condition as to the completeness, modernity or democratic legitimacy of its legal system, their freedom nevertheless stops short of non-state norms such as the *lex mercatoria* or the Unidroit rules for international contracts. These, according to recital 13 of the recast Rome I Regulation, may merely be 'incorporated by reference' into the contract, where they are necessarily subject to the contrary provisions of the governing law. Underlying this second restriction is the idea that the contract law of liberal states is presumptively interchangeable, because it is deemed to be based on shared conception of societal needs (albeit largely facilitative and exclusive of specific regulatory interference), whereas norms of purely private origin cannot be supposed to implement similar conceptions. In other words, according to this vision, it was important that the parties should not escape the network of state regulation.

The fear inspired by the concept of 'private legislation'[45] may or not be justified: it could well be, as frequently argued, that the content of the new *lex mercatoria* has now developed sufficiently so as to present a coherent, reasonably

---

[45] On the (more forbidding) concept of lawless contracts, see above section 2.

complete and generally acceptable set of operative principles; it is also arguable that carefully thought-out principles of substantive contract law drafted at an international level may be more valuable and adjusted to the needs of cross-border trade than many state laws which might be less progressive, less clear, more parochial, etc. In economic terms, the burden of over-regulation could be an evil greater than excessive freedom in the international sphere. But the point here is that if the mandatory social and economic policies of connected states are implemented whenever it makes sense to do so in functional terms, then the quality of whatever non-state contract norms the parties may have chosen – in the unlikely event they have committed themselves to incomplete, incoherent or non-progressive principles – hardly matters. In the absence of a specific regulatory interest, which would trump any other chosen rule anyway, the choice of non-state law does not endanger the public policies of potentially concerned states, of which, on the other hand, the protection is inadequately ensured by the sole requirement that the parties choose a state law. Excessive focus on the latter has signified, paradoxically, that party autonomy has ceased to imply subordination of private actors to state authority.

5. "CHANGES OF STATE": THE REVERSAL OF THE RELATIONSHIP BETWEEN LAW AND MARKET

Private actors are empowered to attain 'regulatory lift-off'[46] because the liberal state has renounced – or has been constrained by competitive economic forces to give up – the means to ensure the primacy of its own, or another's, public policy regulation over 'private legislation'.[47] Indeed, the changing global context[48] in which party autonomy is exercised, and to which it has largely contributed both as a foundational myth and a methodological tool, has induced two significant functions for which it was not initially designed. These 'changes of state' are directly linked to those which affect the relationship between law and market.[49] They also coincide to a large degree with the rise of private dispute resolution, emblematically enshrined in the 1958 New York Convention on the Recognition and Enforcement of Foreign Arbitral Awards.[50] By allowing

---

46 R. Wai, 'Transnational Liftoff and Juridical Touchdown: The Regulatory Function of Private International Law in a Global Age' (2002) 40 *Columbia Journal of Transnational Law* 209.

47 F. Rodi, 'Private Law beyond the democratic order? On the legitimacy problem of "private law beyond the state"' (2008) 56 *AJCL* 743.

48 For this expression, see A. Brett, *Changes of State: Nature and the Limits of the City in Early Modern Natural Law*, Princeton University Press, Princeton 2011.

49 On such changes induced by a competitive market for legal products, see W. Kerber, 'Interjurisdictional Competition within the European Union' (2000) 23 *Fordham Int'l LJ* 217.

50 This is not to say that the early decades (say, from the 1920s until the UN 1958 Conference) of expansion of this new post-Westphalian practice were all smooth sailing. It is our

parties not only to choose the applicable substantive law but also to elect the competent court (choice of forum) or indeed to opt out of any judicial forum – in terms more familiar to economic federalism, to cross jurisdictional barriers[51] unhindered – the principle of free choice reverses the relationship between public regulation and private choice and generates a competitive market for legal products and judicial services.[52]

The first symptom of a reversal of the status of regulation in respect of party choice law, jurisdictional barrier-crossing, results from the combined effect of choice of forum, choice of law and free movement of decisions or awards. The general acceptance of free choice of forum in cross-border litigation, in the name of party autonomy, along with the spectacular rise of arbitration, is traditionally justified in terms of the promotion of international commerce through the benefit of predictability, procedural economy and litigation risk management. Such concerns hold true even when internationally mandatory provisions are at stake: there is no particular reason why courts should not be trusted mutually to uphold the interests of the members of benign community of states and, indeed, the Rome Convention (Art. 7(1)) and Regulation (Art. 9(3)) have gone a long way down this path. Reputedly more flexible, international commercial arbitration presents all these advantages, with the added attraction of confidentiality; furthermore, when political stakes are high, such as in state investment contracts, it offers an appearance of neutrality, its legitimacy being enhanced by increasing institutionalisation. Increasingly commonplace in practice, such agreements have thrived as initial doubts as to the desirability of allowing private actors to appropriate access to the courts have dwindled.

Free choice of forum obviously impacts upon the applicability, and thereby the imperativeness, of the mandatory rules of any state other than the chosen forum (which in the case of arbitration means practically none at all). This is why the liberal scheme on which party autonomy rests presupposes that any extension of the scope of party choice of court, or the enlargement of arbitrability, is compensated for by the right to a 'second look' by the supervising

---

understanding however that the rise of free choice of law on the one hand, and on the other the idea of contractual freedom to opt out either of the local national judicial system (choice of forum) or of any formal judicial system whatsoever (international commercial arbitration), are one of a piece, however rationalised (choice of law in international contract may have received more theoretical attention, particularly in continental European doctrine, than choice of forum or arbitration, often represented as a pragmatic offshoot of contractual freedom).

51 In this context, jurisdictional barrier-crossing refers to the ability of private parties to evade mandatory rules by 'barrier-crossing', i.e. by transferring their relationships to other legal systems through choice of forum.

52 H. Muir Watt and L. Radicati di Brozolo, 'Party Autonomy and Mandatory Rules in a Global World' (2004) 4(1) *Global Jurist* article 2.

or enforcing state over the judgments or awards issuing from the chosen forum. This scheme is apparent in the Supreme Court of the United States' famous dictum in the *Mitsubishi* case, whereby 'in the event that choice-of-law forum and the choice-of-law clauses operated in tandem to as prospective waiver of a party's right to pursue statutory remedies ... for antitrust violations, we would have little hesitation in condemning the agreement as against public policy'.[53] But it rapidly became apparent that the 'second look' was, in many instances, either unrealistic (when no enforcement was required, the parties having settled, for instance), or problematic (when the supervising court is not better equipped than the arbitrator to make an assessment on the merits in economic terms), or indeed practically excluded through deference to the chosen forum (as in cases as notorious as the *Lloyd's* litigation).[54] A powerful economic incentive for states to renounce their 'second look' has been to provide a free zone for the arbitration industry.[55] It is useful to note here, in view of the characterisation (proposed later in this chapter, section 6) of the *lex mercatoria* as a self-constituting constitutional regime, that the extreme liberalisation of arbitration law has come complete with a philosophical doctrine designed to legitimate the regulatory lift-off thus achieved.[56]

Indeed, and secondly, the generalisation of choice-of-court agreements, along with the parallel growth of international arbitration, is now understood as giving rise to a worldwide market in adjudication or dispute resolution. Enhancing global jurisdictional competition would supposedly reap benefits

---

53 *Mitsubishi v. Soler Chrysler-Plymouth*, 473 U.S. 614 (1985). Of course, from an economic perspective, antitrust, just like securities regulation, bankruptcy or indeed eminent domain, is very much about the good old sovereign state intervening top-down into private property rights. These are contemporary expressions (or vestiges) of sovereign intervention that fit the classic, liberal doctrine, based on the sharp vertical divide between public and private. That a special status (a 'second look') should be reserved to public regulatory provisions (*lois de police* in the European vocabulary discussed above) is unsurprising. The point being made here is precisely that such regulation is being disactivated through the process described in the text below.

54 For the *Lloyd's* litigation, see (among many) *Roby v. Corporation of Lloyd's*, 996 F.2d 1353 (2d Cir. 1993); *Bonny v. Society of Lloyd's*, 3 F.3d 156 (7th Cir. 1993). Here, through the combined effect of choice of forum (English courts or arbitration) and choice of law (English law) and liberal rules on enforcement of foreign judgments (in the US), Lloyd's successfully excluded the operation of US securities regulation in an instance where such regulation (with its mandatory provisions on disclosure) might otherwise – in the absence of a combined choice of forum and choice of law – have been expected to apply (here, in order to protect unsuspecting American investors or 'names' from misrepresentation).

55 L. Radicati di Brozolo, 'Mondialisation, juridiction, arbitrage: vers des règles d'application semi-nécessaires?', *Rev. crit. DIP* 2003, 1 and 'Antitrust: A Paradigm of the Relations between Mandatory Rules and Arbitration: A Fresh Look at the Second Look' (2004) *International Arbitration Law Review* 23.

56 E. Gaillard, 'Aspects philosophiques du droit de l'arbitrage international' (2007) *RCADI* 329.

in terms of the improvement of the quality of courts worldwide. However, the real problem lies in the fact that when court access is thus privatised, there is a correlative absence of judicial (or arbitral) regulation of interests beyond those of the parties to the dispute. In this respect, it is instructive to turn to the conclusion, which can hardly be suspected of anti-libertarian bias, reached by Landes and Posner using economic analysis of justice in respect of the domestic judicial system: privately designated judges lack both the legitimacy (conferred by public investiture) and the (private financial) incentive to take account of societal interests in their decision-making process. This conclusion certainly plays out, for instance, in respect of the impact of human rights in investment arbitration, where contractual mandate and choice of law have tended to pre-empt any consideration of wider public or third-party interests.[57] Although of course the public financing of the court system establishes both the legitimacy and the incentive that arbitration lacks in protecting societal interests beyond those of the parties to the litigation, the tendency of courts designated by choice-of-forum agreements to act 'as if they were arbitrators' obviously detracts from this particular regulatory function.

6. CONCLUSION: FOR A DISTRIBUTIONAL ANALYSIS

The centrality of private choice of law in the European tradition is so taken for granted, or at least appears to be so solidly rooted in the history of Western private international law that astonishingly little attention has been paid to the function it fulfils within the changing economic and political environment induced by globalisation. The cloak of tradition is reinforced by more recent law and economics doctrines, which tend to promote party autonomy as efficiency, in the form of predictability, reduced transaction costs or facilitated risk management. No doubt these virtues exist, at least for the party whose skills in contract negotiation and drafting are strongest. It is highly probable however that the interests purportedly served by unbridled freedom of choice, whether cast as those of the market or of a purported community of merchants, do not allow for adequate governance of the cross-border activities of private actors.[58]

---

57 W. Landes and R. Posner, 'Adjudication as a private good' (1979) 8 *Journal of Legal Studies* 235.

58 In this respect, the (in)famous *Lloyd's* litigation serves as a cautionary illustration of the cumulative effect of contract doctrine and private international law theory: *Roby v. Corporation of Lloyd's*, 996 F.2d 1353 (2d Cir. 1993); *Bonny v. Society of Lloyd's*, 3 F.3d 156 (7th Cir. 1993); f. in France, the 'Monster Cable' case: Cass. civ. 1re, 22 octobre 2008, JCP (G) 2008, II, 10187, note L. d'Avout; JCP (E) 2008, 2535, note N. Mathey; Contrats, conc. consom. 2008, comm. 270, note M. Malaurie-Vignal; D. 2009, 200, note F. Jault-Seseke, D. Bureau and H. Muir Watt, 'L'impérativité désactivée? (à propos de Cass civ 1re, 22 octobre 2008)', *Rev. crit. DIP* 2009, 1.

Thus, under a wider perspective than that offered by various dimensions of private law doctrine, it becomes clear that party autonomy no longer serves to free private enterprise from entrenched parochial constraints under the benign supervision of a community of liberal states, but works to transform national public regulation into a disposable private good in a deregulated economy.[59] This holds true even after the various recent financial crises and the disastrous role played by self-regulation in subordinating wider public concerns to speculative interests.

In this respect, once again, the implications of party autonomy must be seen in the context of the various legal tools which provide the private legal infrastructure of global markets and foreign investment. Among these, within the European context, free movement of goods and services entertains a symbiotic relationship with party choice, the latter being the metaphorical expression of cross-border mobility and regulatory arbitrage. While consumer protection has found its place here, neither social rights nor the production chains which supply the European consumer market benefit from similar solicitude. Indeed, more globally, party autonomy also structures transnational production and supply chains (generating what has been described as a 'plug-in effect' in respect of sub-contractors and suppliers),[60] and can moreover be linked in this context to direct investment, of which it supports the international (contractual) regime. The private legal regime thus created is reinforced, on the one hand, by private international law rules in tort, when they work to keep any obligation to pay attention to third-party interests under the sway of local law, itself often constrained to lower the level of reparation by reason of competition to attract foreign investment. On the other hand and furthermore, the private international law regime governing the structure of multinational enterprise reinforces the autonomy of corporate entities when it comes to the duty to care or repair in respect of industrial accidents, environmental damage, or human rights abuse.

At the same time, however, various countervailing tendencies have appeared. Technically, in the current state of the law, the only obvious way of ensuring that law retains its authority when parties have the licence to cross barriers is to make the 'second look' effective at the enforcement stage. This has been made possible within the European Union, where Member States have the obligation to refuse recognition to arbitral awards given in violation of European competition and

---

59 On the use of the notion of distributional effects of legal institutions as a critical tool to understand their often hidden effects in neighbouring spheres, see K. Rittich, *Recharacterizing, Restructuring. Law, Market and Gender in Structural Reform*, Kluwer, The Hague 2002.

60 See H. Muir Watt, "Party Autonomy" in international contracts: from the makings of a myth to the requirements of global governance' (2010) 6(3) *European Review of Contract Law* 250, citing Roger Brownsword, to whom the expression is attributed.

consumer law,[61] and presumably of those fundamental rights which are part of the Union legal order.[62] Party autonomy is therefore severely curtailed in an increasing number of circumstances, albeit within the safe confines of the European internal market. Nevertheless, it may well be that there is need for a more radical reformulation of the issues at stake. In the rapidly changing context of global economy, the real difficulties are not (merely) market practices shaped by stronger parties through free choice of law and forum, but the implications of the expansion of unaccountable private authority in the context of what social theory aptly describes as the increasing functional differentiation of autonomous regimes.[63]

Gunter Teubner illustrates the concept of an autonomous self-constitutionalising system with 'destructive growth tendencies' precisely by reference to the law governing transnational market transactions (the global version of the *lex mercatoria*).[64] Here, a regime of unaccountable private authority, complete with its own inner logic, structuring principles and private jurisdictions, prospers notably through extreme liberalisation of arbitration; it shows furthermore a marked propensity to expand into neighbouring areas such as investment law,[65] where it clashes with other regimes;[66] it has come complete

61 See emblematically (in a competition law case), Case C-126/97, *Eco Swiss China Time Ltd v. Benetton International* [1999] ECR I-3055. Another notable development in the same context is the progressive mainstreaming of consumer protection, which has evolved from the status of exception to the rule in respect of cross-border provision of goods and services. Consumer protection leaves little room to freedom of contract (or, in cross-border contracts, to free party choice of law). This evolution has taken place through the growth of consumer legislation driven by internal market concerns within the EU, and through the additional leverage provided by principles imported from human rights law, such as non-discrimination. Thus, the violation of principles of EU consumer protection can prevent the enforcement of an arbitral award before the courts of an EU Member State: see Case C-168/05, *Mostaza Claro v. Centre Movil Millenium*, ECLI:EU:C:2006:675.

62 K. Ziegler, *Private law and human rights*, Hart Publishing, Oxford 2007.

63 G. Teubner, *Constitutional Fragments: Societal Constitutionalism in Globalization*, Oxford University Press, Oxford 2011. Cf G. Baars, above n. 14, who criticises the focus on criminal liability of people (corporate officers) as opposed to the structural causes of capital accumulation and ensuing alienation and corruption.

64 A. Fischer-Lescano and G. Teubner, 'Regime-Collision: The Vain Search for Legal Unity in the Fragmentation of Global Law' (2004) 25 *Michigan Journal of International Law* 999.

65 In Teubner's words, 'corporate constitutional politics have successfully dismantled nation state production regimes whenever they impede the global expansion of corporate activities': G. Teubner, above n. 62, p. 77. This author also makes another striking claim: 'In a world society with neither apex nor centre, there is just one way remaining to handle inter-constitutional conflicts – a strictly heterarchical conflict resolution. This is not just because of the absence of centralized power, which could be countered by intensified political efforts, but is rather connected with deep structures in society which Max Weber called the "polytheism" of modernity. Even committed proponents of the "unity of the constitution" are forced to agree that the unity of the nationstate constitution is now moving toward a "clash of civil constitutions", toward mutually conflicting rationalities to be defused by a new conflict of laws'. This statement elevates the conflict of laws to a meta-constitutional level.

with a philosophical doctrine designed to legitimate the 'regulatory lift-off' it has achieved in respect of limits contained either in the laws of nation states or indeed, as the context of investment arbitration shows, fundamental rights.[67] All these features are largely 'how private corporate actors govern'.[68] Therefore, if encounters between heterogeneous norms or expressions of diverse types of informal authority are central to the understanding of the normative landscape beyond the confines of state sovereignty, the traditional schemes of intelligibility that underlie private international law as a discipline need to take on board the additional dimensions of global complexity involved in the current expansion of private ordering. Contractual conflicts involving the *lex mercatoria*, as a functionally specialised cross-border regime, seem to be a good place to start, in the context of a wider reflection on transnational economic governance.

To a certain extent, this is unsurprising. After all, the conflict of law's line of business has long been making sense of interactions that cross state boundaries and fall between the gaps between domestic sovereignty and public international law.

66 See H. Muir Watt, 'The contested legitimacy of investment arbitration and the human rights ordeal: the missing link' in W. Mattli and T. Dietz (eds.), *International Arbitration and Global Governance: Contending Theories and Evidence*, Oxford University Press, Oxford 2014, ch. 9.

67 E. Gaillard, above n. 55.

68 D. Danielson, 'How Corporations Govern: Taking Corporate Power Seriously in Transnational Regulation and Governance' (2005) 46 *Harvard International Law Journal* 411.

PART IV

PARTY AUTONOMY AS A BASIS FOR NORMS

AMBIGUITIES OF SELF-REGULATION

Some Illustrative Examples of 'Good' Companies' Certification

Florian Möslein

1. INTRODUCTION

Among the novel ways of creating 'regulatory content' that are currently emerging without or with only limited direct involvement of state legislation, self-regulation plays the lead. In times of globalisation and privatisation, self-regulation has in fact become so important and omnipresent that our age has already been qualified as an 'era of self-regulation'.[1] Concurrently, self-regulation constitutes an established mode of rule-making and has ancient

[1] C. Estlund, 'Rebuilding the Law of the Workplace in an Era of Self-Regulation' (2005) 105 *Columbia Law Review* 319.

origins, for example with respect to the free professions.[2] Its long tradition and widespread use, when taken together, make self-regulation an incredibly broad and challenging field for legal scholarship. Both in the realm of private and (even more so) of public law, the phenomenon of self-regulation has attracted great interest, and many valuable contributions have already been made.[3]

From a private law perspective, and more specifically from the perspective of private autonomy, the various forms of self-regulation pose substantial challenges to the existing conceptual and legal framework, mainly because of their inherent ambiguities. On the one hand, self-regulation by private individuals is based on their private autonomy, but the high-handedness (*Selbstherrlichkeit*) that is immanent in the concept of private autonomy[4] does not fit well with the responsibility for norms that regulation necessarily implies (see section 2). On the other hand, self-regulation never occurs entirely 'without the state'.[5] As a consequence, the concept of self-regulation is also ambiguous due to the variety of different forms of self-regulation, and in particular due the variances of state involvement.[6] Nonetheless it is crucial to distinguish two different subcategories, in particular because the interpretation of rules follows different patterns depending on whether they are induced by the state or not.[7] Drawing the line between these two subcategories turns out to be extremely

---

2 For an extensive (including historical) account, see J. Taupitz, *Die Standesordnungen der freien Berufe*, de Gruyter, Berlin 1991; for a more general historical perspective, see P. Collin et al. (eds.), *Selbstregulierung im 19. Jahrhundert – zwischen Autonomie und staatlichen Steuerungsansprüchen*, Vittorio Klostermann, Frankfurt am Main 2011.

3 For instance, see S. Augsberg, *Rechtsetzung zwischen Staat und Gesellschaft: Möglichkeiten differenzierte Steuerung des Kapitalmarktes*, Duncker u. Humblot, Berlin 2003; W. Berg et al. (eds.), *Regulierte Selbstregulierung als Steuerungskonzept des Gewährleistungsstaats*, Duncker u. Humblot, Berlin 2001; T. Hoeren, *Selbstregulierung im Banken- und Versicherungsrecht*, VVW, Karlsruhe 1995; G. Makowski, *Kartellrechtliche Grenzen der Selbstregulierung*, Nomos, Baden-Baden 2007; K.-D. Sabrowsky, *Selbstregulierung im Wirtschafts- und Unternehmensrecht*, Stollfuß, Bonn 1978; H. Stockhaus, *Regulierte Selbstregulierung im europäischen Chemikalienrecht*, Mohr Siebeck, Tübingen 2015; Z. Talidou, *Regulierte Selbstregulierung im Bereich des Datenschutzes*, Peter Lang, Frankfurt am Main 2005; A.C. Thoma, *Regulierte Selbstregulierung im Ordnungsverwaltungsrecht*, Duncker u. Humblot, Berlin 2008; K. Tonner, *Regulierung und Selbstregulierung im Verbraucherrecht*, Nomos, Hamburg 1994. From a specifically private law perspective, see P. Buck-Heeb and A. Dieckmann, *Selbstregulierung im Privatrecht*, Mohr Siebeck, Tübingen 2010.

4 W. Flume, *Allgemeiner Teil des Bürgerlichen Rechts*, 4th ed., Springer, Berlin 1992, p. 17 (= §1, 9); see also R. Reinhardt, 'Die Vereinigung subjektiver und objektiver Gestaltungskräfte im Vertrage' in *Festschrift for Schmidt-Rimpler*, C.F. Müller, Karlsruhe 1957, p. 116.

5 For a similar form of wording, see G. Teubner, *Global Law without a State*, Dartmouth Publishing, Dartmouth 1997; cf. N. Jansen and R. Michaels (eds.), *Beyond the State: Rethinking Private Law*, Mohr Siebeck, Tübingen 2008.

6 For a recent account of this variety (and its different dimensions), see G.F. Schuppert, *The World of Rules. Eine etwas andere Vermessung der Welt*, Max-Planck-Institut, Frankfurt am Main, working paper available at https://papers.ssrn.com/sol3/papers.cfm?abstract_id=2747385.

7 In more detail F. Möslein, 'Genuine Self-regulation in Germany', *Zeitschrift für Japanisches Recht (ZJapanR)* 10 (2018), 83, 107 et seq.

difficult, however, in particular because of the plurality of distinctive criteria that apply (see section 3). The emerging field of 'good' companies' certification provides illustrative examples of these different ambiguities of self-regulation. A comparative overview of this field shows fundamentally different regulatory approaches which can be neatly arranged according to their degree of state involvement (see section 4). From a conceptual point of view, 'good' companies' certification not only illustrates the cleavages between the different categories of self-regulation but also demonstrates the different arguments that speak both in favour of and against self-regulation. By this means, the entire ambiguity of self-regulation may be brought to light.

From a methodological point of view, the analysis of such ambiguities of self-regulation contributes to research on private law rule-making, a field that increasingly becomes established as a legal sub-discipline in its own right.[8] In fact, there is a growing recognition that private law scholarship should not only focus on the existing rules of substantive law, but that it also needs to support regulators in the selection and design of appropriate legal instruments.[9] In times of globalisation and privatisation, private law is subject to fundamental changes since legal relations between private individuals are increasingly cross-border in nature and occur on the basis of changed patterns of statehood. Legal scholarship must therefore not only examine the material content of specific legal provisions but also needs to analyse the full range of regulatory instruments and strategies, along with comparing them with regard to their regulatory intensity and impact. Legal scholarship must provide for regulatory instruments that are appropriate to solving real-life problems.[10] The discipline of private law is supposed to contribute to the 'art of regulation' (again).[11] Accordingly, an extensive series of recently published monographs aims to measure the effectiveness of specific

---

8 F. Möslein (ed.), *Regelsetzung im Privatrecht*, Mohr Siebeck, Tübingen 2019. In a similar vein, with respect to contract law, see G. Bachmann, 'Optionsmodelle im Privatrecht', *Juristenzeitung (JZ)* 2008, 11, 19 et seq.; H. Eidenmüller, 'Der homo oeconomicus und das Schuldrecht – Herausforderungen durch Behavioral Law and Economics', *JZ* 2005, 216; H. Unberath and J. Cziupka, 'Dispositives Recht welchen Inhalts? – Antworten der ökonomischen Analyse des Rechts', *Archiv der civilistischen Praxis (AcP)* 209 (2009), 37, 39.

9 For general information on peculiar characteristics of current legal scholarship, see C. Engel and W. Schön (eds.), *Das Proprium der Rechtswissenschaft*, Mohr Siebeck, Tübingen 2007; M. Jestaedt and O. Lepsius (eds.), *Rechtswissenschaftstheorie*, Mohr Siebeck, Tübingen 2008.

10 H. Fleischer, 'Die Zukunft der gesellschafts- und kapitalmarktrechtlichen Forschung', *Zeitschrift für Unternehmens- und Gesellschaftsrecht (ZGR)* 2007, 500, 502 et seq.; cf. id., 'Gesetz und Vertrag als alternative Problemlösungsmodelle im Gesellschaftsrecht', *Zeitschrift für das gesamte Handelsrecht und Wirtschaftsrecht (ZHR)* 168 (2004), 673.

11 With reference to the traditional notion (much too narrow today) of *Gesetzgebungskunst* (art of legislation), and from a historical perspective, see S. Emmenegger, *Gesetzgebungskunst: Gute Gesetzgebung als Gegenstand einer legislativen Methodenbewegung in der Rechtswissenschaft um 1900 – Zur Geschichte der Gesetzgebungslehre*, Mohr Siebeck, Tübingen 2006, in particular, pp. 154–83 (on the determination of suitable legislative means).

regulatory instruments, techniques and strategies in different areas of private and commercial law.[12] By taking complex forms of non-state regulation into account, this research approach can help to analyse and understand the various ambiguities of self-regulation, also because it extends far beyond the traditional *Gesetzgebungslehre* (theory of legislation) which traditionally used to be considered a sub-discipline of public law only.[13] Due to its close relationship with private autonomy, self-regulation clearly demonstrates the need for private law scholarship's input to that debate.

2. SELF-REGULATION AND PRIVATE AUTONOMY

2.1. AUTONOMY FROM THE STATE?

Self-regulatory rules are not imposed by state authorities, but are 'by definition developed by those directly involved in the industry or professions'.[14] Some of the advantages commonly attributed to self-regulation are that this regulatory form is relatively flexible, quick and cheap to achieve, that it accurately reflects the issues and needs of specific sectors, and that it creates a sense of a common bond, which in turn increases the likelihood of compliance. On the other hand, there are the various dangers of self-interest coming before public interest, anti-competitive effects and entry barriers, and risks of non-enforcement, in addition to concerns about the lack of democratic legitimacy.[15]

---

12 For instance, see S. Bechtold, *Die Grenzen zwingenden Vertragsrechts – Ein rechtsökonomischer Beitrag zu einer Rechtsetzungslehre des Privatrechts*, Mohr Siebeck, Tübingen 2010; J.-H. Binder, *Regulierungsinstrumente und Regulierungsstrategien im Kapitalgesellschaftsrecht*, Mohr Siebeck, Tübingen 2012; J. Cziupka, *Dispositives Vertragsrecht – Funktionsweise und Qualitätsmerkmale gesetzlicher Regelungsmuster*, Mohr Siebeck, Tübingen 2010; M. Fornasier, *Freier Markt und zwingendes Vertragsrecht*, Duncker u. Humblot, Berlin 2013; T. Haberer, *Zwingendes Kapitalgesellschaftsrecht – Rechtfertigung und Grenzen*, Manz, Vienna 2009; A. Hellgardt, *Regulierung und Privatrecht*, Mohr Siebeck, Tübingen 2016; L. Kähler, *Begriff und Rechtfertigung abdingbaren Rechts*, Mohr Siebeck, Tübingen 2012; F. Möslein, *Dispositives Recht – Zwecke, Strukturen und Methoden*, Mohr Siebeck, Tübingen 2010; R. Podszun, *Wirtschaftsordnung durch Zivilgerichte*, Mohr Siebeck, Tübingen 2014; M. Renner, *Zwingendes transnationales Recht – Zur Struktur der Wirtschaftsverfassung jenseits des Staates*, Nomos, Baden-Baden 2010. From a similarly comparative perspective, see N. Kornet, *Contract Interpretation and Gap Filling: Comparative and Theoretical Perspectives*, Intersentia, Antwerp 2006; V. Lasserre-Kiesow, *La Technique Legislative*, LGDJ, Paris 2002; see also J. Black, *Rules and Regulators*, Clarendon Press, Oxford 1997, pp. 246–250 ('Towards a Theory of Rule Making').

13 G.F. Schuppert, *Governance und Rechtsetzung – Grundfragen einer modernen Regelungswissenschaft*, Nomos, Baden-Baden 2011.

14 C. Harlow and R. Rawlings, *Law and Administration*, Cambridge University Press, Cambridge 2009, p. 325, referring to Better Regulation Task Force, *Self-regulation Interim Report*, London 1999.

15 For more extensive information on both the advantages and disadvantages of self-regulation, see, for instance, A. Ogus, 'Rethinking Self-regulation' (1999) 15 Oxford Journal of Legal

Some public law scholars query whether the exercise of private autonomy in order to set rules qualifies as self-regulation at all.[16] Contrariwise, some private law scholars question whether heteronomous self-regulation, that is self-regulation 'induced by the state',[17] forms part of self-regulation in the proper meaning of the term.[18] The truth lies probably somewhere in the middle. Arguably, self-regulation is not (and can never be) purely autonomous, simply because private autonomy cannot be exercised in the absolute absence of the state. The necessity of some public framework for the exercise of private autonomy has already been underlined by Thomas Hobbes in his famous *Leviathan*:

> If a covenant be made wherein neither of the parties perform presently, but trust one another, in the condition of mere nature (which is a condition of war of every man against every man) upon any reasonable suspicion, it is void: but if there be a common power set over them both, with right and force sufficient to compel performance, it is not void. For he that performeth first has no assurance the other will perform after, because the bonds of words are too weak to bridle men's ambition, avarice, anger, and other passions, without the fear of some coercive power … But in a civil estate, where there a power set up to constrain those that would otherwise violate their faith, that fear is no more reasonable; and for that cause, he which by the covenant is to perform first is obliged so to do.[19]

If even simple exchange contracts will only function reliably with at least some form of state intervention (in order to safeguard the execution of contracts),[20]

Studies 97; R. Van Den Bergh, 'Towards Efficient Self-Regulation in Markets for Professional Services' in C.-D. Ehlermann and I. Atanasiu (eds.), *European Competition Law Annual 2004: The Relationship Between Competition Law and the (Liberal) Professions*, Hart, Oxford 2006, pp. 157 et seq.

16 C. Calliess, 'Inhalt, Dogmatik und Grenzen der Selbstregulierung im Medienrecht', *Zeitschrift für Medien- und Kommunikationsrecht (AfP)* 2002, 465, 466; J. Kühling, *Sektorspezifische Regulierung in den Netzwirtschaften*, C.H. Beck, Munich 2004, p. 27.

17 Cf. J.-H. Binder, 'Self-Regulation Induced by the State in Germany', *ZJapanR* 10 (2018), 127.

18 P. Buck-Heeb and A. Dieckmann, above n. 3, p. 45.

19 T. Hobbes, *Leviathan*, 1st ed., London 1651, §14, paras. 18 et seq. In a similar vein, G. Husserl, *Rechtskraft und Rechtsgeltung: eine rechtsdogmatische Untersuchung*, Springer, Berlin 1925, p. 39, made the following thought experiment: imagine that, by coincidence, two people of different origins, different nationalities and different languages meet in the desert. One of them is thirsty, but has only dried fruits, while the other one is hungry, but has nothing to eat but a coconut. While it might seem beneficial for them to exchange the dried fruits and the coconut, they will probably not conclude such an exchange contract. The reason for the absence of contracting here is that they are both afraid that, immediately after the exchange, the opposing party will steal back what he has just given away. See also G. Manssen, *Privatrechtsgestaltung durch Hoheitsakt*, Mohr Siebeck, Tübingen 1994, p. 141; F.V. Hippel, *Das Problem der rechtsgeschäftlichen Privatautonomie*, Mohr (Siebeck), Tübingen 1936, pp. 91–105 ('*im Naturstande*').

20 For more details, see F. Möslein, 'Privatrechtliche Regelsetzung, Governance und Verhaltensökonomik' (2014) 1 *Austrian Law Journal* 135, 138 et seq.

self-regulation will never entirely occur without the state. This idea that self-regulation can never be purely autonomous but requires at least some state-made legal infrastructure can also be traced back to the jurisprudence of the German Constitutional Court. In the famous *Bürgschaftsurteil*, a decision on the provision of a security, the Court elaborated that safeguarding private autonomy requires enforceability and therefore constitutes a duty on the part of the legislator to provide regulatory tools and mechanisms, which are legally binding and establish legal positions that are enforceable in the case of disputes.[21] The contrary view, which argues that the legal order could restrict itself to simply tolerating private arrangements,[22] has consequently been rejected by Claus-Wilhelm Canaris as completely pointless and inconsistent with the constitutional right on the freedom of action (Art. 2, para. 1, German Basic Law).[23] While the state is necessarily involved to some extent, what may vary is the degree and the manner of state interference. Comparative contract law indeed shows significant differences, namely in the comparison between common and civil law jurisdictions.[24]

2.2. HETERONOMY OF REGULATION

When private autonomy is not only exercised in order to negotiate bilateral contracts, but with a view to regulating behaviour, an additional, inherent tension becomes obvious: 'The term self-regulation is an oxymoron. If all persons affected agree to a set of rules, the problem calling for regulatory intervention disappears. Self-regulation means something different. At least some actors have subdued to group pressure, or the entire group has given in to outside pressure, usually to a threat of the exercise of sovereign powers.'[25] Indeed, if the word fragment 'regulation' is understood as any alteration of socially harmful behaviour, and the word fragment 'self-' is understood as a requirement of consent of all affected

---

21 BVerfGE 89, 214, 231 ('*Nach ihrem Regelungsgegenstand ist die Privatautonomie notwendigerweise auf staatliche Durchsetzung angewiesen. Ihre Gewährleistung denkt die justitielle Realisierung gleichsam mit und begründet daher die Pflicht des Gesetzgebers, rechtsgeschäftliche Gestaltungsmittel zur Verfügung zu stellen, die als rechtsverbindlich zu behandeln sind und auch im Streitfall durchsetzbare Rechtspositionen begründen*').

22 G. Struck, 'Vertragsfreiheit – ein Grundrecht', *Demokratie und Recht* 1988, 39.

23 C.-W. Canaris, 'Verfassungs- und europarechtliche Aspekte der Vertragsfreiheit in der Privatrechtsgesellschaft' in P. Badura and R. Scholz (eds.) *Festschrift for Peter Lerche*, C.H.Beck, Munich 1993, p. 889 (n. 59: '*völlig sinnlos und mit Art. 2 I GG zweifelsfrei unvereinbar*').

24 M. Pargendler, 'The Role of the State in Contract Law: The Common-Civil Law Divide', New York University School of Law Working Paper no. 17-01, available at https://papers.ssrn.com/sol3/papers.cfm?abstract_id=2848886.

25 C. Engel, 'The Role of Law in the Governance of the Internet, International Review of Law' (2006) 20 *Computers & Technology* 201, 202.

parties, the combination of both word fragments is a contradiction in itself. Any change against the will of the involved parties would effectively exclude such consensual agreement. We can only make sense of that combination if such consent is not entirely autonomous, but somehow influenced by outside powers, either by the other party or from outside.

In fact, the approaches to self-regulation vary widely and comprise different degrees of state involvement. Self-regulation is never entirely autonomous in the sense of regulation that takes place without any state interference.[26] Instead, self-regulation itself can be regulated to varying degrees. German administrative lawyers accordingly coined the term 'regulated self-regulation', or *Regulierte Selbstregulierung*, which refers to the title of a *Festheft*, or commemorative booklet, about the well-known legal scholar and former judge of the German Federal Constitutional Court, Wolfgang Hoffmann-Riem.[27] Since its publication, that term has become very common and is used in many different respects,[28] not least because of the impossibility of an entirely autonomous self-regulation.

3. CLASSIFYING SELF-REGULATION

While self-regulation therefore never occurs entirely 'without the state',[29] the different forms of self-regulation vary considerably, just like the different degrees of state involvement.[30] Yet it is crucial to form and distinguish two separate subcategories with regard to the application of the respective rules: the interpretation of rules follows different patterns depending on whether they are induced by the state or not.

For instance, the recent *Elliott* judgment of the ECJ[31] raised the question whether certain private standards require uniform interpretation across Europe, and whether the ECJ is competent under Article 267 of the Treaty on the Functioning of the European Union to decide on that interpretation. In turn, the answer depends on whether the standard qualifies as a provision of

---

26 P. Buck-Heeb and A. Dieckmann, above n. 3, p. 45.

27 W. Berg et al. (eds.), above n. 3.

28 In addition to the monographs by Stockhaus, see Z. Talidou and A.C. Thoma, both above n. 3; see also T. Attendorn, 'Regulierte Selbstregulierung: Gibt es das in der telekommunikationsrechtlichen Zugangsregulierung?', *Die öffentliche Verwaltung (DÖV)* 2008, 715; K.-H. Ladeur, 'Regulierte Selbstregulierung im Jugendmedienschutzrecht', *Zeitschrift für Urheber- und Medienrecht (ZUM)* 2002, 859; T. Weichert, 'Regulierte Selbstregulierung – Plädoyer für eine etwas andere Datenaufsicht', *Recht der Datenverarbeitung (RDV)* 2005, 1.

29 For a similar form of wording, see G. Teubner, above n. 5; cf. N. Jansen and R. Michaels (eds.), above n. 5.

30 For a recent account of this variety (and its different dimensions), see G.F. Schuppert, above n. 6.

31 Case C-613/14, *James Elliott*, ECLI:EU:C:2016:821.

European law, and more precisely whether it ranks among acts 'which, while indeed adopted by bodies which cannot be described as "institutions, bodies, offices or agencies of the Union", are by their nature measures implementing or applying an act of EU law'.[32] The ECJ made clear that this may well be the case, even though the standard is private, but only if it is induced by a European institution:

> While the development of such a harmonised standard is indeed entrusted to an organisation governed by private law, it is nevertheless a necessary implementation measure which is strictly governed by the essential requirements defined by that directive, initiated, managed and monitored by the Commission, and its legal effects are subject to prior publication by the Commission of its references in the 'C' series of the Official Journal of the European Union.[33]

In other words, the ECJ draws a sharp line between two different subcategories of self-regulation, namely genuine self-regulation and self-regulation induced by the state (i.e. the EU). The Court not only emphasises the crucial importance of that distinction with regard to (uniform) interpretation, but also invites the development of specific criteria in order to make such a distinction.

But how can one draw the line between genuine self-regulation and self-regulation induced by the state? What is the decisive criterion? What we already know is that the mere involvement of the state does not play a role: the state is always involved in some form or another when it comes to private rule-making. What we therefore arguably need to consider is not the involvement, but the initiative: on whose initiative does self-regulation take place? Is it the initiative of private parties or is it the initiative of state authorities? Building on the *Elliott* judgment of the ECJ, one can unfold this initiative criterion in three different dimensions: namely, the procedure of rule-making, the substance of rules, and their enforceability. The challenge is to find the respective 'tipping points',[34] i.e. the point where self-regulation rapidly and dramatically changes its character, such that it falls under the alternative respective subcategory, hence the need to define more precise criteria that make the categorical difference between genuine self-regulation and self-regulation induced by the state.[35]

---

32 Ibid., para. 34.

33 See again ibid., para. 43.

34 The idea of such tipping points is extensively explored in other social sciences, namely economics and sociology; see T. Schelling, 'A Process of Residential Segregation: Neighborhood Tipping' in A.H. Pascal (ed.), *Racial Discrimination in Economic Life*, Lexington Books, Lexington 1972, p. 157; M. Granovetter, 'Threshold Models of Collective Behavior' (1978) 83 American Journal of Sociology 1420. Cf. the bestseller from M. Gladwell, *The Tipping Point: How Little Things Can Make a Big Difference*, Little Brown, London 2014: 'The tipping point is that magic moment when an idea, trend, or social behavior crosses a threshold, tips, and spreads like wildfire'.

35 The following considerations are based on F. Möslein, above n. 7, pp. 90–93.

3.1. PROCEDURAL ENABLEMENT

With regard to procedural aspects, the state creates the necessary infrastructure for rule-making: to cite the German Constitutional Court again, the state provides regulatory tools and mechanisms, which are legally binding and establish legal positions that are enforceable in the case of disputes.[36] Several fundamental questions need to be answered in order to define the respective legal positions. Which statements are legally binding? What formalities does self-regulation require? Who is competent to regulate? All these questions concern the legal infrastructure of self-regulation. In fact, private law in general is widely regarded as representing this infrastructure.[37] Its provision by the state does not therefore necessarily speak against genuine self-regulation, but is a necessary precondition for self-regulation of any kind.

But where is the tipping point? What level and what intensity of the respective specifications transform genuine self-regulation into self-regulation induced by the state? A preliminary proposition is that this line is crossed once the state not only provides mechanisms, but also mandates self-regulation.[38] In fact, any such delegated rule-making lacks the necessary degree of private autonomy for it to qualify as genuine self-regulation, since it evolves at the behest of the state, not of private parties. Of course, the 'increasingly dynamic and synergistic interaction

---

36 See the reference, n. 21 above. For more detail on the private law implications, see H. Hanau, *Der Grundsatz der Verhältnismäßigkeit als Schranke privater Gestaltungsmacht,* Mohr Siebeck, Tübingen 2004, pp. 27–29, which claims that enforceability of private arrangements requires a respective order by the state (*Erforderlichkeit eines 'staatliche[n] Geltungsbefehl[s] für private Abreden'*).

37 Above all, see C. Windbichler, 'Neue Vertriebsformen und ihr Einfluss auf das Kaufrecht', *AcP* 198 (1998), 261, 271; cf. G. Bachmann, 'Privatrecht als Organisationsrecht – Grundlinien einer Theorie privater Regelsetzung', *Jahrbuch Junger Zivilrechtswissenschaftler (JJZ)* 2003, 1, 20 et seq.; J. Drexl, 'Zwingendes Recht als Strukturprinzip des Europäischen Verbrauchervertragsrechts?' in M. Coester et al. (eds.), *Festschrift für Hans Jürgen Sonnenberger*, C.H.Beck, Munich 2004, p. 783; S. Grundmann, 'Regulating Breach of Contract' (2007) 3 *European Review of Contract Law (ERCL)* 121, 122; S. Grundmann and F. Möslein, 'Vertragsrecht als Infrastruktur für Innovation', *Zeitschrift für die gesamte Privatrechtswissenschaft (ZfPW)* 2015, 435; K. Riesenhuber and F. Möslein, 'Contract Governance – Skizze einer Forschungsperspektive' in K. Riesenhuber (ed.), *Perspektiven des Europäischen Schuldvertragsrechts*, de Gruyter, Berlin 2008, p. 22. With respect to company law, see H. Fleischer, 'Gesetz und Vertrag', above n. 10, pp. 675–78 and 707 ('*Infrastrukturverantwortung des Gesetzgebers*').

38 For a fundamentally different approach, cf. P. Buck-Heeb and A. Dieckmann, above n. 3, p. 45, referring to state responsibility ('*staatliche Veranwortlichkeit*'), i.e. to the question about whether the state itself has a duty to regulate. What remains unclear, however, concerns the specific requirements with respect to the sources and intensity of such a duty. In fact, there are only a few instances where legislation is (constitutionally) mandatory; see J. Isensee, 'Der Bundesstaat. Bestand und Entwicklung' in P. Badura and H. Dreier (eds.), *Festschrift 50 Jahre Bundesverfassungsgericht*, Mohr Siebeck, Tübingen 2001, pp. 739 et seq. ('*Soweit der Bund die Gesetzgebung in bestimmten Materien hat, hat er die Befugnis, aber nicht die Verpflichtung, Gesetze zu erlassen*').

between public and private ... rule-making systems'[39] tends to make it difficult to distinguish between mandates and mechanisms. The example of 'good' companies' certification will serve as a test case as to whether this distinction is nonetheless workable in practice.

3.2. SUBSTANTIVE LIMITS

In addition to procedural differentiation, a second dimension concerns the substance of self-regulated rules. In this respect, the state can and does define limitations. For instance, the general clause of §138 of the German Bürgerliches Gesetzbuch (BGB), or Civil Code, prohibits extremely unjust or immoral agreements. A more specific example is §276, paragraph 3, of the German BGB, which disallows the exclusion of liability for wilful acts in advance.[40] Such provisions excluding certain (more or less specifically defined) substantive content of private arrangements are commonplace in private law. In particular, they serve to protect the common interest or interests of third parties.[41] As a consequence, such limitations are indeed indispensable for self-regulation to function well, given that self-regulation involves the specific risk of self-interest being put before public interest.[42]

Once again, if substantive limitations are ubiquitous, where is the tipping point? In this substantive respect, the preliminary proposition is that, as long as the state only limits the content of self-regulation, the latter is still within the realm of genuine self-regulation. The line is crossed, however, once the state positively instructs what content self-regulation should comprise. In turn, there are various instances where it is difficult to distinguish between limitations and instructions. Default rules are a prime example: while private parties may, by definition, deviate from them, such rules also serve as focal points, such that deviating from them could prove to be difficult, either for practical reasons or due to legal provisos.[43] But, 'taken as such, default rules do not intrude on autonomy, even if they influence people without persuading them'.[44] In spite of

[39] J. Lister, *Corporate Social Responsibility and the State*, UBC Press, Vancouver/Toronto 2011, p. 29 (illustrating the 'Co-Regulatory Policy Mix' with respect to environmental law).

[40] Various incidental restrictions of that liability remain possible, however; see L. Kähler, 'Mittelbare und unmittelbare Einschränkungen der Vorsatzhaftung', *JZ* 2007, 18.

[41] For more extensive information, see F. Möslein, above n. 12, pp. 164–75.

[42] Cf. the references in n. 15 above.

[43] Such legal and factual barriers are extensively dealt with by F. Möslein, above n. 12, pp. 186–334.

[44] C. Sunstein, 'Autonomy by Default' (2016) 16 *The American Journal of Bioethics* 1. In a similar vein, see F. Möslein, '"Governance by Default" – Innovation und Koordination durch dispositives Recht' in S. Grundmann et al. (eds.), *Festschrift für Klaus J. Hopt*, de Gruyter, Berlin 2010, p. 2861.

the applicability of default rules, which may or may not have an influence on its substantive content, self-regulation may still qualify as genuine.

3.3. ENFORCEABILITY

The third and final dimension concerns the enforcement of self-regulated rules. Hobbes' observations, as well as the reasoning of the German Constitutional Court, demonstrate that safeguarding private autonomy, as in self-regulation, requires some degree of enforceability. Of course, self-regulation can also be of a non-binding nature.[45] To note that codes of conduct, for instance, are not legally binding, however, 'is not to say that they do not influence international economic relations, nor does it mean that they produce no legal effects whatsoever'.[46] The enforcement mechanisms largely differ; they can also involve non-legal, i.e. social or economic, sanctions.[47] Moreover, seemingly 'voluntary' corporate codes may well be enforced by private law means.[48] When distinguishing between the two categories of self-regulation, the specific type of enforcement is relevant. In this respect, the preliminary proposition is that private enforcement (in a very large sense) characterises genuine self-regulation, whereas self-regulation induced by the state is typically also enforced by the state, i.e. publicly enforced.

4. EXAMPLES OF 'GOOD' COMPANIES' CERTIFICATION

While these three dimensions provide an idea of the divide between genuine self-regulation and self-regulation induced by the state, they need to be applied to and tested with different examples. According to the cross-sectoral nature of rule-making theory, one can possibly examine rules in entirely different areas of private law by that yardstick.[49] Building on earlier comparative work,[50] we pick the specific example of 'good' companies' certification here – not simply

---

45 See P. Buck-Heeb and A. Dieckmann, above n. 3, p. 42 (distinguishing between binding and non-binding self-regulation).

46 S. Zamora, 'Economic Relations and Development' in C.C. Joyner (ed.), *The United Nations and International Law*, Cambridge University Press, Cambridge 1997, p. 261.

47 Cf., for instance, A. Ogus and E. Carbonara, 'Self-regulation' in F. Parisi (ed.), *Production of Legal Rules*, 2nd ed., Edward Elgar, Cheltenham 2011, pp. 228–29 et seq.

48 A. Beckers, *Enforcing Corporate Social Responsibility Codes*, Hart, Oxford/Portland 2015.

49 For such additional examples cf. F. Möslein, above n. 7, pp. 94–108.

50 Cf., more extensively: F. Möslein, 'Certifying "Good" Companies: Regulatory Schemes for Corporate Sustainability in a Comparative Perspective' in C. Bruner and B. Sjåfjell (eds.), *Cambridge Handbook of Corporate Law, Corporate Governance and Sustainability*, Cambridge University Press, Cambridge 2020, p. 669.

due to the dynamic development of the respective rules, but mainly because of their significant comparative differences as regards the degree of state involvement.

4.1. REGULATORY NEED

Ensuring sustainability is one of the major challenges of our times, but individual nation states are severely overstretched by this monumental task. It requires a complex mix of different policy actions. What is more, their formal competences end at national boundaries.[51] Since the states' legislative power is limited, the suitable design of regulatory instruments becomes crucial in order to achieve sustainability aims. Market forces need to be activated in order to create incentives for companies to act sustainably. Yet it is one of the basic premises of the market economy that companies prioritise their own profits rather than the welfare of society.[52] Against this backdrop, sustainability goals can arguably only be achieved if sustainable behaviour creates some extra benefits for corporations – at least if the regulatory aim goes beyond the ordinary business case for corporate social responsibility so as to target 'strong sustainability', which requires business practices that conform to planetary boundaries by protecting social and ecological resources also for future generations.[53]

On the other hand, market actors – consumers, investors and workers alike – may have individual preferences for strong sustainability: their decisions to buy products, to make investments or to choose workplaces often not only depend on prices, financial returns or wages, but at least potentially also on the good (or bad) behaviour of corporations, namely on their social, ethical

---

51 On the politics of transnational sustainability laws, cf. P. Paiement, *Transnational Sustainability Laws*, Cambridge University Press, Cambridge 2017, pp. 201–36.

52 That fundamental profit orientation is beyond dispute, at least in principle, even though the more precise definition of corporate purposes is intensively debated both among economists and lawyers; see, for instance, O. Hart and L. Zingales, 'Companies Should Maximize Shareholder Welfare Not Market Value' (2017) 2 *Journal of Law, Finance and Accounting* 247; M. Blair and L. Stout, 'A Team Production Theory of Corporate Law' (1999) 85 *Virginia Law Review* 247; B. Sjåfjell, 'Dismantling the Legal Myth of Shareholder Primacy: The Corporation as a Sustainable Market Actor' in N. Boeger and C. Villiers (eds.), *Shaping the Corporate Landscape*, Hart, Oxford/Portland 2018, p. 77. Even in social enterprises, profit orientation counts among the corporate purposes (so-called dual-purpose, or hybrid, companies), cf. K. Westaway, *Profit & Purpose: How Social Innovation is Transforming Business for Good*, Wiley, Hoboken, NJ 2014, pp. 75–76; D. Brakman Reiser and S. Dean, *Social Enterprise Law*, Oxford University Press, Oxford 2017, p. 27–32.

53 See, for instance, S. Baker, M. Kousis, D. Richardson and S. Young, 'Introduction: the theory and practice of sustainable development in EU perspective' in id. (eds.), *The Politics of Sustainable Development*, Routledge, London/New York 1997, pp. 14 et seq.

and ecological track record. Impact investors, for instance, not only focus on financial returns but also aim at generating social and environmental benefits.[54] While impact-investing funds have amassed well over US$ 100 billion in assets under management, the evaluation of the companies to invest in has proven challenging.[55] These investee companies are highly diverse, spanning various sectors, levels of risk, and expected returns. Even for industry specialists the numerous standards for measuring social and environmental impact are overwhelming. Conscious consumers and workers face similar problems, but even on a larger scale. According to an empirical study, 66 per cent of global consumers are prepared to pay more to support companies committed to making a social and environmental impact.[56] But for consumers, it is even more difficult than for investors to measure sustainable corporate behaviour. Due to these difficulties, information asymmetries arise. Sustainable corporate behaviour therefore does not create the benefits that could otherwise be achieved.[57]

4.2. EMERGENCE OF CERTIFICATION SCHEMES

Certification schemes are a regulatory instrument to overcome this market imperfection. If designed properly they provide a means for sustainable companies to signal their good behaviour to the market.[58] Such signals make it easier for market actors to differentiate when making their respective market choices. While certificates for products (fair-trade coffee, for instance) are widespread and thoroughly researched,[59] certificates for good companies have

---

54 J. Rodin and M. Brandenburg, *The Power of Impact Investing*, Wharton School Press, Philadelphia 2014; see also R. Shiller, *Finance and the Good Society*, Princeton University Press, Princeton 2012.

55 Global Impact Investing Network (GIIN), *Annual Impact Investor Survey*, 7th ed., 2017, pp. III, XII et seq., and 10, available at https://thegiin.org/assets/GIIN_AnnualImpactInvestorSurvey_2017_Web_Final.pdf.

56 The Nielsen Company, *The Sustainability Imperative – New Insights on Consumer Expectations*, October 2015, p. 8, available at https://www.nielsen.com/ssa/en/insights/report/2015/the-sustainability-imperative-2/.

57 In more detail, but with respect to product certification: J. Belson, *Certification and Collective Marks – Law and Practice*, Edward Elgar, Cheltenham 2017, p. 237.

58 On preconditions for the well-functioning of (product) certification, with respect to food safety: C.-F. Lin, 'The Emergence and Influence of Transnational Private Regulation of Food Safety' in S. Halabi (ed.), *Food and Drug Regulation in an Era of Globalized Markets*, Academic Press, London 2015, pp. 192–97; F. Albersmeier, H. Schulze, G. Jahn and A. Spiller, 'The Reliability of Third-Party Certification in the Food Chain: From Checklists to Risk-Oriented Auditing' (2000) 20 *Food Control* 927.

59 On certification regimes like Fair Trade or Forest Stewardship, see S. Guéneau, 'Certification as a New Private Global Forest Governance System' in A. Peters, L. Koechlin, T. Forster and G. Zinkernagel (eds.), *Non-State Actors as Standard-Setters*, Cambridge University Press, Cambridge 2009, p. 379; L. Gulbrandsen, *Transnational Environmental Governance – The*

not yet drawn much academic attention. In business and legal practice, however, various certification schemes have evolved in different jurisdictions. A case in point is the B Corporation certification, a private certification issued by B Lab, a non-profit US organisation that now operates worldwide. To be granted the certification, companies must receive a minimum score on an assessment for social and environmental performance, integrate B Lab commitments to stakeholders into their governing documents, and pay a substantial annual fee.[60] Similar, but less widely known regimes have also developed in other major industrial countries – for instance, in the United Kingdom the 'Social Enterprise Mark' scheme as well as the concurring 'Certified Social Enterprise' badge; in France the two-level ESS/ESUS approval (*qualité d'entreprise de l'économie sociale et solidaire*, and *agrément entreprise solidaire d'utilité sociale*); in Germany, among others, the 'It Works!' label (*PHINEO Wirkt!-Siegel*); and in South Korea the 'Social Enterprises Certification'.[61]

These various regimes of 'good' companies' certification differ widely both in their institutional design and in their substantive content, as well as with respect to their mechanisms of enforcement. 'Good' companies' certification regimes are therefore a prime example to illustrate and analyse the classification and general criteria that we have developed, namely the key element of regulatory initiative and its three different dimensions.[62] In order to assess these various regimes, it is also important to keep the general advantages and dangers of self-regulation in mind that have already been enumerated. On the one hand, self-regulation is relatively flexible, quick and cheap to achieve, it accurately reflects the issues and needs of specific sectors, and it creates a sense of a common bond, which in turn increases the likelihood of compliance. On the other hand, there are the various dangers of self-interest coming before public interest, anti-competitive effects

---

Emergence and Effects of the Certification of Forests and Fisheries, Edward Elgar, Cheltenham 2010; A. Nicholls and C. Opal, *Fair Trade: Market-Driven Ethical Consumption*, Sage, London 2005.

60 In detail: R. Honeyman, *The B Corp Handbook*, Berrett-Koehler, San Francisco 2014.

61 For a survey on these and further (European) regimes, see European Commission (ed.), *A Map of Social Enterprises and their Eco-Systems in Europe – Synthesis Report*, Brussels 2015, pp. 79–86; also A. Triponel and N. Agapitova, *Legal Frameworks for Social Enterprise*, World Bank Group, Washington 2016; on the more recent French regime: J. Lasserre Capdeville, 'Financement alternatif relevant des principes de l'économie sociale et solidaire' in J.-M. Moulin (ed.), *Droit de la Finance Alternative*, Bruylant, Brussels 2017, pp. 47–50; on the South Korean regime: E.Bidet and H.-S. Eum, 'Social enterprise in South Korea: History and Diversity' (2011) 7 *Social Enterprise Journal* 77 et seq. In Germany, additional concurring regimes have been developed both by the technical inspection association (Technischer Überwachungsverein Rheinland, TÜV Rheinland AG) and by a private association dedicated to the economy for the common good (Internationaler Verein zur Förderung der Gemeinwohl-Ökonomie e.V.), see https://www.tuv.com/content-media-files/germany/pdfs/0397-tuv-rheinland-bsci-auditing/tuv-rheinland-broschuere-nachhaltige-unternehmensfuehrung-de.pdf and https://www.ecogood.org/apply-ecg/audit-and-peer-evaluation/.

62 See above section 3.

and entry barriers, and the risks of non-enforcement, in addition to concerns about the lack of democratic legitimacy.[63]

4.3. PROCEDURAL ENABLEMENT: PUBLIC vs. PRIVATE SCHEMES

The certification schemes differ fundamentally with respect to the institutional framework within which they are operating. While the French and the South Korean schemes are administered by state institutions and operate on a legal basis, the US, UK and German schemes are entirely private in nature (with one recent modification, however, in Delaware). Whereas the former regimes are not self-regulatory in nature, but qualify as public regimes, the latter are typical examples of self-regulation. Within these two broad categories, however, important further institutional differences can be identified.

The public regime in South Korea is based on the Social Enterprise Promotion Act, which was enacted in 2007.[64] In its Article 7, that Act provides that 'anyone who intends to run a social enterprise shall be certified by the Minister of Labor after meeting the certification requirements' further specified within that law. More specifically, a Social Enterprise Support Committee within the Ministry of Labour is charged with the certification procedure (Art. 4, para. 1). This Committee is composed of no more than 15 members including the Chairman, who is the Vice Minister of Labor; all other members are appointed by the Minister 'out of persons with deep knowledge and experience concerning public officials of the related central administrative agency and social enterprises determined by the Presidential Decree' (Art. 4, para. 2). While both due to its position under the Ministry and due to its composition, the Korean regime is potentially subject to political influence, the second public regime is much more of an administrative nature. That French system is based on the Act relating to the Social and Solidarity-based Economy of 2014, supplemented by two ministerial rulings of 2015,[65] and it provides for two different levels of certification, ESS and ESUS (the second requiring additional conditions). While various ministries, or public authorities affiliated with ministries, are

63 Above section 2.1.

64 Social Enterprise Promotion Act, enacted by Act No. 8217 as of 3 January 2007, amended by Act No. 8361 as of 11 April 2007; English version available at www.ilo.org/dyn/natlex/docs/ELECTRONIC/78610/84122/F-684569511/KOR78610 Eng 2012.pdf.

65 Loi no. 2014-856 du 31 juillet 2014 relative à l'économie sociale et solidaire, JORF no. 176 du 1 août 2014, p. 12666; Arrêté du 5 août 2015 fixant la composition du dossier de demande d'agrément 'entreprise solidaire d'utilité sociale', JORF no. 185 du 12 août 2015, p. 14004; and Décret du 23 juin 2015 relatif à l'agrément 'entreprise solidaire d'utilité sociale' régi par l'article L. 3332-17-1 du code du travail, JORF no. 145 du 25 juin 2015, p. 10676; all three available at https://www.legifrance.gouv.fr.

responsible for the general implementation of those rules, the commercial register and the regional prefect are the bodies in charge of receiving individual applications for such certifications, and of proceeding with their registration or approval, respectively.

Private regimes, on the other hand, lack both such legislative basis and oversight by public bodies. The most popular certification scheme, B Corporation, is run and administered by B Lab, a non-profit organisation based in Pennsylvania and financed by various private sponsors, such as the influential Rockefeller Foundation, and by annual licence fees to be paid by certified corporations. Since its foundation in 2006, B Lab claims to serve the 'global movement of entrepreneurs using the power of business to solve social and environmental problems'.[66] Its assessment criteria – the preconditions for certification, so to speak – are formulated by the Standards Advisory Council, an independent committee within B Lab composed of about 20 members, including representatives from the business, government and non-profit sectors.[67]

Interestingly, the US state of Delaware recently enacted (public) framework legislation on sustainability certification.[68] That Code only applies to Delaware-governed entities that seek to become certified as reporting entities. It is entirely voluntary and does not mandate specific certification schemes but explicitly allows respective organisations to select their own standards or to tailor them to their specific needs. It does require, though, a formal resolution creating such standards and specifying assessment measures to be taken at the highest organisational level, i.e. the board of directors or equivalent governing body. These rules clearly demonstrate that a public framework legislation does not change the self-regulatory character of the certification scheme itself, and that it does not even transform it into self-regulation induced by the state. Instead, the certification scheme can still be classified into the subcategory of genuine self-regulation since the state legislator only provides certain procedural mechanisms, but does not mandate self-regulation or its specific application.

---

66 Cf. https://www.bcorporation.net/; see also D. Brakman Reiser, 'Benefit Corporations – A Sustainable Form of Organization?' (2011) 46 *Wake Forest Law Review* 591, 594; F. Möslein and A. Mittwoch, 'Soziales Unternehmertum im US-amerikanischen Gesellschaftsrecht' (2016) 80 *Rabels Zeitschrift für ausländisches und internationales Privatrecht* 406 et seq.; K. Engsig Sorensen and M. Neville, 'Social Enterprises: How Should Company Law Balance Flexibility and Credibility' (2014) 15 *European Business Organization Law Review* 280 et seq.

67 In more detail M. Nass, 'The Viability of Benefit Corporations: An Argument for Greater Transparency and Accountability' (2014) 39 *Iowa Journal of Corporation Law* 884 et seq.

68 Certification of Adoption of Sustainability and Transparency Standards Act, House Bill No. 310, available at http://legis.delaware.gov/json/BillDetail/GenerateHtmlDocument?legislationId=26304&legislationTypeId=1&docTypeId=2&legislationName=HB310.

The UK Social Enterprise Mark scheme, which prides itself on being 'the only internationally available social enterprise accreditation',[69] operates within a comparable, but entirely private framework. It is run by a community interest company limited by shares that is owned by a single shareholder, the RISE Legacy Trust, originally set up by Regional Infrastructure for Social Enterprise (RISE) Ltd.[70] Much like its US counterpart, that UK scheme is also financed by licence fees. It also contains an independent body, the Certification Panel, similarly consisting of 'representatives from business, legal and social enterprise experts' (but not from government).[71] This Panel's primary duty consists, however, in overseeing the application and assessment procedure. It performs administrative and also judicial functions rather than regulatory tasks (as opposed to B Lab's Council). The Social Enterprise Mark's criteria, on the other hand, are based on the official definition of social enterprise established by the UK government, namely the UK Department of Trade and Industry, in 2002.[72] In that sense, that private UK scheme has a public element in it, at least at the substantive level. The other UK certification scheme, the Certified Social Enterprise badge, in contrast, is based on a somewhat different institutional structure. While the organisation responsible, Social Enterprise UK, has also the legal form of a community interest company (but limited by guarantee) and maintains close informal ties with various government agencies, it is a membership body, substantively financed by annual membership fees.[73] Moreover, its governance structure is less formal, without any comparable independent committee.

A similar structure is also a feature of the German label issued by PHINEO, a German non-profit company (*gemeinnützige Aktiengesellschaft*). Its governance structure is the same as that of ordinary German stock companies, supplemented by an additional honorary advisory board. Its main shareholders are the Bertelsmann foundation and Deutsche Börse AG, along with other foundations and for-profit companies. As opposed to Social Enterprise UK, however, PHINEO has established an independent advisory body (*Empfehlungskommission*). It is competent to take the final certification decision, but also gives content-related advice.[74] In sum, the institutional frameworks of private self-regulatory regimes

---

69 http://www.socialenterprisemark.org.uk.

70 On the broader background see R. Ridley-Duff and C. Southcombe, 'The Social Enterprise Mark: a critical review of its conceptual dimensions' (2012) 8 *Social Enterprise Journal* 178.

71 A directory of its members is available at http://www.socialenterprisemark.org.uk.

72 Ground-breaking UK Department of Trade and Industry, *Social Enterprise: A Strategy for Success*, London 2002, p. 13; further elaborated, for example, in Department for Business, Innovation & Skills, 'Small Business Survey 2014: SME employers', BIS Research Paper No. 214, March 2015, p. 35.

73 Cf. www.socialenterprise.org.uk, and the accounts stated in Social Enterprise UK, *Impact Report 2016–2017*, London, 2017, pp. 29 et seq.

74 In detail: PHINEO Annual Report (Jahresbericht) 2016, pp. 18–22 (governance structure) and 29 (*Empfehlungskommission*), available at https://www.phineo.org/uploads/Downloads/PHINEO_Jahresbericht_2016.pdf.

range from formalised regimes with nearly state-like divisions of power to informal governance structures that largely correspond to those of ordinary companies. In spite of these differences, all these regimes qualify as genuine self-regulation since none of them is mandated by the state.

4.4. SUBSTANTIVE CONTENT: CERTIFICATION PROCEDURES AND CRITERIA

The substantive content of the certification regimes concerns both the procedure that companies need to follow in order to obtain a specific certificate, and the criteria that they must meet in order to obtain the certificate in question. While these rules differ substantively, the dividing lines interestingly do not correspond to their institutional differences and their (self-)regulatory nature: some certification procedures are much more formalised than others, but private schemes are not necessarily less formal than public schemes. Similarly, the criteria can either be formulated as strictly necessary conditions – where every single condition needs to be fulfilled – or they can constitute a multi-factor model, subject to a more flexible, overarching assessment of all different criteria. Also in this respect, private schemes are not necessarily less formal than public schemes: while the French and the South Korean legal regimes are examples of the first 'tick-the-box' approach,[75] the B Impact Assessment follows the second path, measuring a wide range of different impact factors and requiring an overall score of at least 80 points out of 200.[76]

As regards the certification procedure, the most informal scheme appears to be that of Social Enterprise UK since its membership scheme is simply based on self-certification, i.e. a declaration that the respective company meets the basic certification criteria.[77] In contrast, all other schemes are based on a more objective assessment – not by the certified company, but by the certifying body. They all provide for assessment procedures which only vary in detail. For instance, the PHINEO analysis consists of multiple procedural steps,[78] and the B Impact Assessment is similarly detailed in its specific procedural

---

75 The provisions in Art. L. 3332-17-1 Code du Travail as amended by Art. 11 Loi no. 2014-856 du 31 juillet 2014 (above n. 65) and in Art. 8, para. 1 Social Enterprise Promotion Act (above n. 64) both contain enumerative lists of criteria that need to be fulfilled cumulatively ('*conditions cumulatives*').

76 The assessment ends with a tabular overview that compares the scores in each single category with the general average of all companies (as the benchmark); for an example report see https://bimpactassessment.net/how-it-works/compare-your-impact.

77 Cf. the membership application form at https://www.socialenterprise.org.uk/, requiring the signature of a short statement which contains the relevant criteria.

78 In more detail on these four steps (online questionnaire, disclosure of information material, site review, and decision by the independent recommendatory body): https://www.phineo.org/en/impact-analyses.

requirements, namely with respect to transparency and disclosure, and provides inter alia for complaints procedures, background checks, and site reviews.[79] These procedures are almost administrative in nature. In this respect, they do not differ substantively from public, regulatory schemes such as the French ESUS approval. While the procedures are largely similar, the public schemes provide for publication in official journals or registers, such as the governmental newspaper in South Korea or the *recueil des actes administratifs* of the regional prefecture in France.[80] Another procedural feature concerns the time frames for which certification is granted, but again, that difference does not depend on the public or private character of the institutional framework.[81] The key procedural difference between public and private schemes, and between regulatory and self-regulatory regimes, therefore concerns the certification fees: while the public schemes demand either no fees or at least small, fixed administrative fees,[82] the private schemes usually provide for substantial fees calculated according to the turnover of certified companies.[83] Private schemes simply need to finance themselves, but their desire to generate fees can create substantial conflicts of interests for certifying bodies, even though the fear of sustaining reputational hits in the marketplace may partly mitigate that conflict.[84]

Companies must meet these criteria in order to obtain the certificate in question. In all regimes, these criteria comprise various elements that relate to the legal form, business model, governance structure and financial order of the organisation in question. With respect to the legal form, all certification regimes apply to a variety of different legal structures. Almost all regimes include commercial companies, even though some regimes are (or were) mainly targeted at non-profit organisations.[85] Within the B Impact Assessment, however,

---

79 Cf. the Appendix to the 'Agreement for B Corporation Certification', available in different versions at https://bcorporation.net/certification/legal-requirements.

80 Art. 8, para. 2 Social Enterprise Promotion Act (above n. 64); Art. 3, para. 5 Décret du 23 juin 2015 (above n. 65).

81 While the public scheme in France provides in principle for a validity of five years, the South Korean certificate is valid until cancellation. The private schemes in the UK and the US, on the other hand, provide for annual or biennial renewals, be they re-approvals or re-self-assessments. Cf. in more detail: F. Möslein, above n. 50, p. 674.

82 For South Korea, cf. the information available at http://www.socialenterprise.or.kr. In France, the ESS *immatriculation* involves a fee of €89.80 (while the ESUS approval is seemingly available free of charge).

83 See again the comparative table available at https://www.socialenterprisemark.org.uk/wp-content/uploads/2020/03/Social-Enterprise-Mark-Comparison.pdf. More extensively: F. Möslein, above n. 50, p. 674.

84 The only exception in this respect is the PHINEO analysis: it is free of charge for applicants, and instead financed by PHINEO's shareholders and partners, cf. https://www.phineo.org/en/impact-analyses.

85 In this vein, the French ESS regime used to be confined to associations, foundations and cooperative and mutual organisations, but was subsequently also made available to

charities and non-profit organisations are conversely *not* eligible, as opposed to cooperative and commercial companies: this certificate is exclusively available for legal forms that are designed for for-profit businesses.[86] An important difference between public and private self-regulatory regimes, however, relates to their respective territorial scopes of application: due to conflict-of-law principles, public regimes are obtainable only within their respective jurisdiction.[87] In contrast, private regimes are able to accept international applications.[88] The key substantive condition relates to the business model: as a general rule, only 'social enterprises' are eligible, and applicant companies therefore need to aim at some social benefit or social impact. A more precise specification of that qualification, however, varies considerably between the different certification schemes. Most public regimes focus on the corporate objective and have more or less specific preconditions. Private self-regulatory regimes, on the other hand, have a broader focus, but are often less specific. An interesting case in point is the Social Enterprise Mark, since its criteria are based on the government definition of a social enterprise, despite its self-regulatory nature. Still, it is satisfied with any 'social and/or environmental objective', as long as this purpose is clearly articulated within the legal objects of the organisation.[89] The B Corporation scheme, in contrast, is broad and more specific at the same time: it does not stipulate any specific corporate purpose, but requires a commitment to the triple bottom line approach to business to be incorporated in the company's governing documents, usually 'an objects clause which states that [the company] exists to promote the success of the business for the benefit of its shareholders but also to have a material positive impact on society and the environment'.[90]

---

commercial companies through the 2014 legislative reform; for a historic account see Y. Blein and D. Fasquelle, *Rapport d'information sur la mise en application de la loi n 2014-856 du 31 juillet 2014 relative à l'économie sociale et solidaire,* Paris 2016, p. 9.

86 In more detail R. Honeyman, above n. 60, p. 175.

87 The French regime at least builds on the entry in the commercial register, see Art. 1, para. 3 Loi no. 2014-856 du 31 juillet 2014 (above n. 65). On both theories in general, see for instance: S. Rammeloo, *Corporations in Private International Law: A European Perspective,* Oxford University Press, Oxford 2001, pp. 9–20; S. Grundmann, *European Company Law,* 2nd ed., Intersentia, Cambridge 2012, pp. 125–129 (§7, paras. 6–10).

88 B Lab, in particular, has established a global network of partner organisations in order to make B Impact Assessments available for companies worldwide, see https://www.bcorporation.net/b-corp-community-0/global-partners; for a similar initiative of the Social Enterprise Mark cf. http://www.socialenterprisemark.org.uk/international-applications/#applications. Its Impact Assessment is 'available to any business in the world, regardless of its existing legal structure or location of incorporation', see R. Honeyman, above n. 60, p. 5.

89 See the Social Enterprise Mark Eligibility Criteria, available at https://www.socialenterprisemark.org.uk/wp-content/uploads/2020/11/SEM-Qualification-criteria-Nov-20.pdf (criterion A, even if with some specifications in the footnote).

90 In this sense (with respect to UK law): https://bcorporation.uk/certification; see also D. Hunter, 'The Arrival of B Corps in Britain' in N. Boeger and C. Villiers (eds.), *Shaping the Corporate Landscape,* Hart, Oxford/Portland 2018), pp. 259 et seq.

Nevertheless, it evaluates the effectiveness of corporate behaviour using its multi-dimensional performance test, assessing the overall impact of a company on its various stakeholders, in particular workers, the community, the environment and future generations.[91] In this manner, the relevant business models are tested both on paper and in substance, whereas all other schemes focus on the legal documents.

Another condition relates to the governance structure of the companies to which these schemes apply. Certification schemes require, on the one hand, a reliable corporate structure that fosters unbiased, transparent management decisions, in particular by providing for effective governing bodies, control and compliance mechanisms, disclosure of corporate information, and for a 'democratic' distribution of power among the different corporate bodies, for instance with regard to appointment decisions. Whereas some private self-regulatory regimes are not very specific in this respect, both public certification schemes stipulate participation requirements that are much more ambitious. A final set of conditions relates to the applicant company's financial order. Above all, profit distribution clauses are required by most regimes; they demand that a significant proportion of the organisation's annual profits is reinvested towards its social or environmental objectives. In this respect, the dividing line is not so much between public regimes and self-regulation, but between the US and the European approach: the US B Corp scheme is much less demanding than its counterpart.[92]

4.5. ENFORCEABILITY: LEGAL PROHIBITIONS vs. TRADEMARK REGISTRATION AND UNFAIR COMPETITION RULES

While procedural frameworks and substantive criteria do not differ significantly between public and private self-regulatory schemes, the decisive difference would seem to relate to the legal effects of certification: only public bodies are able to amend the applicable legislative framework in order to mandatorily provide for such effects. But then again, private schemes are based on the binding force of self-commitments,[93] and legislators are by no means prevented from attaching legal consequences to private certification (even though they should do so with

---

91 Extensively on this assessment R. Honeyman, above n. 60, p. 175; see also K. Engsig Sorensen and M. Neville, above n. 66, p. 280.

92 Its (already flexible) threshold is as low as 20 per cent of annual profits, or 2 per cent of sales, see R. Honeyman, above n. 60, p. 139.

93 Cf., with regard to codes of conduct in general: P. Leyens, 'Self-Commitments and the Binding Force of Self-Regulation with Respect to Third Parties in Germany', European Corporate Governance Institute (ECGI), Law Working Paper No. 379/2017, available at https://ssrn.com/abstract=3087417.

care, as the use of credit ratings in financial ratings has shown).[94] Taking this a step further, the private B Corp scheme requires certified companies to 'support B Lab's public policy objectives of passing benefit corporation legislation',[95] and the widespread enactment of such legislation in almost all of the states in the US (and also in Europe, so far in Italy) indicates that private certification schemes have a surprisingly strong influence on public law-makers.[96] As a consequence, that seemingly clear dividing line between self-regulation and public regulation is becoming increasingly blurred.

The core legal effect of certification is that only certified companies can make use of the respective certificate, and any unauthorised use is prohibited. This principle is explicitly stated in the applicable laws of both public regimes, in part along with supplementary rules on fines that apply in the case of violations.[97] Private schemes accomplish very similar results on the basis of either trademark registration or unfair competition rules. Under the intellectual property law of most countries, there are provisions on the protection of certification marks as signs of supervised quality, and of collective marks that indicate membership in a group.[98] The US B Corporation certificate as well as the UK Social Enterprise Mark are registered as trademarks, and are therefore legally protected against infringements since only accepted licensees are permitted to use the respective certificates.[99] Other schemes, namely Social Enterprise UK and PHINEO, seemingly did not seek trademark protections for their badges. Unauthorised use is nonetheless prohibited by unfair competition law and its general prohibition of misleading statements.[100]

Beyond the prohibition of unauthorised use, supplementary legal effects can (but do not need to be) attributed to certification, in particular as incentives to opt into such regimes and to comply with their respective rules of corporate conduct.

---

94 In more detail C. Bruner, 'States, Markets, and Gatekeepers: Public-Private Regulatory Regimes in an Era of Economic Globalization' (2008) 30 *Michigan Journal of International Law* 125, 136–39; C. Bruner and R. Abelal, 'To Judge Leviathan: Sovereign Credit Ratings, National Law, and the World Economy' (2005) 25 *Journal of Public Policy* 191, 207–09.

95 Cf. the agreements for B Corporation Certification applicable to corporations located in states where benefit corporations are not yet available at https://www.bcorporation.net (Legal Requirements).

96 More extensively F. Möslein and A. Mittwoch, 'above n. 66, pp. 410 et seq. ('*kreiert … eine Art kollusiven Rechtsformzwang*'). On the recent introduction of benefit corporations in Italy see, for instance: D. Lenzi, 'Le società benefit' (2016) 43 *Giurisprudenza commerciale* I, 895.

97 Cf. F. Möslein, above n. 50, p. 678 (with references in n. 65).

98 In much more detail, for instance: J. Belson, above n. 57.

99 With respect to B Corporation Certification, cf. the respective agreement (n. 95); the Social Enterprise Mark Licence Terms & Conditions are available at https://www.socialenterprisemark.org.uk/wp-content/uploads/2019/08/Licence-Terms-and-Conditions_August-2019.pdf.

100 With regard to CSR declarations in general, cf. the contributions in: R. Hilty and F. Henning-Bodewig (eds.), *Corporate Social Responsibility – Verbindliche Standards des Wettbewerbsrechts?*, Springer, Heidelberg 2014.

The aim of such supportive efforts is to ensure the recognition of social enterprises and to foster their positive societal and environmental impact, as well as their impact on long-term sustainability in general. Correspondingly, the French ESS certificate gives access to a variety of public finance schemes, for instance within the framework of so-called *projets d'investissement d'avenir.*[101] In addition, investors of ESUS-certified companies enjoy tax benefits, and national law provides for additional political support at the regional and local level.[102] While in France public support is linked to public certification schemes, such support does not necessarily presuppose public certification, as the UK example shows: the Public Services (Social Value) Act 2012 provides in its section 1(3) that procuring authorities must 'consider (a) how what is proposed to be procured might improve the economic, social and environmental well-being of the relevant area, and (b) how, in conducting the process of procurement, it might act with a view to securing that improvement'.[103] Despite its unspecific wording, this requirement is generally regarded as preferential for certified companies. Certification serves as a (rough) proxy for social value – regardless of the private character of both UK certification schemes.[104] Even though public support is thereby linked to a private scheme, this link is less specifically tailored than the link in the French public scheme. Certification serves as a proxy for social value, but is not a necessary condition for the support in question.

5. CONCLUSION

Dealing with the ambiguities of self-regulation, this contribution proposed a three-dimensional grid of criteria in order to distinguish between genuine self-regulation and self-regulation induced by the state. The three dimensions relate to the procedure, the substance and the enforcement of self-regulation. 'Good' companies' certification then served as an example in order to test and to apply these different criteria. As a special type of signalling instrument – implemented not by the producer, but by a third party – certification can help

---

101 See https://www.caissedesdepots.fr/programme-dinvestissements-davenir; other forms of financial support are listed in this note published by the Conseil National des Chambres Régionales de l'Économie Sociale et Solidaire: https://www.cress-pdl.org/wp-content/uploads/CNCRES-Note_Societes_commerciales_ESS_Oct2016-1.pdf, p. 3.

102 Conseil National des Chambres Régionales de l'Économie Sociale et Solidaire, ibid., p. 4.

103 In comparison to similar rules in other countries: M. Camilleri, 'CSR 2.0 and the New Era of Corporate Citizenship', IGI Global, Hershey PA 2016, p. 65.

104 See, for instance, J. Barraket, R. Keast and C. Furneaux, *Social Procurement and New Public Governance,* Routledge, London 2016, p. 115: 'The Social Enterprise Mark makes it easy for commissioners and procurement managers to identify when social value is being delivered'.

to prevent market failures that would otherwise occur. Interestingly, the various regimes of companies' certification differ widely in their institutional design, in their substantive content and with respect to their mechanisms of enforcement. However, the difference between public regimes and self-regulatory schemes has surprisingly little effect on their regulatory design: both with respect to certification procedures and criteria, private self-regulatory schemes are not necessarily less formal than public regimes. Even with respect to the legal effects of certification, in particular its enforcement, the functional similarities of the different regimes are striking. As a consequence, the ambiguities of self-regulation – and its contrast to public regulation – may have less effect on the specific design of rules than one would commonly assume.

CONTRACT LAW UNDER REGULATORY SIEGE – REVIVAL OF CONTRACT LAW?

Standardisation, Regulation and Consent

Hans-W. Micklitz*

1. CONTEXT, CLAIM, ARGUMENT

Regulation and standardisation are conceptually and logically dependent on one another: without regulation no standardisation, and without standardisation no regulation. Regulation can take different forms, as standardisation can. Regulation may be legally binding or not, and may be public or private or both. Whoever is responsible for it, regulation is unthinkable without a particular purpose. Standardisation de-individualises whatever phenomenon is submitted to standardisation – a product, a service, the addressee of the standardisation, the substance or the procedure, even a technology. Contract is Janus-faced: contracts can be subject to standardisation, usually through standard terms, or they can be subject to individual negotiations and end in tailor-made rules for the parties. Contracts are bound to a regulatory purpose, which differs

* I would like to express my gratitude to Stefan Grundmann and Mateusz Grochowski for demonstrating incredible patience in my constant requests for an extension of the deadline.

according to whether the contract is standardised or individualised. The purpose can be private, public or private/public.

My perspective is a European transnational one. Contract law is under regulatory siege, but the question is what remains of consent as the basis for contract law? The 'elephant in the room' is the issue of the public interest vs. the private interest.[1] Who is best suited to promote public interests through contract – the public regulator who narrows the freedom of the contracting parties through mandatory standards, or the private regulator, in spite of their self-interest in contracts that are supposed to neglect public interests? Or is the engagement of both the public and the private needed? The standard assumption seems to be that the public regulator is better suited to promote public interests, being equated with the ideal of the Western democratic nation state. In private law beyond the nation state, there is no democratic regulation. What remains is the extraterritoriality or the external extension of national public regulation.[2] The intellectual umbrella is the law and theory of transnational law. However, there are surface and below-surface cracks in the well-established patterns of discourse. There is doubt as to the wisdom of the public regulator, not only with regard to the feasibility of achieving public interest through contract regulation, but also, and much more deeply, the political and economic implications that result from the instrumentalisation and functionalisation of contract law.[3] If contract can be instrumentalised and functionalised for public interests, then contract can also be used for any other political purpose, both 'good' and 'bad'. Hand in hand with a growing distrust for public regulation in the name of 'public' interests, there is a move in legal practice and legal theory to stress not only the autonomy but the responsibility of private parties in the negotiation and conclusion of contracts.[4] From such a perspective, contract is not materialised only so as to safeguard the autonomy of the private parties. The individual parties bear a deeper interpersonal responsibility, which is understood as an integral part of the realisation of autonomy. This kind of legal thought opens pathways to think about the feasibility of going beyond interpersonal responsibility, which takes at least third-party interests into account.

The legitimacy and the binding effect of a contract is based on the idea of the mutual consent of two individual and autonomous parties. They voluntarily

1 For an early account B.A. Weisbrod, J.F. Handler and N.K. Komesar, *Public Interest Law. An Economic Institutional Analysis*, University of California Press, Berkeley 1978.

2 J. Scott, 'Extraterritoriality and Territorial Extension in EU Law' (2014) 62 *American Journal of Comparative Law* 87.

3 P. Kjaer (ed.), *The Law of Political Economy: Transformations in the Function of Law*, Cambridge University Press, Cambridge 2020.

4 H. Dagan, 'Between Regulatory and Autonomy-Based Private Law' (2016) 22 *European Law Journal* 644; H. Dagan and M. Heller, *The Choice Theory of Contracts*, Cambridge University Press, Cambridge/New York 2017.

engage in negotiations that ideally end up in an agreement that meets the interests of the parties concerned. The purpose of the contract is what the parties have agreed upon. Private law theory considers such negotiated contracts to be 'just' – the result is contractual justice.[5] Such an understanding unites all private law orders around the world. However, there is a well-known mismatch between the idea of consent and the functionalisation and the instrumentalisation of contract through private and public regulation,[6] where the idea of mutual consent and negotiations between two parties on the same level risks turning into 'ideology of consent'. Contract is reduced to its external form; the consent is no longer bound to individual negotiations, but to the formal approval of a standardised contract model.

The long-standing debate on standard terms[7] serves as the theoretical and conceptual background for structuring three more recent forms where standardisation and regulation intermingle with contract: transnational private regulation, European Union contract regulation, and co-regulation, a combination of binding public and non-binding private regulation. Lately, two particular manifestations of contract regulation have attracted attention: first, the use of contracts and codes of conduct in the organisation of transnational economic transactions,[8] in particular through global value and global supply chains;[9] and second, the use of contract law for the completion of regional markets, with the EU at the forefront in what I have coined European regulatory private law.[10] The first can be associated with transnational private regulation,

---

5 S. Grundmann, 'Negotiation, the Function of Contract and the "Justice of Consensus"' in S. Grundmann, H.-W. Micklitz and M. Renner, *New Private Law Theory: A Pluralist Approach*, Cambridge University Press, Cambridge, forthcoming 2021.

6 With regard to transnational regulation, F. Cafaggi, 'Rethinking Private Regulation in the European Regulatory Space' in F. Cafaggi (ed.), *Reframing Self-Regulation in European Private Law*, Kluwer Law International, Alphen aan den Rijn 2006, pp. 3–75; F. Cafaggi, 'New Foundations of Transnational Private Regulation' (2011) 38 *Journal of Law and Society* 20–49. With regard to national and European regulation, see H. Collins, *Regulating Contracts*, Oxford University Press, Oxford/New York 1999.

7 The literature on standard terms is vast. Some of the classics are, in chronological order: L. Raiser, *Das Recht der Allgemeinen Geschäftsbedingungen*, Hanseat. Verl. Anst., Hamburg 1935; F. Kessler, 'Contracts of Adhesion. Some Thoughts about Freedom of Contract' (1943) 43 *Columbia Law Review* 629; H.-J. Pflug, *Kontrakt und Status im Recht der Allgemeinen Geschäftsbedingungen*, C.H. Beck, Munich 1986; H. Collins, above n. 6.

8 Very useful in structuring the different strands of academic scholarship: T.C. Halliday and G. Shaffer, *Transnational Legal Orders*, Cambridge University Press, Cambridge 2015.

9 J. Salminen and M. Rajavuori, 'Transnational sustainability laws and the regulation of global value chains: Comparison and framework for analysis' (2019) 26 *Maastricht Journal of European and Comparative Law*, 602; K.H. Eller, 'Private governance of global value chains from within: lessons from and for transnational law' (2017) 8 *Transnational Legal Theory* 296.

10 G. Comparato, H.-W. Micklitz and Y. Svetiev, 'The Regulatory Character of European Private Law' in C. Twigg-Flesner (ed.), *Research Handbook on EU Consumer and Contract Law*, Edward Elgar, Cheltenham 2016, pp. 35–67.

the second with public regulation beyond the nation state.[11] What is much less in the limelight is a third form of contract regulation through a combination of public and private regulation.[12] In co-regulation, the public regulator establishes a frame which is filled and operationalised through private regulation. Whilst co-regulation is in theory open to be used for contract regulation, in practice it is fully operational only in the field of technical standards.[13] It will have to be shown that technical standards must be understood as a third form of contract regulation. The instrumentalisation and functionalisation of technical standards for contract regulation is less visible and less well known, but seems apt to become an efficient and effective tool of 'contract regulation without contract'.

This chapter makes two claims. Firstly, a common analytical frame is needed to better understand the rationale for and the interaction between the three patterns of regulation. This is done under the heading 'analytical design' in order to make the 'regulatory siege' of contract law visible and understandable. The second step is devoted to the specificities of the three patterns of regulation and how consent in traditional private law is maintained, defended or revitalised. The chapter concludes with a preliminary outlook of the possible consequences.

2. ANALYTICAL DESIGN

Confronting the three forms of regulation with regard to the functional and instrumental use of contracts requires clarification of the analytical design, in terms of the interaction between the three types of regulation – private, public and co-regulation – and the impact on the regulatory frame in which the individual contract is embedded and the role and function of consent within the individual contract. Firstly, there are various ways to distinguish the two levels: the European way seems to differentiate between contractual practice (the regulatory level) and contract law (the individual level); the American way between private ordering (the regulatory level) and contract law (the individual level). My preference is for the European terminology. The second feature relates to the form and content of private, public and co-regulation so as to lay down the parameters for the comparison between the three. The third

11 R. Michaels and N. Jansen, 'Private Law Beyond the State? Europeanization, Globalization, Privatization' (2006) 54 *American Journal of Comparative Law* 843.

12 H. Schepel, *The Constitution of Private Governance*, Hart Publishing, Oxford 2005.

13 H. Schepel and J. Falke, *Legal Aspects of Standardisation in the Member States of the EC and EFTA*, Volume 1: *Comparative Report*, Volume 2: *Country Reports*, Volume 3: *Rechtliche Aspekte der Normung in den EG-Mitgliedstaaten und der EFTA*, Office for Publication of the European Communities, Luxembourg 2000.

feature is meant to prepare the ground for the more theoretical and conceptual conclusions through highlighting the various forms of private and public regulatory failures and the move towards technical standardisation.

2.1. CONTRACT LAW vs. PUBLIC, PRIVATE AND CO-REGULATION

The distinction between standardisation through regulation and consent through negotiation is made via the lenses of the law and theory of standard terms. It is the intellectual pattern, or in today's language the imaginary, which serves as a blueprint against which the three types of regulation are analysed. Any instrumentalisation and functionalisation superimposes a regulatory layer over and on the parties' individual contract dominated by the law of contract. This additional layer frames the conditions under which and in which the private parties operate. The layer is most visible in private regulation when business organisations are involved in the drafting of the contract, to the benefit of the members of the sector or even in coordination with other business sectors.[14] The individual agreement contract law has to face reaches from 'take it or leave it' to more substantial re-negotiation and adjustment to the particular business rationale of the respective economic sectors. Think of the building of a global supply chain through contract. Contractual practice has a quasi-'binding' effect on all those who are operating within the respective sector. Contractual practice can be institutionally and procedurally anchored or it can be derived from an ad hoc decision of the business sector(s) to engage in the creation of a sector- or business-related model.

Contractual practice looks different when contract regulation forms an integral part of public regulation. In the private law beyond the nation state, nation states get together to conclude multilateral conventions or bilateral agreements which rely on the existence of contract. There is no cross-border trade without contract law. GATT, later the WTO, the European Economic Union, Mercosur and NAFTA all aim at the establishment of a market – whether a worldwide market or a regional market – usually without even mentioning private law and contract law. Trade law depends entirely on the role and function of national contract law orders and international private law for the coordination of jurisdiction and the applicable law. With the exception of the EU and to some extent Mercosur, international and supranational agreements do not directly interfere with contract law through regulation.

The nation state – the statutory public regulator – has a responsibility for the development of a trade law that not only serves the overall regulatory purpose

---

14 H.-W. Micklitz, *Der Reparaturvertrag*, München: Schweitzer, 1984 on double collectivisation of standard terms in the service sector.

of market-building but that also provides for a legal framework that balances out public regulation and contract law. This is the place for the potential existence and the outlook of a regional economic or even an international economic constitution.[15] Global and regional multilateral conventions leave it to their members to engage in public interest regulation and to demonstrate their commitment not only towards the rationale of market integration but to policy objectives beyond the market. Trade law and contract law are seen as related but disconnected legal fields. The transformation of the economic order into global supply chains breaks down the boundaries between the two fields of law, via contractualisation, and allows for rethinking their relationship and the responsibilities of private parties.[16] Co-regulation, thought of as regulation of technical standards, is at the interface between contractual practice and contract law. Technical standards may be instrumentalised for all sorts of purposes – for standardising product or services, for regulating a market or sector of the economy, or for cutting across sectors and markets through procedural rules. At the same time, technical standards could be understood as contractual practice.

All three forms of regulation rely on contract law, on consent, which complements contractual practice. Contract law is the lifeblood of market economies – not the regulated contract but the individually and autonomously negotiated contract. If public regulation interferes directly with contracts through mandatory rules, the consent of the parties in contract law is partially replaced by regulation. The result is regulated contract. Co-regulation neatly distinguishes between the development of technical standards as an integral part of contractual practice and the insertion of technical standards into contracts via consent. The first relates to contractual practices and the second to contract law. If public regulation ties lawfulness to compliance with private technical standards, the public law requirements and the private regulation are formally interconnected. The legal mechanism is presumed defectiveness or presumed non-conformity of products in the event of non-compliance with technical standards. Apart from the rather limited scope of regulatory private law, contractual practice and consensual contract law stand side by side. It remains for courts and extrajudicial bodies to engage with the interrelationship between private, public and co-regulation and contract. The imaginary of standard terms highlights what is at stake. Contractual practice, standard terms or even codes of conduct may be submitted to some sort of ex post judicial review. The impact of public contract regulation may be tested

---

15 Here is the place for the vast literature on the European Economic Constitution and on the International Economic Constitution. For an overall discussion, see H.-W. Micklitz, 'Multi-Level Governance and Economic Constitution' in S. Grundmann, H.-W. Micklitz and M. Renner, above n. 5.

16 R. Ravalli, 'Contract and communication in GVCs: a new role for consumer protection', forthcoming ECRL.

against constitutional requirements. This happens in litigation before the WTO Appellate Body and before the ECJ in Luxembourg, when private parties invoke market freedoms against national public regulation.[17]

Contract-specific regulation opens the way for judicial review. The legislation on unfair terms could serve as a blueprint. Many states around the world have introduced the possibility of submitting standard terms to ex post judicial review *in abstracto* without touching upon contract law. Co-regulation – the interplay between public regulation and contractual practice – may be submitted to constitutional review. Here courts are involved in the legality of the division between public law requirements and delegated private regulation.[18] The technical standards themselves, though, are not generally submitted to a similar judicial review to standard terms, although recent developments indicate a certain trend towards this. If technical standards are formally integrated into the contract through an explicit consensual agreement, judicial scrutiny clashes with the technicity of the technical standards. The following chart is meant to make what follows easier to understand and to assess. The details will be discussed below.

Table 1. The Macro-Perspective: Contract vs. Private, Public and Co-Regulation

	Private Regulation	**Public Regulation**	**Co-Regulation**
Contractual practice and responsibility	Standard terms codes of conducts	Trade conventions and regulatory contract law	Public law requirements + private regulation
Contract law, consent and autonomy	Insertion through formal consent Negotiation	Overrules consent Ex post re-establishment of autonomy	Insertion through explicit consent Objective standard of conformity
Interaction	Ex post (extra) judicial review	Ex post constitutional review and ex post judicial review	Ex ante participation but no or limited ex post judicial review

2.2. INSIDE PRIVATE, PUBLIC AND CO-REGULATION

The distinction between the three forms of regulation and their relationship to contractual practice in its framing effects for the law of contract provides for a kind of macro-picture. A look into the inner world of the three regulatory patterns delivers the micro-picture. The analytical categories are derived from transnational and standard terms law and theory.

---

[17] H.-W. Micklitz and C. Sieburgh (eds.), *Primary EU Law and Private Law Concepts*, Intersentia, Cambridge/Antwerp 2017; no equivalent for WTO and GATT.

[18] T. Tridimas, 'Community Agencies, Competition Law and ECSB Initiatives' [2009] *Yearbook of European Law* 216.

Regulation with and through contracts necessarily implies a change in perspective away from the idea of consent in traditional contract law. Regulation is not done for nothing; there is always a particular *purpose* behind. In standard terms it is historically the rationalisation, in today's language the gain in economic efficiency of contract regulation through the standardisation of the way in which private relations are shaped. Contract thereby changes its *form*, from individually negotiated terms to standardised terms. Rationalisation requires the elaboration of contractual standards that do justice to the rise of mass production and mass consumption in the 20th century. The *function* differs with regard to the regulator, collective business entity or single company. If standard terms are meant to cover a business sector or a particular kind of goods and services, the regulator might be a business organisation, but it might also be an individual company which takes the lead in its sector of activities. The governance debate has added a new analytical layer to private regulation. It harks back to a century-old debate on the institutional dimension of private law and private regulation.[19] *Governance* opens the door to the way in which the rules are made, by whom and under what kind of procedure. The participation of non-governmental organisations which claim or are claimed to represent the public interest are in the limelight of the institutional architecture, its accountability, its transparency and its legitimacy.[20] Most of the more conceptual and theoretical debate turns around the status of standard terms, whether standard terms can be regarded as 'law', and if they can be regarded as 'law', where the legitimacy of privately produced 'law' can be derived from and whether the standard terms must be publicly accessible for free. The mainstream answer seems to be that standard terms are not 'law', therefore standard terms gain legitimacy only through their integration into the contract via the consent of the other party.

The derived analytical frame can be used for all sorts of private regulation, whether through standard terms or through codes of conduct. Public regulation has to implement the common interest[21] of the peoples; co-regulation tries to combine rationalisation and the realisation of public interests. All three are

---

19 See O. Gierke, *Die soziale Aufgabe des Privatrechts. Vortrag gehalten am 5. April 1889 in der juristischen Gesellschaft zu Wien*, Springer, Berlin 1889, English translation by E. McGaughey, 'The Social Role of Private Law' (2018) 19(4) *German Law Journal* 1017; but also S. Grundmann, 'Institutional Economics', in S. Grundmann, H.-W. Micklitz and M. Renner, above n. 5, as well as S. Grundmann, F. Möslein and K. Riesenhuber (eds.), *Contract Governance. Dimensions in Law and Interdisciplinary Research*, Oxford University Press, Oxford 2015.

20 B. Kingsbury, N. Krisch and R.B. Stewart, 'L'émergence du droit administratif global' [2013] *Revue internationale de droit economique* 37.

21 D. Kelemen, *Eurolegalism. The Transformation of Law and Regulation in the European Union*, Harvard University Press, Cambridge, MA 2011; H.-W. Micklitz, 'The Interest in Public Interest Litigation' in H.-W. Micklitz and N. Reich, *Public Interest Litigation before European Courts*, Volume 2, VIEW Schriftenreihe (book series of the Institut für Europäisches Wirtschafts- und Verbraucherrecht – Institute for European Economic and Consumer Law), 1996, pp. 21–38.

united in the change of form towards standardising. Public contract regulation addresses collective entities, the group of companies and persons that are claimed to be in need of regulatory intervention. Co-regulation, on and through technical standards, focuses on the development of technical specifications not for a particular company, but for a whole economic sector or a particular group of products or services. The institutional safeguards for the representation of the public interest is traditionally weak in private regulation, strong in public regulation and foreseen in co-regulation. Private regulation is not equated with law. Social practice might turn into law through adjudication, but such an assessment is subject to controversy.[22] Co-regulation breaks down into binding public law requirements and non-binding technical standards. This does not mean that the non-binding standards do not have legal implications. Overall, compliance with standards is presumed to meet legal rules, subject to proof of the contrary.

Table 2. The Micro-Perspective: Contract vs. Private, Public and Co-Regulation

	Private Regulation	**Public Regulation**	**Co-Regulation**
Purpose **Business and public policy**	Rationalisation Public Interest	Common interest	Rationalisation Public interest
Form **Standardisation**	Standard terms Codes of conduct	Collective entities	Technical standards Technical specifications
Function **Company and sector**	Sectorial standard terms Company terms	General laws and Special laws	Sectorial technical standards Product- or service-specific standards
Structure **Governance**	Private bodies Participation of non-governmental organisations	Democratic institutions	Standards bodies Institutional participation
Status **Law – non-law**	Non-law	Law	Presumed law

2.3. REGULATORY FASHIONS AND REGULATORY FAILURES

The three forms of regulation are strongly interconnected through the failure rhetoric. Standard terms and technical standards mirror the economics and politics of regulation. The development of standard terms for mass contracts is understood as an expression of party autonomy and freedom of contract. From the 1920s on, courts started to submit standard terms to judicial review via

22 G.-P. Calliess and M. Renner, 'Between Law and Social Norms: The Evolution of Global Governance' (2009) 22 *Ratio Juris* 260.

reference to general principles of contract law.[23] There were and still are today considerable differences between national private law orders around the globe. However, overall courts compensated to a certain degree for the imbalance of information, the imbalance of negotiating power or simply the abuse of power. The literature fills libraries. Israel was the first country to adopt legislation in 1964, Germany followed in 1976, and the EU in 1993. In the Western European Member States, the call for a legislative framework went hand in hand with the rise of the welfare state, in the EU with the adoption of the Single European Act that empowered the EU to take legislative measures to complete the internal market with a social face. Judicial review in individual litigation was claimed not to suffice to cleanse the market of unfair contract terms. The political debates turned around the pros and cons of introducing legislation to remedy the failures that resulted from the one-sided use of private autonomy and freedom of contract to the detriment of the weaker economic party, be it a consumer or a small or medium-sized company. Recent years have demonstrated a growing concern for whether the exercise of judicial review over standard terms is economically efficient and socially effective.[24] Empirical research guided by law and economics, behavioural economics and behavioural science highlights all sorts of deficiencies that demonstrate the difficulty of realising public interests through public contract regulation.[25]

The regulation of standard terms – the move from self-regulation and judicial review towards a legislative framework that distinguishes between the possibility of reviewing standard terms independently from individual use and the ongoing judicial review in individual litigation – did not in any way set a precedent for other, newer forms of private regulation, with the exception of the EU regulation on unfair trading practices that detrimentally affect small and medium-sized suppliers in the global food chain.[26] A possible candidate for a new form of regulation would have been the rise and ever-wider spread of codes

---

23 F.A. Wieacker, *History of Private Law in Europe*, translated by T. Weir, Clarendon Press, Oxford 1995.

24 F. Gómez, J. Ganuza and M. Artigo, *Standard Contract Terms and Legal Controls: A Reconstruction from the Law and Economics Theory of Contract*, 2018, available at https://www.upf.edu/documents/6764143/93632110/13+SEPTEMBER+GOMEZ+GANUZA+ARTIGOT+STANDARD+TERMS+NET.pdf/7b4559fd-a197-a803-a038-68afaf40c0b0; Y. Bakos, F. Marotta-Wurgler and D.R. Trossen, 'Does Anyone Read the Fine Print? Consumer Attention to Standard Form Contracts', New York University Law and Economics Research Paper No. 195, 2014; H. Luth, *Behavioural Economics in Consumer Policy. The Economic Analysis of Standard Terms in Consumer Contracts Revisited*, Intersentia, Antwerp 2010); H. Collins (ed.), *Standard Contract Terms in Europe. A Basis for and a Challenge to European Contract Law*, Kluwer Law International, Alphen aan den Rijn 2008).

25 A.-L. Sibony, 'Data and arguments: empirical research in consumer law' in H.-W. Micklitz, A.-L. Sibony and F. Esposito (eds.), *Research Methods in Law and in Consumer Research*, Edward Elgar, Cheltenham 2018, pp. 165–216.

26 Directive 2019/633/EU of the European Parliament and of the Council of 17 April 2019 on unfair trading practices in business-to-business relationships in the agricultural and food

of conduct in all business sectors to demonstrate corporate social responsibility (CSR) and now digital corporate responsibility. CSR has a long history, one that dates back to industrialisation and the emergence of the labour movement in the 19th century. Even after nearly 40 years of discussion, there is no consensus on its definition, however. In 2001, the EU defined CSR as 'a concept whereby companies integrate social and environmental concerns in their business operations and in their interaction with their stakeholders on a voluntary basis'.[27] Much of the debate turns around voluntariness and what exactly that means.

Private regulation also governs the re-organisation of international trade along the lines of global value chains.[28] The intensification of globalisation has offered new business opportunities facilitated by private law and private regulation beyond the nation state, but also new business responsibilities. Companies, NGOs and international organisations have used the space opening up to promote CSR, though in very different ways. The OECD and the UN have highlighted CSR as a prominent field of political action through the development of Guidelines (by the OECD), the UN Global Compact and, more ambitiously, the 17 UN Sustainable Development Goals. The EU has followed its own agenda. Since 2018, Directive 2014/95/EU requires large companies to disclose information on the way they operate and manage social and environmental challenges. However, this reporting duty, although mandatory, is miles away from introducing a legal framework in order to exercise control over the content of the contract. There is intense academic debate on the possibility of enforcing CSR standards through EU contract law and the EU Directive on unfair commercial practices.[29] Less spectacular, but no less important, are the efforts of companies that try to enforce CSR standards using contract law in supply chains.[30] In comparison to the fully fledged review mechanism for standard terms, the regulatory attempts of international and supranational organisations to introduce a legislative framework for CSR seems to be stuck halfway. Whilst reporting has been made mandatory, no enforcement mechanisms have been foreseen.

---

supply chain [2019] OJ L111/59; Cf. M. de la Cuesta, 'SMEs in the (Food) Global Value Chain. A European Private Law Perspective', PhD, European University Institute 2020.

27 European Commission, *Green Paper: Promoting a European framework for Corporate Social Responsibility*, 18.07.2001, COM (2001) 366 final, p. 1.

28 R. Baldwin, *The Great Convergence: Information Technology and the New Globalization*, Harvard University Press, Cambridge, MA 2016.

29 A. Beckers, *Enforcing Corporate Codes: On Global Self-Regulation and National Private Law,* Hart Publishing, Oxford 2015; A. Beckers, 'The regulation of market communication and market behaviour: Corporate social responsibility and the Directives on Unfair Commercial Practices and Unfair Contract Terms' (2017) 54 *Common Market Law Review (CMLR)* 475; A. Beckers, 'Environmental Protection meets Consumer Sales The Influence of Environmental Market Communication on Consumer Contracts and Remedies' (2018) 14(2) *ECRL* 157.

30 F. Cafaggi, 'The regulatory functions of transnational commercial contracts: new architectures' (2013) 36(6) *Fordham International Law Journal* 1557.

As for co-regulation, it is a relatively young approach, whereas the history of standardisation dates back to the Roman Empire. In the current context, it suffices to recall that standardisation has gone hand in hand with industrialisation in the 19th century and the consumer society in the 20th century. Standardisation is a form of self-regulation, very similar in its form and function to the creation of standard terms. The business sector established standards bodies; the public sector – in particular, the national administration – became dependent on business expertise in the heyday of industrialisation. This was the beginning of a complex relationship between business and politics, which gained paced when standardisation went far beyond measuring and weighing, and began to engage with policies.[31] The widespread use of electricity required technical standardisation that took the health and safety of workers and users into account. The benchmark around which co-regulation developed was the EU Low Voltage Directive, adopted in 1974. After the EU had succeeded in reducing and abolishing customs even earlier than planned, the non-tariff barriers to trade – i.e. the differences in national technical standards – thus became visible. The political response was to adopt European Directives that regulate the technical details of products and services. This approach failed miserably, as politics got lost in parliamentary debates about technical details. The Low Voltage Directive preceded the new approach, beginning in 1985, to technical standards and regulation. Under the new approach, public regulation is limited to laying down binding legal requirements that are concretised through non-binding technical standards elaborated by the two European standards bodies, CEN and CENELEC. Voluntary compliance documented via a certificate guarantees access to the internal market. The Memorandum of Agreement between the European Commission and the standards bodies lays down how the cooperation between the public and the private sector should operate. The rationale is that the European Commission is entitled to mandate the elaboration of technical standards in exchange for co-financing. These are called harmonised European standards. Non-governmental organisations were involved, but only gained formal status as observers in 1995. The new approach boosted the elaboration of technical standards in the EU, but not only in the EU: the Low Voltage Directive and the new approach impacted the elaboration of the GATT TBT Agreement and later the WTO SPS Agreement. In this way, the combination of binding public regulation coupled to non-binding private regulation became the worldwide model for merging politics and economics even beyond the regulation of mere technicalities.

[31] On the following C. Joerges, J. Falke, H.-W. Micklitz and G. Brüggemeier, 'European Product Safety, Internal Market Policy and the New Approach to Technical Harmonisation and Standards (Reissued)' (2010) 6(2) *Hanse Law Review*, Special Issue, available at http://hanselawreview.eu/wp-content/uploads/2016/08/HanseLRVol6No02.pdf.

But what about contracts? What about the relationship between contract and technical standards? I will come back to this issue later.

What remains to be clarified is how the enforcement mechanisms of technical standards look like. Quite similar to codes of conduct, the monitoring and surveying of compliance is very much put into the hands of the business sector itself. Self-certification or third-party certification are the means through which the business sector documents compliance. Public regulation defines when third-party certification is required, as well as the conditions for the accreditation of certification bodies. For decades, neither standardisation nor certification reached the courts This has now changed. Interestingly enough, all the cases the ECJ has had to decide in this area have a private law background. *Fra.bo*[32] concerns the liability of a German certification body to pay compensation for the claimed illegal withdrawal of a certificate that had permitted access to the internal market, *Elliott*[33] dealt with the legal effects of flawed construction materials that did not meet the contractually agreed technical standards, and *Schmitt* is part of the PIP saga,[34] where women are seeking compensation from the German certification bodies for the failure to properly monitor and survey the production of breast implants that turned out to be made out of industrial silicone.

3. CONTRACT REGULATION VERSUS CONSENT

The common analytical frame demonstrates how the regulation of and through contracts has dominate debates over the past decades. The traditional idea of contract remained very much in the realm of the national private law orders, whereas the three patterns of regulation reached out to the private law beyond the nation state. In the following analysis, the tensions between the three patterns of regulation and the idea of consent in traditional contract law will be put into the limelight. This requires a stock-taking and a critique of academic scholarship, which has been swimming with the tide.

3.1. PRIVATE REGULATION, CONTRACTUALISATION AND CONSENT

Today's economic reality is characterised by the increased role of 'contract' and 'codes of conduct', in particular when it comes to transnational economic

32 Case C-171/11, *Fra.bo*, ECLI:EU:C:2012:453, has made it to a website which tells the full story, https://www.frabo.com/eng/frabo/the-frabo-case.

33 Case C-613/14, *Elliott*, ECLI:EU:C:2016:821.

34 Case C-219/15, *Schmitt*, ECLI:EU:C:2017:128.

relations, let alone the organisation of global supply chains. The phenomenon has been termed the 'contractualisation' of economic relations. Non-statutory entities, business organisations and multinational companies are pursuing first and foremost business interests, i.e. the search for economically efficient contractual relations. Scholarship, for its part, is very much focused on the degree to which private regulators are taking over public interests, worker protection, consumer and environmental protection, and human rights in the shaping of their contractual relations. The more private regulation intermingles with public policy concerns, the more private contractual regulation crosses the line towards public regulation through nation states or supranational and international regulation.

However, contrary to statutory legislation and supranational and international conventions, private contractual regulation is not per se publicly accessible. This is true at both levels: at the level of contractual practice and at the level of contract law. Those who would like to understand what private regulators are doing in their respective fields of economic activities, what kind of regulatory purposes they are pursuing and how the contracts are shaped to meet that overall purpose are dependent on gaining access to the respective 'regulatory business community'. No access means no information on contractualisation, whether and to what extent public policy concerns are taken into consideration, surveyed and monitored, and what contract law that follows contractual practice looks like, for example whether the individual contracts concluded are copy-pasted from contractual practice or whether they are individually negotiated. In short, all that we know about private regulation is the result either of scholarly research or of theoretical and conceptual considerations.

The ever-increasing amount of 'case studies' on particular economic sectors or particular phenomena is testament to the difficulty of understanding what contractualisation means in practice. Overall it seems easier to analyse contractual practice than to get access to contract law along the supply chain, even if the researcher manages to get access to the regulatory business community. The case studies have mainly helped to create an understanding of the regulatory purpose, form, function and the governance structure – in short what I call the 'inside of private, public and co-regulation' beyond the nation state. This kind of knowledge is rather stable, although the information, collected under difficult and time-consuming circumstances, can seem rather useless. It might already be outdated by the time it is collected, as private regulators are free to constantly adjust contractual practice to increase economic efficiency and/or to upgrade or downgrade public policy requirements. What is true for contractual practice is even more important for an understanding of contract law in individual cases, especially the way in which the standard terms or codes of contracts are reflected, connected and copy-pasted into the individual relations. What is then needed is access not only to the private regulator but to all actors along the global supply chain, both upstream and downstream. This is a painful and near-impossible exercise, at least if the expectation is to be able to study the contracts as they are concluded, the contractual practice and the role and function of contract law.[35]

There are two solutions – ever more case studies and/or engaging with theories of transnational law. Whilst social empirical research by way of case studies is always ongoing, thereby turning the patchwork knowledge of contractual practice into knowledge of whole business sectors, theories on transnational seem stuck.[36] What seems to be empirically and theoretically somewhat under-researched is the role and function of consent, i.e. of the traditional idea of contract in the organisation of transnational economic relations, in terms of the degree to which business parties downstream and upstream voluntarily agree, and of whether and to what extent there is leeway for negotiation between the lead company and the other parties. The similarities between the debate on the imposition of standard terms on the weaker economic party in B2B and B2C relations and the organisation of the supply chain by the private regulator to suit particular business needs are obvious. The theoretical discourse on private regulation beyond the nation state which incorporates public policy implicitly or explicitly relies on a strong and powerful private regulator that imposes public policy regulations downstream and upstream. There seems to be a kind of low-profile and implicit sympathy with a 'good and strong private regulator', be it a collective business or an individual, often multinational, company, a kind of thinking which is equally found in the discourse on the role and function of the public regulator – the 'good' welfare state against the 'bad' neo-liberal state, the 'good' interventionist EU against the 'bad' neo-liberal trend, or more broadly in Hall/Soskice's distinction between coordinated and liberal market economies, even if they claim not to take sides.[37]

However, there is an alternative to the 'good' private regulator which imposes 'good' private regulation on those who are unwilling or economically unable to resist the pressure. In theory, private regulation which takes public policy concerns seriously could be the product of individual or even collective negotiations as well, be it at the level of contractual practice or at the level of contract law.

35 There are a few examples beyond L. Bernstein, 'Opting out of the Legal System: Extralegal Contractual Relations in the Diamond Industry' (1992) 21(1) *Journal of Legal Studies* 115; F. Cafaggi and P. Iamiceli, 'Inter-firm Networks in the European Wine Industry', EUI LAW Working Paper 2010/19; with regard to the methodological dimension this type of research requires, A. Beckers, 'From Corporate Personality to Corporate Governance: The Transformation of International Human Rights Protection in Corporate Governance Structures' in N. Bhuta and R. Vallejo (eds.), *Human Rights and Global Governance*, Oxford University Press, Oxford, 2020, also available at https://ssrn.com/abstract=3573755.

36 For an attempt to open a new path, R. Vallejo, 'After Governance: The Idea of a Private Administrative Law' in P. Kjaer (ed.), above n. 3, pp. 320–47.

37 H.-W. Micklitz, 'Organisations and Public Goods' in S. Grundmann, H.-W. Micklitz and M. Renner, above n. 5.

In such a case, the instrumental and functional character of contractualisation gives way to consensual private negotiations. It seems that it is this kind of contractualisation through negotiations that theories on transnational law have in mind.[38] There are scholarly proposals on how consensual regulation could and should be organised so as gain legitimacy. From a purely sociological perspective, the problem arises that the more private regulation is shaped along the same lines as public regulation, through the input and participation of public interest organisations and 'democratic' majority decision-making, the more private regulation loses its advantages that result from the rationale of the respective regulatory community. There are lessons to learn from the regulation of alternative dispute resolution mechanisms as quasi-courts.[39]

3.2. PUBLIC REGULATION, REGULATORY CONTRACT LAW AND CONSENT

The way in which the EU has been instrumentalising private law and in particular contract law to build the internal market and promote European integration has been studied doctrinally and theoretically.[40] The European experience is unique and has no comparable counterpart in other regional organisations, let alone international organisations. Over the past decades, the EU has built a dense set of public regulation that frames the role, function and application of the Member States' national private law orders within the territory of the EU and even beyond.

The EU has no genuine competence in the field of contract law; it is only empowered in relation to the economic and social policy fields in which contract law matters. The public interest dimension is enshrined in the search for appropriate worker, consumer and environmental protection rules. This bounded competence means that European regulatory private law cannot and does not deal with the conclusion of contracts and more explicitly with consent. Directive 93/13/EEC might serve as a blueprint for this. Otherwise, there is a disclaimer – i.e. 'the directive or regulation does not affect national rules on the conclusion of the contract' – that is part of the standard repertoire of European regulatory private law, appearing for instance in

---

38 G. Teubner (ed.), *Global Law Without a State*, Dartmouth, Aldershot 1997; G.-P. Calliess and P. Zumbansen, *Rough Consensus and Running Code. A Theory of Transnational Private Law*, Hart Publishing, Oxford 2010; G.-P. Calliess and M. Renner, above n. 22.

39 D. Eidmann, *Schlichtung. Zur Logik außergerichtlicher Konfliktregelung*, Nomos, Baden-Baden 1994.

40 H. Collins, 'The Revolutionary Trajectory of EU Contract Law towards Post-national Law' in S. Worthington, A. Robertson and G. Virgo (eds.), *Revolution and Evolution in Private Law*, Hart Publishing, Oxford 2017, pp. 315–36; H.-W. Micklitz, *The Politics of Justice in European Private Law*, Cambridge University Press, Cambridge 2018.

Directive 2005/29/EC on unfair commercial practices. The exception to the rule is the regulation of 'consent' in the European General Data Protection Regulation. Consent to a data privacy policy, though, is claimed to be neatly disconnected from the role and function of consent in contractual agreements on digital services.[41]

The politics of European regulatory private law can be condensed into the formula that the European rules surround and embed the conclusion of the contract through an ever-denser web of rules on pre-contractual, contractual and post-contractual information requirements, and on the means of concluding a contract, both through the regulation of online and offline business outside business premises, and through the regulation of the use of particular communication technologies. From such an instrumental and functional perspective, there is no space for the idea of consent and its role and function for contract law. What matters, seen through the regulatory lens, is whether the policy objectives behind the piecemeal regulation – sectorial policies and social protection for workers, consumers and environmental sustainability – can be achieved at all, this means in the language of the European legislature whether the European regulatory private law is economically efficient and socially effective. The 'Better Regulation' approach[42] and the steady fine-tuning of EU private and contract regulation to better achieve the twin objectives of efficiency and effectiveness – the building of the internal market at a high level of (consumer) protection – document how instrumentalism and functionalism prevails over the ideal type of contract relying on two parties who engage in negotiations and consensual agreement.

Thinking the instrumental approach through, consent is no longer needed – it is not 'contracted out', but 'regulated out'. In the search for innovative legal doctrines, Elizalde[43] hypothesises that EU law *de lege lata* is developing core rules for the formation of contracts that could end up in a harmonised mandatory system (MEUCL), yet one that is of 'a different colour to the dominating theories of private autonomy and free will'. In its most radical form, European regulatory private law deprives contract law of the requirement of consent. What matters

---

41 P. Schmechel, 'Verbraucherdatenschutzrecht in der EU Datenschutzgrundverordnung' in G. Joost, H.-W. Micklitz, L.A. Reisch and H. Zander-Hayat (eds.), *Verbraucherrecht 2.0 – Verbraucher in der digitalen Welt*, Nomos, Baden-Baden 2017, pp. 265–302; Regulation (EU) No. 2016/679 of the European Parliament and of the Council of 27 April 2016 on the protection of natural persons with regard to the processing of personal data and on the free movement of such data, and repealing Directive 95/46/EC (General Data Protection Regulation) [2016] OJ L119/1.

42 https://ec.europa.eu/info/law/law-making-process/planning-and-proposing-law/better-regulation-why-and-how_en.

43 F. de Elizalde, 'Standardisation of agreement in EU law. An adieu to the contracting parties?' in T. Tridimas and M. Durovic (eds.), *New Directions in European Private Law*, Hart Publishing, Oxford, forthcoming 2020.

is no longer the will or the autonomy of private parties, but the regulatory function that the contractual relation between two parties has to meet. Functionalism prevails over the idea of a contract. Seen in this way, the question whether the EU pursues neo-liberal objectives alone or combined with social policies does not matter anymore. In both variants, consent is downgraded, if not completely lost. Whether such a relationship can still be called contract, or should be better understood as quasi-contract or as-if contract, is a matter of definition only. It should be recalled that private law theory has been discussing the existence of de facto agreements for more than 70 years. In de facto agreements, the typical social behaviour of two parties allows for the normative conclusion that there is a binding legal relationship.[44] The idea of a contract without consent has been critically reviewed by Palka[45] in his analysis of the digital economy.

There are notable counter-movements, not only with regard to the critique of European instrumentalism and functionalism, i.e. of the use and usefulness of mandatory contract law to protect the weaker party, but also in the search for alternatives at the EU level and in terms of the interaction between the European legal order and the national private law orders. Hugh Collins has presented a model for the development of a European contract law from the bottom up, through the representatives of civil society.[46] This type of thinking overlaps with private regulation that is not imposed on the parties downstream and upstream, but is rather negotiated between the parties concerned. The European Commission had started half-hearted attempts to initiate the development of standard contracts for particular branches through business and civil society organisations. The discussion in the 1980s on how collective agreements could be made binding on individual parties could have served as a source of inspiration.[47] However, the European Commission did not seriously consider collective negotiations as an alternative to public regulation through European Directives and Regulations.

---

44 G. Haupt/H. Sieber, *Über Faktische Vertragsverhältnisse*, Weicher, Leipzig 1941. In a famous judgment the Federal German Supreme Court recognised the existence of a de facto agreement: BGHZ 21, 319. However, not least due to the criticism raised in legal doctrine, the Supreme Court did not develop the idea of a contract without consent. See on the German debate and the relevant case law: http://lorenz.userweb.mwn.de/urteile/njw00_3429.htm.

45 P. Palka, 'Terms of Service are not Contracts – Beyond Contract Law in the Regulation of Online Platforms' in S. Grundmann (ed.), *European Contract Law in the Digital Age*, Intersentia, Cambridge/Antwerp 2018, pp. 161–204.

46 H. Collins, *The European Civil Code: The Way Forward*, Cambridge University Press, Cambridge 2008.

47 Commission de refonte du droit de la consommation, 'Proposition pour un nouveau droit de la consommation. Rapport de la Commission de la refonte du droit de la consommation au secrétaire d'État auprès du ministre de l'Économie, des Finances et du Budget chargé du Budget et de la Consommation', 1985.

More recently, the legal discourse has shifted away from the analysis of European regulation as designed through the European Union in the legislative procedure and has put the European Court of Justice into the limelight. In the aftermath of Lehman Brothers and the euro crisis, Member States courts have referred an ever-growing number of questions to the ECJ on the interpretation of European contract law. In the meantime, the ECJ has passed more than 100 judgments, most prominently in the field of unfair terms and unfair commercial practices.[48] A detailed reconstruction of the relevant case law of the European Court of Justice demonstrates that the ECJ is not willing to accept that the public regulation – specifically the policy objectives of social protection – prevail over the autonomy of the parties.[49]

There is a clear trend in the case law of the ECJ that the consumer should have the last word on whether the elimination of unfair contract terms in the contract is in her interest. What the ECJ in fact proposes is a kind of ex post restoration of private autonomy. The position of the ECJ seems to reflect a change in legal scholarship, away from the pros and cons of European functionalism and instrumentalism towards an emphasis on the need to strengthen individual autonomy, if needed, against the instrumental and functional collective solutions foreseen in the European contract regulation. This strand of research leads back to the traditional role of contract law, thereby willingly or unwillingly revitalising traditional contract law values – autonomy and freedom – against publicly promoted policy objectives. The relationship between public regulation that downgrades consent in contract law and the practical application of public regulation in individual cases *ex post factum* will have to be rethought. Has the regulatory ideology now been replaced by the autonomy ideology? Are we running in circles or is it a loop?[50]

3.3. CO-REGULATION, TECHNICAL STANDARDISATION AND CONSENT

Technical standards, in particular after the EU's new approach to technical standards and regulations and the GATT/WTO TBT and SPS Agreements, have enjoyed a great deal of attention in legal scholarship. The institutional, constitutional and administrative implications of co-regulation have been

---

48 B. Kas and H.-W. Micklitz, 'Rechtsprechungsübersicht zum Europäischen Vertrags-und Delikts-recht (2014–2018)', (2018) *Europäische Zeitschrift für Wirtschaft und Steuerrecht (EWS)* 181–219 and 241–300 (Teil I und Teil II).

49 C. Leone, 'The Missing Stone in the Cathedral of unfair terms in employment contracts and coexisting rationalities in European private law', PhD, University of Amsterdam, June 2020.

50 D. Kennedy, 'The Stages of the Decline of the Public/Private Distinction' (1982) 130 *University of Pennsylvania Law Review* 1349.

analysed in much detail.[51] Most of the research is conceptual and theoretical. However, as for the connections between technical standards and contract law, these seem to be much more at the margins of scholarly attention.[52]

Like with private regulation, there is an access problem. In private regulation, while standard terms or codes of contracts are available online and can be easily studied, what is missing is access to the drafting process and to the individual contracts. In technical standardisation, the rules and procedures which govern standardisation are accessible *in abstracto*, but what is not available are the technical standards themselves. This is true even for harmonised European standards. The institutional and procedural rules on technical standardisation resemble the creation process for a European Directive or Regulation: the mandate from the business sector or exceptionally from the European Commission, the background research behind the mandate, the establishment of a working committee, the first draft, the hearings, the consultation and the voting. The dense set of rules can be downloaded online. The abstract rules and procedures form the core of the conceptual and theoretical analysis of technical standards. In public regulation, the European Commission has set today's benchmark for the online accessibility of the drafting process of public regulation in its various steps, from the very beginning, through the drafts, up to the final version, public hearings and voting in the Council and the Parliament. Technical standards are developed behind closed doors in a club-like mentality, however. The standards bodies publish the projects they are working on, usually a list of the technical committees. Only in the case of harmonised standards are the different steps published online, referring to the procedure, but without any of the content. Whilst awareness of the mandate makes it possible to get an idea of what standards bodies are working on and in what fields, two major pieces of information are missing: the drafting process that discloses the internal debates, and the final result. Therefore, accessibility requires de facto membership of the standardisation community, as a full member or as an observer of the relevant working committees.

The reasons for this is not only secrecy, but also business interests.[53] Technical standards are copyright-protected.[54] The standards bodies finance their activity

---

51 H. Schepel, 'The Empire's Drains: Sources of Legal Recognition of Private Standardisation Under the TBT Agreement' in C. Joerges and E.U. Petersmann (eds.), *Constitutionalism, multilevel trade governance and international economic law*, Hart Publishing, Oxford 2011, pp. 397–409: P. Delimatsis (ed.), *The Law, Economics and Politics of International Standardisation*, Cambridge University Press, Cambridge 2015.

52 For a rare exception, see B. van Leeuwen, *European Standardisation of Services and its Impact on Private Law*, Hart Publishing, Oxford 2017.

53 L. Bernstein and O. Ben-Shahar, 'The Secrecy Interest in Contract Law' (2000) 109 *Yale Law Journal* 1885.

54 H.-W. Micklitz and R. van Gestel, 'European Integration through Standardisation: How Judicial Review is Breaking down the Club House of Private Standardisation Bodies' (2013) 50 *CMLR* 145.

through the sale of technical standards, and each and every company that wants to base its production process on technical standards has to buy them. Even where the standards body's financing comes from the European Commission under a Memorandum of Agreement, and even if the respective technical standards reach beyond technicalities and cover sensitive policy issues, such as safety at work or safety of products and services, third parties still have no cost-free access to the standards. In fact, there are two barriers. The first is access to the standardisation community, specifically the working group in charge of drafting the respective standard. But even if this hurdle can be cleared, there is a second and even more effective barrier: anyone who wants access is required to buy the technical standard(s) they want to investigate. Amazingly this is true even for the harmonised standards mandated and sponsored by the European Commission. The financial barrier, i.e. needing to buy the standard(s), might help to explain why there is little research on the substance of technical standards as well as on the circumstances in which these standards are developed.[55]

When it comes to the relationship between technical standards and contract law, it is crucial to recall two major phenomena that have contributed to a substantial increase in the role and function of technical standards in the shaping of contracts. The first has already been mentioned, namely the move from the pure technicity of weighing and measuring to the integration of non-economic policies, first and foremost health and safety at work and consumer safety. Functionally, standardisation replaces public regulation – or to put it differently, public regulation and co-regulation, through technical standards, compete over the best approach to handling the tension between economic efficiency and public interests. Product safety-related standards are either linked to the contractual conformity of the product or serve as benchmark for assessing the legitimate expectation of customers in liability claims. The second phenomenon is the move to the service society. Today more than 60 per cent of Europe's gross income comes from services. The 200-year-old distinction between *obligations de résultat* and *obligations de moyen*, which governs contract law on services, has undergone a transformation that has led to an ever-deeper fragmentation of services, along the lines of either particular economic sectors or particular types of services.

In contracts for services, the parties cannot rely on a set of default rules which are comparable to a sales contract. Contracts for services are to a much

---

55 I have twice had the chance to get access to the standardisation community and to the standards themselves, first as an observer representing the consumer interests in the 1980s and secondly via ANEC, which commissioned a study on the standardisation of services in 2006: H.-W. Micklitz, 'Services Standards: Defining the Core Elements and Their Minimum Requirements', study commissioned by ANEC, 2007, available at http://www.anec.eu/attachments/ANEC-R&T-2006-SERV-004final.pdf.

larger degree dependent on how the parties tailor their rights and obligations with regard to the particular service. They need to concretise the performance and counter-performance. That is why contracts for services are a prominent field for standard terms. It suffices here to consider insurance contracts, where the standard terms determine what the insurer and the insured owe each other outside and beyond the dense network of insurance law. However, the service society has opened up space for technical standardisation in the wide variety of services outside and beyond services that are subject to specific European public regulation. The link between the European regulation of services and the role and function of standardisation is enshrined in the Service Directive 2006/123/EC. The original idea behind the Service Directive was to open up the internal market through the principle of mutual recognition. Under pressure from the Member States and non-governmental organisations – the infamous Polish plumber, who is taking the internal market by storm, served as a deterrent – the European Commission had to step back from its initial overambitious and somewhat radical proposal. The version of the Directive that was finally adopted laid down a rather vague regulatory framework for technical standardisation in un-regulated fields of services. It needed two further regulatory steps to promote standardisation of services, the adoption of Regulation 1025/2012[56] and the Standardisation Package of June 2016, in which the European Commission prioritised and incentivised the development of voluntary European service standards.[57]

What can be seen from the inner world of the standardisation of services demonstrates a certain degree of similarity with European public regulation in the field of contract law.[58] A systematic analysis of European public regulation and European technical standards in the fields of tourism, care for the elderly, furniture removal, postal services and transport covers the following six elements: (1) education and skills; (2) equipment and premises; (3) the pre-contractual and conclusion stages of contracting; (4) the content of the contract, including affordability, minimum content, safety, quality, payment, rights and remedies, withdrawal, compensation and liability; (5) the post-contractual stage, including after-sales services, handling of complaints, dispute resolution,

---

56 Regulation (EU) No. 1025/2012 of the European Parliament and of the Council of 25 October 2012 on European standardisation, amending Council Directives 89/686/EEC and 93/15/EEC and Directives 94/9/EC, 94/25/EC, 95/16/EC, 97/23/EC, 98/34/EC, 2004/22/EC, 2007/23/EC, 2009/23/EC and 2009/105/EC of the European Parliament and of the Council and repealing Council Decision 87/95/EEC and Decision No 1673/2006/EC of the European Parliament and of the Council [2012] OJ L316/12.

57 https://ec.europa.eu/growth/single-market/services/service-standards_en.

58 The following insight into the impact of standardisation on service contracts is based on H.-W. Micklitz, above n. 55; P. Delimatsis received an ERC grant in 2016 – https://www.tilburguniversity.edu/staff/p-delimatsis – which very much focuses on the relationship between trade and standardisation.

collective redress and protection against insolvency; and (6) monitoring and inspection. The closer the standards get to touching on the content of the contract, the more vague they become. Service standards by and large regulate access to the relevant profession and the pre-contractual and in particular the post-contractual stages. In the pre-contractual stage, they might overlap with public regulation, although the service standards are much more context-specific and tailor-made with regard to the particular information requirements in the respective service sector. In the post-contractual stage, they fill gaps left by public regulation.

Within the scope of EU co-regulation, the use of technical standards is voluntary. Companies are free to rely on technical alternatives, provided they meet the binding legal requirements laid down in EU Directives. A company has to decide whether or not to base its services on technical standards. If the company does so, it has to certify its compliance with the EU standard via the CE mark.[59] In *Fra.bo*, the ECJ had to deal with the de facto barriers which resulted from the pressure put on an Italian producer to get his product certified by a German national body so as to gain access to the German market.[60] Voluntariness turned into de facto bindingness. In *Fra.bo*, the ECJ argued that an implied term to respect national certification requirements functions as a barrier to trade and infringes market freedoms. Access to the market goes hand in hand with quality requirements that determine the content of the contract. It would be interesting to know what the contracts look like after *Fra.*bo more generally. The conflict between the Italian producer and the German certification body was settled. The German certification body had to compensate Fra.bo for barring its access to the German market.

One might wonder, however, whether the ECJ would come to a similar conclusion in the case of litigation regarding service standards that precede the contract or complement post-contractual duties. The *Fra.bo* rationale would require that mainstream business practice is to take voluntary service standards as a benchmark for offering, for example, tourism services, care of the elderly, postal services or transportation. Without compliance with technical standards, access to the respective market is not guaranteed. A possible candidate to ensure compliance might be the existence of a complaint-handling system or after-sales services.

Policy-wise, technical standards and contract terms remain legally separate. Technical standards only become part of the contract if the two parties explicitly

---

59 https://ec.europa.eu/info/business-economy-euro/product-safety-and-requirements/eu-labels_en.

60 *Fra.bo*, above n. 32, para. 30: 'Thirdly, the referring court takes the view that, in practice, the lack of certification by the DVGW places a considerable restriction on the marketing of the products concerned on the German market. Although the ABVWasserV merely lays down the general sales conditions as between water supply undertakings and their customers, from which the parties are free to depart, it is apparent from the case-file that, in practice, almost all German consumers purchase copper fittings certified by the DVGW'.

turn them into a reference point for the contractually owed performance. In *Elliott*, however, the ECJ decided that harmonised European standards come under the scope of the jurisdiction of the Court and are therefore subject to judicial review. It is not at all clear how far the judicial review reaches – whether a kind of judicial review of the content will be exercised – but *Elliott* brings the judicial review of technical terms conceptually close to the *abstract* judicial review of standard terms. There is a second major message enshrined in *Elliott*. Conformity of products with harmonised European standards provides a presumption of fitness for the purposes of free circulation of goods in the EU, but does not affect the contractual obligation to supply products of 'merchantable quality', as required by the Irish law on the sale of goods at issue in *Elliott*. Consequently, neither the Directive nor the harmonised technical standard 'harmonises the national rules applicable to proof in the context of a contractual dispute … or [the] method establishing the conformity of a product with contractual specifications or the time of establishing conformity.'[61] Conformity with a harmonised standard cannot shield a party from the contractual obligation to supply goods of merchantable quality and payment of damages for failing to comply with this duty. In this respect, there is no difference between contract and tort.[62]

One might interpret the ECJ as preserving the autonomy of the parties, but this is not the end yet. In May 2019, the European Parliament and the Council adopted two Directives concerning B2C contracts: Directive 2019/770/EU on the supply of digital content and digital services[63] and Directive 2019/771/EU one online and other distance sales of goods.[64] Both Directives revise the conformity test. Whilst party agreement still plays a role, the Directives strengthen the need to rely on objective requirements. According to Article 7(1)(a) Directive 2019/771, products shall 'be fit for the purposes for which goods of the same type would normally be used, taking into account, where applicable, any existing Union and national law, technical standards or, in the absence of such technical standards, applicable sector-specific industry codes of conduct.' For the first time, the legislature explicitly recognised the role that technical standards play in the conformity test besides the individual agreement of the parties on the quality of the product. This is co-regulation in contract law. It shifts the contract away from party agreement towards objective criteria enshrined in the technical standards. Objectivisation makes it easier for the EU not only to define common standards for getting access to the internal market,

---

61 *Frau,bo*, above n. 32, para. 52

62 C. Hess, 'Die Bedeutung von Normen für den Rechtsvollzug am Beispiel der Produktsicherheit und -haftung' in T. Brönneke, A. Wilburger und S. Bietz (eds.), *Verbraucherrechtsvollzug – Zugang der Verbraucher zum Recht*, Nomos, Baden-Baden 2020, pp. 167–374.

63 [2019] OJ L136/1.

64 [2019] OJ L136/28.

but at the same time also to tie market access and conformity requirements together. However, the technical standards exist side by side with the contractual agreement and the consumer's autonomy is protected in Article 7(5), in that the seller has to inform the consumer explicitly if the product deviates from the relevant technical standards. The new rule seems to be in line with the ex post restoration of autonomy through the ECJ in the judicial review of unfair terms. Autonomy prevails over the potential judicial review of objective standards. But the legislature had opened the door for a new balancing exercise between what the parties require and what the market needs – common objective standards which give the supplier the security that compliance with EU and national standards will shield him from liability claims.

4. PRELIMINARY CONCLUSIVE THOUGHTS

The first lesson to be learnt from the comparison of the three regulators – the public, the private and the co-regulator – is that all of them, whatever the purpose of the regulation is, come into conflict with contract law, specifically the idea that parties engage voluntarily and autonomously in contractual relations. Private regulation pursues first and foremost the purposes of rationalisation and efficiency, in which there is not much room for deviating behaviour through autonomous decision-making. Public regulation, guided by social policy purposes, runs into similar difficulties. Political intentions might clash with the endeavour of private parties to reject interference with their autonomous decision-making. In both private and public regulation, courts are the gatekeepers of contract law. They use the idea of contract as the starting point for submitting standard terms to a more or less intensive judicial review. Where the legislator takes over responsibility for this and introduces a quasi-legislative judicial review *in abstracto*, even courts might run the risk of disconnecting contractual practice from contract law. Judicial review then turns into a kind of phantom review, with limited relevance for the autonomy of the parties.[65] What might be true for the nation-state level is not correct for the European Union. Whilst the EU has introduced judicial review *in abstracto*, the European treaties do not foresee the possibility for the ECJ to make a final judgment on the legality of incriminated standard terms. This is not the place to discuss whether the ECJ acts like a European civil court.[66] What matters is that the ECJ has established

---

65 H.-W. Micklitz, 'Some Considerations on Cassis de Dijon and the Control of Unfair Contract Terms in Consumer Contracts' in K. Boele-Woelki and W. Grosheide (eds.), *The Future of European Contract Law*, Kluwer, Alphen aan den Rijn 2007, pp. 387–410, reprinted in H. Collins (ed.), above n. 24, pp. 19–42.

66 C. Schmid, 'The ECJ as a Constitutional and a Private Law Court: A Methodological Comparison', Zentrum für Europäische Rechtspolitik (Centre for European Legal Policy – ZERP), ZERP Discussion Paper 4/2006, available at https://d-nb.info/119024845X/34.

a kind of *ex post factum* restoration of contract law via the right of the user of standard terms to reject the identified unfairness, even to her detriment, if she so decides. The more recent developments in co-regulation demonstrate that there is a common denominator. The ECJ is not ready to accept that harmonised European standards should remain free from review. The 'co-' in the regulatory approach does not prevent the ECJ from submitting technical standards to some sort of judicial review. It is not without reason that this view has been subject to massive criticism in the technical standards community.

What are the escape strategies for regulators? Private regulators tend to invent ever more forms of private regulation below the radar of standard terms, meaning that they are exempt from judicial review. Codes of conduct fit perfectly well into the picture. The public regulator is not ready to treat standard terms and codes of conduct alike, independent of the difficulty of vague wordings. Those who argue in favour of some sort of judicial review of codes of conduct should refer to the existing set of European legislation, either the Standard Terms Directive or the Unfair Commercial Practices Directive.

Co-regulation is a relatively young field that merges public and private regulation and public and private regulators. It seems to be the perfect alternative to private and public regulation, as it theoretically allows the interests of both regulators to be combined and makes it possible to overcome the tension between rationalisation and public interests through the inclusion of non-governmental organisations in the making of technical standards. It is alarming that co-regulation through technical standards is legally designed so as to fully disconnect contract practice – i.e. the development of technical standards – from contract law. The regulatory goals which are inherent in co-regulation are exempted from judicial review apart from a constitutional review of the delegation mechanism. With its judgment in *Elliott*, the ECJ broke a taboo which shattered the regulatory model and opened pathways for laying down procedural requirements for the development of harmonised European standards that might compensate for the technicity of the standards which impact the rights and duties of the parties. There is room for doctrinal imagination. Who should have standing? Is it possible to deduce from the action for injunction as the European minimum standard that the 'entities' mentioned in the unfair terms Directive and the unfair commercial practices Directive should have standing?

The tension between regulation and standardisation – between contractual practice and the law of contract – is timeless, however. The interaction resembles the fable of the tortoise and the hare. The regulators are constantly inventing new strategies for realising all sorts of regulatory purposes; the courts, however, remain in the background, always ready to exercise their adjudicative power to preserve contract law. This might explain the move away from the courts towards all sorts of out-of-court settlement mechanisms. But even such a strategy has to face the fact that courts might be just as ready to look into dispute settlement mechanisms as they are ready to look at other forms of contractual practice that are subject to private or co-regulation. From a more conceptual and theoretical perspective, one might raise the question whether we are running in circles or whether instead the circle is in fact an upward spiral towards an ever higher and more sophisticated degree of interaction between the three patterns of regulation and contract law.

DEFAULT RULES BEYOND A STATE

Special-Purpose Lawmakers in the Platform Economy

Mateusz GROCHOWSKI*

1. INTRODUCTION

Undoubtedly, default rules[1] constitute one of the most characteristic regulatory instruments of contract law, and encapsulate its most crucial concepts

---

* I would like to express my deep gratitude for several colleagues and mentors who contributed to this chapter with their remarks and advice. I am particularly grateful to the Yale Law School community, especially Professor Daniel Markovits, Professor Alan Schwartz and Professor Jack Balkin, as well as to the Affiliates of the YLS Information Society Project and the Fellows and Faculty of the Edmond J. Safra Center for Ethics and the Blavatnik Interdisciplinary Cyber Research Center at the University of Tel Aviv. In particular, I feel much indebted to Professor Hanoch Dagan, Professor Roy Kreitner, Professor Yotam Kaplan, Dr Tomer Shadmy and Dr Fabrizio Esposito. Last, but absolutely not least, I am also truly obliged to the participants of the European Society of Contract Law (SECOLA) Conference in Warsaw in 2018, who were kind enough to provide me with questions and comments on my research. The text is partly based on the results of a research project financed by the Polish National Science Center No. 2016/20/S/HS5/00458. The usual disclaimers apply.

1 The chapter uses the notions of 'default rules' and 'non-mandatory rules' interchangeably. It should be, however, kept in mind that it is possible to draw more detailed conceptual

concerning the relation between a legal rule and an individual. Under the conventional assumption, default rules are intended to facilitate contracting by providing parties with a choice of pre-set alternatives for the content of an agreement. Current markets, however, alter this general picture to a certain extent. Instead of a general and universal community of contractors, they develop parallel close-knit communities, which are typically brought together through the use of IT tools in order to facilitate contracting amongst their members. They give rise to more constrained and tighter regulatory communities, which develop more specific sub-majorities of preferences. Many of these communities set forth various self-regulatory frameworks, which attempt – at least to a certain extent – to respond to these preferences. Amongst the diverse types of rules that result, there are an increasing number of optional rules, which in many respects resemble classic default rules in contract law.[2] As opposed to the more classic defaults, however, the default rules generated by these private regulators are created for closer regulatory communities about which these private regulators have much more information. They therefore address and reflect the 'fractioned' majorities' preferences.

Although similar occurrences have also been recognised in classic market settings,[3] the clusters of contractors created currently in electronic commerce seem particularly exemplary for this phenomenon and – at the same time – in many respects specific in terms of identifying and aggregating preferences of individuals. Therefore, the main point of reference for the text are rules developed by online intermediary platforms in the sharing economy – which seem to embody many of the peculiarities of fractioned majorities.[4] From this perspective, the matter of fractioned majoritarian defaults merits and necessitates a more comprehensive theoretical account on at least two levels.

distinctions between these terms, building on various theoretic assumptions; cf. e.g. M. Hesselink, 'Non-Mandatory Rules in European Contract Law' (2005) 1 *European Review of Contract Law (ERCL)* 43.

2 The notion of default rules is traditionally referred to as a tenet of the state-created contract law; see however F. Möslein, 'Dispositive Regeln im transnationalen Privatrechtsverkehr: Same same, but different?' in G.-P. Calliess (ed.), *Transnationales Recht. Stand und Perspektiven*, Mohr Siebeck, Tübingen 2014, who provides a theoretic framework for the question of default rules that are created beyond a sovereign state's monopoly on international trade.

3 See e.g. R.C. Ellickson, *Order without Law. How Neighbors Settle Disputes*, Harvard University Press, Cambridge, MA/London 1991.

4 Generally, on fractioned market communities, see also L. Bernstein, 'Beyond Relational Contracts: Social Capital and Network Governance in Procurement Contracts' (2015) 7 *Journal of Legal Analysis (JLA)* 561; L. Bernstein, 'Private Commercial Law in the Cotton Industry: Creating Cooperation through Rules, Norms and Institutions' (2001) 99 *University of Michigan Law Review* 1724; L. Bernstein, 'Opting Out of the Legal System: Extralegal Contractual Relations in the Diamond Industry' (1991) 21 *Journal of Legal Studies* 115; L. Bernstein, 'Social Norms and Default Rules Analysis' (1993–94) 3 *Southern California Interdisciplinary Law Journal* 59.

A more detailed analysis is required regarding its exact nature and variations, in respect of current market phenomena. A deepened analysis is also required in terms of its relation with the existing body of contract law rules – both in terms of legislation, and in terms of pertinent case law.

2. 'SPONTANEOUS' DEFAULT RULES

2.1. DECENTRALISED CREATION OF DEFAULT RULES

State-centred law-making is traditionally the most important field in which default rules emerge – and in which the classic theories of default rules can be primarily put to use. Default rules are also, however, ubiquitous in private law and are commonly created outside state-oriented settings.[5] As opposed to the former, classic way of rule-making, private defaults are created to regulate particular, usually precisely limited, spheres of contracting. Typically, they emerge in those domains in which the establishment of default rules by a state is too costly (e.g. due to low availability of relevant data or enforcement deficiency), but at the same time in which the entirely independent creation of contracts (without any pre-existing legal framework) may lead to substantial inefficiency, or a lack of contracting at all.[6] In these instances, the market tends to generate 'superstructures', which organise individual contracting and provide a privately made regulatory framework. This situation can lead to the emergence of two patterns.

In the first of them, a regulatory advantage offered by privately created defaults may result from a substantial inequality of costs of obtaining information necessary for creating optimal rules. Many of the bodies that set forth default rules in fact operate as organisers or facilitators of particular spheres of the market, and consequently possess privileged access to information about

5 Generally, on creation of default contract provisions by private actors, see also M. Cohen and A. Sundararajan, 'Self-Regulation and Innovation in the Peer-to-Peer Sharing Economy' (2015–16) 82 *University of Chicago Law Review Dialogue* 116; and S. Grundmann and P. Hacker, 'Digital Technology as a Challenge to European Contract Law. From Existing to Future Architecture' (2017) 13 *ERCL* 255, 274. On the related problems of privately created default rules, see also e.g. R. Rubb, P. Corrigan and P.L. Warren, 'A Behavioral Contract Theory Perspective on Retirement Savings' (2015) 47 *Connecticut Law Review* 1317.

6 More generally, on privatisation of tasks in contract law, see M.J. Radin, 'The Deformation of Contract in the Information Society' (2017) 37 *Oxford Journal of Legal Studies* 505, 505–06. The general outline of regulatory questions posed by the platform economy is not entirely novel. Also before the emergence of the platform economy, the involvement of non-state actors in cooperative regulation was quite an ubiquitous phenomenon – M. Cohen and A. Sundararajan, above n. 5, p. 121 seem to make a stronger claim in this respect: '[p]rior to the emergence of sharing-economy platforms, governmental intervention was a natural solution to market failure in traditional peer-to-peer businesses.'

the regulatory needs and ways of addressing them in the most adequate way. Illustrative for this model are professional associations (e.g. trade chambers)[7] that take up regulatory competence in particular spheres of industry. Typically, they are formed in the collective way – i.e. by a group of professionals who aggregate their interest by establishing a stable regulatory framework. The resulting frameworks are often much cheaper and more efficient regulators than those that result from those generated by separate parties to contracts, in which governing rules were considered in isolation.

In the second such pattern, privately created default rules can arise in those spheres in which the creation of detailed contracts would be unreasonably costly for the 'monadic' contractors and, therefore, it is advantageous to centralise rule-setting aptitude and to delegate it to a specialised entity, separate from contracting parties.[8] This situation seems particularly typical for low-value contracts, for which the pace of concluding and executing an agreement is typically more essential than its completeness. As a result, in some instances markets seem to organise themselves naturally around a limited number of entities (sometimes only one of them), which are the cheapest 'governors' of the particular spheres of economy.[9] One of the most vivid examples of this situation is the current shape of the sharing economy, in which particular domains of the market (e.g. short-term apartment rental prices) are to a great extent organised around online platforms (like Airbnb or Uber).[10] These entities, as opposed to the first genre of bodies mentioned above, tend to operate as typical market players – i.e. companies that base their business model on putting together a community of suppliers of goods or services and clients.[11]

The majority of rules created by those online platforms have a mandatory (inalienable) character that is binding upon members of the community. However, a fraction of these rules is of a default nature – allowing parties to contract around them. The emergence of privately created default rules poses a complex question of the extent to which majoritarian theory – foundational for default rules in state-created contract law – can be considered relevant for the extra-state sphere. In other words, since the majoritarian theory is to be perceived as a fundament of the concept of default rules, private regulation in turn presents a problem of whether privately created defaults

7 L. Bernstein, 'Private Commercial Law …', above n. 4, p. 1724.

8 On the difference between classic trade associations and self-regulatory institutions see also M. Cohen and A. Sundararajan, above n. 5, p. 124.

9 On the similar phenomenon see also A. Schwartz and R.E. Scott, 'Third Party Beneficiaries and Contractual Networks' (2015) 7 *JLA* 325, 330.

10 On the regulatory activity of platforms see e.g. J. Tanz, 'How Airbnb and Lyft got Americans to Trust Each Other', *Wired*, 23 April 2014, https://www.wired.com/2014/04/trust-in-the-share-economy/; A.J. Casey and A. Niblett, 'Self-Driving Contracts', (2017) 43 *Journal of Corporation Law*, 1.

11 See also M. Cohen and A. Sundararajan, above n. 5, p. 124.

resemble classic default rules only formally (i.e. by providing optional and non-binding regulatory designs) or also in substantive terms (i.e. by playing similar or at least comparable roles on the market).

2.2. DOES MAJORITARIAN THEORY REALLY MATTER?

In the classic theoretical accounts, default rules are considered to be a soft regulatory instrument, designed to frame the process of contracting by supplying pre-defined solutions (framed either as opt-in or opt-out provisions) for a contract's content. Under this fundamental assumption, legislative defaults should typically provide an optimal or, in some sense, 'average' and 'basic' set of responses to particular issues that emerge in market practice. The classic concept of contract law, mostly in the European tradition, organises default rules into structured groups and supplements them incidentally by mandatory or semi-mandatory regulation,[12] thereby creating contract types.[13] The idea of default rules as a response to the expected preferences of their addressees – who should obtain through such rules an aid in designing their individual contracts – rests on this fundamental assumption, labelled as the 'majoritarian' concept. It assumes that optimal default rules should respond to the most typical or widespread preferences of the relevant community of contractors. This general premise is intrinsic to the concept of default rules as such, and defines their most inherent and 'proper' nature.

It does not seem, however, that this classic framework can be applicable to default rules that are not established by classic state actors. In its traditional shape, it has been created to explain sources and legitimisation of default rules imposed in a general and abstract way by law-makers or courts. It was not intended to describe defaults that are set by private actors for other participants within the market. Under closer scrutiny, differences between those two ways of setting rules seem, however, much less. Privately created defaults typically emerge in triangle-shape settings, in which parties to a particular contract are subordinated to another entity that plays a governing role over their relation. As a result, the link between the bottom edges of the triangle (i.e. parties to a sale or service contract) and the top edge (i.e. the private regulatory entity, to which parties subordinated their relation) resembles in many respects the relation between the state law-making agent and the addressees of its rules.

This basic observation does not give, however, a final answer to the question of whether defaults created by non-state entities comply to any extent with the

---

12 Further on the types of optional rules in the continental European tradition of private law, G. Bachmann, 'Optionsmodelle im Privatrecht', 63 (2008) *Juristenzeitung*, 11.

13 See also M. Hesselink, above n. 1, p. 47.

majoritarian theory. The feasible responses seem to be different for the two model categories of non-state regulatory entities distinguished above.

The first of the models discussed above has much more deliberative nature. Self-regulatory bodies of this sort produce regulation typically in a 'collective' way (through direct consent of members of a professional association or delegation of representatives that has been bestowed with the necessary competence to enact such rules). Furthermore, in many instances, the process of rule-setting by these bodies is entirely or partially non-formal. They often support spontaneous creation of default rules (e.g. by enforcing 'local' customs or rules of conduct that emerge within the community)[14] amongst the members rather than impose them from above. Notably, the rule-setting entities – both the entire community and its specialised agents (such as committees drafting codes of conduct and arbitrators) – represent in these situations the aggregated interests of the community and do not have any a priori self-interest and biases.[15]

In the case of defaults created by the sorts of entities described above as the second alternative model to state-centred law-making, the situation differs much more strongly from the classic contract law concept of establishment and operation of default rules. As has been discussed, in this situation rules are created not *by* but *for* the community which gathers around a particular commercial actor (e.g. an online intermediary platform). In other words, as opposed to the previously mentioned instance, in which default rules emerge within a fully self-regulatory community, in this case members of the community enter a pre-set 'marketplace', the regulatory framework of which has been provided ex ante by the governing entity. Moreover, in those situations, the actor who organises this marketplace typically has a direct economic interest in providing regulation of a particular shape and content. Therefore, default rules established in this way are not preference-neutral, but quite the opposite: they tend to manifest the one-sided economic interest of their creators (who set up the market communities to accrue direct profit from transactions concluded between their members).

These details do not mean, however, that default rules created in this type of economic setting lack the majoritarian dimension. Despite all the peculiarities described above, apparently most of the default rules generated within this sort of setting also seem to fit the majoritarian concept, albeit in a less obvious

---

14 On the classic accounts of the self-regulatory potential of usages developed by fractioned market communities, see e.g. R.C. Ellickson, above n. 3, pp. 188–206; L. Bernstein, 'Merchant Law in a Merchant Court: Rethinking the Code's Search for Immanent Business Norms' (1996) 144 *University of Pennsylvania Law Review (UPLR)* 1765.

15 This claim does not suggest, obviously, that bodies creating default rules in this type of situation are totally bias-free. They can be subject to a variety of factors that can skew their final decision – see also A. Schwartz and R.E. Scott, 'The Political Economy of Private Legislatures' (1995) 143 *UPLR* 595, 650–52.

way. Their existence within this circumstance can be explained in terms of interconnected preferences. By establishing those rules, 'authoritarian' governors of a market aim to maximise their own utility. In doing so, however, such governing platforms have to develop mechanisms enhancing the efficiency of particular horizontal contracts. The peculiarities of a specific market – especially in contemporary online contracting – create a few premises that may support the creation of efficient default rules in this way.[16]

First of all, privately set default rules allocate in a different way the costs of regulation. Law-makers who act in fractioned market communities such as online platforms typically have strong sector-specific expertise, as well as much easier access to data that is relevant for designing efficient contract law rules, than state legislators. Therefore, this decentralised way of regulating market issues may in many instances render results that are more efficient and adequate than those produced through state-provided law-making.[17] In some instances private communities are, moreover, not only the best acquirers of regulatory expertise, but are also the only entities that may feasibly access this data, as they are either the only actors or the most vividly predominant actors in the particular spheres of the market (e.g. Airbnb for short-term apartment rentals). In many instances, private rule-makers can also be strongly incentivised to care about the quality and efficiency of privately created rules. They are naturally inclined not only to attract the broadest possible array of clients, but also to encourage them to behave proactively and to willingly engage in contractual transactions.[18] As a result, they may try to limit possible failures of the market as much as possible – especially those possible failures which could act as discouraging factors to the possible contracting parties.[19]

---

16 More generally, on the particular competence of private entities to develop efficient default rules, see also L. Bernstein, 'Private Commercial Law ...', above n. 4, p. 1741. On self-regulation as a remedy for deficiencies of state regulation in the context of the sharing economy, see also C. Koopman, M. Mitchell and A. Thierer, 'The Sharing Economy and Consumer Protection Regulation. The Case for Policy Change' (2015) 8 *Journal of Business, Entrepreneurship & the Law* 529, 543.

17 Cf. M. Cohen and A. Sundararajan, above n. 5, p. 133; C. Marzen, D.A. Prum and R.J. Aalberts, 'The New Sharing Economy: the Role of Property, Tort and Contract Law for Managing the Airbnb Model' (2016) *New York University Journal of Law and Business* 295, 318–20.

18 M. Cohen and A. Sundararajan, above n. 5, p. 121.

19 Cf. M. Cohen and A. Sundararajan, above n. 5, p. 121; in a similar way also A. Malhotra and M. Van Alstyne, 'The Dark Side of the Sharing Economy ... and How to Lighten It. Improving the sharing economy will require addressing myriad problems' Viewpoints vol. 57 n. 11, November 2014: 'Platforms are closer to the action; and they have an incentive to look after their communities.' In the context of sharing economy, the same scheme can also be applied in some instances to 'vertical' contracts, concluded between a platform and its participants. Agreements of this kind allow particular contracts to be shaped idiosyncratically and to thereby set forth an organisational framework for participation in a platform. In practice, rules of this sort typically provide an option for the platform's participant – and allow her to choose the most suitable regulatory scheme.

In doing so, private regulators are much more apt to create tailor-made solutions which address directly the needs of a particular regulatory community. Depending upon the particular platform and sector of the market, the level of specificity of these rules can vary from 'general' defaults set for the entire community to more or less specialised ones. In some instances, this may amount even to the creation of fully personalised rules, specifically created for particular contractors[20] (with regard to their previous 'contractual history' in particular, via the community and other data collected by a private regulator). The emergence of a fractioned creation of default rules in contract law means, hence, a certain shift in the long-lasting way of development of contractual practice towards depersonalisation.[21]

All in all – from the perspective of the second model described above – default rules supplied by private actors aim also to address the preferences of suppliers and clients, as well as to produce rules that would optimally address their suppliers' and clients' interests. From this vantage point, the lack of neutrality of a rule-setter does not necessarily undermine the majoritarian view of default rules. Moreover, also in those settings, the governing entities typically leave (deliberately or de facto) some space for spontaneously created default rules and standards. In particular, they allow the community to develop bottom-up regulatory schemes, based especially on trust (which in the current economy is very often formalised by various feedback and reputational systems, based on IT tools).[22]

3. FRACTIONED MAJORITY IN USE: THE CASE OF THE PLATFORM ECONOMY

3.1. PLATFORM COMMUNITIES AS REGULATORY COMMUNITIES

As has been preliminarily noted above, one of the most illustrative and comprehensive instances of fractioned contractual communities are clutches of

20 On personalisation of rules by private actors, see especially A. Verstein, 'Privatizing Personalized Law' (2019) 86 *University of Chicago Law Review* 551.

21 An exemplary observation of this phenomenon was made over 70 years ago, at the time of intensive emergence of standardised contracting, by F. Kessler, 'Contracts of Adhesion – Some Thoughts About Freedom of Contract' (1943) 43 *Columbia Law Review* 629, 631: '[a] standardized contract, once its contents have been formulated by a business firm, is used in every bargain dealing with the same product or service. The individuality of the parties which so frequently gave color to the old type contract has disappeared. The stereotyped contract of today reflects the impersonality of the market. It has reached its greatest perfection in the different types of contracts used on the various exchanges.'

22 On the regulatory role of trust cf. C. Busch, 'Crowdsourcing Consumer Confidence. How to Regulate Online Rating and Review Systems in the Collaborative Economy' in

parties that gather around online intermediary platforms.[23] The creation of such groups is in the strong and direct interest of online platforms, which typically ground their business models upon involving broad groups of suppliers and clients and increasing the scale of exchange between them. In consequence, platforms are intrinsically interested in construing the most well-structured and appealing 'infra-markets'[24] for the clusters of contractors who access them.

A part and parcel of the market model of every intermediary platform is its internal regulatory design, i.e. the clusters of rules that govern relations within the market domain that each platform governs. This framework is most often supplied by typical contract law means, and binds all involved parties by virtue of the individual consent of each individual supplier and client. From a functional perspective, however, the regulatory framework of platform 'infra-markets' is created in an entirely imperious fashion. Such regulatory frameworks are imposed unilaterally by platforms, and framed as a take-it-or-leave-it regulatory proposal, which must be adhered to by individuals who join the platform-created market. Typically, they are framed as standard contract terms ('User Agreement', 'Terms of Use', etc.), provided for platform users as click-wrap or browse-wrap.

Rules of this kind typically work in two dimensions. Most obviously, they address the vertical relation between a platform and its participants. They govern matters related to the structure of the community (e.g. entry and exit rules for its members) and frame the entitlements of a platform and individual members vis-à-vis each other (as regards, for instance, transaction fees, managing user accounts etc.). At the same time, rules created by platforms also operate in a horizontal dimension, by creating entitlements and duties for individual 'supplier–client' relations. At this level, rules created by platforms usually dictate both the classic matters of the contract's design (such as the formation of an agreement, the quality of performance and the delivery of goods), as well as other issues related to an exchange within a platform-established market (for instance, consumer protection and non-discrimination).[25]

In practice, although all platforms require by nature a relatively strong vertical regulatory scheme, they differ substantially in terms of the scope and intensity of their horizontal regulation. At the most general level, platforms differ in terms of the general propensity towards pre-establishing contractual design

A. de Franceschi (ed.), *European Contract Law and the Digital Single Market. The Implications of the Digital Revolution*, Intersentia, Cambridge/Antwerp 2016, p. 227–28; M. Grochowski, 'Spontaneous Order in the Sharing Economy? A Research Agenda' (2018) 13 *Studia Prawa Prywatnego* 75, 80–82.

23 As M. Cohen and A. Sundararajan, above n. 5, p. 119, assert, 'platforms should be viewed as part of the solution, rather than part of the problem, and they should be included as key actors in a self-regulatory regime.'

24 Cf. e.g. O. Lobel, 'The Law of the Platform' (2016) 101 *Minnesota Law Review* 87, 146–56.

25 See e.g. J.K. Winn, 'The Secession of the Successful: The Rise of Amazon as Private Global Consumer Protection Regulator' (2016) 58 *Arizona Law Review* 193.

with an effect for all the contracting parties. The differences and resemblances in this regard are particularly sharp for the platforms that operate in the same sphere of the economy. For instance, while the car-sharing industry (e.g. Uber, Lyft and Bolt) is relatively unified in its proclivity towards strong regulatory framing of horizontal contracts, auction platforms are generally much more divergent. They differ from platforms which implement broad and direct governance of horizontal agreements (such as Amazon), to those that limit their focus to selected elements of contractual design (e.g. eBay) to the least interventionist ones, which frame themselves as pure facilitators and organisers of marketplaces and leave the bulk of the rules of the game to individual contractors (e.g. Alibaba). The market hence provides several models of 'fractioning' of contracting communities, in which a platform shares – to various degrees – contract governance tasks with its users. The division of governance tasks between a platform and its individual contractors means enhancing the de facto autonomy of suppliers, who typically enjoy a stronger bargaining position over clients, and thus form the second tier of regulatory design in platform communities.

Regardless of the particular model of governing horizontal relations, regulatory schemes established by platforms create a challenging situation for understanding the institutional design of contract law. The platform economy emerged to a great extent in a regulatory 'no man's land'. Due to the specificity of its overall model, as well as to peculiar features of market relations in the platform–supplier–client triangle, the entire sector cannot be easily encompassed by the existing regulatory schemes (e.g. by consumer or labour law). As a result, the platform economy has a strong self-regulatory flavour and – in its current regulatory design – builds predominantly upon the schemes created by platforms to fill in the regulatory vacuum, beyond the spectrum of state-created law. In this sense, platforms gain a strong de facto sovereignty over the online market,[26] supplementing those regulatory tasks that (due to a deliberate choice) have not been properly performed by the regulatory sovereigns in the classic sense. In these terms, platforms operate in fact as 'special-purpose sovereigns',[27] whose regulatory toolboxes and range of market impacts are limited to frames of the particular contracting communities.

---

26 See also S. Grundmann and P. Hacker, above n. 5, p. 274 who observe that '[w]hen platforms supply default contractual terms or provide for specific support for certain users, they act as de facto "lawmakers" for the platform environment.'

27 The term was used for the first time by Balkin to label the de facto regulatory aptitude of social media platforms in terms of freedom of expression: '[i]n fact, the largest owners of private infrastructure are so powerful that we might even regard them as special-purpose sovereigns. They engage in perpetual struggles for control of digital networks with nation states, who, in turn, want to control and coopt these powerful players. The practical ability to speak in the digital age is shaped by the results of these struggles for control and cooptation': J.M. Balkin, 'Free Speech in the Algorithmic Society: Big Data, Private Governance, and New School Speech Regulation' (2018) 51 *U.C. Davis Law Review* 1149, 1153.

In this regard, the platform economy can be allocated as a further component of a broad array of market communities that produce rules for themselves, supplementing (or in fact replacing) those that are state-supplied. The realities of the online market changes, however, the typical design of such communities, altering their structures from the 'consensual' towards the 'autocratic'. The ability both to organise broad communities of contractors and to minimise transaction costs by use of IT design allows the most powerful players on the market – the companies that set up the most-used platforms – to maximise their own economic impact, by dictating terms of exchange for horizontal contractors. For these reasons, the earlier attempts to explain the nature of contractual relations in the platform economy as a regulation established by community of peers[28] seem relatively unconvincing. The private regulatory schemes created by platforms are, in fact, much closer to other internet-based communities, such as social media users. They are also typically organised through the imperious establishment of rules by an external entity, with varying levels of involvement of individual participants – and, hence, have a strong vertical spine.

From the perspective of contract law, online platforms function, hence, as quasi-law-makers, which are apt to introduce rules that shape agreements concluded amongst particular clients and suppliers. From the structural perspective, each of the platforms creates in fact an idiosyncratic type of a contract, offering it to their own actual and potential users. Platforms that operate on the same market may, moreover, compete over regulatory design, trying to attract new participants (or to increase the volume of exchange between existing ones) by providing contracts that better fit the regulatory needs of the particular community.[29] As a result, instead of a 'centralised' model of a contract, regulated and enforced predominantly by a state, the platform economy offers a picture of 'distributed' regulation, whereby each of the market players, powerful enough to gather a community of horizontal contractors, may construe a new, granular type of agreement.[30]

3.2. HETEROGENEITY OF CONTRACT LAW

The shift of the model in question also entails a significant change within the classic concepts of autonomy and optionality in contract law. Classic contract law

---

28 A. Sundararajan, *The Sharing Economy. The End of Employment and the Rise of Crowd-Based Capitalism*, The MIT Press, Cambridge, MA/London 2017, pp. 151–52.

29 On contract design as a field of competition, see also, generally, D. Gilo and A. Porat, 'Viewing Unconscionability Through a Market Law' (2010) 52 *William & Mary Law Review* 133, 162–70.

30 See also V. Mak, *Legal Pluralism in European Contract Law*, Oxford University Press, Oxford 2020, 94ff.

(understood through the lens of the positivist theory of law-making) has been concerned mostly with guaranteeing parties' autonomy and the possibility of self-determination at the level of choosing the regulatory design for a particular agreement concluded between parties. For these reasons, classic contract law has been typically averse towards mandatory command-and-control regulation and opted rather towards default rules as a less intrusive (and hence, more autonomy-preserving) solution. The crucial regulatory choices in this regard were centred around the optimal architecture of default rules at the substantive level and the intensity of altering constraints and behavioural framing.

Online contracting alters this setting by removing the focus from autonomy facilitated by 'internal' choice (i.e. by the possibility to contract around default rules that constitute particular types of contracts) towards greater consideration of the 'external' decision to adopt one of the concurring types of a contract available in a parallel way on the market. While in the classic model parties to a sales contract could typically make a choice about the conditions of delivery or warranties – adhering to a default rule or replacing it with an independently created clause – in online commerce they may choose between a few concurring designs of sales agreements, as supplied by various platforms.

The decision in the latter regard rests mostly on the choice of the regulation provider. In practice, it may take place on a few levels. First of all, it is a choice between pledging obedience to the 'general' or, rather, to one of the 'special-purpose' sovereigns. In this field, individual contractors may decide whether they wish to conclude an agreement with the use of a domestic platform (which is more strongly linked to a particular state-centred jurisdiction and thus to the classic enforcement modes) or instead to a transnational platform (which, in typical instances, will develop stronger self-regulatory tools). Secondly, the choice in question may turn upon a direct choice between two, at least roughly comparable, designs of the same contract type. In this regard, parties may choose, for example, between transport agreements supplied by Uber and Lyft, building on their nitty-gritty details and attempting to choose the type that would represent their preferences in the most accurate possible way. Finally, the essence of choice may focus upon selecting between rules provided by a platform or rules created by particular suppliers. In this way, clients may choose, for instance, between the 'Amazon'[31] subtype of a sales contract and one of several subtypes of sales contracts created by particular sellers on the (much more regulation-averse) Alibaba. At the same time, most of the rules supplied by platforms are mandatory in nature: once set, they cannot be easily altered by parties to a specific platform-facilitated contract.

---

[31] In practice, the regulatory model adopted by Amazon is a bit more complex. The platform allows individual sellers to frame their own contract rules, but at the same time effectively excludes most of them at the stage of finalising the order and processing the client's payment.

In consequence, contract law in the platform economy turns from a classic unitarian system based upon default rules into a set of parallel universes, composed of in mandatory rules that are offered by the market as alternatives to be opted into. In other words, a one-size-fits-all contract law becomes increasingly heterogeneous, divided between various domains, governed by state and non-state actors.

For obvious reasons, the realities of particular segments of the online market may blur the premises of choice in all of these dimensions. Decisions taken by average contractors may be driven by other types of inclinations than sheer preference of one contract type over the other. The decisive role in this regard may be played, for obvious reasons, by the price of a particular good or service or the accessibility of a platform through an internet search.[32] As a result, the ways of expressing (and ex post identifying) preferences, which underpin choice between contract types, may be much less obvious or concealed beneath other circumstances. This does not mean, however, that this level of preference-revealing is utterly inoperable; and, indeed, preference-revealing may nonetheless have its cognitive value. The actual premises of parties' choices in many instances is the effect of the regulatory design provided by a platform, especially the limitation of transaction costs or the more favourable framing of particular rights and duties (e.g. terms of delivery). It is also possible that the subtype of contracts created by platforms may act in favour of one group of parties (e.g. clients) and thus to the relative detriment of other parties. In this regard, the choice made by contractors may also operate as a clear cognitive indicator of more detailed preferences.

3.3. THE TYPICAL NON-MANDATORY RULES

The most inherent type of optionality created by the platform economy – multiplication of contract types available for contractors – is accompanied by default rules, which remain close to the classic understanding of this notion. As opposed to the previously described 'wholesale' optionality, in this case electability of rules has a targeted character and is limited to particular elements of the platform's regulatory design. Construed in this way, default rules operate as exceptions to the generally mandatory character of provisions created by platforms.

---

32 Alternatively, platforms may tend to create their own efficient search engines, which could provide users with comprehensive data on the goods and services in the entire partition of the market – for this phenomenon in the case of Amazon see L.M. Kahn, 'Amazon's Antitrust Paradox' (2016) 126 *Yale Law Journal (YLJ)* 710, 714, 773; *ea*, 'The Separation of Platforms and Commerce', (2019) 119 *Columbia Law Review*, 973.

Default rules set by platforms naturally involve this community in a regulatory process, providing it with the aptitude to co-create rules for itself. The rule creation in question usually takes place through particular horizontal contracts (although some patterns may become so sufficiently widespread in the community that many parties contract around a default rule in the same or a similar way). Moreover, making use of default rules is, by nature, a cooperative undertaking, since (with minor exceptions) it can take place only upon an agreement. Default rules provided by platforms take various forms and operate in a variety of ways. From the structural point of view, they can be expressed in two model ways.[33]

Typically, they are introduced through various sorts of standard terms agreements, in the relation between the facilitator of the 'infra-market' and each of the participants who enter it. The rules of this kind are formally not binding upon the horizontal contracts concluded between platform members. Nevertheless, they impact this relation indirectly, by creating an obligation on each of the individual contractors, towards the market 'governor', to adopt particular behaviour vis-à-vis the other contractor[34] (e.g. to provide a particular warranty for goods offered within an auction or to offer certain cancellation terms), unless both parties agree otherwise. They may be framed either as binary alternatives[35] (where parties are given a choice between two exclusive options)[36] or as menus, consisting of a number of solutions to be chosen.[37]

---

33 See generally V. Katz, 'Regulating the Sharing Economy' (2015) 30 *Berkeley Technology Law Journal* 1067, 1100–01: '[m]oreover, sharing platforms standardize transactions such that providers no longer clearly occupy a superior bargaining position. In many cases, the terms of the platform govern all aspects of the transaction, leaving both providers and users only the freedom to accept or reject a potential match. In other cases, the platform provides a default contract or baseline set of terms, but allows users and providers to negotiate privately.'

34 Gap-filling defaults are also present in contract relations between the platform and its members. They are relatively less frequent in this respect (the relation between the platform and its users is governed typically by inalienable rules). Sometimes, however, platforms decide to introduce in this respect a particular degree of optionality; one of the most peculiar examples of this solution is eBay's rule on the alienability of the user's feedback history – see also B. Rietjens, 'Trust and Reputation on eBay: Towards a Legal Framework for Feedback Intermediaries' (2006) 15 *Information & Communications Technology Law* 55, 72. According to the eBay Terms of Use, the transfer of feedback is prohibited without the platform's consent. The consent in question (or, more precisely, the agreement constituted by user request and the platform's consent) allows the inalienability the thereby be repealed and the feedback made transferable.

35 See e.g. Airbnb's ODR procedure: https://www.airbnb.com/help/article/767/what-is-the-resolution-center?_set_bev_on_new_domain=1599842957_NzljYWJlNGE1OWYw&locale=en, which is available on request (opt-in), after complying with certain formal requirements.

36 In many instances, default rules are not expressed only in the wording typical of contract terms, but in a 'narrative' form. In this way, for instance, eBay imposes a default rule that allows to set a 'reserve price' – following this general provision with an instruction, which specifies an altering rule: 'A reserve price is the lowest price you're willing to sell an item for. By using a reserve price you can set a low starting price for your auction – and boost

Secondly, in much more rare instances, members of a 'fractioned' market community are provided with a pattern of clauses that can be introduced in horizontal contracts between them (sometimes with ready-to-take templates, which need only to be filled-in with the personalised data of contractors and the key elements regarding the agreement's subject matter). In fact, the clauses in question are functionally similar to default rules – as they give parties a(n opt-in) way to choose pre-set provisions to frame a contract concluded between them.

Most often, default rules introduced by online platforms play a role typical of classic (state-created) defaults, i.e. they are intended to fill in gaps in horizontal agreements. This type of optional regulation also provides the most illustrative instance of the fractioned majorities phenomenon. By introducing these rules, platforms (at least assumptively) try to respond to the average preferences of the horizontal contractors, who belong to the particular market community. Rules of this kind regulate both substantive[38] and procedural issues,[39] and play mostly organisational and framing roles, safeguarding the proper operation of a market created by a platform.[40] The existence of those rules seems particularly important

interest in your item – but without the risk of having to sell your item for less than you think it's worth.': https://www.ebay.co.uk/help/selling/listings/selling-auctions/reserve-prices?id=4143#:~:text=A%20reserve%20price%20is%20the,than%20you%20think%20it's%20worth.

37 One of the simplest menus of this sort is provided by Airbnb regarding whether there is a smoke detector in the dwelling. The host is given a choice: to install the detector or leave the dwelling without one, with a duty to disclose this fact to clients in the offer available online: https://airbnb.com/help/article/515/i-m-a-host--am-i-required-to-have-a-smoke-and-co-detector-installed.

38 See e.g. eBay's rules on the cancellation policy, based on a default component and allowing sellers to introduce individually tailored rules: '[s]ellers can create rules to automate replacements, returns, and refunds under certain circumstances. For all new sellers, in listings where returns are accepted, eBay will set a default rule that automates the return process. Sellers may remove or customize their return preferences in their account settings within My eBay. Where settings have been set to automatically accept requests for returns or replacements, an eBay-generated return shipping label will be provided to your buyer. You agree to comply with our returns policy.' (https://www.ebay.com/help/policies/member-behaviour-policies/user-agreement?id=4259#Returns). Default character was also attributed to the term of delivery of a reward, under the Kickstarter Terms of Use. According to the caveat made by Kickstarter, '[t]he estimated delivery date is the creator's estimate. The date listed on each reward is the creator's estimate of when they will provide the reward – not a guarantee to fulfill by that time. The schedule may change as the creator works on the project. We ask creators to think carefully, set a date they feel confident they can work toward, and communicate with backers about any changes.'

39 E.g. eBay's rule on identifying the user who won the auction (which is explicitly labelled in scholarship as a default rule – see M.R. Albert, 'E-Buyer Beware: Why Online Auction Fraud Should Be Regulated' (2002) 39 *American Business Law Journal* 575, 588).

40 In particular, platforms adopt various regulatory policies aiming to safeguard the smooth functioning of the community and attract new members (e.g. by enhancing trust between horizontal contractors and redressing certain imbalances between suppliers and clients) – see also A.G. González, 'eBay Law: The Legal Implications of the C2C Electronic Commerce

for platforms that deal with small-value or everyday-life contracts, the parties to which may have a stronger preference for the quick and smooth conclusion and execution of an agreement than for the completeness of its content.

As a result, in order for a platform to enhance the efficiency of its horizontal contracts (and, consequently, the functionality of its entire business model), it needs to introduce its own regulation to supplement the contract terms. Some of those rules are shaped as opt-out defaults, applicable in the event that parties do not regulate particular issues idiosyncratically. The platform economy evidences a high diversity of default rules. They allow platforms to shape ensuing contractual relations in a way that is optimal from the perspective of these platform, while still leaving parties a margin of freedom (which may vary significantly between particular rules) to provide their own rules.[41]

3.4. OTHER GENRES OF OPTIONALITY

Some of the default rules imposed by platforms are typically based on the opt-in model. They provide parties with additional options that could be introduced, on their choice, to the particular relation. Some of them function as typical opt-in defaults, widely known already from traditional private law settings. They allow parties to supplement their rights and obligations with an additional element (sometimes chosen out of a broader menu of options).[42] In many instances, the opt-in mechanism functions in a different way and entails more complex consequences.

In the simplest model, opting into a non-mandatory solution can be connected with using additional IT tools provided by a platform. For instance, if a passenger who takes an Uber ride decides to tip the driver, she can use a dedicated facility within the Uber payment service.[43] Choosing a default rule entails, in this instance, procedural consequences, 'channelling' performance of a chosen option by a technical framework.

Model' (2003) 19 *Computer Law & Security Review* 468, 469, who notes that eBay 'must attempt to achieve some balance between providing as much freedom for its users as possible, and the imposition of enough restrictions to safeguard them from fraud, which may drive some of them away.'

41 See, for instance, the compound default rules on international sales via eBay. According to the eBay User Agreement, sellers may restrict geographical rage of potential clients by excluding certain countries or regions in the personal account settings (https://www.ebay.com/help/policies/selling-policies/international-selling-policy?id=4689).

42 See e.g. the menu of shipping modes and shipping costs provided in eBay's rules. The provisions in question list various options that could be chosen by parties on a take-it-or-leave-it or take-it-or-amend-it basis: https://www.ebay.com/help/selling/shipping-items/shipping-rates-sellers?id=4087.

43 See https://help.uber.com/h/8459a496-5ed2-4f9d-b15c-d8afd9ccf34f.

In more complex settings, the choice of default rules is then connected with choosing particular services rendered (for one or both parties to a horizontal contract) by a platform or its subcontractor. In other words, opting in has in those situations twofold consequences: (a) opting into a default rule (and, hence, introducing additional elements into contractual relation) and (b) opting into a separate agreement with a platform or another contractor. Typical of this model are various ways of securitisation of performance offered by platforms (e.g. the escrow fund on eBay[44] or security deposit on Airbnb[45]).

Lastly, default rules may also function in the disguise of 'pure' services accessible for a platform's user. In these situations, choosing a particular facility or tool that is offered by a platform entails further consequences, which are connected in an implied way with this conduct. For instance, it may be presumed (although this claim needs further verification) that this sort of implied default has been contained in the Airbnb 'Verified images' service.[46] It allows hosts to ask Airbnb for a professional photo service of a dwelling, rendered by a person designated by Airbnb. By sending this person to the host's premises (regardless of whether she acts as an employee or independent contractor) Airbnb, however, creates for itself an opportunity to learn about actual conditions of a dwelling and neighbourhood. As a result, selecting the 'Verified images' option by a host can entail the responsibility of Airbnb for the quality of performance in a rental contract. The presence of the platform's authorised representative (even if that representative was delegated only to take photographs) provides a plausible ground for a claim that Airbnb can bear responsibility for any defects that were evident at the moment of taking photographs and that would have a substantial impact on the expected quality of an apartment.

Finally, some of the default rules introduced by platforms seem to play a much more peculiar role within a community's regulatory design. The structure of some default rules introduced by platforms may suggest that they are introduced to incentivise parties to introduce their own, tailor-made rules. For instance, the eBay User Agreement contains an optional provision on replacement, return and cancellation (labelled *explicitly* as a 'default'). At the same time, however, as the wording and construction of the provision may suggest, the actual aim of the platform is to encourage parties to regulate particular issues idiosyncratically and to make a default non-sticky. Finally, such regulation-incentivising defaults can also provide platforms with more accurate information about the preferences of their communities.[47] From a long-term perspective, this can allow platforms

---

44 See also B. Rietjens, above n. 33, p. 57.

45 Rule 7.2.2. of the Airbnb Terms of Service.

46 Rule 5.6. of the Airbnb Terms of Service.

47 According to the provision, every new seller (i.e. one joining the platform for the first time and not having previously had the chance to set up its own terms of contract) is entitled to create individual 'rules to automate replacements, returns, and refunds under certain

to adjust their internal policy measures in a more adequate way – building upon data which would hardly be obtainable through any other means.[48]

4. MARKET ACTORS AS REGULATORY INTERMEDIARIES

While it is one of the tenets of private law that contractual rules have classically been set and dictated by class law-making bodies, there are also phenomena of fractioned majorities, including private governors of the market and, more recently, online platforms, setting forth their own regulatory schemes through private intermediaries. This is especially common in instances in which the more traditional regulatory schemes are less applicable, or do not reach with specificity the particularities of the markets or communities. These types of privately set, and non-classical, regulatory schemes often serve both to illuminate and cater to the preferences of the distinct market communities that they serve, and, as a result, the regulatory frameworks that they develop can serve as patterns for developing a broader-array regulation that is created in the more classical ways. Especially in cases of default rules set by platforms, a more careful and precise look is warranted, in order to gain a fuller understanding of a spontaneous, and precisely calibrated, market order.

The preference-revealing role of private intermediary regulators of fractioned majorities can entail two (typically interconnected) outcomes. Firstly, they can provide relatively close insight into the particular configuration of preferences and needs for regulation that exist in a particular community. Secondly, they are potentially well situated to gather, synthesise and respond to information about the preferences of the communities they serve, which are then reflected in the regulatory rules that are consequently developed by private rule-setters. Contractual rules generated by these fractioned majorities – either through private governors of the market or through online platforms – thus provide relatively precise indices about the most suitable instruments that should be used to address and handle particular regulatory problems, and about these instruments' exact usage.

---

circumstances'. The provision also indicates precisely the steps which need to be followed in order to alter the rule.

48 This observation may at first sight approximate the concept of 'penalty defaults', focused on the information-revealing potential of default rules – see especially I. Ayres and R. Gertner, 'Filling Gaps in Incomplete Contracts: An Economic Theory of Default Rules' (1989) 99 *YLJ* 87, 89. In the discussed example of platform-set defaults, revealing information (preference) is based, however, not on a penalty measure, but rather on economic or cognitive incentives to replace a default rule with a solution individualised for a particular horizontal contractor.

Rules developed to address preferences of particular fractions of contractors can, hence, serve as small-scale domains, where particular solutions can be observed and scrutinised in the environment of real contracting. As a result, the regulatory frameworks developed by and for specific communities can provide patterns for developing a broader-array regulation that is created in the classic terms, i.e. by legislation and case law. In this way, platforms and similar private governors of the market may play the role of regulatory intermediaries, staying halfway between the classic sovereign regulators and the market.[49] The actual vector of this relation may be twofold. First of all, private intermediaries may be deliberately 'outsourced' with a competence to set and enforce rules (which is for example the case for private standardisation bodies).[50] Secondly, private intermediaries may set and pursue 'regulatory' goals on their own (for example by balancing risks of contracting parties, combatting segregation and discrimination in contracting, etc.) – providing thereby a more spontaneous market order. The second instance is particularly relevant for default rules set by platforms and deserves a more precise look.

The possibility of construing better-aligned matches between regulatory needs and the regulatory toolbox may reinforce the crucial function of contract law[51] – i.e. by providing market actors with a menu of regulatory options that address their preferences in the optimal way.[52] The regulatory framework that emerges out of the fractioned communities scarcely provides independent and fully-developed types of contracts. Instead, this framework rather engages in more compound relationships that comprise both spontaneous contractual practice on the one hand, and the existing typology of contracts that exists in the state law on the other hand. Consequently, these communities' regulatory frameworks function – to generalise somewhat – as an 'intermediary'

---

49 See e.g. K.W. Abbott, D. Levi-Faur and D. Snidal, 'Introducing Regulatory Intermediaries' (2017) 670 *Annals of the American Academy of Political and Social Science* 6; C. Busch, 'Self-Regulation and Regulatory Intermediation in the Platform Economy' in M. Cantero Gamito and H.-W. Micklitz (eds.), *The Role of the EU in Transnational Legal Ordering: Standards, Contracts and Codes*, Edward Elgar, Cheltenham 2020.

50 On the place of standardisation in the framework of European private law, see further R. van Gestel and H.-W. Micklitz, 'European integration through standardization: How judicial review is breaking down the club house of private standardization bodies' (2013) 50 *Common Market Law Review (CMLR)* 145.

51 Cf., especially, H. Dagan and M. Heller, *The Choice Theory of Contracts*, Cambridge University Press, Cambridge 2017, pp. 72, 115–16. On the factors that drive parties' choice within the menu of options for contract design, see also T.R. Adler, R.F. Scherer, S.L. Barton and R. Katerberg, 'An empirical test of transaction cost theory: Validating contract typology' (1998) 7 *Journal of Applied Management Studies* 185, 197–98.

52 Further on the premises of optimal array of contract types, see O. Bar-Gill and C.P. Gillette, 'On the Optimal Number of Contract Types', paper presented at the conference 'Freedom, Choice and Contracts', University of Columbia Law School, 13–14 October 2017, manuscript on file with the author, pp. 4–6; see also H. Dagan and M. Heller, above n. 50, pp. 128–30.

phenomenon between spontaneity and traditional typology. Typically, they provide more detailed rules, based upon the actual preferences of the communities they serve, and thereby supplement and enhance the general framework, which in the classic contract law is provided by particular types of contracts.[53]

Therefore, and although it seems hardly probable (at least taking into account the phenomena currently observable on the market), the data gathered from self-regulatory processes in these 'fractioned' communities seems poised to re-shape and refine the existing structure of classic contract types – in order to make pertinent contracts more sensitive to the actual needs and preferences of market participants. In fact, this data, and the preferences it makes manifest, can be a basis for elaborating more or less expanded subsets of rules, supplementing the existing contractual framework. The result could resemble solutions either adopted by these fractioned communities or which could respond to the externalities that arise upon the privately set rules.

Of course, this attitude is quite similar to some previous regulatory attempts in private law, based on data concerning contractual practice collected from the market. As has already been noted in the doctrine, a large proportion of existing contract types originally emerged on the basis of spontaneous contractual practice – observed, however, from the perspective of the market as a whole.[54] The emergence of fractioned regulatory communities on the online market alters, however, this picture to a certain extent. It allows for more precise lessons and knowledge about the detailed regulatory needs of contractors and their distribution amongst contracts – not only about their aggregated outcome, which can be seen in the classical approach towards mining regulatory data from the market. Consequently, the same general type of contract (such as a rental or sales agreement), observed from the perspective of fractioned preferences developed by particular communities, may have various regulatory 'tones'. In particular, even when using the same legal framework (i.e. the same formal set of rules) this type of contract may embody and manifest

---

53 For instance, Airbnb's intensive regulatory activity in the sphere of rental contracts can be considered – from this perspective – as a way of amending the existing set of state-made rules, which constitute the general structure of a rental contract. In other words, contracting within the general framework established in the state-made contract law encompasses a few subcategories of rental contract, some of them (like Airbnb agreements) co-created by statutory law and private regulation (see also above, point 3.2).

54 The current discussion on the need and way to regulate franchise contracts in EU law is a good illustration of this issue. Its fundamental question is how to absorb the current widespread market occurrences and frame them legally in a way that would diminish existing negative externalities (especially the outcomes of substantially unequal bargaining power between contractors) – cf. e.g. European Parliament, Directorate General for Internal Policies, Policy Department A: Economic and Scientific Policy, *Proceedings of the Workshop on Relations between franchisors and franchisees: regulatory framework and current challenges*, IP/A/IMCO/2016-03 (2017), http://www.europarl.europa.eu/RegData/etudes/STUD/2016/595340/IPOL_STU(2016)595340_EN.pdf.

various kinds of interests and create diverse externalities, depending upon the particular type of community of contractors who are using and working within this framework.

5. THE CHALLENGE FOR EUROPEAN CONTRACT LAW

Privately created default rules emerge by nature in a spontaneous way, as a 'pure' creation of markets. They are not supported by any pre-established concept or intentional public policy aim, but they rest mostly on the natural transformation of contractual dealings, triggered by more sophisticated tools of collecting and processing data about individual contractors. Any similarities between particular regulatory communities, which have been discussed above, are a result of common functionalities of the economy, as well as of the use of similar technological tools for bringing contractors together and recognising their preferences. The rising ubiquity of the 'fractioned majorities' on the market opens, however, a question of whether this phenomenon should not be organised and framed 'from above', by a certain sort of regulatory actions.

In particular, communities formed around platforms are often characterised by a number of inequalities and inefficiencies.[55] Private law-makers typically enjoy a dominant position within a community. They organise entire clusters of clients and suppliers, and have almost exclusive governing competence over these participants. As a consequence, they can quite easily use – and abuse – their power over participants to maximise their profits by exploiting one or both contractors (for instance, by imposing inefficient pricing,[56] unbalanced allocation of risk[57] or provision of inconvenient terms of supply or of rendering services[58]). In the outcome, the broadly considered quality of default rules set by 'special-purpose sovereigns' depends upon several contingencies and certainly departs quite far from a somewhat utopian view of a fully workable 'spontaneous order' on the market. As a result, the cognitive function of private setting of default rules may also be questionable and cannot be taken for granted. In particular,

---

55 See also, generally, O. Bar-Gill and C.P. Gillette, above n. 51, pp. 4–6.

56 One of the most vivid instances of this issue can be the setting of personalised prices, established through algorithmic analysis of big data – cf. e.g. F.Z. Borgesius and J. Poort, 'Online Price Discrimination and EU Data Privacy Law' (2017) 40 *Journal of Consumer Policy (JCP)* 347, 350–55.

57 On the illustrative instances of such schemes see e.g. L.A. DiMatteo, 'Regulation of Share Economy: A Consistently Changing Environment' in R. Schulze and D. Staudenmayer (eds.), *Digital Revolution: Challenges for Contract Law in Practice*, Nomos/Hart Publishing, Baden-Baden/Oxford 2016, p. 99–101; T.G. Loucks, 'Travelers Beware: Tort Liability in the Sharing Economy' (2015) 10 *Washington Journal of Law, Technology & Art. 329*, 335.

58 See C. Busch, H. Schulte-Nölke, A. Wiewiórowska-Domagalska and F. Zoll, 'The Rise of the Platform Economy: A New Challenge for EU Consumer Law?' (2016) 5 *Journal of European Consumer and Market Law* 3, 5, 7.

the shape of rules established by platforms and other private governors may embody only preferences of the rule-setters, resting on their predominant power in setting forth rules for horizontal contractors.

This creates an imminent question of whether – and, if so, to what extent and by what means – the deficits of the private setting of default rules should be framed or regulated through state-originated intervention. Notably, such possible state-generated regulation can have a twofold effect. Self-evidently, it can increase the quality of regulation produced by fractioned communities, acting to the benefit of general efficiency of the contracts concluded between their members. At the same time this sort of intervention into a particular community's regulatory design can also – indirectly – enhance the majoritarian dimension of privately created default rules and, hence, increase their informative aptitude.

This issue, discussed globally,[59] takes its very idiosyncratic shape from the perspective of the EU contract law. It pertains both to the existing framework of the common European rules on contracts (with particular regard to consumer agreements), as well as to the new embodiment of the overall goals of the EU contract law policy, within the Digital Single Market scheme. The institutional structure of the online market – with particular regard to the platform economy – constitutes one of the focal points of this agenda.[60] In addition, the existing legislative drafts[61] and policy discourses[62] evidence quite clearly that the platform economy has come right into the spotlight of EU regulatory interests at the common ground of contract, privacy and competition law. At the same time, however, the self-regulatory dimension of the platform economy still remains on the remote margins of the current regulatory discourse. As a result, the 'private' default rules, which currently are supplied most massively by the online market, seem to avoid any more precise political and regulatory grasp.

All of the feasible solutions to this lack of classical state regulatory oversight of platform economy contracts are currently mostly speculative. As has been

---

59 See e.g. M. Cohen and A. Sundararajan, above n. 5; A. Stemler, 'Feedback Loop Failure: Implications for the Self-Regulation of the Sharing Economy' (2017) 18 *Minnesota Journal of Law, Science & Technology* 673, 703–12; H. Berkovitz and A. Souchaud, '(Self-)Regulation of Sharing Economy Platforms Through Partial Meta-organizing' (2019) 159 *Journal of Business Ethics* 961.

60 See more at https://ec.europa.eu/digital-single-market/en/online-platforms-digital-single-market; see also G.F. Frosio, 'Reforming Intermediary Liability in The Platform Economy: A European Digital Single Market Strategy' (2017) 112 *Northwestern University Law Review Online* 19.

61 See especially Proposal for a regulation promoting fairness and transparency for business users of online intermediation services, 2018/0112 (COD).

62 Cf. the European Law Institute draft model rules on online intermediary platforms: https://www.europeanlawinstitute.eu/projects-publications/current-projects-feasibility-studies-and-other-activities/current-projects/online-platforms/; C. Busch, G. Dannemann, H. Schulte-Nölke and A. Wiewiórowska-Domagalska (eds.), *Discussion Draft of a Directive on Online Intermediary Platforms. Commentary*, Jagiellonian University Press, Cracow 2019.

explained above, the emergence of 'fractioned majorities' results, to a great extent, from shortcomings within the existing regulatory frameworks at the national and transnational level. It is possible, however, to distinguish four hypothetical and classical regulatory approaches, which may support the creation of more efficient and majority-based default rules within fractioned communities.

First of all, it is possible to imagine an ex post control of contract terms introduced by online platforms. EU contract law provides a clear illustration of this attitude in the control of unfair terms, under Directive 93/13/EEC.[63] This scheme is directly applicable to the bulk of the contractual rules established by platforms and – as the existing case law confirms[64] – can be effectively used to frame and constrain one-sidedness of rule-setting by private market actors. This mechanism is, however, substantially inefficient as a general response to some of the major problems of the private setting of contract rules in the online markets. Above all, the sharp boundaries between the EU law concepts of consumer and professional are naturally blurred in the online context.[65] This significantly complicates a possible application of the control tools, making it costly and unpredictable from the very outset (notwithstanding the fact that a major part of the platform economy is based on peer-to-peer rather than business-to-consumer agreements). Moreover, the scrutiny of contract terms offered by Directive 93/13/EEC is by definition selective and limited only to the instances in which a competent agent (an individual or a regulatory body that acts on an individual's behalf decides to enforce proactively the control of contract terms.[66] The existing model of verification of consumer contracts also does not allow for a full ex ante check and can be applied mostly after a particular agreement has actually occurred on the market.

Secondly, instead of a general check, based upon an open-ended standard (such as good faith under Directive 93/13/EEC), it is also possible to speculate about blacklisting particular terms and conditions that cannot be introduced into privately made sets of rules[67] (similarly to the list of prohibited commercial practices in the meaning of Directive 2005/29/EC).[68] This sort of mandatory

---

63 Council Directive 93/13/EEC of 5 April 1993 on unfair terms in consumer contracts [1993] OJ L95/29.

64 See especially Case C-95/04, *Verein für Konsumenteninformation v. Amazon EU Sàrl*, ECLI:EU:C:2016:612, where the CJEU carried out a direct review of Amazon's standard terms, building on the control mechanism in Directive 93/13/EEC.

65 See e.g. V. Hatzopoulos and S. Roma, 'Caring for Sharing? The Collaborative Economy under EU Law' (2017) 54 *CMLR* 81, 88–90.

66 Cf. also H.-W. Micklitz, P. Pałka and Y. Panagis, 'The Empire Strikes Back: Digital Control of Unfair Terms of Online Services' (2017) 40 *JCP* 367, 370–72.

67 On the rationale for this sort of intervention, cf. M. Cohen and A. Sundararajan, above n. 5, pp. 131–32.

68 Directive 2005/29/EC of the European Parliament and of the Council of 11 May 2005 concerning unfair business-to-consumer commercial practices in the internal market and amending Council Directive 84/450/EEC, Directives 97/7/EC, 98/27/EC and 2002/65/EC

regulation can also operate in a different mode: as a catalogue of compulsory elements that should be introduced into user agreements by platform operators or at least offered to users as an element of a menu, open to individual choice (like the optional 'plain vanilla' mortgage in US consumer contracts).[69] Finally, mandatory rules can be introduced as thresholds (e.g. with respect to transparency or quality of goods) that cannot be contracted out of by privately created defaults, but which would preserve self-regulatory autonomy in other regards.

The third feasible approach is introducing schemes of scrutiny of default rules provided by private regulators, without direct interventions into their content. The control in question could be possibly focused on meeting, by rules, the requirements of justice (e.g. avoidances of substantial imbalances in allocation of rights and duties) and efficiency (especially, addressing through these requirements the rudimentary and evident preferences of the community). The scrutiny may be applied ex ante (in a form of pre-approval) or ex post and could be conducted by administrative authorities[70] or courts,[71] or, instead, be delegated to private bodies.

Fourthly, instead of any regulatory intervention, it is possible to adopt a more *laissez-faire* attitude, providing for the smooth operation of private rule-setters within the internal forum. At the same time, it seems possible to frame the market by competition rules (that could guarantee efficiency and fairness of inter-platform relations) and by incentivising 'meta' self-regulatory structures (e.g. associations of platforms, which provide cross-scrutiny of their regulatory schemes). This opens a further question, namely whether private rule-makers can be deliberately considered to be 'regulatory intermediaries' in the proper sense of this word, i.e. as entities that can (either by way of soft steering or simply spontaneously) supplement a state in carrying out its regulatory agenda. This quandary, however, would undoubtedly require a much deeper and more comprehensive data and analytical framework.

6. CONCLUSIONS

The phenomenon of default rules that emerge beyond the state provides a substantial challenge for the landscape of rule-making in contract law, which

of the European Parliament and of the Council and Regulation (EC) No 2006/2004 of the European Parliament and of the Council [2005] OJ L149/22.

69 On the use of mandatory rules in this context, see e.g. N. Leong and A. Belzer, 'The New Public Accommodations: Race Discrimination in the Platform Economy' (2017) 105 *Georgetown Law Journal* 1271, 1319.

70 Cf. M. Cohen and A. Sundararajan, above n. 5, p. 131.

71 See also S. Grundmann and P. Hacker, above n. 5, p. 275.

itself is quite well established in the classical literature and the EU policy agenda. Instead of the unitarian structure of contract law, privately regulated default rules offer by contrast a heterogeneous and fragmented picture, one in which state-made legislation is one of many centres of governance of market agreements and is supplemented by private actors, who – due to their economic positions and shortcomings of the existing contract law – are powerful enough to take on the role of quasi-sovereigns within the relevant markets. At the same time, the phenomena discussed pose more detailed questions for the theory of default rules, as the main component of the classic body of contract law. The clear translation of the existing contract law concepts onto the privately made rules would be, certainly, quite misleading. This pertains especially to the majoritarian concept, which in the landscape of privately created defaults turns out to be idealistic and far from the actual reality of power dynamics on the market. Although creation of default rules beyond the state-based law-making schemes may allow one to speak of 'fractioned' majorities, established with regard to more detailed and precisely framed needs of particular market communities of different origins and scale, in fact these majorities and their privately generated regulations may follow the interests of their creators and not necessarily the interests of the entities that they regulate (which is vivid, for example, in the case of privately created nudging default rules).

This creates a plea for possible state-based regulatory intervention, which could frame the self-regulatory processes of the market and aim to improve the 'quality' of default rules established in this way – or, if possible, to embody them within the state-made policy agenda. This question is particularly pressing for EU contract law, which has begun to pay increasing amounts of attention to the platform economy as one of the principal fields for regulatory action.[72]

The current policy debate in the EU seems clearly to miss the link between existing EU law and the massive emergence of self-regulatory phenomena on the market. Beyond doubt, state- and privately set default rules may (and indeed do) operate in parallel, supplementing one another. Especially in those instances in which state-made regulation is not applicable (e.g. due to the transnational scale of the particular industry), privately created rules may be a much more effective tool of governing pertinent contractual relations. At the same time, state-made rules very often provide a basic conceptual and regulatory framework for privately established schemes, facilitating their

72 See in particular the provisions on consumer agreements concluded via platforms introduced by Directive (EU) 2019/2161 of the European Parliament and of the Council of 27 November 2019 amending Council Directive 93/13/EEC and Directives 98/6/EC, 2005/29/EC and 2011/83/EU of the European Parliament and of the Council as regards the better enforcement and modernisation of Union consumer protection rules (OJ L 328, 18.12.2019, p. 7–28); see also P. Iamiceli, 'Online Platforms and the Digital Turn in EU Contract Law: Unfair Practices, Transparency and the (pierced) Veil of Digital Immunity' (2019) 15 *ERCL* 392.

creation and application. Moreover, it is also possible that regulatory structures created by markets themselves may diffuse into EU contract law, providing rules that can be absorbed by the legislation or the case law (and which have been pre-verified by and through market practice). Finally, 'fractioned' market communities can be used purposefully as regulatory 'laboratories', by which public authorities may introduce particular rules to be tested in practice.

PART V

CASE LAW AND CREATION OF NORMS

EUROPEAN CONTRACT LAW IN THE EU COURT OF JUSTICE'S CASE LAW

Camelia Toader*

1. INTRODUCTION

The question as to whether it is admissible or even just advisable that courts are involved in the creation of legal norms remains, to the present days, highly controversial. Indeed, much has changed from the times when Montesquieu developed his metaphor of the judge as '*la bouche de la loi*'. With the emergence of new international actors, most notably of the EU, the Court of Justice has acquired a key role in ensuring the functioning of a system of multi-layered governance in general and of European contract law in particular.

As we all know, EU Directives have been of crucial importance for the harmonisation of private law in Europe. However, by their very nature, Directives lack the specificity which conversely characterises instruments that have direct application, leaving Member States a margin of discretion as to how to translate the aim of the Directive into national law. And it is precisely in relation to this margin of discretion that the 'creative vocation' of the Court of

* This chapter is based on the speech given by the author on 23 June 2018 in the framework of the SECOLA Conference on 'European Contract Law and the Creation of Norms', which took place on 22–23 June in Warsaw, Poland, and it was updated on 10 December 2018.

Justice case law manifests itself. Within this framework, the Court makes use of general principles of EU law – in particular the principles of effectiveness and proportionality – to pursue and establish legal policies through its case law.[1]

For the purpose of this chapter, 'the creation of norms' will be understood as the contribution of the Court of Justice to the construction of European contract law. Three main areas of activity will be identified. Firstly, the Court contributes to the creation of European contract law by marking its outer limits, that is by defining the scope of application of each of the several instruments which compose this body of law (section 2). Secondly, even though the Court of Justice will never, by definition, interpret a private law contract, it may nonetheless guide national judges in assessing its compliance with domestic legislation, interpreted in the light of EU law (section 3). Finally, the most creative contribution of the Court of Justice in the field of European contract law arguably consists in setting up a procedural framework capable of ensuring the effectiveness of European contract law (section 4).

2. THE IDENTIFICATION OF THE PERSONAL SCOPE OF APPLICATION OF EU INSTRUMENTS OF EUROPEAN CONTRACT LAW

The delimitation of the personal scope of application of an instrument of European contract law entails a delicate balance between private autonomy and mandatory rules of European origin. I will focus my analysis on four of these instruments: Directive 2008/48/EC on consumer credit (CCD), Directive 93/13/EEC on unfair terms in consumer contracts (UCTD), Directive 1999/44/EC on certain aspects of the sale of consumer goods, and, finally, the protective jurisdictional regimes set forth by Regulation (EU) 1215/2012.

In interpreting the scope of application of these instruments, the Court of Justice starts from a common assumption. The consumer, understood as a person who acts outside the scope of his profession or trade, is regarded as being in a weaker position vis-à-vis the professional with respect to his financial capacity, his bargaining power and his level of knowledge. This common protective intent is, however, nuanced by the Court in the light of the specific objectives pursued by the specific instrument submitted to its interpretation. The definition of the outer limits of European contract law is therefore largely influenced both by its piecemeal character and by instances of individual protection.

Let us take, for example, Directive 2008/48/EC on consumer credit. This instrument seeks to ensure that borrowers have to hand, when the credit agreement

---

1 E. Poillot, 'The ECJ and General Principles Derived from the Acquis Communautaire' in J. Rutgers and P. Sirena (eds.), *Rules and Principles in European Contract Law*, Intersentia, Cambridge/Antwerp 2015, pp. 33, 42.

is concluded, relevant information concerning the obligations entailed, so as to prevent them from assuming commitments which are unfair. In the light of this specific objective, the Court excluded, in *Berliner Kindl Brauerei*,[2] from its scope of application the situation of a third person who provides security for the repayment of loans granted by the lender to the principal debtor for the purpose of carrying out a commercial activity. According to the Court, a guarantor cannot be considered a consumer within the meaning of the CCD, even if, in the specific instance, that guarantor was a natural person with little bargaining power and a limited level of knowledge. Since the primary concern of the guarantor is the solvency of the principal debtor, rather than receiving adequate pre-contractual information on the conditions of the credit agreement, his protection falls outside the scope of application of the CCD. The finding of the Court, in that instance, whereby the specific objectives of the CCD prevailed on the individual protection of the guarantor, did not prevent, however, a characterisation of a guarantor as 'consumer' under other instruments of European contract law, and namely Directive 93/13/EEC. The personal scope of application of this Directive is considerably wider, applying to 'all contracts' concluded in the course of activities outside a trade, business or profession. In *Tarcău*,[3] *Dumitraş*[4] and *Michael Tibor Bachman*,[5] the Court held that the guarantor can be considered a consumer within the meaning of the UCTD, insofar as said guarantor acts outside his trade or profession when providing security. This holds true even when he guarantees an obligation of a commercial company, the requirement being, in that case, that he does not provide the security in the course of his own business and does not have a functional link with that company. As it is, the personal situation of this guarantor perfectly fits the – different – objective pursued by the UCTD, which is protecting consumers from terms drawn up in advance by the seller or supplier, the content of which they were structurally unable to influence. According to the Court, a contract providing security concluded between a banking institution and a consumer entails a personal commitment of the guarantor which involves onerous obligations, its effect being to subject that person's own property to a financial risk which is often difficult to quantify. This guarantor therefore deserves the protection that the UCTD vests upon 'consumers'.

The purposive or functional interpretation of EU legislation explains, as well, the treatment that the Court of Justice Court has reserved to lawyers under the UCTD. In *Costea*,[6] the Court held that a lawyer who concludes a credit agreement for private purposes can be considered a 'consumer' under

2 Case C-208/98, *Berliner Kindl Brauerei*, ECLI:EU:C:2000:152.
3 Case C-74/15, *Dumitru and Ileana Tarcău*, ECLI:EU:C:2015:772.
4 Case C-534/15, *Pavel and Mioara Dumitraş*, ECLI:EU:C:2016:700.
5 Case C-535/16, *Michael Tibor Bachman*, ECLI:EU:C:2017:321.
6 Case C-110/14, *Horaţiu Ovidiu Costea*, ECLI:EU:C:2015:538.

the UCTD, irrespective of the specific knowledge and expertise that this person indisputably has. In *Šiba*,[7] however, a lawyer who provides a legal service to a natural person and who uses, for these purposes, standard terms drafted in advance by himself or by his professional association, has been considered a 'seller or supplier' under the UCTD. There is no contradiction in the Court of Justice's reasoning. It recalls, in fact, that under the UCTD the same person can act as a consumer in certain transactions and as a seller or supplier in others. The concept of 'consumer' is objective in nature and is distinct from the concrete knowledge the person in question may have, or from the information that person actually has. It solely depends on the personal capacity in which the parties act while concluding a contract. Analysed from this standpoint, the factual situations underlying *Šiba* and *Costea* are hardly comparable. *Šiba* involved a lawyer acting in his professional capacity and who, in spite of his professional knowledge, freely decided to use standard terms which did not reflect mandatory statutory or regulatory provisions within the meaning of Article 1(2) of Directive 93/13/EEC. In *Costea*, conversely, the lawyer was contracting vis-à-vis a bank for purposes which were not linked to the exercise of his profession. He had therefore, vis-à-vis that professional, a weaker bargaining power.

A teleological interpretation of the EU consumer acquis has recently prompted the Court of Justice to take an expansionist approach to the interpretation of the Consumer Sales Directive.[8] This instrument applies to contracts for the sale of consumer goods concluded between 'a seller' and 'a consumer'. In the *Sabrina Wathelet* case,[9] the Court was asked whether this Directive applied also to a 'private' sale, where a consumer – Ms Wathelet – bought a second-hand car from a garage. This garage, however, never owned the car, but was acting instead as a mere intermediary on behalf of another consumer. Nonetheless, specific and consistent circumstantial evidence indicated that Ms Wathelet had not been informed that there was a private sale, believing that her counterpart was the garage, as a professional dealer. The Court initially remarked that, according to the letter of the Directive, the notion of seller does not generally cover intermediaries. However, its purposive interpretation implies that this should cover traders who act as intermediaries (regardless of whether they are remunerated for their services) but present themselves as professional sellers to consumers, giving consumers the false impression that they are concluding a B2C contract. The opposite interpretation would in fact have deprived consumers of the protection granted by the Consumer Sales Directive, within which the concept of 'seller' serves precisely to limit the circle of persons against whom consumers may take action in order to enforce the rights granted therein.

---

7 Case C-537/13, *Birutė Šiba*, ECLI:EU:C:2015:14.

8 Directive 1999/44/EC of the European Parliament and of the Council of 25 May 1999 on certain aspects of the sale of consumer goods and associated guarantees [1999] OJ L171/12.

9 Case C-149/15, *Wathelet*, ECLI:EU:C:2016:840.

The Court deems that only the ex ante provision of due and complete information on the identity of the seller intermediary could have eliminated the information imbalance between the parties, preventing the application of the Consumer Sales Directive. Here lies the 'creative' potential of this judgment: in its aftermath, traders who act as intermediaries on behalf of private individuals shall inform consumers in clear and unequivocal terms of the fact that they are not the owner of the goods sold, and provide adequate information on the identity of the real seller. If they fail to do so, they may be held liable under the Consumer Sales Directive if the goods sold are not in conformity with the sale contract.

Yet another approach to the identification of the personal scope of application of specific contractual regimes of EU origin can be found in the field of private international law. The Brussels I *bis* Regulation[10] lays down protective jurisdictional regimes for contracts characterised by a structural imbalance between the parties. For these reasons it grants to a consumer, a policyholder or an employee a *forum actoris* which is otherwise contrary to the logic underlying that Regulation.

The personal scope of application of the jurisdictional regime applicable to B2C contracts is to be determined according to the criteria most recently identified by *Hobohm*.[11] In addition to the evident requirement that one of the parties to the contract must be a consumer, acting in a context which can be regarded as being outside his trade or profession, contracting with a professional, said contract must have been effectively concluded, and must fall within one of the categories referred to in Article 15(1)(a)–(c) of the Brussels I Regulation. Building on the derogatory nature of said provision, the Court upheld a strict interpretation of these requirements, particularly as concerns the need for the conclusion of a contract with the professional himself. In *Kolassa*,[12] a consumer, who acquired a bearer bond on the secondary market through an intermediary, claimed rights against the issuer of the bond. While Mr Kolassa submitted that, in such circumstances, the aim of consumer protection would have required the adoption of an economic approach and the finding that a contract had indeed been concluded between him and the issuer of the bond, the Court took a different view. In a chain of contracts through which certain rights and obligations of the professional in question are transferred to the consumer, the applicability of Article 17 of the Brussels I Regulation cannot be triggered.

Relatively more lenient is the assessment, by the Court, lying behind the identification of a 'consumer' for the purposes of that regime. The problem emerges, in particular, with respect to dual-purpose contracts. Whereas in *Gruber*[13]

---

10 Regulation (EU) No. 1215/2012 of the European Parliament and of the Council of 12 December 2012 on jurisdiction and the recognition and enforcement of judgments in civil and commercial matters [2012] OJ L351/1.

11 Case C-297/14, *Rüdiger Hobohm*, ECLI:EU:C:2015:844.

12 Case C-375/13, *Harald Kolassa*, ECLI:EU:C:2015:37.

13 Case C-464/01, *Johann Gruber*, ECLI:EU:C:2005:32.

the Court adopted a strict interpretation, whereby the consumer concept could only apply if 'the trade or professional purpose is so limited as to be negligible in the overall context of the supply', in the more recent *Schrems* case[14] the Court nuanced its approach. It recognised, in particular, that some contracts, such as those relating to services of a digital social network, 'are intended to be used over a long period of time', so that there might be subsequent changes in the use which is made of those services. Such was the situation of Mr Schrems, a data protection activist, who initially used a Facebook account exclusively for private purposes. Starting from 2011, however, he has also used a Facebook page to promote his activities of publishing books, lecturing, operating websites, fundraising and collecting the claims of numerous consumers for the purpose of their enforcement. According to the Court of Justice, nonetheless, these activities do not entail the loss of the status as a 'consumer' within the meaning of Article 17 of the Brussels regime.

On the one hand, this judgment confirms that, even within the framework of the Brussels I *bis* Regulation, the notion of 'consumer' is objective in nature and is distinct from the concrete knowledge the person in question may have, or from the level of information that person actually has. On the other hand, the Court seems to lower somewhat the standard established in *Gruber*, at least in the case of long-term contracts. The Court in fact reinstates a purposive and consumer-biased approach in the interpretation of the head of jurisdiction set out by Article 17. It remarks, in fact, that an interpretation of the notion of 'consumer' excluding activities of the kind of those at issue in *Schrems* would have the effect of preventing an effective defence of the rights that consumers enjoy in relation to their contractual partners who are traders or professionals, including those rights which relate to the protection of their personal data. In particular, the Court adds, 'such an interpretation would disregard the objective set out in Article 169(1) TFEU of promoting the right of consumers to organise themselves in order to safeguard their interests'.

Finally, the protective regime for insurance contracts lies at the heart of two recent judgments of the Court of Justice. Despite it also being a derogatory regime vis-à-vis the 'general' rule of jurisdiction under Article 4 and the special rules of jurisdiction under Article 7, the Court of Justice has been keen to propound a wider interpretation of the regime's scope of application. After having included, with *FBTO Schadeverzekeringen*,[15] 'the injured party' in the list of plaintiffs entitled to profit from the more favourable head of jurisdiction under Article 9(1)(b) of the former Brussels I Regulation, the Court clarified that the notion of 'weaker party' has a wider acceptance in matters relating to insurance than the notion of 'consumer' or 'employee' have in their respective

---

14 Case C-498/16, *Maximilian Schrems*, ECLI:EU:C:2018:37.

15 Case C-463/06, *FBTO Schadeverzekeringen NV*, ECLI:EU:C:2007:792.

jurisdictional regimes. On this basis, the *MMA Iard* case,[16] decided in July 2017, extended this status to the employer of the actual victim of a road traffic accident, who subrogated in his rights against the insurer. On the contrary, the more recent *Hofsoe* case,[17] decided in January 2018, excludes from the scope of this protective jurisdictional regime a professional who carries out an activity of claims recovery against insurance companies, to whom the actual victim of the accident assigned his claim. Since the assignment of claims to a professional has the effect of overcoming the imbalance, in terms of economic capacity but also of level of information between the parties which the Brussels Regulations aims to correct, there is no longer any need to resort to a protective and derogatory jurisdictional regime.

Again, in interpreting the personal scope of application of this specific set of contractual rules, the Court of Justice took into account the specific objectives of the instrument to which they belong. Since the Brussels I *bis* Regulation aims at the expeditious identification of the court having jurisdiction, the identification of the 'injured party' does not require a case-by-case assessment of whether or not the employer or the professional in question are, de facto, in an economically weaker position vis-à-vis the insurer. An approach relying on an individual assessment of the economic situation of each party would in fact give rise to legal uncertainty, and it would run counter to the objective of expeditiousness underlying that Regulation.

3. THE 'CONTRACT' AS A SOURCE OF RIGHTS AND OBLIGATIONS IN THE CASE LAW OF THE COURT OF JUSTICE

Moving on to the second conception of 'the creation of norms' presented by this chapter, it is time to assess the role that a 'contract', as the tool through which the parties construe the legal regime governing their private relationships, may play before the Court of Justice. As I have already mentioned, the Court of Justice will, by definition, interpret a private law contract only to the extent necessary to guide national judges in the interpretation and application of relevant instruments of EU law.

To remain within the framework of the Brussels I *bis* Regulation, the Court is often confronted with the difficult question of delimiting the respective scope of application of the heads of jurisdiction under current Article 7(1) and (2), concerning, respectively, 'matters relating to a contract' and 'matters relating to tort, delict or quasi-delict'. From the standpoint of contract law, an interesting

16 Case C-340/16, *Landeskrankenanstalten-Betriebsgesellschaft – KABEG*, ECLI:EU:C:2017:576.
17 Case C-106/17, *Paweł Hofsoe*, ECLI:EU:C:2018:50.

issue arose in the recent *Granarolo* case.[18] The case concerned a claim for damages for abrupt termination of an established business relationship, which developed over approximately 25 years in the absence of any framework contract or exclusivity agreement. The question therefore arose as to whether a legal relationship of this kind should be classified, under the Brussels I *bis* Regulation, as a matter relating to a contract or a matter relating to a tort.

As is well known, long-standing and well-established case law of the Court of Justice requires these notions to be construed as autonomous concepts of EU law, having regard to the scheme and objectives of Brussels I *bis* Regulation and to the general principles of law common to the legal systems of the Member States.[19] In the *Granarolo* case, the Court built on the latter approach by looking into the legal traditions of Member States in the field of contract law.[20] For these purposes, the Court commissioned a comparative analysis of the solutions decided, at domestic level, by eight Member States in relation to the abrupt termination of an established business relationship. This revealed, in the first place, that, in accordance with a well-established principle of European contract law,[21] the absence of a framework contract concluded in writing does not prevent the possibility of identifying an oral or even implicit contract. The existence of the latter cannot nonetheless be presumed, but must result from a consistent body of corroborating evidence. Secondly, this analysis also revealed that in most Member States the abrupt termination of an established business relationship gives rise to contractual liability if such a framework contract can be identified. On this basis, the Court of Justice concluded in *Granarolo* that former Article 5(1) of the Brussels I Regulation (current Article 7(1) of the Brussels I *bis* Regulation) does not require a contract to be concluded in writing, even though a contractual obligation must nevertheless be identified in order for that provision to apply.

The Court of Justice, in its guiding role, clarified that to regard such an obligation as having tacitly arisen, national courts shall seek to identify 'unequivocal acts expressing the intention of the parties' as proven by 'a body of consistent evidence, which may include in particular the existence of a long-standing business relationship, the good faith between the parties, the regularity of the transactions and their development over time expressed in terms of

18 Case C-196/15, *Granarolo SpA v Ambrosi Emmi France SA*, ECLI:EU:C:2016:559.

19 Case 29/76, *LTU Lufttransportunternehmen GmbH & Co. KG*, ECLI:EU:C:1976:137, para. 3, referring to 'the general principles which stem from the corpus of the national legal systems'.

20 *Granarolo*, above n. 17, para. 23: 'In a significant proportion of the Member States long-standing business relationships which have formed without a contract in writing may, in principle, be regarded as falling within a tacit contractual relationship, breach of which is liable to give rise to contractual liability'.

21 Principles of European Contract Law (PECL), Article 2:101, §2: 'A contract need not be concluded or evidenced in writing nor is it subject to any other requirement as to form. The contract may be proved by any means, including witnesses'.

quantity and value, any agreements as to prices charged and/or discounts granted, and the correspondence exchanged'. Only where this condition is satisfied may a tacit contractual relationship exist between the parties for the purposes of Article 7(1) of the Brussels I *bis* Regulation.

The Court of Justice is often also confronted with a private law contract within the – very different – framework of Directive 93/13/EEC, which aims at preventing abuses of standard form contracts. As is well known, Article 4(2) of the Directive explicitly excludes from the unfairness check contractual terms which define the 'main subject matter of the contract' or the 'adequacy of the price and remuneration'.

Unsurprisingly, several questions relating to the notion of the 'main subject matter of the contract' have been submitted to the Court of Justice over the years. The Court of Justice, for its part, has established a few general guidelines, meant to steer all national courts in the interpretation of Article 4(2), as well as more detailed instructions concerning specific kinds of contracts. As for the general guidelines, the Court held, in particular, that that provision must be strictly interpreted, since it lays down an exception to the mechanism for reviewing the substance of unfair terms. Moreover, the Court set out the general definition of the concept of the 'main subject matter of the contract', thus assisting the interpreter in the identification thereof. This notion encompasses only those contractual terms that lay down the essential obligations of the contract and, as such, characterise it. Such assessment must be carried out having regard to the nature, general scheme and the stipulations of the contract and its legal and factual context. In the *Van Hove* case,[22] the Court had to apply these general principles to the specificities of an insurance contract, namely to a term intended to ensure that loan repayments will be covered in the event of the borrower's 'total incapacity for work'. The main finding of the Court in this case was, however, that, in order to fall within the exemption from the unfairness check, the term relating to the main object of an (insurance) contract must be drafted in 'plain, intelligible language'. To comply with this condition, a contractual term shall not only be grammatically intelligible, but it shall also set out, in a transparent manner, the functioning of the arrangements it establishes as well as the relationship existing between those arrangements and the arrangements laid down in other contractual terms. The objective thus pursued is to put the consumer in a position to evaluate, on the basis of precise, intelligible criteria, the economic consequences which derive from the term. It must be recalled here that the Court has recently developed this second condition in a considerable number of cases relating the widespread practice of loans undertaken in a foreign currency.[23] The Court expressly acknowledged that a term providing that a loan

22 Case C-96/14, *Van Hove*, ECLI:EU:C:2015:262.

23 Case C-186/16, *Andriciuc*, ECLI:EU:C:2017:703; Case C-126/17, *ERSTE Bank Hungary*, ECLI:EU:C:2018:107; Case C-119/17, *Lupean and Lupean*, ECLI:EU:C:2018:103.

shall be repaid in the same foreign currency as that in which it was contracted lays down an essential obligation characterising those kinds of contract.[24] For such a term to be formulated in plain and intelligible language, however, the amount and type of pre-contractual information provided by the bank is of fundamental importance. The Court provides specific guidance in this respect. It not only reasserted the general principle whereby regard shall be had for all the relevant facts, including the promotional material provided by the lender in the negotiation of the loan agreement. It additionally referred to a Recommendation of the European Systematic Risk Board to set, *in concreto*, the minimum amount of information that a borrower shall be given prior to the conclusion of a loan in a foreign currency.[25]

The 'creative' role that the Court undertakes in constructing notions which are left undefined by the EU legislator is not confined to the UCTD. Directive 2008/48/EC on consumer credit has undergone a similar development. In *CA Consumer Finance*,[26] the Court filled a gap left open by the EU legislator: while the Directive recognises that the creditor's pre-contractual obligations are of fundamental importance in the attainment of its objectives, it omits nonetheless to set out specific rules concerning the burden of proof of compliance. In ordinary circumstances, this gap shall be filled by the domestic procedural rules of the forum, having regard of the principles of effectiveness and equivalence. However, by building on a purposive interpretation of the Directive, the Court proceeds in that case to set a uniform European standard. According to the Court of Justice, in fact, the effectiveness of the Directive would be undermined if the burden of proving the non-performance of the obligations laid down therein lay with the consumer. Rather, the effective exercise of the rights conferred by Directive 2008/48/EC could only be ensured by a national rule requiring the creditor to prove to the court that those pre-contractual obligations have been fulfilled. As a result, the margin of discretion which in theory lies with domestic legislators in the application of the principle of procedural autonomy may be, in practice, considerably curbed by the creative interpretations of the Court, carried out under the aegis of the principle of effectiveness. This does not mean,

---

24 *Andriciuc*, above 22, para. 37.

25 In *Andriciuc*, above n. 22, para. 49. Pursuant to this Recommendation, this information shall, at least, concern the impact on instalments of a severe depreciation of the legal tender of the Member State in which a borrower is domiciled and of an increase of the foreign interest rate. The Court additionally refers to the Opinion of the Advocate General, stating that the borrower must be clearly informed of the fact that, in entering into a loan agreement denominated in a foreign currency, he is exposing himself to a certain foreign exchange risk which will, potentially, be difficult to bear in the event of a fall in the value of the currency in which he receives his income. Moreover, the bank must be required to set out the possible variations in the exchange rate and the risks inherent in taking out a loan in a foreign currency, particularly where the consumer borrower does not receive his income in that currency.

26 Case C-449/13, *CA Consumer Finance*, ECLI:EU:C:2014:2464.

however, that this should always be the case. In other instances, the effectiveness of EU legislation can peacefully coexist with the creative prerogatives of national legislators. For example, in *Home Credit Slovakia*,[27] the Court recognised that the effectiveness of the CCD did not preclude national legislation from laying down additional formal requirements, namely the need for a credit agreement, drafted 'on paper' in accordance with that Directive, to be signed by the parties.

4. PROCEDURAL FRAMEWORK: THE ROLE OF THE COURT OF JUSTICE VIS-À-VIS THE EX OFFICIO APPLICATION OF EU LAW

Coming towards the conclusion of this chapter, we cannot ignore what was probably the most 'creative' contribution of the Court to European contract law, namely the establishment of the obligation of ex officio application of EU consumer law. Again, this was done in the name of the principle of effectiveness of EU law: in the landmark *Océano Grupo* case,[28] the Court established that the protection provided for consumers by the UCTD entails that a national court shall be able to determine of its own motion whether a term of a contract before it is unfair. In *Pannon*,[29] it was clearly stated that the national court is required to examine, of its own motion, the unfairness of a contractual term in cases where it has enough legal and factual elements at its disposal for performing that task. Shortly after, *Pénzügyi*[30] took this obligation even further, by holding that a national court is obliged to investigate of its own motion whether a term in a contract concluded between a seller or supplier and a consumer falls within the scope of the UCTD and, if so, to assess of its own motion whether such a term is unfair. In the same vein, in *Faber*,[31] the Court required a national judge to investigate on its own motion whether or not, in relation to a contract, the purchaser can qualify as 'a consumer'. This entails, in practice, that the protection granted to consumers by EU law will apply irrespective of the effective reliance of individuals on this status.

More recently, in May 2018, the Court confirmed in *Karel de Grote*[32] that its case law also applies to default proceedings. Furthermore, in *Profi Credit Polska*,[33] it arrived at the same result in the case of order for payment procedures.

---

27 Case C-42/15, *Home Credit Slovakia a.s.*, ECLI:EU:C:2016:842.
28 Case C-240/98, *Océano Grupo Editorial SA*, ECLI:EU:C:2000:346.
29 Case C-243/08, *Pannon GSM Zrt*, ECLI:EU:C:2009:350.
30 Case C-137/08, *VB Pénzügyi Lízing Zrt*, ECLI:EU:C:2010:659.
31 Case C-497/13, *Froukje Faber*, ECLI:EU:C:2015:357.
32 Case C-147/16, *Karel de Grote – Hogeschool Katholieke Hogeschool Antwerpen VZW*, ECLI:EU:C:2018:320.
33 Case C-176/17, *Profi Credit Polska*, ECLI:EU:C:2018:711.

These recent cases evidence that the procedural implications of EU contract law, as interpreted by the Court, lead to changes in the Member States' domestic judicial systems. This is further evidenced by *Lintner*,[34] in which the Court of Justice detailed what it specifically means when consumer rights are examined ex officio. For national courts, and in the case of the UCTD, it implies that they are required to review, of their own motion, other terms of the contract insofar as these terms are connected to the subject matter of the dispute before them. To do so, they may take investigative measures in order to obtain the necessary legal and factual elements.

As it is, default and order for payment procedures are generally meant to dispose, in an expedited manner and with no prior extensive control as to the merits, of uncontested cases. Against this backdrop, the implementation, in default and expedited procedures, of the positive obligations established by the Court – requiring the competent authorities, it is worth stressing, not only to check, but also 'to investigate' – may indeed conflict with the objectives pursued by domestic procedural systems. Firstly, in the light of the considerable number of default cases introduced annually in matters covered by the UCTD, re-establishing compliance with the Court of Justice's case law may require Member States to invest considerable financial resources in their civil justice systems to ensure the proper performance of the prior checks and inquiries meant to ensure the effective enforcement of European consumer law. Secondly, if these obligations were effectively extended to order for payment procedures, this may require many Member States[35] to rethink their domestic procedures, to the extent these are based on a strict implementation of the no-evidence model.[36] This because the standard of review imposed by the Court is indisputably high, concerning, inter alia (a) the existence of the status of consumer, (b) the existence of a significant imbalance between the parties, as resulting from the concrete facts of the case, and (c) the consequences of a term under the law applicable to the contract.[37] A procedure based on the no-evidence model is unlikely to provide the national judge with enough information to assess compliance with all these requirements, and will likely trigger the 'obligations to investigate'

---

34 Case C-511/19, *Lintner*, ECLI:EU:C:2020:188.

35 Especially those who deal with the first *ex parte* phase of the procedure by means of an IT system, such as Germany and Hungary.

36 Green Paper on a European order for payment procedure and on measures to simplify and speed up small claims litigation, COM/2002/0746 final.

37 Cases C-482/13, C-484/13, C-485/13 and C-487/13, *Unicaja Banco SA*, ECLI:EU:C:2015:21, recently recalled in Case C-613/15, *Ibercaja Banco SAU*, ECLI:EU:C:2016:195. As concerns the CCD, the Court has specified, in Case C-377/14, *Radlinger*, ECLI:EU:C:2016:283, that a national court is required to examine of its own motion whether the obligation to provide information laid down in Article 10 of the Directive has been complied with and to establish the consequences under national law of an infringement of that obligation.

envisioned by the Court. How these should be reconciled with the summary character of said procedures will be an issue for national legislators to solve.

Another aspect of the ex officio assessment which will likely be further developed by the Court of Justice in the foreseeable future concerns the powers conferred upon the national court when dealing with a term considered as being unfair. As is well known, EU law prevents a national court from modifying the contract by revising the content of the term deemed invalid,[38] but allows for the substitution of that term with a supplementary provision of national law.[39] The Court refined that line of reasoning in Joined Cases C-70/17 and C-179/17, *Abanca and Bankia*,[40] by stating that Articles 6 and 7 of UCTD, first, preclude a contractual clause that has been found to be unfair from being maintained in part, with the elements which make it unfair removed, where the removal of those elements would be tantamount to revising the content of that clause by altering its substance. However, second, these provisions do not preclude the national court from compensating for the invalidity of such an unfair term by replacing that term with the new wording of the legislative provision on which it was based, which is applicable where the parties to the contract so agree, provided that the concerned contract cannot continue its existence if that unfair term is removed, and that the annulment of the contract in its entirety would expose the consumer to particularly unfavourable consequences.

5. CONCLUDING REMARKS

The evolution of European contract law has been shaped by a number of transformations, among which a major role has been played by the Court of Justice's action in interpreting and enforcing EU law. As we showed above, the contribution of the European Court of Justice to the 'creation' and further development of European contract law occurs in different ways depending on the type of provision of EU law submitted to its interpretation. Firstly, the 'creative' activity of the Court manifests itself in the delineation of the 'variable geometry' of European contract law. By interpreting the scope of application of the several instruments which compose this body of law, the Court engages in a balancing exercise between domestic laws and mandatory provisions of EU law, the concrete outcome of which will finally depend on the assimilation and 're-working', by the Court of Justice, of the political objectives set by the European legislator.

In the interpretation of a contract as a 'source of private regulation', the *Granarolo* case shows that the Court of Justice is often best placed to identify

---

38 Case C-618/10, *Banco Español de Crédito SA*, ECLI:EU:C:2012:349.

39 Case C-26/13, *Kásler and Káslerné Rábai*, ECLI:EU:C:2017:54.

40 Joined Cases C-70/17 and C-179/17, *Abanca and Bankia*, ECLI:EU:C:2019:250.

the existence of commonalities or divergences in national legal cultures, and to provide for an authoritative solution to the conflicting interpretations arising therefrom. The cases on the notion of the 'main object of the contract' and on the requirements of transparency of unfair terms emphasise, instead, the role of active guidance that the Court takes upon itself in filling gaps or specifying concepts of European contract law. This undoubtedly contributes to the construction of 'European contract law' as a branch of law which is, at once, autonomous from and intertwined with domestic contract law and domestic procedural law. In parallel, the authoritative interpretations rendered by the Court of Justice under the aegis of the principle of effectiveness often impinge on the procedural autonomy that Member States shall in principle retain, thus contributing to the further approximation of the Member States' legal cultures.

On top of that, the case law of the Court of Justice often triggers important legislative reforms in the Member States. This has happened, for example, with respect to the Spanish Law on Civil Procedure (LEC) in the aftermath of the mortgage enforcement crisis, or with respect to the Hungarian law on consumer loan agreements.[41] Similar changes might concern, in the foreseeable future, the structure of order for payment and default proceedings in some Member States, insofar as is necessary for ensuring the implementation of ex officio control in default proceedings. This role of the Court as a catalyst for legislative reforms can also be seen as a manifestation of the larger phenomenon of 'the creation of norms'.

Finally, the recent Spanish cases concerning mortgage enforcement and the line of (Hungarian and Romanian) cases on loans contracted in a foreign currency can be ascribed to yet another form of interaction identified in the academic debate.[42] It has been submitted, in this respect, that the Court of Justice is nowadays often called, in an unprecedented way, to assist national courts in providing an answer to social needs affecting wide portions of the population. By doing so, the Court of Justice sets – that is, creates – its own policies, by acting in accordance with the political rationale lying behind EU law.

To conclude, this contribution was meant to evidence that, at present, the preliminary ruling procedure remains an extremely flexible and, above all, inherently 'creative' tool. Far from being limited to the interpretation of EU law, it additionally contributes to shaping, monitoring and enforcing EU contract law, within the framework of a strategic interaction between EU institutions, national legislators and national courts.

---

41 The changes to the Hungarian legislation and their origin were exhaustively explained in the Opinion delivered by Advocate-General Wahl on 18.01.2018 in Case C-483/16, *Zsolt Sziber*, ECLI:EU:C:2018:367.

42 See, in particular, F. Gómez and K. Lyczowska, 'Spanish courts, the European Court and consumer law: some thoughts on their interaction' in F. Cafaggi and S. Law (eds.), *Judicial Cooperation in European Private Law*, Edward Elgar, Cheltenham 2017, p. 93.

POTENTIAL AND HURDLES FOR THE CJEU'S JURISPRUDENCE IN DOMESTIC LEGAL ORDERS

A Polish Case Study

Aneta Wiewiórowska-Domagalska

1. INTRODUCTION

1.1. GENERAL OVERVIEW

EU law is only able to achieve its goals if the Member States ensure its effective application at a national level. Considering how EU legal instruments and norms are constructed, it is obvious that they very often require judicial interpretation that allows them to be properly understood and applied at a national level. This is particularly important for the open, general norms, as well as for the lacunas that require filling in at an national level. Since the effectiveness of EU law is measured in its operation in practice, it is critical to ensure that the CJEU's case law is applied at a national level. In order to reach this point, the CJEU's case law must become part of the national legal reality. National courts are the guardians of this process. They hold very powerful tools that allow them to control market practice as well as the implementation of EU law. National courts often also play a correctional function when confronted with the inaccurate transposition of EU rules. Their function as guardians is an active one: in order to build a European legal sphere, national courts of all instances must engage in meaningful dialogue with the CJEU. While effective cooperation between the national and the European judiciary is indispensable for implementing EU law, many characteristics of EU law make this process rather challenging.

1.2. THE FOCUS OF THE CHAPTER

Bearing in mind the importance of national courts for ensuring the proper functioning of EU law, the primary focus of this chapter is the hurdles (and much less so the potential) when it comes to the integration of the CJEU's jurisprudence into national judicial practice. The chapter is divided into two parts. The first presents the external perspective, i.e. the construction of the EU judicial system in which national courts function, focusing on the characteristics that impede fruitful dialogue between the European and national judiciary. These include the structure and specific features of EU law, the way the CJEU operates and the effects it has on the national courts. The second part presents an example of a national perspective in the form of a case study that deals with the application of the Unfair Contract Terms Directive to consumer loans denominated or indexed in Swiss francs in the Polish legal system. As, in practice, the effectiveness of EU law depends not only on the legal, but also the social, economic and political environment in which national courts function, the case study shows a national, internal perspective on the challenges faced by national courts applying EU law.

1.3. METHODOLOGICAL REMARKS

It is important to emphasise the constraints of the analysis in this chapter. The first part strives to comment on the construction and the functioning of the EU judiciary, and in doing so it presents a view that might probably be shared by the Member States in general. The case study, however, serves an illustrational purpose only. The national characteristics that the case study presents are unique for each Member State and depend on the construction of the national legal system as well as on the functioning of the given society as such (sociological, economic and political factors). Hence, the functioning of the CJEU's jurisprudence in every legal system is the result of many components, most of which relate to the legal culture of the given system. How does the national legal system function? How far is the implementation of EU law granted by the public administration, and to what extent does this duty fall upon the courts? How effective is the executive branch? As the national courts are normally the last resort when it comes to assuring that EU law is applied, putting the courts in the position where they have to correct the actions (or omissions) of the legislative and executive branches of power creates additional stress factors for the national jurisprudence.[1] Depending on the national situation, far greater pressure might be imposed on the national courts than arises from the need to overcome the differences in the construction and functioning of the national legal system and EU law (which in itself is already very difficult). The court culture is equally important. How do the national judges approach cooperation with other state bodies and cooperation with other courts? This is a necessary element for creating an effective system of ensuring the correct application of EU law. How intensive and how well organised is the professional training of judges, with the aim of introducing the EU methodology and keeping the national judiciary up to date with EU developments? And last, but not least, there is the question of how efficient the judicial system is in general. So, while the case study identifies critical factors for ensuring the proper application of the CJEU's case law in the national practice, it does so from a Polish perspective, without presupposing whether and to what extent these factors are equally relevant in other Member States.

1 On that, see a very interesting analysis of the interaction between Spanish courts and the Spanish government in the context of the referrals to CJEU: F. Gómez Pomar and K. Lyczowska, 'Spanish Courts, the Court of Justice of the European Union, and Consumer Law: A Theoretical Model of their Interaction', DLA Piper Spain, October 2014.

2. THE CHARACTERISTICS OF EU LAW THAT IMPACT ITS FUNCTIONING AT A NATIONAL LEVEL

2.1. OVERVIEW

Considering its construction and functioning (the effect that the Member States are expected to achieve), EU law is difficult to understand and apply correctly at a national level. The multi-layered composition of EU law, and its unavoidable intertwining with national legal systems, creates a complicated structure that escapes easy categorisations from a national perspective. EU law cannot be ordered according to the traditional national methodologies and with the dogmatic tools used to address national law issues. Apart from its constructional distinctiveness, the application of EU law is simply much more complicated than the functioning of a purely national legal system.

2.2. DISTINCTIVE AIMS OF EU LAW

The element that primarily distinguishes EU legislation from national legislation is its pan-national character. It is obvious that EU law pursues aims that are not naturally present at a national level. While the great codifications have always had the aim of unifying national legal systems (which has long been achieved), national private law is traditionally oriented towards reducing transactional costs. Although EU law also pursues reductions in transactional costs, it is always done in a cross-border context and along with other aims (building the market while protecting consumers). Moreover, what the EU legislator has sought to achieve so far is not a coherent legal system (of private law), but rather to meet EU objectives, such as an efficiently functioning internal market (Article 3(3) TEU), or establishing the EU as an area of security and justice (Article 3(2) TEU). The true aim of the EU legislator is therefore to create EU market standards, and at a precisely established level. While trying to achieve this aim, the EU legislator struggles with the restrictions imposed by the limited competences of the European Union and the political choices of the Member States to allow or to restrict the full utilisation of those competences (for example, the consumer-driven development of private law for the internal market). Moreover, sometimes the effective fulfilment of the EU law aims would require a much higher level of harmonisation, or a more far-reaching adjustment of the legal systems than is officially admitted (the famous 'does not infringe' declarations contained in EU Directives).

2.3. DEPARTURE FROM 19TH-CENTURY DOGMATICS

The European Union perceives law as a measure to advance the effective functioning of the EU internal market. Despite the highly demanding legislative process, EU law is therefore much closer to the market, and more responsive to the evolving market situation than national laws usually are. In addition, due to the global character of the ongoing market changes (such as digitalisation and climate concerns), the EU is much better equipped to provide an appropriate regulatory response than individual Member States.[2] In doing so, EU law makes use of economic tools to describe rather than to structure and categorise the market phenomena it addresses. In this process, EU law disregards the traditional national distinctions recognised by the national legal systems and the national law-making methodology. This characteristic makes EU law very difficult for the national legal systems to absorb, as they must deconstruct European norms in order to be able to fit them within their national ones, which are normally based on 19th century dogmatic constructs.

2.4. EU LAW'S AXIOLOGICAL DRIVE

Another characteristic that might be alien from the perspective of the national judiciary is the strong axiological drive of EU law, which results in a different balance between axiology and structure (the dogmatic construction). The social engineering aspect, inherent in EU law, is normally much less visible at the national level. EU law strives to achieve positive effects on the market (a market that functions and where consumer rights are implemented in practice), to create rather than to eliminate or reduce negative effects. This translates into the undisputed precedence of teleological interpretation, which overrules all other interpretation methods and constitutes an unceasing driver of EU law, clearly identifiable in the CJEU's jurisprudence. These axiology-based solutions pursued by the CJEU are often very challenging for the traditional dogmatic thinking of national (continental) lawyers, in particular considering that applying such solutions is supposed to lead to achieving aims that are also new for the national judges. In other words, national judges are expected to pursue aims they do not know (or do not fully understand) using legal instruments they are not acquainted with.[3]

A good *a contrario* illustration could be provided by two CJEU judgments that were relatively easy for national legal systems to accept. The first is *Leitner*,[4] which clarified that for organised package tours, the *ex contractu* damage also includes non-material damage for lost holidays. According to the judgment in

---

[2] C. Lübberding, H. Schulte-Nölke, M. Thase and A. Wiewiórowska-Domagalska, 'Contribution to Growth: Legal Aspects of Protecting European Consumers', Study requested by the IMCO committee, April 2019, pp. 77–94.

[3] On this problem in the Polish context, see: E. Łętowska, *Znajomość treści prawa czy biegłość w metodach jego poznawania. Głos w dyskusji nad stanem prawoznawstwa*, in *Studia i Rozprawy. Księga jubileuszowa dedykowana profesorowi Andrzejowi Całusowi*, ed. A. Janik, Warsaw 2009, pp. 83–95.

[4] Case C-168/00, *Leitner*, ECLI:C:2002:163.

the second case, *Weber/Putz*,[5] it is the seller who has to pay for the removal of defective goods that were installed, along with the costs of installing new ones. What these cases have in common is that, even though they are axiology-driven (ensuring extensive protection of the consumer), they propose specific, challenging, but not ground-breaking, changes to the national dogmatic constructions. Nevertheless, their internalisation for the Polish legal system required specific actions. For the *Leitner* case, it was a resolution of the Supreme Court of 19 November 2010 (III CZP 79/10), confirming that, indeed, damages in the case of package tours includes damages for the non-material damage (before this judgment, the lower-instance courts would normally reject consumer claims for non-material damage). *Weber/Putz*, on the other hand, simply triggered a legislative change introduced as part of the sales law reform in 2014.[6]

Very often, however, EU law (and the CJEU) require national courts to simply make sure that *in casu* the high level of consumer protection and the market-building mechanisms are in place in national law. That includes, for example, the *ex officio* review of unfair contract terms, removing the procedural or substantial obstacles that prevent consumers from exercising their rights, or even interpreting contractual terms in a specific manner. The difficulty of such an approach rests on the fact that it focuses on the *effet utile* that must be achieved. In addition, the burden to make sure that EU law functions properly (i.e. according to the CJEU's jurisprudence) is often placed on the national courts (see the case study, section 5 below). The CJEU's instructions directed to national courts might be seen as a challenging support tool, as they often run counter to the approach traditionally present in the national legal reasoning, in terms of their content as well as the presentation (formulation).

3. THE CJEU'S JURISPRUDENCE OPERATION IN PRACTICE: THE ACCESS PROBLEM

Establishing how the CJEU's jurisprudence functions at a national level constitutes a considerable challenge for the researcher, mainly due to the lack of available data. This implies that the level of knowledge when it comes to verifying the real impact of the CJEU's case law on national law is simply insufficient.

How then does one find out how far the national courts observe the case law of the CJEU, and to what extent they use the possibility and observe the duty to address the CJEU with a preliminary referral? The process of genuinely assessing this would necessitate screening national judgments *en masse*. At this point, the

5 Joined Cases C-65/09 and C-87/09, *Weber/Putz*, ECLI:EU:C:2011:396.

6 Act on Consumer Rights and Changes to the Civil Code of 30 May 2014, Journal of Laws 2014, item 827.

question of access appears. While most Member States (maybe even all at the moment) allow internet access to national jurisprudence, and internet-based translation services solve the language barrier to a large extent, case selection remains a significant problem. In other words, how can national cases that have an EU element (which national courts might or might not have noticed) be distinguished from purely national cases? If national systems of case designation for statistical purposes were to require an 'EU designation' (which is not the case), the access problem would theoretically become much less significant. Yet even then, the question of whether or not the case designation is correct would require verification.[7]

Even if the search of national case law were limited to the judgments of the national supreme courts, it would require a case-by-case verification in 28 Member States, as there is no EU database that gathers and organises the case law with EU relevance from all the Member States. In the New Deal for Consumers Agenda,[8] the EU Commission announced actions aimed at (among other things) collecting cases and creating a consumer law database, but this useful tool is not fully operational yet (it does not contain the collection of national cases). In addition, the analysis would not only have to include the cases where the national courts noticed and acted on the EU character of the case, but would likewise have to verify in how many cases the EU character of the judgment went unnoticed, i.e. where the court either did not apply the EU solution or did not address the CJEU with a preliminary referral. However, even full knowledge of the jurisprudence of a supreme court in a given Member State does not provide an answer to the question of how the CJEU's case law operates, neither in the context of the national market nor in the context of the national jurisprudence. First, the jurisprudence of the lower-instance courts does not reflect the market practice, as not all instances of consumer rights/contract violations are brought to court.[9] Likewise, the supreme courts' case law does not necessarily reflect the legal practice of the lower courts. This is the case for two reasons. First, for procedural reasons (the low value of the case), the vast majority of cases

7 In a case study that was supposed to establish how Directive 1999/44/EC functions in practice, which the author of this chapter conducted in 2014, out of 200 researched cases, 173 had a clearly incorrect designation, while for four there were doubts whether the designation was correct and for one it was impossible to establish what the designation was. This means that only 11 per cent of cases were correctly qualified. See: A. Wiewiórowska-Domagalska, 'Refleksje na tle orzecznictwa sądów powszechnych w zakresie sprzedaży konsumenckiej' (Reflections on the basis of consumer sales cases decided by ordinary courts) (2014) 20 *Prawo w działaniu* 219.

8 Communication from the Commission to the European Parliament, the Council and the European Economic and Social Committee, 'A New Deal for Consumers', COM (2018) 183 final, p. 13.

9 The Green Book, COM (2008) 794 of 27 November 2008, p. 4, indicates that that for half of EU15 consumers, a claim worth €200 would not be worth pursuing, and for 20 per cent a claim of €1,000.

(very often of those concerning consumers) do not reach the supreme courts. Second, the characteristic inertia of national jurisprudence always requires verification of how effective and swift the impact of a supreme court's decision is on the practice of the lower courts in a given country.[10]

4. THE SYSTEM OF PRELIMINARY REFERRALS TO THE CJEU

According to Article 19(1) sentence 2 TEU, the CJEU's duty is to ensure compliance with the law when interpreting and applying the Treaties. Article 267(1) TFEU provides the CJEU with an instrument to perform this duty, i.e. the preliminary ruling procedure. The CJEU's 2016 recommendations to national courts and tribunals in relation to the initiation of preliminary ruling proceedings[11] clarify that the initiation of the preliminary ruling proceedings should be used when a question of interpretation is raised before the national court or tribunal that is new and of general interest for the uniform application of EU law, or where the existing case law does not appear to provide the necessary guidance in a new legal context or set of facts.

Article 267 TFEU establishes a system of cooperation between the CJEU and the national courts.[12] It follows very clearly from the CJEU's jurisprudence that

---

10 The Re-Jus Casebook 'Effective Justice in Consumer Protection' provides interesting examples in this respect. It reports that there are 'no noteworthy cases regarding the issue of ex officio examination of contract terms by the courts, from the perspective of consumer protection and, in particular, of unfair contract terms' (pp. 20–21). However, a Polish study of 200 consumer sales cases of first- and second-instance courts shows that the courts of first and second instance did not undertake *ex officio* control in any of the cases, even though in eight cases there was a very strong prima facie indication of unfairness of a contract term. A. Wiewiórowska-Domagalska, above n. 7, pp. 236–242. Similarly (p. 123), according to Re-Jus, '[d]eclaration of the unfairness of a clause occurs *ex lege* and has an *ex tunc* effect, which has been referred in multiple examples of case law (see e.g. judgments: of the Supreme Court of 30 May 2014, III CSK 204/13 and of 14 May 2015, II CSK 768/14, of the District Court in Gdansk of 19 June 2015, III Ca 970/14, of the Regional Court in Warsaw-Śródmieście of 19 July 2016, VIII C 2064/15).' It continues: 'Since the declaration of unfairness of a contract term and its non-binding nature is made with regard to the time of concluding the contract, it is a natural consequence that this provision is declared ineffective from the very outset. Therefore, under this assumption, the professional is obliged to refund the consumer in full, i.e. the total sum that he/she had paid on the basis of that provision.' However, firstly, for a long time there was no stable line of Supreme Court jurisprudence when it comes to the consequences of declaring a term unfair, and, second, the consequences of finding a term unfair constitutes one of the most important problems in the practice of the lower-instance courts (see sections 5.10 and 5.11 on that). This means that either the methodology of the research is not properly selected for the aims of the research, or the performance is need of improvement.

11 [2016] OJ C439/01, para. 5.

12 Case C-322/16, *Global Starnet Ltd*, ECLI:EU:C:2017:985, para. 22, and Case C-5/14, *Kernkraftwerke Lippe-Ems*, ECLI:EU:C:2015:354, para. 35 and the case law cited.

the Court's aim is to create a set of procedural assurances to guarantee that the system, where the initiative to address the CJEU with a preliminary referral rests entirely in the hands of the national courts, might work. However, despite the numerous attempts of the CJEU, the distinctiveness of the construction of the EU and national judicial systems makes it difficult for the national courts to enter into and navigate through the EU judicial system.

First, the decision of whether or not to address the CJEU belongs entirely to national courts. The CJEU stresses[13] that it is solely for the national court before which a dispute has been brought, and which assumes responsibility for the subsequent judicial decision, to determine, in light of the particular circumstances of the case, both the need for a preliminary ruling in order to enable it to deliver a judgment, and the relevance of the questions that it submits to the CJEU.[14] The discretion of national courts is replaced by an obligation for courts of final instance, subject to certain exceptions recognised[15] by the Court's case law.[16] Such an approach means that a national court in every case that potentially involves the application of EU law should establish whether the existing EU law (including jurisprudence) provides a sufficiently clear answer to the legal question at stake. This means that, if the submitted questions concern the interpretation of Community law, the CJEU is, in principle, bound to give a ruling.[17]

Second, national courts should be free to refer any question to the CJEU for a preliminary ruling that they consider necessary,[18] and should enjoy the widest discretion in referring questions to the Court involving the interpretation of relevant provisions of EU law.[19] According to the CJEU, this freedom prevails over the national rules of varying nature (substantive as well as procedural rules). This all means that national law cannot prevent or limit the possibility of national courts using this discretion[20] or complying with this obligation.[21] It refers equally to national rules imposed by legislation or national case law that

---

13 Case C-83/78, *Redmond*, ECLI:EU:C:1978:214, para. 25; Case C-338/85, *Pardini*, ECLI:EU:C:1988:194, para. 8; Case C-212/04, *Adeneler and Others*, ECLI:EU:C:2006:443, para. 41; Joined Cases C-261/07 and C-299/07, *VTB-VAB NV/ Galatea BVBA*, ECLI:EU:C:2009:244, para. 32; and Case C-494/16, *Santoro*, ECLI:EU:C:2018:166, para. 20.

14 Inter alia, Case C-379/98, *PreussenElektra* [2001] ECR I-2099, para. 38; Case C-18/01, *Korhonen and Others* [2003] ECR I-5321, para. 19; and Case C-295/05, *Asemfo* [2007] ECR I-2999, para. 30.

15 Case 283/81, *Cilfit and Others*, ECLI:EU:C:1982:335, para. 21 and operative part.

16 Similarly, ibid., para. 21; Case C-348/89, *Mecanarte*, ECLI:EU:C:1991:278, para. 42; Case C-689/13, *PFE*, ECLI:EU:C:2016:199, para. 32.

17 Inter alia, *PreussenElektra*, above n. 14, para. 38; *Korhonen and Others*, above n. 14, para. 19; *Asemfo*, above n. 14, para. 30.

18 *Global Starnet Ltd*, above n. 12, para. 22; *Kernkraftwerke Lippe-Ems*, above n. 12, para. 35 and the case law cited.

19 Case 166/73, *Rheinmühlen-Düsseldorf*, ECLI:EU:C:1974:3, para. 3.

20 Ibid., para. 4; Joined Cases C-188/10 and C-189/10, *Melki and Abdeli*, ECLI:EU:C:2010:363, para. 42; Case C-173/09, *Elchinov*, ECLI:EU:C:2010:581, para. 27.

21 *Rheinmühlen-Düsseldorf*, above n. 19, para. 3; Case C-210/06, *Cartesio*, ECLI:EU:C:2008:723, para. 88; *Melki and Abdeli*, above n. 20, para. 41; *PFE*, above n. 16, para. 32.

cannot interfere with this discretion or obligation.[22] National courts are also not bound by the hierarchical structure of the national judicial system, should that prevent them from exercising their discretion to address the CJEU. According to the CJEU, not only are national courts free to address it at whatever stage of the proceedings they consider appropriate, even at the end of an interlocutory procedure for the review of constitutionality,[23] but also the existence of a rule of national law whereby courts against whose decisions there is a judicial remedy are bound on points of law by the rulings of a court superior to them cannot, on the basis of that fact alone, deprive the lower courts of the discretion to address the CJEU.[24] The CJEU clarified that a court not ruling at final instance must be free, if it considers that a higher court's legal ruling could lead it to give a judgment contrary to European Union law, to refer to the Court questions that concern it.[25] In the *Ełczinow* and *Križan and others* cases, the CJEU made it clear that national courts, if necessary, must disregard the rulings of the higher court if it considers, in light of the interpretation given by the CJEU, that these rulings are not consistent with European Union law.[26] The rules of national law, even of a constitutional order, cannot be allowed to undermine the unity and effectiveness of European Union law.[27] Those principles apply equally to relations between a constitutional court and all other national courts.[28]

The decentralised[29] system of judicial cooperation that the CJEU establishes on the basis of Article 267(1) TFEU places very high demands upon national courts. It requires them to independently and *ad casu* decide whether there is a need to refer to the CJEU. The criteria that a national judge must apply are rather vague, and when verifying their application, the national judges of lower instances are expected to disregard national substantive and procedural provisions (should a need arise). Likewise, the national judge must disregard national case law and the binding force of judgments of the higher-instance

---

22 *PFE*, above n. 16, para. 34.

23 *Global Starnet Ltd*, above n. 12, para. 22; *Kernkraftwerke Lippe-Ems*, above n. 12, para. 35 and the case law cited.

24 *Melki and Abdeli*, above n. 20, para. 42.

25 *Elchinov*, above n. 20, paras. 25 and 27; Case C-396/09, *Interedil*, ECLI:EU:C:2011:671, para. 35; *Rheinmühlen-Düsseldorf*, above n. 20, para. 4; Case C-378/08, *ERG and Others*, ECLI:EU:C:2010:126, para. 32; Case C-180/11, *Bericap Záródástechnikai*, ECLI:EU:C:2012:717, para. 55; Case C-42/13, *Cartiera dell'Adda*, ECLI:EU:C:2014:2345, para. 27; *Melki i Abdeli*, above n. 20, para. 42.

26 *Elchinov*, above n. 20, para. 30; Case C-416/10, *Križan and Others*, ECLI:EU:C:2018:8, para. 69.

27 Case 11/70, *Internationale Handelsgesellschaft* [1970] ECR 1125, para. 3; Case C-409/06, *Winner Wetten* [2010] ECR I-8015, para. 61.

28 *Melki and Abdeli*, above n. 20, paras. 41–45; *Elchinov*, above n. 20, para. 30; *Križan and Others*, above n. 26, para. 69.

29 On that, see: J. van Dorp and P. Phoa, 'How to Continue a Meaningful Judicial Dialogue About EU Law? From the Conditions in the CILFIT Judgment to the Creation of a New European Legal Culture' (2018) 34(1) *Utrecht Journal of International and European Law* 75.

courts (including the constitutional court) in its country. All this should be done in a procedure that is rather difficult to fit into the national hierarchical construction of the juridical system – the EU system stresses that the system under Article 267 TFEU is based on cooperation between the CJEU and national courts in their capacity as courts responsible for the application of EU law.[30]

Given that the CJEU is not a higher-instance court, it might be challenging for the national courts (particularly for the final-instance courts) to implement the referrals into the hierarchically structured rules of case precedence within the hierarchically constructed system of courts. National courts are expected to constantly act as rebels within their own legal system – rebels against the rules that contradict EU law and rebels against the higher-instance courts that violate EU law. This is, indeed, also a difficult task from a human perspective (lower-instance judges will normally aspire to become higher-instance judges). Moreover, these revolutionary actions are supposed to be undertaken in consumer cases, often of a very low value,[31] which would normally not make it to the highest instance court in a national legal system. Lower-instance courts must have expertise that will allow them to formulate the referral (normally they do not have clerks at their disposal),[32] suspend the pending case and wait on average 15.6 months (data for 2017)[33] to receive an answer, which really is just an instruction on how the case should be decided when applying national law, rather than a real solution. The courts cannot share experience when it comes to applying the CJEU's judgments, because there is no information available outside the CJEU on how the referring court subsequently decided to apply the answer of the CJEU.[34] In other words, every judge of every court in the EU is expected to present a level of knowledge, expertise, organisational capabilities and independence of thinking normally expected of judges of supreme courts. While as a principle this is a very noble approach, the reality of the lower-instance courts might seriously impede its – even partial – realisation.[35] This might be reflected in the numbers of preliminary referrals to the CJEU: in 2017 there were 533[36] and in 2018 568,[37] which, considering that the CJEU acts for 500 million EU citizens, seems to be a surprisingly low number.

---

30 Joined Cases C-72/14 and C-197/14, *X and van Dijk*, ECLI:EU:C:2015:564, para. 54; Case C-3/16, *Aquino*, ECLI:EU:C:2017:209, para. 32.

31 The value of the claim was €69.97 in the *Quelle* case.

32 See: M. Glavina, 'To refer or not to refer, that is the (preliminary) question. Why Member States' judges do not participate in the preliminary ruling procedure', available at https://www.leuvenpubliclaw.com/to-refer-or-not-to-refer-that-is-the-preliminary-question-why-member-states-judges-do-not-participate-in-the-preliminary-ruling-procedure/.

33 https://curia.europa.eu/jcms/upload/docs/application/pdf/2018-03/cp180036en.pdf.

34 During the conference, judge Camelia Toader explained that follow-up information is available for the CJEU.

35 M. Glavina, above n. 32.

36 See the reference in n. 33 above.

37 https://curia.europa.eu/jcms/upload/docs/application/pdf/2019-03/cp190039en.pdf.

5. CASE STUDY

5.1. INTRODUCTION

This case study presents the legal, economic and political considerations that have contributed to creating the problem with the currency loans market in Poland (consumer mortgage secured loans, either denominated or indexed in Swiss francs) and at the moment have a fundamental impact on how the case law of the CJEU in the area of consumer law is received and applied by Polish courts.[38] This issue has already given rise not only to a massive amount of national case law,[39] but also to a stream of cases before the CJEU.[40] On the basis of national case law, one might risk saying that the CJEU's jurisprudence concerning the unfairness control has, in principle, established itself in the legal practice of Polish courts regarding currency mortgage loans.[41] At the time of writing the initial version of this chapter the Polish market was impatiently awaiting the CJEU's judgment in the *Dziubak* case.[42] The case study shows how long and complicated the process of striving towards accepting the CJEU's jurisprudence is,[43] as well as how complex and intertwined are the factors that had to come into existence in order for the CJEU's jurisprudence to overcome the resistance of the national market actors and effectively enter into the national legal sphere.

---

38 M. Wilczek, 'Polish homebuyer's lawsuit raises risk for banks and government', available at https://www.politico.eu/article/polish-homebuyers-lawsuit-raises-risk-for-banks-and-government/?fbclid=IwAR3a4m72KcDQjp8Kf629pva5up2aHM-S0nv7Ja3-08b1G4ckns0WXS33O7Q.

39 The estimation of the number of cases on the basis of available data suggests that there are 18,800 cases pending at the moment in the Polish courts, https://www.money.pl/banki/frankowicze-zalewaja-pozwami-sady-ponad-18-tys-spraw-przeciw-najwiekszym-bankom-6556700710914752a.html.

40 Case C-537/15, *Euro Bank SA*, ECLI:EU:C:2016:143; Case C-176/17, *Profi Credit Polska*, ECLI:EU:C:2018:711; Case C-632/17, *Powszechna Kasa Oszczędności*, ECLI:EU:C:2018:963; Case C-260/18, *Dziubak*, ECLI:EU:C:2019:819; Case C-266/18, *Aqua Med*, ECLI:EU:C:2019:282; Case C-383/18, *Lexitor*, ECLI:EU:C:2019:702; Case C-419/18, *Profi Credit Polska*, ECLI:EU:C:2019:702; joined Cases C-419/18 and C-483/18, *Profi Credit Polska*, ECLI:EU:C:2019:930; joined Cases C-84/19, C-222/19 and C-252/19, *Profi Credit Polska*, ECLI:EU:C:2020:631; or C-779/18, *Mikrokasa*, ECLI:EU:C:2020:236.

41 Although one can still find very recent judgments that contradict the EU approach, for example: Appeal Court Białystok, judgment of 9 May 2019 (I ACa 47/19); District Court Toruń, judgment of 12 August (I C 517/18); District Court Łódź, judgment of 28 March 2019 (III Ca 1889/18), as well as referrals to the CJEU that disclose deep misunderstanding of EU consumer policy, see: C-212/20 *A. S.A.*, or C-198/20, *X Bank*.

42 *Dziubak*, above n. 40.

43 Preliminary referrals C-19/20, *Bank BPH*, C-212/20 *A. S.A.*, or C-198/20, *X Bank* illustrate that the process has not been concluded yet.

5.2. HOW DID THE PROBLEM ARISE?

The Polish market for mortgage-secured loans is relatively young. Such contracts appeared in the mid-1990s and became popular among consumers around 2000.[44] In 2002, a law of exchange[45] was adopted that allowed loans in a foreign currency. The beginning of the 2000s was a period of a rapid increase in wealth and optimism among Polish consumers, which translated into increased interest in buying apartments and homes[46] (in the aftermath of the communist period, the ownership level was low). However, at that time loans in Polish zloty were expensive (the annual interest rate was up to 20 per cent), because of the high interest rates, caused by the disinflation policy of the Polish government.[47] Foreign currency loans (i.e. loans indexed to or denominated in a foreign currency, in particular in Swiss francs) were not only much cheaper (based on the lower interest rate), but also much more available: the lower value of a loan payment calculated on the basis of the Swiss franc, which was very cheap at that time, allowed greater creditworthiness to be established for consumers who wanted to conclude such loan.

The low exchange rate of foreign currencies, combined with the aggressive promotional policy of banks, led to almost one million loan contracts being concluded. According to the data provided by the Supreme Audit Office (*Najwyższa Izba Kontroli*, NIK), by the end of 2017 there were 985,700 loan contracts with a currency risk, 81 per cent of which constituted loans indexed or denominated in Swiss francs.[48] The peak popularity of loan contracts with a currency risk was between 2006 and 2008. In this period, Polish banks concluded 476,000 contracts, of which 192,100 (more than 760 a day) came in 2008.[49] In the aftermath of the financial crisis of 2008, those numbers dropped by 80 per cent in 2009 (39 100),[50] while in 2012 just 8,422 loans were concluded and in 2013 957.[51]

The market problem revealed itself when, at the beginning of 2015, the Swiss Central Bank freed the rate of the Swiss franc, and as a consequence, the franc rapidly rose in value. Between 2007 and 2016, the average franc to zloty rate increased by 90.5 per cent, from 2.1614 zloty per 1 franc to 4.1137 zloty per 1 franc (during the same period, the euro rate rose 23.5 per cent).[52] The decrease

44 R. Kata, 'Kredyty hipoteczne w Polsce w kontekście stabilności finansowej i makroekonomicznej', Zeszyty Naukowe PWSZ w Płocku, Nauki Ekonomiczne, t. XXII, 2015, p. 185.
45 Act of 27 July 2002, Law of Exchange, Journal of Laws No. 141, item 1178.
46 'Biała księga kredytów frankowych w Polsce Związek Banków Polskich', Warsaw 2015, p. 8.
47 Ibid.
48 NIK, *Ochrona praw konsumentów korzystających z kredytów objętych ryzykiem walutowym, Informacja o wynikach kontroli, Najwyższa Izba Kontroli*, Warsaw 2018, pp. 32–33.
49 Ibid., p. 34.
50 Ibid., p. 35.
51 Ibid., p. 60.
52 Ibid., p. 33.

in the value of the zloty meant that the loans indexed or denominated in Swiss francs not only lost their financial attractiveness, but for some consumers they became very cumbersome. While loans in Swiss francs were very cheap at the moment of concluding the contract, they burdened consumers (who were not always aware that it would be the case) with an unlimited risk of the Swiss franc gaining value against Polish zloty. The decrease in value of the Polish zloty meant that, after several years of paying off the loan, the consumer might have debt (in Polish zloty) that was higher than the initial debt (also in Polish zloty). For some debtors, it was also impossible to pay off the loan by selling the apartment the loan was taken to purchase, because the value of the loan became higher than the value of the property (LTV factor >100 per cent). In 2015–2016, the value of the property was lower than the value of the debt for about 50 per cent of all loans in Swiss francs.[53] In 2017, the situation improved: for banks that had a housing loan portfolio worth over 100 million zloty, it was 20.1 per cent of contracts (34.4 per cent of the credit value of CHF loans), and in 2018 it is 20 per cent (34.3 per cent of the value).[54] For loans in Polish zloty, the same factor in 2018 was 6.09 per cent.[55]

5.3. REACTION OF THE MARKET AUTHORITIES

The developments in the mortgage loan sector did not go unnoticed by the market and market authorities. As early as 2005, the Polish Main Banking Inspector pointed out the dangers that the mass offering of foreign currency loans raises for Polish banks.[56] At the end of 2005, the self-governing organisation of banks (the Polish Bank Association – *Związek Banków Polskich*, ZBP) requested the introduction of a legislative prohibition on foreign currency housing loans.[57] At the same time, in 2006 some of the banks (also those in favour of a legislative ban) intensified their credit action in foreign currency, which reached its peak in 2008.

The Main Banking Inspector restricted its actions to adopting non-binding recommendations, claiming that it was impossible to implement hard law prohibitions, due to its lack of competence, but also because this solution would

53 Ibid., p. 38.

54 Ibid., p. 38.

55 Komisja Nadzoru Finansowego, *Wyniki badania portfela kredytów mieszkaniowych i konsumpcyjnych gospodarstw domowych według stanu na koniec 2018, aneks do 'Raportu o sytuacji banków w 2018'*, Urząd Komisji Nadzoru Finansowego, Warsaw 2019, pp. 11–12.

56 Publications that refer to oral statements of the Main Banking Inspector in this regard: A. Myczkowska and E. Więcław, 'Kredyty walutowe są zbyt ryzykowne', Rzeczpospolita, 25.11.2005; M. Krześniak, 'Nadzór ostrzega', Gazeta prawna, 17.03.2005, available at http://www.nbp.pl/home.aspx?f=aktualnosci/wiadomosci_2005/ginb 09122005.html.

57 'Biała księga kredytów frankowych w Polsce Związek Banków Polskich', Warsaw 2015, pp. 33–34.

give preference to the banks that had a large deposit base. As he stressed in 2018, 'the position presented by the economists, politicians and society when it comes to the availability of such contracts' also prevented any possibility of acting in practice. Over the years, the Financial Supervision Authority (*Komisja Nadzoru Bankowego*, KNF, which replaced the Main Banking Inspector) issued a number of recommendations. Recommendations S of 2006, 2008, 2011 and 2013 dealt with the management of credit exposure secured by means of mortgages, and Recommendations T of 2010 and 2013 with good practices in managing retail risk. The recommendations gradually increased the requirements for banks that offered currency risk loans. For example, in 2008, banks were supposed to offer the consumer a loan in Polish zloty first, and only later, after receiving a written declaration from the consumer that he chooses to accept such an offer in fully understanding of the associated risks, a loan in foreign currency. According to the 2013 S Recommendation, loans indexed or denominated in a foreign currency could only be offered to the consumers that earned in such currencies.

Despite its non-binding character, the 2006 Recommendation S was met with a very negative reaction by politicians and economists. The Prime Minister 'did not understand' and 'would not agree with the policy of limiting access to loans'.[58] Politicians belonging to the party governing at the time (Prawo i Sprawiedliwość) claimed that it was against the interests of poorer consumers, and its introduction was motivated by support for the large banks that offer loans in Polish zloty.[59] While the President of the Office of Competition and Consumer Protection (*Urząd Ochrony Konkurencji i Konsumentów*, UOKiK) admitted that the argument referring to consumer protection is correct, limiting access to foreign currency loans would be too far-reaching. In his opinion, the proper solution would be to educate consumers and increase the banks' informational duties.[60] The economists (*Instytut Globalizacji*) called upon the supervisory authorities to sustain competition on the mortgage market, claiming that restricting the availability of mortgage-secured loans was a result of the actions of bank lobbyists who pursue their own interest and the maximisation of profit, rather than the well-being of consumers.[61]

---

58 Rekomendacja S – nowe wymogi do kredytów walutowych, Gazeta Ubezpieczeniowa, 03.07.2016.

59 Komunikat Klubu Parlamentarnego PiS dotyczący zalecenia Komisji Nadzoru Bankowego of 01.07.2006, as in 'Biała księga kredytów frankowych w Polsce Związek Banków Polskich', Warsaw 2015, pp. 38–40.

60 'UOKiK: Każdy sam powinien decydować o wyborze kredytu', Money.pl, 04.07.2006, as quoted in Komisja Nadzoru Finansowego, 'Przypomnienie publicznej dyskusji o kredytach walutowych', 10.03.2015, p. 4.

61 Report published by Instytut Globalizacji, that concluded an action 'Wolność dla marzeń, wolności dla kredytu' (Freedom for dreams, freedom for credit), August 2006, as referred to in Komisja Nadzoru Finansowego, 'Przypomnienie publicznej dyskusji o kredytach walutowych', 10.03.2015, p. 5.

The 2018 review by NIK proves that, despite the radical evaluation by politicians and economists, the restrictions introduced by the recommendations were neither challenging, nor respected. For example, the 2008 Recommendation S requested that banks present customers with four simulations of the payments in a currency risk loan. These simulations were to include the decrease in the zloty's value in relation to the currency of the loan, in a scale reflecting the difference between the maximum and minimum zloty value in relation to the currency of the loan in the last 12 months without a change to the interest rate, and with an interest rate identical to the interest rate for loans in Polish zloty, but with the amount of the credit increased by 20 per cent. According to NIK, these simulations did not properly reflect the risks related to changes in the value of the foreign currency, in the context of long-term loans, sometimes concluded for 30 years. NIK pointed out that in 2008 there was not a single currency of any OECD state that, over the previous 30 years, had value fluctuations lower than 25 per cent. In fact, for 28 out of 35 countries, the changes were greater than 70 per cent, and for 20 countries greater than 150 per cent. The Polish zloty fell in value against the Swiss franc by more than 400 per cent, but if one considers the entire period of the last 30 years (i.e. the crises of the 1980s and 1990s), it would be more than 1.1 million per cent.[62] The approach of the KNF is very well illustrated by its reaction to the changes proposed in 2018 by NIK in Recommendation T. NIK suggested that the banks should inform consumers about the risks associated with the foreign currency value changes, on the basis of historical data for the period reflecting the length of the proposed loan contract, and not the last 12 months. The KNF rejected this, arguing that it would change the current practice of the banks, which provide data for the last 12 months regardless of the period of the loan under consideration. The KNF also feared that consumers would mistake information about the risk covering the period of the loan for information about interest.[63]

The recommendations were also not effectively applied in practice, as was proven by the results of 104 inspections carried out by the KNF.[64] While the situation improved over time, the inspections revealed irregularities in the implementation of the recommendations in all the banks inspected. However, since the recommendations were not binding, the KNF was only able to issue post-inspection suggestions and – if the irregularities were serious – reminders. According to Article 138, para. 2, of the Banking Law, the inspection recommendations would not apply to contracts that had already been concluded, but only to contracts concluded in the future.

The KNF concentrated on the economic aspects of the market for loans in Swiss francs: the chance of the debtors paying the loans off to ensure the stability

62 NIK, above n. 47, p. 57.
63 Ibid., p. 118.
64 Ibid., pp. 61–65.

of the financial sector. The unfair character of provisions in the loan contracts, as well as the legal risk associated with banks using unfair contract terms over a very long period of time, remained outside the scope of the KNF's interest. According to the KNF's analysis (October 2017), the banking sector was resilient to the depreciation of the value of the currency, the quality (i.e. whether or not the debtor pays their dues on time) of the home loans was stable, the currency risk loans did not generate risks that would jeopardise the stability of the financial sector, and reductions in interest rates introduced by the Swiss Central Bank neutralised, to a large extent, the effects on consumers of the increase in the value of the Swiss franc.[65] A similar evaluation was presented by the National Bank of Poland and the Committee for Financial Stability (*Komitet Stabilności Finansowej*). As of 2015, on the basis of a study, the KNF has introduced additional capital requirements for 14 banks with the largest portfolios of foreign currency loans, to cover the risks associated with loans in Swiss francs and euros.[66] As of 2017, these additional requirements also take into account the legal risks, like the estimated number of open court cases within a one-year period, the number of cases lost by the bank or the reserves for pending cases. The additional capital requirements for 14 banks amounted to 303 million zloty.[67]

UOKiK, the office responsible for developing and implementing consumer policy in Poland, initially did not recognise the scale of the threats to the foreign currency loans market. Between 2005 and 2007, there were no investigations initiated by UOKiK in this area, which – according to NIK – suggests that the market was not being properly monitored.[68] Until 2016, the abstract control of unfair contract terms had to be initiated in the Court of Competition and Consumer Protection in Warsaw. In 2008, UOKiK initiated five such cases, which resulted in nine entries into the Register of Unfair Contract Terms that it holds.[69] The effectiveness of such actions was, however, limited, and did not have the desired preventive effect, because entering a trader into the Register, according to the case law of the Supreme Court, is effective only against the trader against whom proceedings were initiated, and not against any other trader that uses identical clauses. In 2014, personnel changes in the presidium of UOKiK brought about changes in the approach of the Office. In 2015, UOKiK conducted investigations into 27 banks, which led to the issuing of decisions concerning practices infringing collective consumer interests in relation to eight banks. In 2016, UOKiK managed to increase its competences[70] in the area of

---

65 NIK, above n. 47, p. 67.
66 NIK, above n. 47, p. 66.
67 Ibid., p. 67.
68 Ibid., p. 40.
69 Ibid., p. 41.
70 Act of 5 August 2015 on changing the Act on Competition and Consumer Protection and some other acts., Journal of Laws, item 1634.

the control of unfair clauses. Among other things, UOKiK received the ability to impose a penalty of up to 10 per cent of the turnover of the trader in the year preceding the fine, and the ability to issue a relevant opinion in pending cases, in order to present arguments important for the case, sharing with the courts the knowledge and case law from the area of consumer protection. By 30 November 2017, the UOKiK had presented 217 relevant opinions in the currency risk loans cases.[71]

In its 2018 report, NIK accused UOKiK of insufficient activity and prolixity of proceedings. UOKiK explained that its lack of personnel means it cannot carry out more effective actions. This is a rational explanation: in 2017 UOKiK employed 198 lawyers, and in 2018 184. Given that UOKiK is responsible for competition policy, consumer protection and monitoring and ensuring security of products, this truly is an insufficient number for a society of 38 million people. After UOKiK's scope of activity and competences was expanded in 2016, no new positions were created that would allow these competences to be properly carried out without having to limit its activities in other areas.

5.4. LEGISLATIVE INTERVENTIONS

Three legislative Acts have been introduced to deal with the problem of foreign currency loans. First, in 2011, i.e. still before the rapid increase in the value of the Swiss franc, an 'anti-spread' Act[72] was adopted that allowed consumers who had concluded loan contracts indexed or denominated in a foreign currency to pay the loan off directly in that currency. Consumers became independent from the exchange rates set by banks, and consequently from the unfair contract terms that dealt with the spread charged by the banks.

Next, in 2015,[73] came an Act on support for debtors in a difficult financial situation who had incurred home loans. It established a Debtor Support Fund consisting of 600 million zloty contributed by banks. The fund was supposed to help people in an extremely difficult financial situation who were obliged to pay off their home loan in zloty or in a foreign currency. The support offered in the Act included an interest-free loan for up to 18 months, and up to 1,500 zloty per month. The impact of the fund turned out to be illusory as, according to the available data, only 833 people managed to successfully apply for the financial support. There were two factors that contributed to this. Firstly, the

71 NIK, above n. 47, pp. 85–86.

72 Act on Amending the Banking Law and Certain Other Acts of 29 July 2011, Journal of Laws 2011, No. 165, item 984.

73 Act on Support for Debtors in a Difficult Financial Situation, who Incurred Home Loan of 9 October 2015, Journal of Laws 2015, item 1925.

criteria that had to be met by the debtor to make use of the fund were extremely demanding. Secondly, the banks were not interested in the effective use of the fund (applications were to be submitted to the banks by the end of 2018, and any unused funds were to be returned to the banks).

The Act of 2015 was changed by an Act proposed by the President (who in his first electoral campaign promised to help people who concluded loans in Swiss francs). The new Act of 2019[74] extends the operation of the Debtor Support Fund, raises the income threshold permitting access to the fund, increases the monthly support to 2,000 zloty, and extends the support period as well as the pay-off period of the loan provided from the fund. During the parliamentary work on the Act, at the request of the representatives of the governing party, provisions on establishing a Conversion Fund were removed from the proposal.[75] The Conversion Fund, which was also based on the banks' contributions, was supposed to be used to convert foreign currency loans to loans in Polish zloty. Not only were the banks against the Conversion Fund (they estimated it would cost 3 billion zloty), but the embassies of Germany, Austria, Spain and Portugal (banks from these countries have their daughter companies in Poland, with a large portfolio of foreign currency loans) also warned that such a fund may infringe the protection of investment agreements.[76]

Lastly, 12 years after the problem arose, in 2017, an Act on mortgage loans[77] was adopted that practically eliminated the possibility of concluding a foreign currency loan. A mortgage loan can currently be concluded or indexed only in the currency in which the consumer receives most of his/her income or owns most of his/her financial means or other assets.

5.5. CONSUMER SUPPORT SYSTEM

While the Polish legal system offers two forms of direct support to consumers, they both lack the effectiveness that the EU expects. Consumer debtors can turn to the Financial Ombudsman (an office established in 2015, as a successor to the Ombudsman of the Insured) or municipal and district consumer ombudsmen (the

---

74 Act Amending the Act on Support for Debtors in a Difficult Financial Situation, who Incurred Home Loan of 4 July 2019, Journal of Laws 2019, item 1358.

75 'Dodatkowe Sprawozdanie Komisji Finansów Publicznych o przedstawionym przez Prezydenta Rzeczypospolitej Polskiej projekcie ustawy o zmianie ustawy o wsparciu kredytobiorców znajdujących się w trudnej sytuacji finansowej, którzy zaciągnęli kredyt mieszkaniowy oraz ustawy o podatku dochodowym od osób prawnych (druk nr 1863)', Druk nr 3247-A, https://www.sejm.gov.pl/Sejm8.nsf/druk.xsp?nr=3247-A.

76 https://forsal.pl/artykuly/1398759,niemcy-austria-hiszpania-i-portugalia-interweniuja-ws-ustawy-frankowej-news-dgp.html.

77 Act on Mortgage Loans and the Supervision of Agents of 23 March 2017, Journal of Laws 2017, item 819.

ombudsmen network consists of 371 individuals).[78] The Financial Ombudsman is responsible for informing consumers and helping them to claim their rights. However, the Financial Ombudsman does not have any discretionary powers over banks, which has a strong impact on the attitude of the banks towards the Ombudsman's actions, translating into them being of only limited effective. The Financial Ombudsman can address the Supreme Court with a motion to adopt a resolution, and it has successfully used this option, asking the Court about which moment in time is relevant for establishing the unfairness of a contract term, which has caused a lot of problems in the practice of Polish courts.[79] The Financial Ombudsman took a clear stand not only in relation to the problem of consumer loans in Swiss franks,[80] but also to the problems that consumers experience on the financial market in general. In particular, the Financial Ombudsman decided to sue one of the banks, accusing it of using unfair commercial practices, because the bank addressed the consumers demanding remuneration for the use of the bank's capital after the loan contracts have been annulled by courts.[81] Moreover, the Ombudsman initiated a high-profile misselling case against GetBack S.A.[82] In 2019 and 2020, the Financial Ombudsman became probably the most active administrative body in the area, taking over the role of UOKiK. In September 2020, the government declared its intentions to liquidate the position of the Ombudsman and merge its office with the UOKiK's,[83] which led to protests from various bodies supporting consumers.[84]

Legal advice can also be given by the municipal and district consumer ombudsmen. The consumer ombudsmen are entitled to contact banks and initiate individual and group actions in court. However, the inadequate number and fluctuations of staff, as well as the insufficient financial support received by ombudsmen, renders their actions rather ineffective. The Warsaw ombudswoman, who is particularly active, has initiated three individual and

---

78 UOKiK, 'Działania powiatowych i miejskich rzeczników konsumentów w roku 2017', Warsaw 2019, p. 11.

79 The content of the motion: https://rf.gov.pl/pdf/Wniosek_SN_klauzule_abuzwyne.pdf; it led the Supreme Court to adopt Resolution III CZP 29/17, available at http://www.sn.pl/sites/orzecznictwo/orzeczenia3/iii%20czp%2029-17.pdf.

80 Between 2016 and 2019, the Financial Ombudsman issued 1664 learned opinions (*istotne poglądy*) in consumer court cases relating to the CHF credit contracts (755 of which in 2019), https://archiwum.rf.gov.pl/sprawy-biezace/Coraz_wiecej_istotnych_pogladow_w_sporach_frankowiczow_z_bankami_23150, in 2020 it published a very comprehensive legal analysis relating to the legal situation in the CHF consumer credits area that clearly and strongly supported position of consumers, anchoring consumer protection in the EU law, https://rf.gov.pl/2020/09/29/kredyty-frankowe-2020/.

81 https://rf.gov.pl/2020/04/30/3924/.

82 https://rf.gov.pl/2020/08/25/pierwszy-pozew-rzecznika-finansowego-w-sprawie-getback/.

83 https://www.prawo.pl/prawo/likwidacja-rzecznika-finansowego-uderzy-w-kosnumentow,502886.html.

84 https://www.prawo.pl/prawo/likwidacja-rzecznika-finansowego-uderzy-w-kosnumentow,502886.html, https://www.rpo.gov.pl/sites/default/files/Wystąpienie%20do%20premiera%20ws.%20likwidacji%20Rzecznika%20Finansowego%2C%2030.09.2020.pdf.

three group proceedings.[85] In the 2018 report,[86] NIK accused her of delays in the cases in which she was involved. The ombudswoman explained the delays by the inadequate number and rotation of her staff. In response, NIK suggested that introducing binding internal deadlines would diminish the delays for the cases. In Krakow, on the other hand, the ombudsman has tried to avoid filing claims for consumers, because the appeal courts in Krakow in other cases have several times charged the costs of the case to the ombudsman when dismissing the action. These costs were borne by the Krakow municipality, which was a very serious burden for the municipality (the officially-allotted budgetary means of the municipality for such instances would have been insufficient to cover even one case).

In addition, in September 2019 the Polish Commissioner for Human Rights established an expert group called the 'Consumer Forum' with a view to supporting consumers and disseminating EU consumer law concepts.[87] It gathered academics, consumers' and debtors' associations, professional representatives of consumers and judges. Until autumn 2020, the Ombudsman, who holds the same procedural powers as a prosecutor as a result of the Forum's activities joined several high-profile national cases,[88] as well as preliminary referrals to the CJEU.[89] Moreover, the Forum elaborated and disseminated among courts commentaries of a number of CJEU judgments crucial from the perspective of the Polish market that not only clarify the solution explained by the CJEU itself, but also the Court's methodology and axiology underpinning EU consumer policy.[90] Since the term of the Ombudsman ends on 9 September 2020, it should be expected that the Forum's activities will be halted. Plans are already in place, however, to continue the work on a municipal level.

5.6. STRATEGIES OF THE MARKET PLAYERS

In response to the inadequate actions of public administration, the debtors began to organise themselves, trying to exert pressure on the public bodies, courts and banks. The debtors established several associations, created groups on social media, entered into cooperation with lawyers that represent them,

---

85 On 15 July 2020, she has had a spectacular success in group proceedings involving 1,247 consumers, when a bank, after proceedings that lasted 10 years withdrew its appeal, see section 5.11 for more information.

86 NIK, above n. 47, pp. 118–119.

87 https://www.rpo.gov.pl/pl/content/forum-konsumenckie-przy-rpo.

88 https://www.rpo.gov.pl/pl/content/rpo-przestapil-do-sprawy-panstwa-dziubakow-kredyt-tzw-frankowy, https://www.rpo.gov.pl/pl/content/pozew-zbiorowy-frankowiczow-rpo-przystapil-do-sprawy-arbuzowej.

89 In cases: C-19/20, *Bank BPH*, C-212/20 *A. S.A.*, and C-198/20, *X Bank*.

90 See for example: https://www.rpo.gov.pl/pl/content/wyjasnienia-na-tle-orzeczenia-tsue-c-41918-c-48318-profi-credit-ii.

began collecting and analysing court cases (which is very important, considering that the court statistics insufficiently identify cases). They became engaged in the public discourse, by appealing to the public administration bodies, commenting on the proposed legislation, putting forward their own proposals, organising protests in front of courts, and calling on the courts to observe Directive 93/13/EEC. One of the organisations addressed the European Commission, accusing Poland of violating Directive 93/13/EEC.[91]

The strategy adopted by the banks clearly follows from the data on dispute resolution held by the Financial Ombudsman. The banks were trying to avoid settling cases with consumers and insisted on confrontations in court. Between 1 January 2017 and 30 September 2017, there were 728 out-of-court proceedings regarding foreign currency, of which only six reached amicable resolution.[92] In the opinion of the Financial Ombudsman, such cases are not fit for successful dispute resolution, because of (among other things) the polarised positions of the parties. The banks are not willing to compromise, since continuing the dispute in court is much more burdensome for consumers than for the banks. It is thus not surprising that the attempts by the Ombudsman or UOKiK to solve the problem amicably failed. At the same time, in 2015 the banks offered so-called 'six-pack' assistance to their clients, taking into consideration the negative LIBOR rate, the decrease in the spread value, and the option to increase in the period to pay off the loan or to temporarily suspend the payments.[93]

The line of argumentation of the banks refers to the danger that will be posed to the stability of the Polish banking sector should the demands of consumers be met. The banks have estimated that transforming a Swiss francs loan into a loan in Polish zloty, with the interest rate due for a loan in Swiss francs would cost the sector 60 billion zloty. As a part of their campaign they, for example, informed Prime Minister Morawiecki (who in the past, as a CEO of a bank, was initially openly against banks offering loans in a foreign currency) that it was necessary for Poland to present additional remarks in the *Dziubak* case, claiming that if the judgment followed the opinion of the Advocate General, the value of foreign currency loans could, in the long term, drop by more than 50 per cent of their current estimated value. The banks also stress that the interest rate is currently negative, so in many cases the interest on such loans would be close to zero. This would, in the opinion of the ZBP, lead to inequality between the debtors who obtained loans in Swiss francs and in zloty. This argument (the inequality of treatment of CHF and PLN debtors) was also raised in one of the decisions of the Polish Supreme Court.[94]

---

91 https://obserwatorpolityczny.pl/czy-polska-zaplaci-za-wyroki-sadow-sprzeczne-z-postanowieniami-tsue/.

92 NIK, above n. 47, pp. 93–94.

93 https://zbp.pl/public/repozytorium/archiwum/Prezentacja_ZBP_konferencja_prasowa.pdf.

94 Decision of the Supreme Court of 18 September 2019 (V CSK 152/19).

5.7. CASE LAW STATISTICS

At certain moment it became clear (also in the eyes of the politicians) that pursuing their rights in court is the only viable option for the debtors. In February 2017, Jarosław Kaczyński (officially the chairman of the governing party, but *de facto* the Polish head of state) encouraged the debtors to bring their cases to court,[95] explaining that the government could not initiate actions that would endanger the banking system. The debtors seem to be following his advice. The 14 banks with the largest portfolio of foreign currency loans have approximately 6,900 contracts engaged in cases pending before the courts. More than 80 per cent (5,653) of these contracts were concluded by two banks. In 2018, according to the statistics of the Ministry of Justice, 7,212 claims were initiated in court, and the continued increase of the number of CHF credit cases is clear and undisputable.[96] The debtors started to win more and more often: of the 400 individual cases against seven banks that had ended (this number includes the judgments that are still lacking the force of law) as of the end of April 2017,[97] there were 266 cases (66.5 per cent) in which the courts ruled in line with the debtors' claims in full or partly. Advocate Czabański (one of the representatives of the debtors) concluded, on the basis of 300 cases, that while in 2016 only 25.93 per cent of cases ended in the debtors' favour, in 2019 such judgments amounted to 87.50 per cent.[98]

5.8. PROBLEMS WITH ESTABLISHING A COMMON APPROACH IN CASE LAW

So far, despite the hundreds of judgments that have been passed, no clear uniformity of solutions has been achieved in the case law. The cases are typically based on unfair contract terms that enable banks to calculate the payments on the basis of exchange rate tables that were created by the banks, and over which consumers had no influence, to change the interest rate on the basis of unclear modification clauses, or to introduce extra payments to insure the debtor's low-value deposit. EU rules that apply to the unfairness control are grounded on different principles from Polish law, which is very liberal in its approach.

---

95 https://www.polskieradio.pl/13/53/Artykul/1726088,Sygnaly-Dnia-10-lutego-2017-roku-rozmowa-z-Jaroslawem-Kaczynskim.

96 There are reports of a 300% increase in the number of cases in the courts in Warsaw, comparing the periods between January and April in 2019 and in 2020 respectively, and of 401% when comparing April 2019 and April 2020, see https://serwisy.gazetaprawna.pl/finanse-osobiste/artykuly/1484971,sad-frankowicze-pandemia-koronawirusa-wzrost-liczby-spraw.html.

97 NIK, above n. 47, p. 81.

98 https://pomocfrankowiczom.pl/?p=1206.

To apply EU law properly, the courts must demonstrate European sensitivity when approaching consumer issues, in accordance with the European axiology. The system of protection introduced by Directive 93/13/EEC is based on the idea that the consumer is in a weak position in relation to the seller or supplier, in terms of bargaining power at negotiations and level of knowledge.[99] Only by the courts adopting such an approach can the objective of Directive 93/13/EEC be assured, i.e. restoring the balance between the position of the consumer and of the trader. In the long term, Directive 93/13/EEC aims to prevent the continued use of unfair terms in contracts with consumers though the dissuasive effect on sellers or suppliers 'of the straightforward non-application of those unfair terms'.[100] Hence, the sanctions applied by the courts not only have to be effective and proportional, but must also have a dissuasive character, preventing the use of the unfair contract terms in the future.

Adjudication that allows these aims to be met is challenging for the Polish courts, as it departs from their traditional libertarian approach. Polish law would normally strive to restore the balance between the parties, but with a very strong emphasis placed on the principle of freedom of contract, based on the formally understood equality of parties. The structural weakness of consumers, as well as the dissuasive effect of the European sanction, is in clear contradiction with such an approach. For the Polish judges, applying EU law correctly means breaking away from a position towards market actors that was established as an after-effect of the socialist era in Poland.[101]

5.9. LEGAL AID TOOLS IN PROCEEDINGS

Both banks and consumers have at their disposal legal tools that aim to facilitate the assertion of claims during court proceedings. For consumers, this is above all the group actions that allow consumers to pursue their claims together with other consumers. They are rather popular among debtors: as of November 2017 there were eight group proceedings against four banks, with regard to 8,853 credit contracts.[102] Representatives of the debtors claim that for some debtors this is the only way they considered pursuing their claims, due to the high costs of individual proceedings. Group proceedings, however, take far longer than individual proceedings. The average length of civil proceedings, according

99 Case C-70/17, *Abanca Corporación Bancaria*, ECLI:EU:C:2019:25, para. 49.

100 Case C-618/10, *Banco Español de Crédito*, ECLI:EU:C:2012:349, para. 69.

101 On that see: M. Safjan and A. Wiewiórowska-Domagalska, 'Political Foundations of European Private Law: Rethinking the East–West Division Lines' in R. Brownsword, H.-W. Micklitz, L. Niglia and S. Weatherill (eds.), *The Foundations of European Private Law*, Hart Publishing, Oxford 2011, A. Wiewiórowska-Domagalska and M. Grochowski, *Consumer Law in Poland or There and Back Again*, forthcoming 2021.

102 NIK, above n. 47, p. 24.

to data from the Ministry of Justice, was approximately eight and a half months, and the group action in which the Warsaw consumer ombudswoman represented debtors lasted 40 months, counted from the moment of filing the claim in the court. The first instance proceedings alone lasted 30 months, of which the formal phase of the proceedings took 23 months.[103] Not only are the judges not prepared to manage group proceedings, but also for a very long time none of the group proceedings initiated since 2009 (when this option was introduced) have been particularly successful. This discouraged potential group representatives, primarily law firms, from organising group actions. The length of the proceedings generates high costs and causes problems with evidence. In July 2020, however, consumers won one of the most publicised group proceedings against bank (cassation judgment of 14 May 2015 (II CSK 768/14), see section 5.11 for details). The bank withdrew its appeal after the Human Rights Commissioner has joined the case, leaving the consumers with the initial judgment, in which the court adjudicated according to the consumers' demands. Another, even larger case involving a group of 5,000 consumers is pending at the moment in Warsaw. If this is also resolved in accordance with the consumers' wishes, the group proceedings may actually become a more effective enforcement tool, despite the problems associated with this form of proceedings.

The banks, on the other hand, were for a long time able to use (or are sometimes still using) a privileged position, which they enjoy as institutions of the public trust (i.e. people tend to trust them). Until November 2015, the banks had the ability to issue bank enforcement titles on the basis of the banking books. Such enforcement titles enabled the banks to enforce their dues without the need to go through court proceedings and without a court judgment constituting in an enforcement title. Banks could proceed with the debt collection after the court granted an executory title, which lasted up to three days. When repealing this option in 2015, the Constitutional Tribunal[104] stressed that it was an exceptional privilege granted only to banks that a document issued by a private economic subject could replace a judgment. In other words, a bank could be the judge in its own case. For a long time the banks were massively exploiting the possibility introduced in 2000 (Article 485(3) Polish Code of Civil Proceedings) of receiving a payment order in specialised proceedings aimed at receiving such an order, on the basis of a signed excerpt from the banking books and proof of having delivered a written call for payment to the debtor. The court would issue the order in a closed session (i.e. without the participation of the debtor), on confirmation that there are grounds for issuing it, and after one quarter of the court fee has been paid. Once the order was issued, it constituted a security warrant enforceable without the need for the court to grant an executory title. A payment order against which pleas have not been effectively made had the effect of a final judgment.

[103] Ibid., p. 100.
[104] Judgment of the Constitutional Tribunal of 14 April 2015, P45/12.

The possibility of obtaining the payment order in this way was eliminated when the changes made to Article 485(3) of the Polish Code of Civil Proceedings to the Code of Civil Proceedings entered into force in 2019.

5.10. COURTS OF THE FIRST AND THE SECOND INSTANCE

In 2018, NIK distinguished four types of judgments in the currency risk loans cases.[105] First, the courts have claimed that the entire contract collapses as result of finding the contract term unfair. Most often, such terms dealt with establishing valuation rates for the payments, without references to any objective data. The courts would then say that it is impossible to perform such a contract after declaring the term unfair, and at the same time reject the idea of transforming the contract into a loan in Polish zloty, but with interest calculated according to the LIBOR for the Swiss franc (plus the margin of the bank), i.e. the contract would have to be annulled (this is the solution suggested by the Court of Justice of the European Union in the *Dziubak* case).

Second, courts have declared that, while the valuation clause is not binding, the parties are bound by the contract in its remainder, which includes interest calculated according to the LIBOR (plus the margin of the bank). The loan contract was still against remuneration (as required by Article 69 of the Bank Law), despite the fact that most probably the bank would not have concluded a loan in Polish zloty with interest calculated based on the LIBOR. The debtor, as a result, is placed in a more favourable position than normally offered on the market, which follows from the collapse of the unfair contract term that the bank decided to include in the contract (this was also the option favoured by the AG in the *Dziubak* case).

Third, some courts decided that there is no foundation for establishing that the unfairness of specific contract provisions should lead to the removal of the entire indexation mechanism from the contract, which would result in the contract being transformed into one for a loan in Polish zloty, with interest as in a foreign currency loan. Since the common intention of the parties was to conclude a contract denominated or indexed in a foreign currency, such a transformation would constitute too far-reaching an intervention into the content of the contract. The payments of the debtor should still be valued as in the parties' agreement, i.e. according to the Swiss franc value. On the basis of Article $385^1(2)$ of the Polish Civil Code, unfair contract terms do not bind the parties, unlike the rest of the contract, which remains binding. Eliminating the unfair contract term that deals with the valuation mechanism of the consumer's performance does not eliminate the provision that introduces the valuation as

---

105 NIK, above n. 47, pp. 83–85.

such into the contract. Referring to the case law of the Supreme Court, which on the basis of Article 56 of the Polish Civil Code[106] allowed such solution,[107] the courts would change the valuation rules included in the contract into a valuation based on the average value of the National Bank of Poland, or the market value, arguing that since the intention of the parties was to conclude a contract denominated or indexed in a foreign currency, transforming the loan contract into one in Polish zloty would be a too far reaching interference.

Fourth, in some cases the courts dismissed the claim, arguing that the debtor was not a consumer (for example, because a flat was bought for rental purposes), did not prove that s/he should bear lower credit costs as a result of the collapse of the clauses, or decided (usually incorrectly) that the valuation clauses in the contract are clear and so not unfair. The courts argued that the reference to the exchange rate table of the bank, used to establish the amount of the loan (and subsequently the value of the payments) did not give the bank the unacceptable freedom to establish obligations of consumers. The courts in such judgments tended to ignore the fact that there were no clear rules on establishing the exchange rate in the exchange rate tables of the banks.

The judgment in the *Dziubak* case of 2019 had a very strong impact on the position of consumers and courts alike. Before the judgment, the most frequent demand of consumers was to maintain the loan contract, which after the elimination of the unfair term would transform into a loan in Polish zloty, with the LIBOR-based interest rate (the first type judgment discussed above). As of the *Dziubak* case, most of the consumers demand annulment of the contract, and most often the courts agree to that solution (the second type of judgment). Moreover, the *Dziubak* case made it clear that from the perspective of EU law supplementing the contract (in order to maintain it as such, or to maintain its content unchanged as far as possible), by using national provisions other than those defined by the CJEU is clearly inacceptable. However, the *Dziubak* judgment solved only some of the issues that appear in Polish legal practice, relating to the first phase of the process of assessing the unfairness of the term. At the moment, the most important problem in the practice is the question of further claims that banks claim to have against consumers after the annulment of the contract, for the use of the bank's capital.[108] This is the issue that is addressed simultaneously to both, the Court of Justice of the European Union and the Polish Supreme Court.[109] A related issue is what is the scope of the information duty of the court, which adjudicates in a case, where the contract is annulled (i.e. if remuneration

---

106 Article 56 of the Polish Civil Code reads: 'An act in law will have not only the effects expressed in it, but also those that follow from statutory law, the principles of community life, and the established customs.'

107 Judgment of 27 February 2019, II CSK 19/18.

108 On that see: A. Wiewiórowska-Domagalska, *Unfair contract terms in CHF mortgage loans, Case C-260/18 Dziubak – where do we go from here?*, EuCML 5/2020, forthcoming.

109 C-19/20 *Bank BPH*; Decision of 22 January 2020 III CZP 11/20.

claims pursued in separate proceedings would be allowed, how would it be possible for the court to inform the consumer about the consequences of the contract annulment?). At the same time, some Polish courts, clearly inspired by the banks, formulate preliminary referrals to the Court of Justice, which (from the perspective of the Polish market practice) clearly aim at limiting the scope of unfairness control of the terms falling under Article 4(2) Directive 93/13/EEC by restricting and partitioning the transparency control,[110] or by suggesting, that the consumer does not in fact deserve protection, due to the fact that she or he did not pay sufficient attention to the content of the contract at the time of the contract conclusion.[111]

5.11. IMPACT OF THE SUPREME COURT

One factor that had a very significant impact on the currency loan market, the approach of banks and the judgments of the lower-instance courts was the unstable line of judgments by the Supreme Court. Unfortunately, for a rather long time the Supreme Court case law handicapped the position of debtors, as the Court decided in clear contradiction to the CJEU's case law, or rejected the possibility that the CJEU offered in terms of increasing the efficiency of EU law in Poland.

As stressed by Advocate General Pitruzzella[112] when interpreting Directive 93/13/EEC, the CJEU takes a position that if national courts find that contract terms are unfair, they should draw all the consequences that follow under national law so that those terms do not produce effects with regard to the consumer, unless the consumer objects to the removal of those terms.[113] This radical approach stems from the assumption taken by EU law that the consequences that traders bear for using unfair contract terms must have a dissuasive character. Therefore, the court is not entitled to intervene as regards the content of the term that it finds to be unfair. Article 6(1) of Directive 93/13/EEC must be interpreted as precluding national legislation allowing a national court to modify the contract by revising the content of that term.[114] It is clear that allowing the courts such

---

110 Referrals C-19/20, *Bank BPH*, C-19/20 *Bank BPH*, see also: A. Wiewiórowska-Domagalska, *How Does the Unfair Contract Terms Directive Penetrate National Legal Systems? A Case Study Based on Mortgage-Secured Loans for Housing Purposes, Indexed or Denominated in CHF in Poland.*, Osteuropa-Recht, 1/2020, pp. 54–74.

111 C-212/20 *A. S.A.*, C-198/20, *X Bank*.

112 *Dziubak*, above n. 40, para. 29.

113 *Abanca Corporación Bancaria*, above n. 86, para. 52; *Banco Español de Crédito*, above n. 87, paras. 63 and 65; Case C-243/08, *Pannon GSM*, ECLI:EU:C:2009:350, para. 35. See, more generally, Case C-40/08, *Asturcom Telecomunicaciones*, ECLI:EU:C:2009:615, para. 58; Case C-453/10, *Pereničová and Perenič*, ECLI:EU:C:2012:144, para. 30; and Case C-76/10, *Pohotovosť*, ECLI:EU:C:2010:685, para. 62.

114 *Abanca Corporación Bancaria*, above n. 86, para. 53; *Banco Español de Crédito*, above n. 87, para. 73; Case C-26/13, *Kásler and Káslerné Rábai*, ECLI:EU:C:2014:282, para. 77.

an intervention would compromise the long-term objective of the Directive, i.e. deterring sellers or suppliers from using unfair terms.[115] Sellers or suppliers could be tempted to use those terms in the knowledge that, even if they were found to be invalid, the contract could nevertheless be modified, to the extent necessary, by the national court. The CJEU did develop an exception, however. In the *Kásler* case,[116] it permitted the unfair contract term to be substituted by a supplementary provision of national law if, under the national law, the non-application of the term declared unfair entails the annulment of the contract, and such annulment exposes the consumer to particularly unfavourable consequences.[117]

The Polish Supreme Court has experienced serious problems with internalising these EU principles and introducing them into the Polish legal system. The case that has had probably the greatest impact on the functioning of the CJEU's jurisprudence in Poland, as it strongly influenced the position of banks (i.e. strengthened their resistance towards resolving disputes with consumers amicably), was the judgment of 14 May 2015 (II CSK 768/14) in group proceedings that involved 1,247 debtors represented by the Warsaw ombudsman. In this case, the Supreme Court departed from the CJEU's jurisprudence on two important points. First, with regard to the consequences of deleting the unfair term from the contract, the Supreme Court stated that it might not result in changing the content of the contract (in this case, the Court refused to change the variable interest rate into a fixed interest rate). This was in a stark contradiction to the judgment in *Banco Español*, where the CJEU recognised that the only change allowed in the content of the contract in the process of fairness control is a change that results from deleting the unfair contract term.[118] Second, the Supreme Court decided that to eliminate the unfair character of the contract term, the term should be 'split like a watermelon'.[119] Hence, the Supreme Court divided the term into a parametric (economic) part and a competence (decision-making) part, which it declared to be unfair. While doing so, the Supreme Court did not argue that the parametric part was not abusive, but stressed that declaring the entire clause unfair would result in the impossibility of deciding whether the debtors were liable towards the bank, and what the exact amount of the debt is. This reasoning also contradicts the *Banco Español* judgment, in which the CJEU clearly articulated[120] that Article 6(1) of Directive 93/13/EEC cannot be understood as allowing the national court to

---

115 *Abanca Corporación Bancaria*, above n. 86, para. 54; *Banco Español de Crédito*, above n. 87, paras. 69 and 70; *Pohotovosť*, above n. 98, para. 41 and the case law cited there.

116 *Kásler and Káslerné Rábai*, above n. 99.

117 Ibid., para. 83.

118 *Banco Español de Crédito*, above n. 87, para. 64.

119 A comparison used in the oral presentation of the judgment.

120 *Banco Español de Crédito*, above n. 87, para. 71.

revise the content of an unfair contract term, rather than merely setting aside its application to the consumer.

The II CSK 768/14 judgment never refers explicitly to the *Banco Español* case, but it describes the unfairness control mechanism introduced therein as an 'extensive interpretation of the legal consequences of finding the clause unfair, which cannot be justified even considering that its aim is remarkably pro-consumer'. The Supreme Court stressed that the foundation of the parametric part of the clause is 'the element of economic profitability of offering mortgage loans of this type with a variable interest rate', so the bank may refer to the costs of offering the credit, even though there is no mention of this element in the clause itself. The case lasted a further five years after the cassation judgment (almost ten years in total). It ended only when, on 15 July 2020, the bank withdrew its appeal against the first instance judgment. It seems that the decision of the bank was influenced by the changed demand of the consumers, who decided to request the annulment of the contract. The demand of consumers was supported by the Commissioner for Human Rights, which joined the case at the request of the consumers, and who claimed that the court should respect only these parts of the cassation judgment, which are in accordance with EU law, and set aside those which contradict it. What followed, since the Supreme Court established that the loan contract cannot exist after eliminating the unfair contract term, is that the court adjudicating after the cassation should annul it.[121]

Case II CSK 19/18 of 27 February 2019 also had a disadvantageous effect. In this judgment the Supreme Court accepted the possibility of replacing the unfair contract term that established a valuation mechanism in a loan denominated in Swiss francs with the average rate of the National Bank of Poland on the day of the claim maturity, despite the fact that, as follows from the *Kásler* case, the Court of Justice allows the replacement of the unfair term only with national law of a supplementary character, and only in exceptional circumstances, i.e. when the contract cannot continue to exist after the unfair contract term has been set aside.[122] According to the CJEU, the continuing existence of the contract must have penalising consequences for the trader, because otherwise the trader might not be dissuaded from inserting such terms into contracts.[123]

While the Supreme Court took note of the *Kásler* case, it allowed the lacuna in the contract that appears after deleting the unfair contract term to also be filled in other circumstances. The Supreme Court referred to its previous judgment of 14 July 2017 (II CSK 803/16).[124] This case concerned a loan concluded in 2001 (i.e. before Poland joined the EU), but the Supreme Court decided to apply

121 The Polish version of the Commissioner's position is available at https://www.rpo.gov.pl/sites/default/files/Pismo%20procesowe%20RPO%2C%2030.06.2020.pdf.

122 *Kásler and Káslerné Rábai*, above n. 99, para. 85.

123 Ibid., para. 84.

124 OSNC 2018, Nos. 7–8, item 79.

EU law. Yet, in doing so, it allowed the lacuna left after deleting the unfair contract term to be filled by (a) reconstructing the common intention of the parties on the basis of the remainder of the contract, or (b) applying *per analogiam* provisions of law that would not normally apply to the contract. Importantly, the Court also allowed such adaptations when the contract could continue to exist without the unfair contract term. In case II CSK 19/18, the Supreme Court suggested the application of a modified *rebus sic stantibus* principle as the practical inability of the borrower to assess the economic consequences of a loan indexed/denominated in a foreign currency could be qualified as a fundamental change of circumstances. In the eyes of the Supreme Court, the problem that remains in such a situation is establishing what exchange rate should be applied to calculate the total amount of the consumer's debt. Here the Supreme Court pointed out Article 358(2) of the Civil Code, according to which the value of foreign currency is determined according to the average exchange rate announced by the National Bank of Poland for the day of the claim maturity, unless the law, court order or act in law stipulates otherwise. Even though this provision was not in force at the time when the loan contract was concluded, according to the Supreme Court it might be one of the guidelines to resolve the problem. The Supreme Court also referred to another judgment of 1 March 2017 (IV CSK 285/16, not published), in which it opted against removing the indexing mechanism from the contract, even though it was unfair, because it would lead to changing the 'legal nature' of the contract (like in the II CSK 768/14 judgment), and stressed that the indexing mechanism used in the contract was in fact a variation of the valuation clause dealt with in Article 358^1 of the Civil Code (known as the 'small' *rebus sic stantibus* clause), and when establishing the amount or the way of carrying out the performance, the court must take into consideration the interests of the parties and the principles of social coexistence.

This line of reasoning contradicts the judgment in *Asbeek Brusse*,[125] in which the CJEU established a conflict of law rule regarding the relation between Directive 93/13/EEC and national general rules of contract law. According to this judgment,[126] Article 6(1) of Directive 93/13/EEC does not allow the national court, where it has established that a penalty clause is unfair, merely, as is authorised by national law, to reduce the amount of the penalty imposed on the consumer by that clause, but requires it to exclude the application of that clause in its entirety with regard to the consumer. The action suggested by the Polish Supreme Court, which would lead to the adjustment of the unfair clause, on the basis of a national law provision, instead of simply deleting it from the contract, stands in glaring contradiction to the solutions introduced in the CJEU's jurisprudence.

---

125 Case C-488/11, *Asbeek Brusse*, ECLI:EU:C:2013:341.

126 Ibid., para. 60.

The Supreme Court has also blocked attempts by UOKiK to undertake more effective actions against banks, with a view to eliminating unfair contract terms from the market. The Supreme Court has repeatedly rejected UOKiK's cassation notions,[127] which – if approved – would allow the judgment in *Partner*[128] to be applied in Poland. Until 2015, following the abstract control of unfair contract terms (at the time conducted by the Regional Court of Warsaw, the Competition and Consumer Protection Court), the terms were entered into the Register of Unfair Contract Terms held by UOKiK. On the basis of Article 24 of the Act on Competition and Consumer Protection, UOKiK tried to impose fines on traders who were using clauses identical to the terms entered into the Register because this is classified as a practice that violates the collective interests of consumers. The fines, unlike the potential consequences of entering the terms into the Register, were rather severe, as they could amount up to 10 per cent of the trader's turnover in the year preceding the fine. Questions concerning the effect on traders of using a clause identical to one entered into the Register were disputed several times by the Polish Supreme Court, and the subsequent judgments were not coherent. While the Supreme Court agreed that the entry into the Register should be effective against all consumers who concluded a contract with a given trader (no matter whether or not they participated in the proceedings), depending on the judgment the Court either denied or accepted that the entry also has effect against other traders that use identical terms (or terms that have an identical effect to those entered into the Register) but did not participate in the proceedings that led to the entry. Finally, in 2015 the Supreme Court issued resolution III CZP 17/15 of 20 November,[129] in which it stated that entry into the Register is only effective against the trader who was a party to the proceedings.

When referring to the *Partner* case in the decision of 7 March 2017 (III SK 13/15), the Supreme Court stated that EU law does not preclude the possibility of accepting the extended effectiveness of the entry into the Register, but at the same time it does not require that Member States adopt this approach. The Court considered that, since the practice of a trader that violates the collective interests of consumers under Article 24 of the Competition and Consumer Protection Act must be unlawful, and Article 24 is not a self-standing source of the unlawfulness, the source of the unlawfulness of the trader's practice must be established on the basis of another act. Using a term identical to one entered into the Register is not unlawful, in the sense that it does not violate Article 479[43]

[127] Resolution of the Supreme Court of 7 March 2017, III SK 13/15; resolution of the Supreme Court of 11 January 2019, I NSK 29/18.

[128] Case C-119/15, *Partner*, ECLI:EU:C:2016:987.

[129] OSNC 2016/4/40.

of the Civil Procedure Code, which constitutes the basis of entering the term into the Register. According to the Supreme Court, considering that the *Partner* case does not make it mandatory to introduce the extended effectiveness of the entry, when deciding a case based on Article 24 of the Competition and Consumer Protection Act the national court is not obliged to apply a pro-European interpretation to ensure compliance with EU law, so the unlawfulness of the trader's behaviour could be recognised solely on the basis of Article 24. Hence the Polish Supreme Court chose a solution that is less effective (and with no dissuasive effect) but which it has developed itself. As a result, UOKiK lost an instrument that could effectively encourage the banks to modify their approach towards consumers. What is particularly paradoxical is that the *Partner* case was the result of a preliminary referral of a Polish court, and the procedural safeguards of traders' rights could easily be met in the Polish legal system.

Recently, the approach of the Supreme Court seems to be evolving in a direction more in line with the CJEU's approach. Due to discrepancies in the case law of the lower-instance courts, on 20 June 2018 the Supreme Court issued a seven-judge resolution (III CZP 29/17), in which it explained that an evaluation of whether a term is unfair is to be made as of the moment of concluding the contract, so the subsequent performance of the contract cannot remove the initial unfairness of the term. The Court is also changing its attitude when it comes to the consequences of setting a term aside. In judgment II CSK 632/17 of 24 October 2018, the Supreme Court rejected the possibility of supplementing a contract in order to protect the interests of the trader. The Court referred to the European nature of the provisions applied in the case, and the need to implement them as sanctions. It stressed that the sanctions are introduced with a view to protecting consumer interests, and not those of traders who are violating the law, and should be interpreted accordingly. In the next step, cases III CSK 159/17 of 4 April 2019 and I CSK 242/18 of 9 May 2019 emphasised that the collapse of the term that regulates the indexing mechanism means that the parties are bound by the contract in its remainder, which includes the method of calculating the interest (i.e. a loan in Polish zloty with the interest typical of a loan in a foreign currency).

To sum up, what needs to be stressed is that the problems the Polish courts (including the Supreme Court) had to face were much deeper than simply overcoming the constructional and axiological differences between Polish and EU law, although this in itself would be a very challenging process. The other actors (the legislator and the administrative bodies) either did not act at all, acted too late or did not act effectively enough. Moreover, the problem that from a legal point of view can easily be reduced to establishing a practice of a correct application of CJEU case law and identifying national solutions that can complement the EU scheme, due to the huge value of the cases involved became heavily politicised. At a certain point it became clear that the problems were inevitable, and still the legislative actions were merely illusory.[130] It is clear that the Polish courts needed to overcome not only the inertness of the legislator and the executive branch, but also the heavy lobbying of the sector (which is still a novelty for the Polish courts, see section 5.12 below). In other words, the judiciary had to act with an efficiency that would combine the effectiveness of the legislative, administrative and judicial branches.

5.12. PROBLEM OF THE LEGAL DOCTRINE

The problem with foreign currency loans has revealed the close links that exist in Poland between business and academia. In the Polish legal system, the doctrine has traditionally played a corrective function, pointing out the social problems that stem from the improper application of law, and critically scrutinising case law. Academia has also been very present in the law-making process when it comes to the area of private law, as most of the Civil Law Codification Committee members[131] came from universities. The courts were therefore accustomed to the situation, where the doctrinal analysis would offer an objective (yet axiologically motivated) solution that the courts could apply.

Yet, in the public debate on foreign currency loans, for a very long time, representatives of academia to a large extent simply repeated the positions of the parties, instead of presenting axiologically motivated yet independent views. Due to the glaring disproportion in salaries between business and academia, most academics in Poland are also engaged in legal practice, either in their own legal firms or preparing legal opinions in court cases. Naturally, academics usually present the positions of the banks, who have better resources that allow them to, for example, sponsor conferences or buy out a large part of a publication. This means that it was often difficult to decide whether a given public appearance by an academic is made as a part of their academic work, with its specific methodology, or as a legal representative of one of the parties (also a possibility). The position of the borrowers is normally presented in public discourse by their legal representatives (practising lawyers).[132] For courts, accustomed to the traditionally impartial position of legal writing, distinguishing between the academic, dogmatic arguments and those that support a specific party to the

---

[130] For more on the swift reactions of the legislator, see T. Josipović, *Ad hoc legislation in the financial crisis (Croatian model of the fight against over-indebtedness of citizens), 'Ad hoc legislatíva v súkromnom práve'*, ed. Kristian Csach, pp. 158–184.

[131] A body acting under the Minister of Justice, which prepared and gave opinions on the most important Acts in the area of private law. The Commission does not exist at the moment; it was dissolved by the Minister of Justice in 2015.

[132] This situation is very well described and commented on by E. Łętowska, *Co ujawnia dyskurs o kredytach frankowych, czyli o świadomym i nieświadomym uwikłaniu prawników*, Europejski Przegląd Sądowy, April 2020, pp. 4–14.

legal dispute is still challenging. This had a very deep impact on the situation in Poland. In legal systems with a longer tradition of lobbyists, it is probably much easier for the courts to distinguish lobbyists from academic opinions. In addition, in such systems academia probably better understands the need to act with the utmost caution when mixing theory and practice. In Poland, this process has not yet taken place.

6. CONCLUSIONS

The main conclusions of this chapter concern not only the lack of certainty when it comes to the functioning of the CJEU's jurisprudence in the national legal systems, but also the lack of instruments that help discover how it functions. It is possible to identify factors that make EU law such a complicated construct from the point of view of national legal systems, and such factors are most probably at least similar for all Member States (i.e. the differences in the construction of EU law and national legal systems). However, the factors that set up the internal situation are unique for each Member State and depend on the functioning of the national system – not only from the legal but also from the social, political and economic points of view. The legal and court cultures of a given state (above all: the culture of cooperation) heavily contribute to how the CJEU's jurisprudence is received at the national level. How the jurisprudence of the CJEU functions at a national level depends on the attitudes of all the actors responsible for ensuring the proper functioning of EU law. How great a task this is for the national courts very much depends on how much of the implementation is secured through proper legislation and administrative enforcement.

EU law expects a lot from national judges, primarily a willingness and capacity to break from the constraints of their own legal system in order to ensure the effectiveness of EU law. This might often be seen as going against one's legal tradition. If the construction and the functioning of the national legal system make this burden even heavier, the process of ensuring the effectiveness of EU law (including the proper functioning of the CJEU's jurisprudence) becomes even more challenging.

INDEX

EUROPEAN CONTRACT LAW AND THEORY SERIES

1. *Rules and Principles in European Contract Law*, Jacobien Rutgers and Pietro Sirena (eds.)
2. *European Contract Law and the Charter of Fundamental Rights*, Hugh Collins (ed.)
3. *European Contract Law in the Digital Age*, Stefan Grundmann (ed.)
4. *European Contract Law in the Banking and Financial Union*, Stefan Grundmann and Pietro Sirena (eds.)